The UK Economy
A Manual of Applied Economics

The UK Economy
A Manual of Applied Economics

Eighth Edition

Edited by

A.R. Prest M.A. Ph.D.
Professor of Economics, London School of Economics
and

D.J. Coppock B.A. (Econ.)
Stanley Jevons Professor of Economics, University of Manchester

Weidenfeld and Nicolson
London

© 1966, 1968, 1970, 1972, 1974, 1976, 1978, 1980 by A.R. Prest, D.J. Coppock, M.C. Kennedy, N.J. Gibson, J.R. Cable

© 1972, 1974, 1976, 1978, 1980 by David Metcalf and Ray Richardson

© 1974, 1976, 1978, 1980 by J.S. Metcalfe

First published 1966
Second impression 1967
Third impression 1968
Second edition 1968
Second impression 1969
Third edition 1970
Second impression 1971
Fourth edition 1972
Fifth edition 1974
Sixth edition 1976
Seventh edition 1978
Eighth edition 1980

Weidenfeld and Nicolson
91 Clapham High St, London SW4

ISBN 0 297 77858 7 cased
ISBN 0 297 77859 5 paperback

Text set in 10/11 pt IBM Press Roman, printed and bound
in Great Britain at The Pitman Press, Bath

CONTRIBUTORS

Chapter 1
> M.C. Kennedy *B.Sc. (Econ.) (London)*
> *Lecturer in Economics, University of Manchester*

Chapter 2
> N.J. Gibson *B.Sc. (Econ.), Ph.D. (Belfast)*
> *Professor of Economics, The New University of Ulster*

Chapter 3
> J.S. Metcalfe *B.A. (Econ.), M.Sc. (Manchester)*
> *Professor of Economics, University of Manchester*

Chapter 4
> J.R. Cable *B.A. (Nottingham), M.A. (Econ.) (Manchester)*
> *Senior Lecturer in Economics, University of Warwick*
> assisted by I. Tonks *M.A. (Warwick), University of Warwick*

Chapter 5
> David Metcalf *M.A. (Econ.) (Manchester), Ph.D. (London)*
> *Professor of Economics, University of Kent*
> and
> Ray Richardson *B.Sc. (Econ.) (London), Ph.D. (Columbia)*
> *Reader in Industrial Relations, London School of Economics*

Contents

Contents   *ix*

TABLES

Chapter 4

Chapter 5

FIGURES

STATISTICAL APPENDIX

ABBREVIATIONS

(1) Economic Terms

CAP	Common Agricultural Policy
CET	Common External Tariff
c.i.f.	Cost including Insurance and Freight
DCE	Domestic Credit Expansion
FIS	Family Income Supplement
f.o.b.	Free on Board
GDP	Gross Domestic Product
GNP	Gross National Product
MCA	Monetary Compensation Adjustments
MLH	Minimum List Headings
NSA	Non Sterling Area
NS	North Sea
OSA	Overseas Sterling Area
PAYE	Pay as you Earn
PDI	Personal Disposable Income
PRT	Petroleum Revenue Tax
PSBR	Public Sector Borrowing Requirement
R and D	Research and Development
RPM	Resale Price Maintenance
SDRs	Special Drawing Rights
SIC	Standard Industrial Classification
SITC	Standard Industrial Trade Classification
TCF	Total Currency Flow
TFE	Total Final Expenditure at Market Prices

(2) Organizations, etc.

CBI	Confederation of British Industry
CSO	Central Statistical Office (UK)
DE	Department of Employment
DI	Department of Industry
ECE	Economic Commission for Europe
ECSC	European Coal and Steel Community
EEA	Exchange Equalization Account
EEC	European Economic Community
EFTA	European Free Trade Area
FAO	Food and Agriculture Organization
GATT	General Agreement on Tariffs and Trade
IFC	International Finance Corporation
IMF	International Monetary Fund
MC	Monopolies Commission
NBPI	National Board for Prices and Incomes
NEB	National Enterprise Board

NEDC(O)	National Economic Development Council (Office)
NIESR	National Institute of Economic and Social Research
NRDC	National Research Development Corporation
OECD	Organization for Economic Cooperation and Development
OPCS	Office of Population Census and Surveys
OPEC	Organization of Petroleum Exporting Countries
PC	Price Commission
TUC	Trades Union Congress
UN	United Nations
UNCTAD	United Nations Commission for Trade and Development
WB	World Bank

(3) Journals, etc.

AAS	*Annual Abstract of Statistics* (HMSO)
AER	*American Economic Review*
BB	*British Business* (formerly *Trade and Industry*)
BEQB	*Bank of England Quarterly Bulletin*
BJIR	*British Journal of Industrial Relations*
BLS	*British Labour Statistics, Historical Abstract* (HMSO)
BTJ	*Board of Trade Journal* (HMSO)
DEG	*Department of Employment Gazette* (HMSO)
EC	*Economica*
EJ	*Economic Journal*
ET(AS)	*Economic Trends (Annual Supplement)* (HMSO)
FES	*Family Expenditure Survey* (HMSO)
FS	*Financial Statistics* (HMSO)
IFS	*International Financial Statistics*
JIE	*Journal of Industrial Economics*
JPE	*Journal of Political Economy*
JRSS	*Journal of Royal Statistical Society*
LBR	*Lloyds Bank Review*
LCES	*London and Cambridge Economic Service*
MBR	*Midland Bank Review*
MDS	*Monthly Digest of Statistics* (HMSO)
MS	*The Manchester School of Economic and Social Studies*
NIBB	*National Income Blue Book* (HMSO)
NIER	*National Institute Economic Review*
NWBQR	*National Westminster Bank Quarterly Review*
OEP	*Oxford Economic Papers*
QJE	*Quarterly Journal of Economics*
RES	*Review of Economic Studies*
REST	*Review of Economics and Statistics*
ROT	*Report on Overseas Trade* (HMSO)
SJPE	*Scottish Journal of Political Economy*
ST	*Social Trends* (HMSO)
TBR	*Three Banks Review*
TER	*Treasury Economic Report* (HMSO)
TI	*Trade and Industry* (HMSO)

Foreword to the Eighth Edition

In 1966, when the first edition of this book was published, the foreword began as follows:

> The central idea behind this book is to give an account of the main features and problems of the UK economy today. The hope is that it will fulfil two functions simultaneously, in that it will be as up to date as possible and yet will not be simply a bare catalogue of facts and figures. There are many sources of information, official and otherwise, about the structure and progress of the UK economy. There are also many authors to whom one can turn for subtle analyses of the problems before us. Our effort here is based on the belief that there is both room and need for an attempt to combine the functions of chronicler and analyst in the confines of a single book.
>
> The contributors to these pages subscribe rather firmly to the belief that economists should practise, as well as preach, the principle of the division of labour. The complexity of a modern economy is such that, whether one likes it or not, it is no longer possible for any individual to be authoritative on all its aspects; so it is inevitable that the burden of producing work of this kind should be spread among a number of people, each a specialist in his or her particular field. Such a division carries with it obvious dangers of overlap and inconsistency. It is hoped that some of the worst pitfalls of this kind have been avoided and there is reasonable unity of purpose, treatment and layout. At the same time, it is wholly undesirable to impose a monolithic structure and it is just as apparent to the authors that there are differences in outlook and emphasis among them as it will be to the readers.
>
> The general intention was to base exposition on the assumption that the reader would have some elementary knowledge of economics – say a student in the latter part of a typical first year course in economics in a British university. At the same time, it is hoped that most of the text will be intelligible to those without this degree of expertise. We may not have succeeded in this; if not, we shall try to do better in the future.

Despite the usual extensive re-writing, we should still regard this as an accurate description of our intentions.

Chapter 1, 'The Economy as a Whole', is concerned with questions of applied macroeconomics: fluctuations in demand and employment, the management of demand, inflation and economic growth. The chapter ends with a section on the economic prospects in the near future. Chapter 2, 'Monetary, Credit and Fiscal Policies', starts with a brief discussion of the general theoretical background and then analyses in detail the theory and practices of monetary, credit and fiscal policies in the UK in recent years. The final section discusses the policy record and some policy implications of membership of the EEC. Chapter 3, 'Foreign Trade and the Balance of Payments', deals with the importance of foreign trade and payments to the UK economy and assesses UK balance of payments performance over the last two decades or so. It then looks at current problems and policies in this field and ends with a discussion of the reform of the international monetary system. Chapter 4, 'Industry and Commerce', starts with a brief summary of various theories of the behaviour of firms and the structural characteristics of UK industry. Various aspects of public policy towards nationalized industries, competition policy and consumer protection, regional problems and so on are then discussed, all with due regard to the implications of EEC membership. A final section deals with industrial efficiency, including such issues as planning agreements and price control. The last chapter, 'Labour', analyses employment and unemployment among the UK labour force, and then discusses problems of wealth, income distribution and pay. The final sections are concerned with trade unions and wage inflation.

Whilst we try to minimize unnecessary overlapping between chapters, we quite deliberately aim at complementary treatment of some topics. Thus different aspects of EEC membership are discussed in the relevant chapters; similarly, wages-inflation relationships appear in both Chapter 1 and Chapter 5. To minimize the use of space, factual material or definitions appearing in one chapter but relevant to another are not always duplicated and so it must be understood that to this extent any one chapter may not be self-contained.

Each chapter is accompanied by a list of references and further reading. The Statistical Appendix has seven tables dealing with different aspects of the UK economy. There is an index as well as the detailed list of headings and sub-headings given in the Contents pages.

We acknowledge the great help given to us by all those who have rendered secretarial or computing assistance.

London School of Economics   A.R. PREST
University of Manchester   D.J. COPPOCK

April 1980

1

The economy as a whole
M.C. Kennedy

I   INTRODUCTION
I.1   Methodological Approach

This chapter is an introduction to applied macroeconomics. It begins with a brief
description of the national income accounts and goes on to discuss the multiplier,
the determination of national expenditure and output in the short run, the policy
problems of maintaining full employment, the causes of inflation and of economic
growth. It cannot claim to give all the answers to the questions raised, but aims to
provide the reader with a basis for further and deeper study.

In principle there is no essential difference between applied economics and
economic theory. The object of applied economics is to explain the way in which
economic units work. It is just as much concerned with questions of causation
(such as what determines total consumption or the level of prices) as the theory
which is found in most elementary textbooks. The difference between theoretical
and applied economics is largely one of emphasis, with theory tending to stress
logical connections between assumptions and conclusions and applied economics
the connections between theories and evidence. Applied economics does not seek
description for its own sake, but it needs facts for the light they shed on the
applicability of economic theory.

At one time it used to be thought that scientific theories were derived from
factual information by a method of inference known as *induction*.[1] Thus it was
supposed that general laws about nature could be deduced from knowledge of a
limited number of facts. From the logical point of view, however, induction is an
invalid procedure. For example, the fact that ten men have been observed to save
one-tenth of their income does not entail the conclusion that the next man will
do so. The conclusion may be true or false, but it does not rest validly on the
assumptions. Inductive conclusions of this kind simply have the status of
conjectures and require further empirical investigation.

More recently it has come to be accepted that scientific method is not inductive
but *hypothetico-deductive*. A hypothesis may be proposed to explain a certain
class of event. It will generally be of the conditional form 'if p then q', from which
the deduction follows that any particular instance of p must be accompanied by an
instance of q. Thus the hypothesis is tested by every observation of p; it is
corroborated whenever p and q are observed together; and falsified if p occurs in
the absence of q.

---

1   For a highly readable introduction to the problems of scientific method the reader is
    referred to P.B. Medawar, *Induction and Intuition in Scientific Thought*, Methuen, 1969,
    and the more serious student to K.R. Popper, *The Poverty of Historicism*, Routledge and
    Kegan Paul, 1961, and *Conjectures and Refutations*, Routledge and Kegan Paul, 1963.
    For a treatment of methodological problems in economics, see I.M.T. Stewart, *Reasoning
    and Method in Economics*, McGraw-Hill, 1979.

It will be clear that this concept of scientific method places the role of factual information in a different light from the inductive approach. Facts, instead of being the foundation on which to build economic or scientific theories, become the basis for testing them. If a theory is able to survive a determined but unsuccessful attempt to refute it by factual evidence, it is regarded as well tested. But the discovery of evidence which is inconsistent with the theory will stimulate its modification or the development of a new theory altogether. One of the purposes of studying applied economics is to acquaint the theoretically equipped economist with the limitations of the theory he has studied. Applied economics is not an attempt to bolster up existing theory or, as its name might seem to imply, to demonstrate dogmatically that all the factual evidence is a neat application of textbook theory. Its aim is to understand the workings of the economy, and this means that it will sometimes expose the shortcomings of existing theory and go on to suggest improvements.

The discovery that a theory is falsified by factual observation need not mean that it must be rejected out of hand or relegated to total oblivion. Economists, as well as natural scientists, frequently have to work with theories that are inadequate in one way or another. Theories that explain part but not all of the evidence are often retained until some new theory is found which fits a wider range of evidence. Frequently the theory will turn out to have been incomplete rather than just wrong, and when modified by the addition of some new variable (or a more careful specification of the *ceteris paribus* clause), the theory may regain its status. The reader who notices inconsistencies between theory and facts need not take the line that the theory is total nonsense, for it may still hold enough grains of truth to become the basis for something better.

It is often argued that our ability to test economic theories by reference to factual observations is sufficient to liberate economics from value judgments, i.e. to turn into a *positive* subject. This position has more than an element of truth in it: when there is clear evidence against a theory it stands a fair chance of being dropped even by its most bigoted adherents. Nevertheless, it would be wrong to forget that a great deal of what passes for factual evidence in economics is infirm in character (e.g. the statistics of gross domestic product or personal saving), so that it is often possible for evidence to be viewed more sceptically by some than by others.

The discussion of economic policy which also figures in this chapter is partly normative in scope, and partly positive. The normative content of policy discussion consists in the evaluation of goals and priorities. But the means for attaining such goals derive from the positive hypotheses of economics. They involve questions of cause and effect, the hypothetical answers to which are appraisable by reference to evidence. In making recommendations for the achievement of policy goals, however, the economist treads on thin ice. This is partly because his positive knowledge is not inevitably correct, but also because it is seldom possible for him to foresee and properly appraise all the side-effects of his recommendations, some of which have implications for other policy goals. When economists differ in their advice on policy questions it is not always clear how much the difference is due on the one hand to diagnostic disagreements, and, on the other, to differences in value judgments. Indeed it is seldom possible for an economic adviser to reveal all the normative preferences which lie behind a policy recommendation. Thus policy judgments have to be scrutinized carefully for hidden normative assumptions. The reader of this chapter must be on his guard against the author's personal value judgments.

I.2   Gross Domestic Product

Most of the topics discussed in this chapter make some use of the national accounts statistics. A complete explanation of what these are and of how they are put together is available elsewhere.[1] It will be useful, however, in the next few pages to remind the reader of the main national accounting categories in so far as they affect this chapter.

The most important concept of all is gross domestic product (GDP). This is the value of the total output of the whole economy. Its significance can be most readily appreciated by imagining that the economy is like some simple productive enterprise, such as a farm. Suppose that a farm produces only wheat, the total production during a single year being 100 bushels and the price £1. The value of total production is therefore £100. This is the sum which is divided as income between the various factors of production. It is distributed in the form of rent to the land-owners, wages to the labour force and profit to the farmer. Thus total output is equal to total income. Furthermore, total output is equated to total expenditure on the output under the accounting convention that any output which is not sold is recorded as an addition to stocks, and as such regarded as investment expenditure by the farmer. Thus the income and output of the farm and the expenditure on its output are evaluated so as to make them identically equal to each other.

The GDP of the UK, by analogy with the simple production unit, can also be added up in three different ways: from the sides of income, output and expenditure. The first of these, total *income*, measures the sum of all incomes of the residents of the UK earned in the production of goods and services in the UK during a stated period. It divides into income from employment, income from self-employment and profit, and income from rent. These are factor incomes earned in the process of production and are to be distinguished from *transfer incomes*, such as pensions and sickness benefits, which are not earned from production and which, therefore, are excluded from the total. The breakdown of factor incomes for 1978 is illustrated in table 1.1 on page 5.

As with the simple production unit, the value of output accruing in the form of unsold stocks is included in total factor output. But a problem arises when the prices at which stocks are valued in the national accounts vary during the course of the accounting period. When this happens the value of stocks held at the beginning and end of the period will have been reported at two different prices, and it is then necessary to make a special valuation adjustment known as the adjustment for *stock appreciation*. A firm holding stocks of wood, for example, may increase its holding from 100 tons on 1 January to 200 tons on 31 December. If the price of wood was £1.00 per ton at the beginning of the year and £1.10 at the end of the year, the increase in the monetary value of stocks will show up as (£1.10 x 200) − (£1.00 x 100), which equals £120. This figure is inflated by the amount of the price increase and fails, therefore, to give an adequate record of what the Central Statistical Office (CSO) calls 'the value of the physical increase in stocks'. In order to rectify this the CSO attempts to value the physical change in stocks at the average price level prevailing during the period. If, in the example,

---

1   See, for example, S. Hays, *National Income and Expenditure in Britain and the OECD Countries*, Heinemann, 1971; R. and G. Stone, *National Income and Expenditure*, 9th edition, Bowes and Bowes, 1972; H.C. Edey and others, *National Income and Social Accounting*, 3rd edition, Hutchinson, 1967; or the official handbook, *National Accounts Statistics, Sources and Methods*, HMSO, 1968.

the price averaged £1.05 over the period then the value of the physical increase in stocks would be shown as £1.05 (200-100), which equals £105. The difference of £15 between this and the increase in monetary value is the adjustment for stock appreciation. It must be deducted from the reported value of factor incomes in order to reach an estimate of gross domestic income.

GDP is measured from the *production* side by adding up the value of production of the various firms and public enterprises in the country. This procedure presents two types of problem. First, the goods and services produced by one firm may also form part of the output of some other firm. Wheat produced on a farm, for example, is entered as farm output. But it may also be used by a bakery as an input in the production of bread. If so, its value will enter into the value of bread output as well as farm output. To eliminate double-counting of this kind a distinction must be drawn in the production accounts between, on the one hand, total final output, which is sold to final buyers and, on the other hand, intermediate output sold to other productive units. Intermediate output must be excluded before arriving at a firm's contribution to gross domestic product.

A second problem arises in the case of imports which often form part of a firm's production (e.g. imported wheat in bread output), but which are produced by enterprises outside the UK. To arrive at UK domestic output, the value of imports must be deducted from the value of total final output. In table 1.1 the various categories in the output column are all evaluated net of intermediate output.

GDP can also be measured from the side of *expenditure*. Conceptually this total is identical to the income and output totals; but in practice the expenditure statistics are collected from independent sources and do not lead to exactly the same figure. The difference between the two estimates is known as the residual error and is sometimes quite large. In 1978 it was £1,071m, or 0.8% of GDP.

The breakdown of the expenditure total is especially important in the analysis of aggregate demand. Expenditures are undertaken by four types of spending unit: persons, public authorities, firms and foreign residents.[1] Purchases by persons are described as consumers' expenditure, or, more loosely, as consumption. The latter description, however, may be slightly misleading when applied to expenditure on durable goods such as motor cars and refrigerators, the services of which are consumed over several years and not solely in the year in which they are purchased. One form of personal expenditure which is not classed as such is the purchase of new houses. These are deemed to have been sold initially to 'firms' and included under the broad heading of domestic capital formation or gross investment. Fixed investment, other than housing, represents the purchases by firms of physical assets that are not used up in current production, but which accrue as additions or replacements to the nation's capital stock. The preface 'gross' warns us that a year's gross investment does not measure the change in the size of the capital stock during the year because it does not allow for withdrawals from the capital stock due to scrapping, or for wear and tear. The concept of gross capital formation is also carried through into the definition of domestic product itself. Net domestic product is not easily measured but attempts to include only that investment which adds to the total stock of capital. It is less relevant to the level of employment than gross output.

---

1 The distinctions between types of spending units are not always clearcut, e.g. expenditure by self-employed persons is partly consumers' expenditure and partly investment.

TABLE 1.1

GDP and GNP at Current Prices, UK, 1978

FROM INCOME

	£m	% of domestic income[1]
Income from employment	98,156	67.6
Income from self-employment	13,245	9.1
Income from rent	9,842	6.8
Gross trading profits of companies	17,055	11.7
Gross trading surplus of public corporations and other public enterprises	5,596	3.9
Imputed charge for consumption of non-trading capital	1,283	0.9
Total domestic income (before providing for stock appreciation)	145,177	100.0
less Stock appreciation	−4,249	
Residual error	1,071	
Gross domestic product at factor cost	141,999	

FROM OUTPUT

	£m	% of domestic output[1]
Agriculture, forestry and fishing	3,715	2.5
Mining and quarrying	4,467	3.0
Manufacturing	40,690	27.7
Construction	8,610	5.9
Services and distribution	89,544	60.9
Total domestic income (after providing for stock appreciation)	147,026	100.0
Adjustment for financial services[2]	−6,098	
Residual error	1,071	
Gross domestic product at factor cost	141,999	

FROM EXPENDITURE

	£m	% of TFE[1]
Consumers' expenditure	96,086	46.4
General government final consumption	32,693	15.8
Gross domestic fixed investment	29,218	14.1
Investment in stocks	1,528	0.7
Export of goods and services	47,636	23.0
Total final expenditure at market prices	207,161	100.0
less Imports of goods and services	−45,522	
less Adjustment to factor cost	−19,640	
Gross domestic product at factor cost	141,999	
Net property income from abroad	836	
Gross national product at factor cost	142,835	

Source: NIBB, 1979, tables 1.1, 1.2 and 1.10.
1 Percentage figures may not add up to 100.0 because of rounding.
2 Deduction of net receipts of interest by financial companies.

The sum of exports, consumers' expenditure, government final consumption and gross investment is known as total final expenditure at market prices, or TFE for short. Each of the four components contains two elements which must be deducted before arriving at GDP at factor cost. The first is the import content of the expenditure which must, of course, be classified as foreign rather than domestically produced output. The simplest way of removing imports is to take the global import total as given by the balance of payment accounts and subtract it from TFE, and this is the usual method. Estimates do exist, however, for the import content of the separate components of final expenditure in the input-output tables, but they are drawn up much less frequently than the national accounts. The second element of total final expenditure which must be deducted to obtain the factor cost value of GDP is the indirect tax content (net of subsidies) of the various expenditures. This is present for the simple reason that the most readily available valuation of any commodity is the price at which it sells in the market. This price, however, will overstate the factor incomes earned from producing the commodity if it contains an element of indirect tax; and it will understate factor income if the price is subsidized. The deduction of indirect taxes (less subsidies) is known as the *factor cost adjustment*, and is most conveniently made globally since it can be found from the government's records of tax proceeds and subsidy payments. Estimates of its incidence on the individual components of TFE are available annually in the National Income *Blue Book*.[1]

Gross domestic product from the expenditure side is thus obtained by adding up the components of TFE at market prices, and by subtracting imports of goods and services together with the factor cost adjustment. It relates to expenditure on the total production in the UK of the residents of the United Kingdom. It differs from the other aggregate concept, gross national product (GNP), in that it does not include receipts of interest, profits and dividends by UK residents from productive activity carried out overseas; nor does it exclude the profits of foreign-owned enterprises producing in the UK. The balance of these two amounts is known as net property income from abroad and must be added to GDP in order to obtain GNP. It is a small total representing about 0.6% of GDP in 1978.

I.3   Gross Domestic Product at Constant Prices

Table 1.1 summarizes the national accounts for 1978 at the prices obtaining in 1978. As such it is a useful source of information as to the way in which domestic income, output and expenditure were divided in a particular year. If, however, we wish to compare the *volume* of goods produced in different periods we must use a different set of figures. These are the estimates of GDP at constant prices, the expenditure side of which is presented in the Statistical Appendix, table A-1. They show the value of GDP for each year in terms of prices ruling in 1975. Similar estimates are available in index-number form for the income total of GDP and for the output total together with its main industrial components. These totals are derived almost entirely from movements in quantities, the various quantities for each year being added together by means of the value weights obtaining for 1975. The result is three conceptually equal but independently derived estimates of real domestic output, and, as with the current price series, there are often large

---

1 *NIBB*, 1979, table 1.8.

differences between them.[1] The existence of these differences means that there is normally some element of ambiguity as regards both the level of GDP in a particular year and changes between years. Thus the increase in real GDP between 1978 and 1979 was put at 0.3% by the expenditure estimate and at 2.0% by the income estimate. Since most macroeconomic discussion is concerned with expenditure relationships, it is usual to put the main emphasis on this aspect of GDP.

Gross domestic product is an important entity in its own right and changes in its real amount are the best estimates available of changes in UK production. Even so, it must be remembered that it leaves a good deal out of the picture by excluding practically all productive work which is not sold for money. The national income statistics neglect, for example, the activities of the housewife and amateur gardener even though they must add millions of hours to UK production of goods and services. It is also important to recognize that GDP stands for the production of UK residents, not their expenditure. As an expenditure total it measures the spending of all persons, resident or foreign, on the goods and services produced by the residents of the UK. Thus if national welfare is conceived as spending by UK residents, it is incorrect to represent it by GDP. The total appropriate for this purpose is GDP *plus* imports *minus* exports. This total is sometimes referred to as 'domestic absorption', and is equal to the UK's total use of resources, which is the sum of consumption, government expenditure and gross investment. It is an amount which can diminish quite substantially when there is a sharp improvement in the balance of payments.

TABLE 1.2

Personal Income, UK, 1978

	£m
Income from employment	98,156
Income from self-employment	13,245
Rent, dividends and interest	13,671
Current transfers to charities from companies	44
National Insurance benefits and other current grants from public authorities	17,853
Imputed charge for capital consumption of private non-profit-making bodies	244
Personal income before tax	143,213
less	
National Insurance, etc., contributions	10,023
UK taxes on income	19,655
Transfers abroad	218
equals	
Total personal disposable income	113,317
of which	
Consumers' expenditure	96,086
Personal saving (before provision for depreciation, stock appreciation and addition to tax reserves)	17,231

Source: NIBB, 1979, table 1.3.

---

1 These differences are usually referred to as 'the statistical discrepancies' so as to distinguish them from the residual error in the estimates at current prices.

I.4   Personal Income and Personal Disposable Income

Two further concepts, personal income and disposable income, are of importance in
the analysis of consumption and the multiplier. Personal income is not directly
obtainable from the income breakdown shown in table 1.1, although two of the
categories there, employment income and the income of the self-employed, form
part of it. The remainder consists of that part of total rent, dividends and profits
which is actually paid to persons (a part of the total shown in table 1.1) and also
transfer incomes received by persons from the central government and from
charitable institutions. A full breakdown of personal income and personal
disposable income is shown in tables 1.2 (p. 7) and A-3 (in the Statistical Appendix).
It should be noted that the difference between personal disposable income
(derived from the income side of the national accounts) and consumers'
expenditure (derived from the expenditure side) is the most frequently quoted
estimate of personal saving.

II   FLUCTUATIONS IN TOTAL OUTPUT AND EXPENDITURE
II.1   Fluctuations in Output and Employment

The British economy has experienced cyclical fluctuations since the time of the
industrial revolution. During the nineteenth century these appear to have followed
a fairly uniform pattern with a peak-to-peak duration of seven to ten years and a
tendency for 'full employment' (roughly defined) to reappear at each cyclical peak.
After the First World War this pattern ceased, and for nearly twenty years there
were well over one million unemployed. Unemployment reached 12½% of the
work force in the recession of 1926 and 22% in 1932.

The business cycle has been much milder since the Second World War. In the
1950s and 1960s the unemployment rate never rose above an annual figure of
2.3 per cent, and its highest rate in the 1970s was 5.6 per cent (in 1977 and 1978).
But unemployment has been persistently higher in some parts of the UK, notably in
Northern Ireland, Wales, Scotland and the North of England.

Economic fluctuations have not been at all regular. Their duration, measured
from peak to peak, has varied between 4 and 8 years. There was a particularly long
spell of low activity between the peaks of 1965 and 1972, a very sharp upturn in
1973 and renewed recession in 1975 and 1976. The upturns have generally been
associated with faster-than-average increases in GDP. Thus GDP rose by about 4%
per annum in 1955-61 and 1963-5 and by 7% in 1972-3. In 1975-9, however, the
growth of GDP was only about 2.3% a year, which was lower than the trend growth
rate of earlier years, and much lower than the rates normally encountered in cyclical
recoveries. Sharp downturns in GDP have been rare in the postwar period although
there was a decline of 2.5% between 1973 and 1975. In the mildest recessions GDP
did not fall at all, declines in employment being more than offset by increased
productivity.

The best indicators of cyclical activity are the figures for unemployment and
unfilled vacancies as percentages of the labour force (figure 1.1). These indicate
peak levels of economic activity in 1960-1, 1965 and 1973-4, whilst the main
periods of recession are shown as 1963, 1971-2 and 1976-8. The vacancy series
suggest that the pressure of demand for labour was much the same in 1975-7 as in
the earlier recessions of 1963 and 1971, whereas the unemployment figures suggest

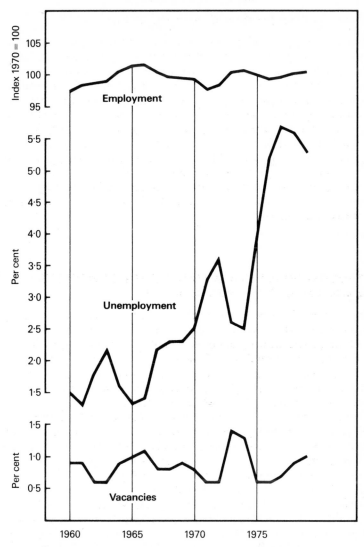

Figure 1.1   Employment, unemployment and vacancies, UK, 1960-79.

that the recession was much more serious than earlier. Thus the two sets of figures are in agreement about the *phases* of the cycle but in conflict as to its *intensity* (see pp. 10-12).

Whilst employment and unemployment move together over the business cycle they seldom display the same relative variations from year to year. In most cycles the proportionate variation in employment exceeds the change in the unemployment percentage. This is probably explained by the presence of 'hidden unemployment', i.e. various groups of workers, such as married women, who do not register as unemployed when they are dismissed. A second common characteristic of cyclical movements in the economy is for the change in total output to be proportionately greater than the change in employment. This implies that productivity tends to rise faster on the upturn of the cycle than on the downturn. It is explained partly by the presence of 'overhead labour', such as managerial and supervisory staff who remain on the payroll despite changes in turn-over, and partly by a tendency for firms to 'hoard' labour, particularly those with scarce skills, during the recession so as to be sure of having it to hand when demand recovers.

Some of these characteristics are illustrated by the upturn of 1972-3 (see table 1.3), when GDP rose much faster than employment, whilst the fall in unemployment was less than the gain in the numbers employed. In the much slower expansion of 1975-9 there was very little rise in employment whilst unemployment was increasing.

TABLE 1.3

Changes in Output, Employment and Unemployment, UK, 1972-9

	1972-3	1973-5	1975-9
GDP (percentage change)	+7.0	−2.5	+9.5
Employment (percentage change)	+2.1	−0.4	+0.4
Change in unemployment rate	−1.0	+1.3	+1.4

Sources: ET(AS) 1980; *NIER*, February 1980; *DEG* (wholly unemployed, excluding school-leavers).

The intensity of peaks and troughs: An accurate measure of the intensity of peaks and recessions is needed for policy purposes. It is important to have complete, sensitive and consistent indicators of inflationary pressure and of the degree of under-utilization of resources. There are some grounds for regarding the unemployment figures as better than unfilled vacancies for this purpose. It can be argued, for example, that unemployment tends to be more completely recorded than vacancies because most of those who register are entitled to unemployment benefit. Unfilled vacancies, by contrast, are recorded only in so far as employers believe it to be worth their while to report them to the employment offices. An employer who has already notified the employment office of vacancies for a particular kind of worker will not always register new vacancies when they arise since the original notice will be sufficient to attract applicants. Thus the vacancy figures are bound to be incomplete, and it is officially recognized that only a part, perhaps one-third, of all new vacancies are notified to the Department of Employment.[1]

In the last fifteen years, however, both sets of statistics have been called in question by a sharp change in the relationship between them. A given level of vacancies is now accompanied by a much higher level of unemployment than it used to be. The extent of the change can be seen from the following comparisons:

1 See *DEG*, February 1980, footnote to chart.

	Unfilled vacancies, GB		Unemployment, GB	
	(000s, percentages in brackets)			
1962-3 (average)	145	(0.6)	461	(2.0)
1965-6 (average)	262	(1.1)	315	(1.4)
1971-2 (average)	137	(0.6)	777	(3.5)
1973-4 (average)	297	(1.3)	576	(2.6)
1975-6 (average)	145	(0.6)	1055	(4.6)
1978-9 (average)	224	(0.9)	1282	(5.5)

The figures illustrate a continuing tendency for unemployment to rise relative to vacancies. The comparison between 1962-3 and 1971-2 shows a rise of 1.5% in unemployment for a constant vacancy rate, whilst that between 1965-6 and 1973-4 (two peak years) indicates a rise in the unemployment percentage of 1.2% during a period when vacancies were hardly changed. The comparison between 1971-2 and 1975-6, moreover, implies a further shift in the relationship, so that by this time a vacancy rate of 0.6% coincided with an unemployment rate some 2.6% higher than would have been observed in the early 1960s. By 1978-9, a vacancy rate of 0.9% coincided with an unemployment rate of 5.5%; 13 years earlier the same vacancy rate would have been associated with an unemployment percentage of about 1.6%. It will be clear that a change of this magnitude makes it very difficult to compare the intensity of the cycle over periods of more than a year or two.

It is possible to point to four different sets of factors which may have been responsible for this dramatic change in the relationship of unemployment to vacancies:

(i)   One explanation is that there has been an increase in the ratio of registered to actual unemployment. Registered male unemployment in 1971 was 71% of the amount recorded by the Census sample of the same date, as against only 56% at the time of the 1966 Census, and 44% of the 1961 Census. The increased reporting rate could have added about 100,000 to the register, or about one-third of the increase noted above. What is not so clear, however, is the underlying reason for the increased reporting rate. It can be argued that it was due to improved monetary incentives to register, such as the earnings-related unemployment benefits introduced in September 1966, and the gradual rise in the ratio of basic benefit to average industrial earnings. But a possible qualification here is that regional figures indicate a higher reporting rate in areas of high unemployment, and this could mean that the rise between the peak of 1966 and the trough of 1971 may have been partly due to the phase of the cycle.

(ii)   A second hypothesis is that better compensation for unemployment could have encouraged workers to spend longer on the unemployment register whilst looking for new jobs, thus raising the unemployment level for any given pressure of demand for labour. It is significant that the shift in the U-V relationship has been almost totally confined to male workers, a high proportion of whom are entitled to unemployment benefit, whereas there has been practically no shift for female workers, large numbers of whom do not qualify for benefit when they lose their jobs.

(iii)   A third hypothesis is the 'shake-out' theory, which rests on the supposition that since about 1968 employers have become much more economical in their use of labour, and, in particular, that the practice of hoarding labour between cyclical peaks was greatly diminished at about this time. The stimulus to greater economy may have been given by the jolt to expectations of recovery after devaluation and by the promise in the Budget speech of 1968 of 'two years' hard slog'. Thus, hoarded labour was shaken out, with the result that recorded unemployment increased relative to vacancies. The fact that output per man rose dramatically in 1968 (by 4.8%) is a point in favour of this hypothesis. But a weakness of the hypothesis is that it seems to imply a change in the relationship of vacancies to unemployment only in the recession of the cycle. One might expect a recovery of demand to be accompanied by a 'shake-in' – a decline in unemployment faster than a rise in vacancies. This, however, did not happen when the recovery came in 1973. Vacancies rose to their previous peak level whereas unemployment did not fall correspondingly.

(iv)   Two converse factors were the raising of the school-leaving age in 1973, which probably produced some increase in vacancies relative to unemployment, and the various improvements in the efficiency of the employment service since about the same date. The latter would have increased the reporting rate for vacancies.

It seems probable that all the factors mentioned have played some part in the shift in the U-V relationship. But their relative importance is difficult to ascertain with confidence. A tentative conclusion is that the vacancy figures probably functioned as a more consistent indication of the pressure of demand on resources over a period running from about 1961 to 1973, but that from then onwards there were factors which impaired their reliability. This would suggest that the recession of 1975-6 was somewhat more severe than those of 1971-2 and 1962-3 despite very similar vacancy rates. It also seems clear that the high vacancy rate in 1978-9 indicated a rather less intense pressure of demand for labour than in 1969 when the vacancy rate was also 0.9%, and this judgment is, of course, confirmed by the much higher unemployment figures in the 1970s. Finally, it is difficult to assert that the degree of hardship indicated by the unemployment figures is greatly exaggerated by factors suggesting a greater degree of 'voluntariness', although there were clearly *some* influences in this direction.[1]

---

1   There is a large volume of literature on the relationship between unemployment and vacancies. It includes A. Evans, 'Notes on the Changing Relationship between Registered Unemployment and Notified Vacancies: 1961-1966 and 1966-1971', *Economica*, May 1977; J.K. Bowers, P.C. Cheshire, E.A. Webb and R. Weeden, 'Some Aspects of Unemployment and the Labour Market, 1966-71', *NIER*, November 1972, pp. 83-5; J. Taylor, 'The Behaviour of Unemployment and Unfilled Vacancies: Great Britain, 1958-71, An Alternative View', *EJ*, December 1972; D.I. Mackay and G.L. Reid, 'Redundancy, Unemployment and Manpower Policy', *EJ*, 1972; D. Gujarati, 'The Behaviour of Unemployment and Unfilled Vacancies: Great Britain 1958-71', *EJ*, March 1972; S.J. Nickell, 'The Effect of Unemployment and Related Benefits on the Duration of Unemployment', *EJ*, March 1979. For an official view, see 'The Unemployment Statistics and their Interpretation', *DEG*, March 1975.

II.2   Expenditure in the Cycle

Fluctuations in domestic output have their origins in movements in total spending and its components. The two main sources are investment demand and exports. Fixed investment has generally grown rapidly in the upswing of the cycle, sometimes by as much as 10% per annum (see table 1.4). But it fell in much of the 1975-8 period, and did not turn up until 1978. Investment in stocks, despite its small size relative to TFE, can move quite violently from year to year. The swing from negative to positive stock investment in 1972-3, for example, was enough to add about 2% to TFE. Export demand depends mainly on the state of world markets and the exchange rate. It has nearly always been an important factor in the business cycle, and was the major source of the 1975-8 upturn.

There is no reason to expect government expenditure to move closely with the cycle or against it. In 1972-3 its increase contributed to the upturn and was part of the government's recovery programme. In the recession of 1955-9, however, the decline in government spending reflected a cutback in defence expenditure, and was not introduced with the express intention of reducing the pressure of demand. Government expenditure can be used for stabilization purposes, but its main movements have originated with changes in social policy or defence.

Whereas government expenditure, investment and exports can be regarded as the principal *autonomous* causes of demand fluctuations, consumption and imports (and also indirect taxes) are often thought to be *dependent* directly upon total income and indirectly upon the autonomous expenditures. This distinction between the autonomous and dependent items cannot be completely watertight since all of the latter are capable of moving autonomously for other reasons. But it is a useful first approximation.

Consumer's expenditure has grown much more evenly than fixed investment on exports. Its rate of increase has not been noticeably faster in the upturn of the cycle than in the downturns. Rates of increase in imports, however, have moved in phase with those of GDP, but their fluctuations have shown a somewhat larger amplitude. This reflects the fact that imports are taken first into stock, and tend to fluctuate with stock-building as well as with GDP.[1]

In the next section we describe some of the main hypotheses which have been advanced to explain movements in the components of total demand.

III   THE DETERMINANTS OF DEMAND

The level of national output is determined in the short run by the level of total expenditure. This is the sum of all demands for domestic output, and thus comprises all the elements of TFE net of their import and indirect tax components. A large area of macroeconomics is devoted to the attempt to explain how these expenditures are determined. Such explanations are essential if we are to understand economic fluctuations and to be able to forecast and control them.

---

1 For a further discussion of cyclical fluctuations see J.C.R. Dow, *The Management of the British Economy, 1945-60*, Cambridge University Press, 1964, chapter 4, and R.C.O. Matthews, 'Post-war Business Cycles in the United Kingdom', in M. Bronfenbrenner (ed.), *Is the Business Cycle Obsolete?*, Wiley, 1969.

III.1 Consumers' Expenditure

Consumers' expenditure is the largest single element in aggregate demand. It accounts for nearly half of TFE (see table 1.1) and, after the removal of its import and indirect tax content, for about the same fraction of GDP at factor cost. Consumption is one of the more stable elements of demand in the sense that its fluctuations are small when measured as percentages of its total. But its total amount is so large in relation to GDP that even quite small percentage variations in it can have important repercussions for output and employment. An understanding of consumption behaviour, therefore, as well as an ability to predict it, are important objectives for economic analysis. A great deal of attention has been given to consumption, both in theory and statistically, although this work has been more heavily concentrated upon consumption in the US where the relevant statistical data are available for a longer period than for the UK.

The starting point for the early studies of consumer behaviour was the well-known statement by Keynes:[1] 'The fundamental psychological law upon which we are entitled to depend with great confidence both *a priori* from our knowledge of human nature and from the detailed facts of experience, is that men are disposed, as a rule and on the average, to increase their consumption as their income increases, but not by as much as the increase in their income.' Keynes was suggesting that current income was the principal, although not the only, determinant of consumers' expenditure in the short run, and that the marginal propensity to consume (MPC), i.e. the ratio of additional consumption to additional income, was positive, fractional and reasonably stable. In point of fact the MPC, when measured crudely as the ratio of changes in the annual value of consumers' expenditure at current prices to changes in personal disposable income, has not been particularly stable, nor always fractional, nor even always positive. Between 1952 and 1974 the value of the MPC varied between 0.7 and 1.2 with an average annual value of 0.9. It was not fractional (i.e. it exceeded unity) in six years.[2]

If we focus attention upon savings rather than consumption, it can be seen (figure 1.2) that the ratio of personal savings to personal disposable income has shown a strong upward trend over the postwar period with deviations from trend which are associated with cyclical fluctuations. The savings ratio was above trend in the peak years of 1956, 1961 and 1965 and below trend in the intervening recessions.

Cyclical movements in the savings ratio can be accounted for in various ways. One possible explanation is that consumer behaviour is driven partly by habit and convention, so that when income declines the individual attempts to maintain his expenditure at its previous level with the consequence that the APC rises and the savings ratio declines. A related explanation can be found in the ideas of the normal-income theorists.[3] Their main proposition is that consumption does not depend upon current income but on normal income, a concept which can be

---

1 J.M. Keynes, *General Theory*, p. 96.

2 Measured at constant prices over the same period, the MPC varied between −0.5 and 2.6. It was not fractional in six years and negative twice.

3 For an examination of these theories, see M.J. Farrell, 'The New Theories of the Consumption Function,' *EJ*, December 1959 (reprinted in Klein and Gordon (eds.), *Readings in Business Cycles*, Allen and Unwin, 1966). The classic reference is F. Modigliani and R. Brumberg, 'Utility Analysis and the Consumption Function' in K. Kurihara, *Post-Keynesian Economics*, Allen and Unwin, 1955.

TABLE 1.4

Growth Rates of Expenditure (at constant prices) during the Main Cyclical Phases, UK, 1955-78
(*Percentage increases per annum*)

	1955-9	1959-61	1961-3	1963-5	1965-72	1972-3	1975-8
Fixed investment	4.6	9.4	0.7	10.7	2.9	6.8	-0.1
Investment in stocks (expressed as % of TFE)	0.0	0.1	-0.2	0.3	-0.1	2.1	0.6
Exports	2.0	4.4	3.2	4.2	5.9	12.1	6.0
Government consumption	-0.9	2.7	2.3	2.1	2.2	4.8	0.8
Consumers' expenditure on goods and services	2.5	3.1	3.2	2.4	2.8	4.6	1.6
Imports	2.6	5.4	3.3	5.5	5.7	11.7	2.9
GDP (average estimate)	1.6	4.0	2.5	4.2	2.4	7.0	2.6

Sources: NIBB, 1977, 1979; *ET*, October 1979.

defined either precisely as the expected lifetime income of the consumer or much more vaguely as his notion of average income over some ill-defined future period. Thus it is changes in the level of expected income which are likely to change consumption. If current income increases then it will raise consumption only in so far as it raises normal income, and the amount by which it does so will depend upon the expected persistence of the income change. Cyclical changes in income are (by definition) not persistent, and the likelihood is that some consumers, perhaps a majority, will recognize them as such. Thus the APC will tend to be high in depressions and low at the peaks, whilst the savings ratio (see figure 1.2) will do the reverse.

It is possible that the normal income hypothesis can also explain the pronounced rise in the savings ratio since 1971 if, as seems plausible, the higher average level of unemployment, the slowing down of real income growth and fears of anti-inflationary policies, have led consumers to revise their long-term expectations downwards. But a further factor after 1975 was the additional uncertainty of real income expectations due to changes in the rate of inflation and in policies to deal with it. The problem with these explanations, however, is the difficulty of finding objective evidence of income expectations or of the degree of certainty with which they are held.[1]

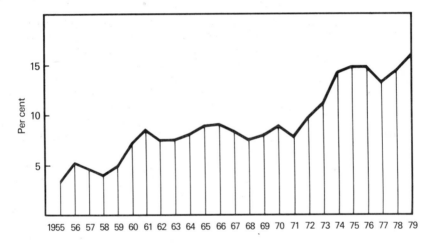

Figure 1.2   Personal saving as a percentage of personal disposable income, UK, 1955-79

Whilst a change in the climate of expectations may have been partly responsible for the climb in the savings ratio between the 1960s and 1970s, it is not clear why there should have been an uptrend in the 1950s when income expectations were improving. Postponed consumption after the Second World War would have explained the very low savings rate in the late 1940s, but it is difficult to believe that it could have been responsible for the savings rate continuing to rise in the

1   In periods when the APS is increasing there is generally an increase in the liquid assets of the personal sector. This is sometimes taken to be the *cause* of the higher savings ratio (see, for example, *BEQB*, March 1976), but in our view is more correctly considered as the *effect*.

1950s. Thus there may be something in the hypothesis that consumer wants tend, as Keynes once suggested, to become saturated as income increases, or at least that the income-elasticity of consumption in general is less than unity. If so, then consumers would appear to have behaved differently in the UK from those in the US where the savings ratio has been much more stable.

An important influence upon consumers' expenditure is the availability and cost of credit, and particularly of credit for financing purchases of durable goods.[1] These goods, which constitute 7.9% of total consumption, are more in the nature of capital equipment than of consumption in that they yield a flow of utility over time. It is natural where income is generally rising that such goods should be bought extensively on credit, and something like one half of their total is financed by hire-purchase. The availability of HP finance used to be regulated through government controls on the minimum percentage downpayment and the maximum repayment period. But these controls have not been used since 1971, and it is now interest rates rather than direct controls which tend to regulate HP borrowing.

III.2 Gross Fixed Investment

Fixed investment or gross domestic fixed capital formation is a heterogeneous total, comprising housing and business investment in both the public and the private sectors. Its breakdown by industry and sector in 1978 is shown in table 1.5. Of the three main components, it is manufacturing investment which is the most volatile. But all three sectors vary enough from year to year to have important effects upon output and employment.

TABLE 1.5

Gross Domestic Fixed Capital Formation, UK, 1978 (£m)

	Private sector	Public sector	Total
Dwellings	3,073	2,162	5,235
Manufacturing	5,414	427	5,841
Other fixed investment	11,453	6,689	18,142
Total	19,940	9,278	29,218

Source: NIBB, 1979, p. 133; current prices.

A hypothesis which goes some way towards explaining the behaviour of manufacturing investment is the capital-stock-adjustment principle. This states that the level of investment is related positively to the level of output and negatively to

---

1 It should be noted that the *Blue Book* definition of durable goods includes cars, motor cycles, furniture, carpets and electrical goods, but, perhaps arbitrarily, does not include clothing, curtains, pots and pans or books.

the existing capital stock (of land, buildings and machinery in productive use). The principle may be expressed as:

$$I_t = aY_{t-1} - bK_{t-1}$$

or, in ratio form, as

$$\frac{I_t}{Y_{t-1}} = a - b \frac{K_{t-1}}{Y_{t-1}}$$

Here I_t stands for gross investment in the current year, Y_{t-1} for last year's level of output, K_{t-1} for the capital stock at the end of the preceding year; and *a* and *b* are constant coefficients. The principle may be interpreted in various ways, one of which is to assume (not too implausibly) that technology dictates a fixed proportional relationship between the stock of capital equipment and the level of output. It follows, since net investment is an increase in the capital stock, that its amount will be planned in relation both to the expected volume of production and to the current size of the capital stock. If it is assumed as an approximation that the expected volume of output is equal to the level most recently experienced, then the expressions above may be seen to hold.[1]

Figure 1.3 illustrates the inverse relationship between the investment ratio and the capital-output ratio implied by the stock-adjustment principle. It shows a fairly close correspondence between peaks in one ratio and troughs in the other. An estimate of the relationship by least-squares regression is as follows:

$$\frac{I_t}{Y_{t-1}} = .381 - .091 \frac{K_t}{Y_{t-1}}$$

where I_t, K_t and Y_{t-1} all refer to manufacturing industry. The equation fits the data moderately well. The residual errors between the estimated and actual data averaged out at the equivalent of 3½% of total manufacturing investment, and they exceeded 10% in four years out of the eighteen. The size of the residuals, however, must be judged in relation to an expenditure total which is highly volatile, and in

---

1 The equations are derived by denoting K_t^* as the desired capital stock, Y_t^* as expected output, R_t^* as desired replacement investment, I_t^* as desired gross investment and I_t as actual gross investment. Then, by definition,

$$I_t^* = K_t^* - K_{t-1} + R_t^*$$

and, by assumption:

$$I_t = bI_t^* = b(K_t^* - K_{t-1} + R_t^*)$$
$$K_t^* = a_1 Y_t^*$$
$$R_t^* = a_2 Y_t^*$$
$$Y_t^* = Y_{t-1}$$
$$\therefore \ I_t = b(a_1 Y_{t-1} - K_{t-1} + a_2 Y_{t-1})$$
$$= b(a_1 + a_2) Y_{t-1} - bK_{t-1}$$
$$= aY_{t-1} - bK_{t-1} \text{ where } a = b(a_1 + a_2)$$

which is the first of the equations in the text.

which year-to-year changes exceed 10% in nine years out of eighteen.[1] It seems possible to conclude that there is at least an element of truth in the stock-adjustment principle, even though, it is difficult to regard its expectational and technological assumptions as more than approximately true.

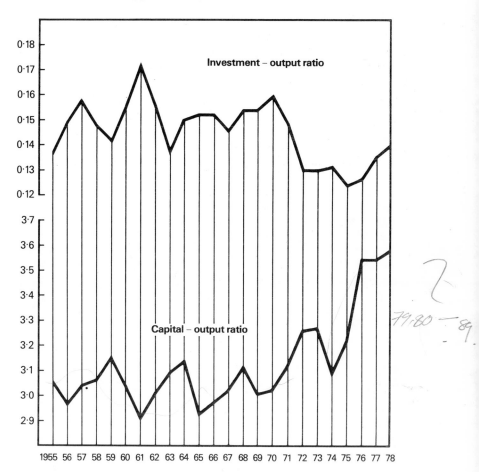

Figure 1.3   Manufacturing investment and capital stock as ratios of manufacturing output, UK, 1955-78

Economic theory suggests that there are a number of relevant considerations ignored by the stock-adjustment principle. One of these is the expected profitability of the investment, which, although related to the volume of expected sales and output, is dependent on other factors too. Expected profitability is likely

---

1   The equation was estimated at 1970 prices for 1953-72. Its other statistical characteristics were $r^2 = 0.57$, t-statistics 7.50 and 4.84 respectively, Durbin-Watson statistic 1.42, standard error of the investment ratio 0.007. The mean prediction error for 1963-72 from a similar equation fitted to 1953-62 data was equivalent to 3.9% of the level of investment. The capital-stock data for 1955-63 were taken from *LCES* and converted into 1970 prices; otherwise *NIBB*, 1966-76.

to be guided by actual profitability which, in recent years, has been exceptionally
low. The rate of return on capital employed fell from 9.6% in 1964-9 to only
4.0% in 1972[1] and there has been a corresponding decline in the ratio of profits to
income:

	Gross trading profits net of stock appreciation as % of total domestic income
1966-9	12.9
1970-2	11.7
1973-5	7.8
1976-8	9.0

(*Source: ET*, October 1979, p. 125)

There is not much doubt that these trends go a long way to explaining why
investment in the 1970s fell so low relative to GDP.

A further factor is the rate of interest which, as the cost of borrowing, can never
be completely ignored as an influence upon the level of investment. Interest must
be paid on all funds that are borrowed from outside the firm and it must be forgone
on internal funds which could have been lent at interest but which, instead, are used
to finance the firm's own investment projects. If interest rates had fluctuated
violently, it would have been necessary to include them as an additional variable in
the determination of investment in the UK. But for many years they showed only
rather modest movements, never rising, for example, by more than 2% in a year
over the period 1958-73.[2] In 1973-4, however, the debenture rate rose from 11.4%
to 16.4% as a result of faster inflation, and this almost certainly affected
investment. It has remained high ever since.

Another factor which must surely be taken into account in any general
explanation of investment behaviour is the availability of funds for investment and
the constraints that from time to time have been imposed by credit policy.
Investment is financed predominantly from internal sources and only partly from
outside credit institutions.[3] As far as internal sources are concerned it must be
accepted that company profits, besides acting as a guide to future profitability, will
also act as a financial constraint upon investment. As for external sources of credit,
there seems little doubt that a tight control of the money supply will constrain the
total amount of investment.

Other business fixed investment does not appear to conform with the
capital-stock-adjustment principle anything like as readily as manufacturing
investment. This may be because the assumption of a fixed relationship between

---

1 *NIER*, February 1976, pp. 83-4. For industry and transport the net rate of return fell from
   10.1% in 1963-7 to 5.8% in 1972-5. See Treasury *Economic Progress Report*, October 1979.

2 This probably explains why so few econometric studies have found interest rates to be an
   important influence on investment in Britain. See D. Savage, 'The Channels of Monetary
   Influence', *NIER*, February 1978.

3 During 1954-63 some 70-90% of company investment was financed from internal sources.
   See 'Internal and external sources of company finance', reprinted from *ET*, February 1966,
   in CSO, *New Contributions to Economic Statistics*, Fourth Series, HMSO, 1967.

capital and output does not hold well in non-manufacturing industries. It is less easy, therefore, to explain investment in these industries, although it must still be the case that expected sales, profits, interest rates and credit availability are relevant influences. Econometric studies have claimed a role for lagged changes in domestic output,[1] whilst short-term forecasts can be made on the basis of investment intentions surveys such as those carried out by the Department of Trade and Industry, the CBI and the *Financial Times*.

Housing investment needs to be divided between the public and private sectors and examined in relation to demand and supply influences in both sectors. The demand for public-sector building comes indirectly from population trends and directly from the policies of the public authorities. The demand for private-sector building depends both upon population characteristics (family formation and size) and also upon expected lifetime income, the cost of mortgage credit, the prices of new houses and of substitute accommodation. It is subject to the important and highly variable constraints set by the availability of mortgage credit which in turn are determined partly by general credit policy and partly by the policies of the building societies. Among the main influences on the side of supply are the size of the building industry and the number of building workers, the price and availability of building land, and stocks of bricks and other building materials. With such a variety of factors at work it is not easy to construct or present a satisfactory model of the determination of housing investment, and we do not attempt the task in this chapter. The problem of predicting housing investment is eased, however, by the statistics of new houses started, which, with an assumption about completion times, makes it possible to forecast housing for at least a short period ahead.

III.3   Stocks and Stockbuilding

Stockbuilding or investment in stocks is the change in a level — the level of all stocks held at the beginning of the period. In any one year stock investment can be positive or negative, whilst the change in stock investment between successive years can exert an important influence upon GDP. The increase in stock investment in 1972-4, for example, was equivalent to 4.6% of GDP, whilst the decline in 1974-5 was equivalent to 1.9% of GDP.

At the end of 1978 the total value of stocks held in all industries was approximately £55,000m, or 26% of the value of GDP in a year. Stocks held by manufacturing industry amounted to nearly £31,000m, or about 72% of the annual value of manufacturing output. Manufacturers' stocks divide into materials and fuel (£10,700m), work in progress (£11,700m) and stocks of finished products (£8,400m).[2]

Stocks of work in progress are held because they are a technical necessity of production, whilst stocks of materials and finished goods are held mainly out of a precautionary motive. They are required as a 'buffer' between deliveries and production; or, more precisely, because manufacturers are wise enough to know that they cannot expect an exact correspondence between the amount of materials

---

1   For example M.J.C. Surrey, *The Analysis and Forecasting of the British Economy*, NIESR and Cambridge University Press, 1971, p. 32, and HM Treasury, *Macroeconomic Forecasting Model, Technical Manual*, 1979.

2   *NIBB*, 1979, table 12.1. The other main holders of stocks are wholesale and retail business.

delivered each day and the amount taken into production, or between completed production and deliveries to customers.

For these reasons it seems plausible to assume that manufacturers carry in their minds the notion of a certain optimum ratio between stocks on the one hand and output on the other. If stocks fall below the optimum ratio they will need to be replenished; if they rise above it they will be run down. The reasoning here is the same as that of the stock-adjustment principle which we have already considered in connection with fixed investment. The principle holds moderately well for manufacturers' stockbuilding, which is by far the most volatile part of stock investment in the UK. Its application is illustrated in figure 1.4, where it can be seen, for example, that the stock investment peaks of 1956, 1960, 1964, 1969 and 1973-4 all coincided with low values of the stock-output ratio.

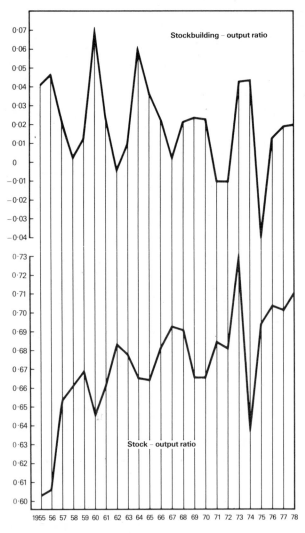

Figure 1.4   Manufacturers' stockbuilding and stock levels as ratios of manufacturing output, UK, 1955-78

A regression estimate of manufacturers' stockbuilding using annual data is:

$$\frac{I_t}{Y_{t-1}} = 0.299 - 0.41 \, \frac{S_t}{Y_{t-1}}$$

where the terms all refer to manufacturing industry and S_t stands for the level of stocks held at the beginning of the year. The quality of this regression equation is less good than that for fixed investment. Its mean residual error (regardless of sign) is about 0.007 in units of the stockbuilding-output ratio, and is equivalent to an average annual error of £80m at 1970 prices. This figure may be put in the perspective of a mean annual change in investment in stocks over the period of £150m.[1] It is probable that this equation would have performed better if we had estimated it for quarterly or semi-annual periods. This is because manufacturers are hardly likely to plan their stock changes for as long as a year ahead.

The stock-adjustment principle is only the beginning of a complete explanation of planned investment in stocks. Other factors are likely to be the level of interest rates, the availability of credit, expected future prices and the degree of uncertainty. *Unplanned* movements in stocks, moreover, will occur whenever sales expectations are falsified. Thus there will be an involuntary accumulation of stocks if sales fall below expectation, and an involuntary run-down of stocks if sales exceed their expected volume.

III.4   Other Expenditures

There are two further components of TFE — exports and public authorities' expenditure on goods and services — and two items which have to be deducted from TFE to obtain GDP — indirect taxes (net of subsidies) and imports of goods and services.

There is little to be said about public current expenditure since its amount is determined by the political aims and priorities of the central government and the local authorities. Exports of goods and services depend upon overseas demand, which in turn is mainly influenced by the volume of overseas income (both in the industrial and primary producing areas), the sterling price of UK exports and the exchange rate.[2] These matters, however, are discussed more fully in chapter 3.

The components of TFE are normally evaluated at their market prices. If we are interested in UK production and factor incomes we must make the factor-cost adjustment, i.e. deduct from these values the sum of indirect taxes net of subsidies. This is usually done for TFE as a whole, but estimates for the factor-cost adjustment for its main components are given in table 1.6.

Most indirect taxes are levied on consumption goods so that the adjustment tends to be higher here than it is for government expenditure, investment or exports.

---

1   The estimation period was 1952-70, but excluded 1960 and 1964 which are both well above estimate: $r^2 = 0.40$, the t-ratios were 3.4 and 3.2 respectively, Durbin-Watson statistic 1.94, and the standard error of the equation was 0.009 in units of the stockbuilding-output ratio. A similar equation fitted for 1952-61 predicted the ratios for 1962-70 with a mean error (regardless of sign) of 0.013; the errors for 1971 and 1972 were large.

2   It can be shown that fluctuations in UK exports correlate fairly closely with the index of world industrial production, and that exports to particular countries are statistically linked to output in those areas.

TABLE 1.6

Domestic Output Content of Total Final Expenditure at Market Prices, 1973

Percentages of market price totals

	Consumers' expenditure	*Government current expenditure*	*Gross domestic fixed investment*	*Exports of goods and services*	*Total final expenditure*
Indirect taxes (less subsidies)	16	4	5	3	10
Imports of goods and services	21	10	27	23	21
Domestic output content	63	86	68	74	69

Source: 'Summary Input-Output Tables for 1973', *ET*, June 1978.

The factor-cost adjustment is one of two deductions which must be made in order to progress from TFE to GDP. The other is imports which, since they are produced by foreign factors of production, cannot constitute UK factor income. In 1973, as the table shows, imports came to 21% of TFE; they were a smaller proportion of government spending than of other types of expenditure.

The main determinants of imports are the level of income, stocks of materials and competitive factors. It is probably this last group which is responsible for the upward trend (see chapter 3) in the ratio of imports of goods and services (at constant 1975 prices) to TFE:

1950-4	16.2%
1955-9	16.9%
1960-4	18.1%
1965-9	19.2%
1970-4	21.8%
1975-8	21.8%

It is possible that this trend can be broken down and explained in terms of price competitiveness, trade policy and other variables, but many forecasting equations for imports have simply extrapolated the trend at its average recent rate of increase.

The influence of stocks upon the volume of imports has been recognized for many years and at one time it was thought that every £100m of stockbuilding would add about £50m to the import bill.[1] More recently, however, the influence of stocks appears to have weakened. A recent estimate suggests an import content of stockbuilding of 0.3 rather than 0.5.[2] The reason for the decline in the coefficients is probably the increased weight of finished manufactures in the import total (see chapter 3).

The underlying explanation of the import content of stockbuilding is to be sought in terms of the stock-adjustment principle which, as suggested above, has a useful part to play in determining stockbuilding and fixed investment. If imports

---

1 See 'Forecasting Imports' by W.A.H. Godley and J.R. Shepherd, *NIER*, August 1965.

2 M.J.C. Surrey, *Analysis and Forecasting of the British Economy*, op. cit.

are found to vary directly with stockbuilding, and if stockbuilding follows the stock-adjustment principle, then imports will vary with the level of income and the initial level of stocks. Thus equations in terms of income and stockbuilding can be recast in terms of income and initial stock levels.[1] The more general point is that approximately one-third of total imports of goods and services consists of items which are used as inputs in the process of production. These are classified in chapter 3 as imports of basic materials, mineral fuels and lubricants, and semi-manufactures. They enter into stocks in the same way as domestically produced iron ore or coal, and they are subject to similar laws of behaviour.

IV   THE MANAGEMENT OF DEMAND
IV.1   Objectives and Instruments

Since the end of the Second World War most governments have striven to influence the level of demand in the economy with the intention of maintaining or restoring acceptable levels of employment. This policy was originally advocated in the White Paper on *Employment Policy* (Cmd. 6527) issued in 1944 by the wartime coalition government. The White Paper stated that:

> The Government believe that, once the war has been won, we can make a fresh approach, with better chances of success than ever before, to the task of maintaining a high and stable level of employment without sacrificing the essential liberties of a free society.

The White Paper recommended that there should be a permanent staff of statisticians and economists in the Civil Service with responsibility for interpreting economic trends and advising on policy. It suggested that the execution of employment policy should be examined annually by Parliament in the Debate on the Budget. The White Paper also foresaw that high levels of employment were likely to endanger price stability, and it pointed out the need for 'moderation in wage matters by employers and employees' as the essential condition for the success of the policy.

The task of maintaining a high level of employment proved to be less difficult than had been expected. The White Paper had not laid down any precise target for the level of employment. But the levels attained in nearly every postwar year (with exceptions in 1947, 1971 and 1975-9) were higher than the authors of the White Paper had hoped. It became apparent, moreover, that high levels of employment were compatible with a fairly moderate rate of inflation. The average rate of retail price inflation in the 1950s, for example, was about 4% per year whilst unemployment averaged as little as 1½% of the labour force.

As we observed in section II (above), however, the postwar economy passed through a series of fluctuations with the annual unemployment rate varying between the limits of 1.0% and 5.7%. Part of the reason for these fluctuations could be found in the different views taken by successive governments (or sometimes by the same government at different times) as to the most desirable

---

1   If $M = mY + nI$ (where M, Y and I are imports, income and stockbuilding respectively, m, the marginal propensity to import and n, the import content of stockbuilding), and if $I = aY - bK$, then $M = (m + na)Y - nbK$. The import ratio is now expressible in terms of the stock-output ratio.

pressure of demand. The aim of high employment has been in some measure of conflict with the objectives of both balance of payments equilibrium and price stability. A conflict with the balance of payments has been present in so far as governments have been unwilling to make use of instruments of policy, such as exchange-rate devaluation or import controls, for dealing with the external balance. Thus fiscal measures, which act upon the level of employment, have at times been directed towards the required balance of payments, with the consequence that the employment objective has taken second place. This conflict of objectives was particularly noticeable in two periods: from 1956 to early 1959 when the government was aiming at a long-term balance of payments surplus and preferred to deflate employment rather than depreciate sterling to achieve it; and also in the period of eighteen months preceding the devaluation of sterling in November 1967.

The employment objective has also been in conflict with that of price stability. Here there is no independent instrument of control to parallel the variability of the exchange rate. Incomes policy, in the sense of voluntary or compulsory guidelines for the rate of increase in wages and prices, has seldom been found to be particularly successful and certainly not successful enough to permit nice percentage variations in the permitted rate of inflation. Thus the absence of an independent instrument for controlling inflation has implied a really genuine conflict of aims. This, together with the balance of payments, helps to explain why the target level of employment has not been stable in the postwar period, but has tended to fluctuate according to the priorities of the government of the day.

It follows that the decision on what level of employment to aim for has normally had to be made on the basis of a compromise with the objectives of price stability and the balance of payments. But once the employment target is settled, the problem of how to attain it becomes a technical issue. It is a matter of how complete and precise is our knowledge of the workings of the economy.

One elementary point concerns the existence of time-lags between the detection of a policy problem and its remedy. This means that it is not sound strategy to wait until unemployment has reached some intolerably high figure before acting or thinking about action to correct it. The unemployment statistics are about a month behindhand; civil servants may take up to six months to advise the appropriate action; Parliament may take three months to enact it; and even after the policy is put into force the full economic effects may not appear for some months afterwards. Thus a strategy based solely upon the observation of past performance can involve a significantly long time-lag (of twelve months or longer) between the observed need for a change in policy and the effects of that change upon the level of employment.

It is partly for this reason that economic management in the UK has been based upon a strategy of looking ahead rather than on response to observed behaviour. This means that the policy-maker relies heavily upon the use of economic forecasts. If he can *correctly* foresee the emergence of a policy problem, then the problem of the delay between the need for intervention and its effects is removed.

There is another reason too, for relying upon forecasts. This is the need to tailor the amount of intervention to the future size of the problem rather than to what is currently observed. The mere observation of high unemployment or excessive inflation in no way guarantees that it will continue in the same degree of seriousness. The problem may get worse or it may get better. Quite clearly it is essential to form some view of what will happen in the future before deciding the degree and the direction of policy intervention required. Failure to produce a correct forecast of the course of employment over the next twelve to eighteen months could result in an *inadequate* degree of corrective policy action. Or it could actually be *destabilizing*,[1] in the sense that the effect of intervention is to remove the level of output still further from target than it would have been without it.

The last three decades have seen a very considerable advance in the various branches of knowledge which bear upon the problems of forecasting and managing the economy. The chief of these have comprised: (i) an enormous improvement, attributable to the CSO, in economic statistics, and particularly the development of quarterly, seasonally adjusted, constant-price, national expenditure figures; (ii) the development of a conceptual framework and quantitative model for forecasting the levels of GDP and employment over a period of about eighteen months; (iii) the development of a conceptual framework and quantitative model for estimating the effects on GDP of tax changes and other instruments of demand management.

IV.2 The Effects of Policy Instruments: Government Expenditure

If fiscal intervention is to be tailored to precise targets for employment and output it is necessary for the policy-makers to make a fairly precise quantitative assessment of the effects of their policy instruments upon the level of domestic output. In this section we shall concentrate upon the effects of three such instruments: changes in government expenditure on goods and services, changes in indirect taxation and changes in personal income tax.

The effects of these changes divide into direct effects upon GDP and indirect effects such as the multiplier and accelerator consequences. In the case of an increase in government expenditure on goods and services measured at market prices, the direct effects on GDP (at factor cost) will be smaller in volume than the expenditure change itself. This is because there are 'leakages' into imports and indirect taxes which do not influence domestic output. For government spending as a whole the indirect tax content averages 4% and the import content 10%,[2] so that £100m added to government expenditure will raise domestic output by £86m if the goods and services purchased are typical of government spending in general.[3] This also means that government expenditure must be raised on average by £116m to add £100m to GDP.

The indirect effects of the additional expenditure cannot be evaluated without an estimate of the size and timing of the *multiplier*; they are common to all three types of policy change. If GDP is raised by £100m by some initial increase in government expenditure, the question to be asked is how much of this will be re-spent on new domestic output. The problem may be tackled by estimating how much of the additional GDP will find its way into personal income, and by asking how this income is distributed between income tax, saving and consumers' expenditure. The addition to consumers' expenditure must be broken down into its

---

1   A more accurate term would be 'perverse', since policy does not necessarily aim to stabilize anything.

2   See table 1.6.

3   If, however, the extra spending is all on the running of a new department in Whitehall, the import content could be well below 9%; if it is all on military spending overseas it could be much higher.

indirect-tax, imported and domestically produced components, and of these it is of course the last which constitutes the second addition to GDP.

The main quantities involved in this calculation are indicated in table 1.7. It can be assumed that none of the additional GDP is distributed as rent, and if the remainder is divided between profits and income from employment in the same ratio as total incomes from profit and employment (see *NIBB*), then the addition to personal income is likely to be about 82%. The increase in disposable income is found by estimating the marginal tax rate for an average income recipient and the increases in consumption by taking the marginal savings ratio. Next, the indirect tax component of consumption is removed in order to obtain consumption at factor cost. Finally, the import component must be subtracted so as to arrive at the domestically produced increase in consumption. On the basis of the assumptions made, this turns out to be quite a small increase − only 31% of the first addition to GDP.

TABLE 1.7

Stages in the Multiplier Process

	£m	Assumed marginal relationships
1st round increase in GDP	100	
Increase in personal income	82	$b_1 = .820$
Increase in personal disposable income	56	$b_2 = .683$
Increase (after a time-lag) in consumers' expenditure at market prices	50	$b_3 = .893$
Increase in consumers' expenditure at factor cost	41	$b_4 = .820$
Increase in domestically produced consumption at factor cost (equals 2nd round increase in GDP)	31	$b_5 = .756$

If the initial increase in GDP of £100m is not sustained, but is confined for example to a single period's duration, then the indirect effects on GDP will be £31m in the second period, 31% of £31m in the following period, and so on. Under these circumstances the effects will tend to die out over time. The sequence of deviations in GDP from the course it would otherwise have followed would be:

£100, 31, 9.6, 3.0, 0.9, 0.3, 0.1 . . . million.

If, however, the increment in GDP is a sustained increase (a continuous injection of demand), then the same sequence is generated in each successive period so that the series of deviations in GDP would be as follows:

£100, 131, 140.6, 143.6, 144.5, 144.8, 144.9 . . . million.

Here the full multiplier effect on GDP is almost wholly realized in four periods after the initial injection, and even by the third period the bulk of the multiplier effect has come through.[1]

---

1 The full multiplier value is 1.449 and is calculated from the marginal relationships set out in table 1.7 as follows:

$$\frac{1}{1 - b_1 b_2 b_3 b_4 b_5} = \frac{1}{1 - \frac{82}{100} \cdot \frac{56}{82} \cdot \frac{50}{56} \cdot \frac{41}{50} \cdot \frac{31}{41}} = \frac{1}{1 - 0.31} = 1.449$$

This is completely analogous with the simple textbook multiplier, save that the marginal propensity to consume is replaced by a composite marginal propensity to re-spend domestic output.

The key to the timing of the multiplier process lies in the lag of one period which is taken to exist between the receipt of GDP in the form of income and the expenditure of this income on additional consumption goods. The length of the period could be anything up to three months, but, in view of the widespread tendency to pay incomes at weekly or monthly intervals, is likely to be shorter than this. Thus the full multiplier effects of a policy change may be realized in only a few months. This, however, presupposes that increased expenditure is matched instantaneously by additional production, which is implausible. It is almost inevitable that the first impact of any increase in consumers' spending will be met out of stocks. So long as stocks behave passively and production responds to expenditure after a short time-lag, the multiplier time path will be delayed but not altered in any fundamental sense. If, however, stocks are not passive but behave according to the stock-adjustment principle, then it is possible that the replenishment of stocks will cause the time path to wobble on its way to equilibrium.[1] The extent of these wobbles is not well established although our consideration of stock-building behaviour in section III.3 suggests that they must be present in some degree. Hopkin and Godley,[2] in their important discussion of the multiplier effects of policy changes, made small notional allowances for the accelerator both in stocks and in fixed investment. It is probably true to say, however, that these effects are not as well known as they ought to be.[3]

The effects of changes in government expenditure have been discussed mainly because their evaluation affords an easy introduction to the concept of the multiplier (which is common to all policy changes). In fact government expenditure was not, until quite recently, used as an instrument for influencing demand. This is mainly because its level is determined by political objectives which are quite independent of the goals of high employment or price stability. Nor is it a particularly appropriate instrument of control since it is difficult to organize changes in its total with any great degree of precision.[4] Nevertheless, cuts in government expenditure provide an opportune method of reducing total demand for a government which regards the size of the public sector as excessive.

IV.3   The Effects of Tax Changes and Other Instruments

The more usual instruments of demand management have been changes in direct and indirect taxes.

The estimation of the effect upon GDP of a change in income tax may be illustrated by reference to the increased allowances and 3p reduction in the basic tax rate introduced in the Budget of June 1979. The effect on the income tax revenue of these changes was estimated by the Inland Revenue to be £4,568m, which implied a reduction in personal disposable income of the same amount.[5]

1 In extreme cases there may be severe oscillations or even an explosive time path. On this the classic reference is L.A. Metzler, 'The Nature and Stability of Inventory Cycles' in R.A. Gordon and L.R. Klein (eds.), *Readings in Business Cycles*.

2 W.A.B. Hopkin and W.A.H. Godley, 'An Analysis of Tax Changes', *NIER*, May 1965. This article is the basis of the discussion above.

3 For estimates of the effects of policy changes based on econometric models, see J.S.E. Laury, G.R. Lewis and P.A. Ormerod, 'Properties of Macroeconomic Models of the UK Economy: A Comparative Study', *NIER*, February 1978.

4 J.C.R. Dow, *The Management of the British Economy 1945-60*, Cambridge University Press, 1964, pp. 180-1.

5 *Financial Statement and Budget Report, 1979-80*, p. 31.

The direct effect of this upon the level of GDP may be found by reference to the coefficients in table 1.7. Thus the change in consumers' expenditure at market prices is obtained by multiplying £4,568m by b_3 (b_3 being the marginal propensity to consume) and the additional consumption of domestic output is this amount multiplied by b_4 and b_5. Thus the initial effect upon GDP, measured at current prices, is £4,568m times $b_3 b_4 b_5$ = £2,529m. This is approximately 1.6% of GDP. The final effect may be found by multiplying this amount by the multiplier value of 1.449, and is about 2.4% of 1979 GDP.[1]

In estimating the effects of changes in indirect taxation the initial effect on GDP can normally be found by taking the additional revenue (as estimated by the Board of Customs and Excise) and applying the coefficients in table 1.7. As an example we may take the increase in VAT from 8 to 15% in the Budget of June 1979. This was estimated to add £4,175m to the revenue in a full year. With no initial change in disposable income or the savings rate this must imply a decline in consumption *at factor cost* of the same amount. The consumption of domestically produced goods will decline by less than this because of the leakage into imports, so that the initial decline in GDP will be £4,175m times the coefficient b_5; this is £3,156, or 2.0% of GDP. With a multiplier value of 1.449 the full effect on GDP works out at 2.9%.[2]

When discussing the effects of tax changes it is advisable to remember that all changes in the budget balance have to be financed either by borrowing from the public or by increasing the money supply. Strictly speaking the effects described above must assume that the method of financing is an expansion of the money supply. This invites the claim that we have not been describing fiscal policy *per se* but a mixed policy of fiscal changes with monetary accommodation. But the name does not matter since the Chancellor of the Exchequer is responsible both for fiscal and monetary policy, and is therefore able to ensure that budget deficits are financed in ways which do not subvert the objectives of policy. It should be noted, however, that if fiscal changes are financed by borrowing from the public there will be consequential increases in interest rates which will tend to inhibit consumer purchases of durable goods and investment by firms. Furthermore, if the rise in interest rates spreads to mortgage rates the effect could be similar to a rise in taxation since every mortgage-holder will find that his pay, after tax and mortgage payments, is less than previously. It follows that reductions in taxation which are financed by borrowing will always be less expansionary than those financed through increases in the quantity of money.

The alternative to fiscal policy is often taken to be monetary policy, but, as we have seen, fiscal expansion may be financed by an increase in the money stock. Debt management, however, may be used to accomplish a change in interest rates without any marked alteration in the budget balance. The effects of interest changes on investment are likely to be delayed for many months and their main impact will fall outside the normal forecasting horizon of twelve to eighteen months. But the effects on consumers' expenditure through higher mortgage rates and HP payments may operate more swiftly. Monetary policy can also affect spending directly through increasing or decreasing the availability of credit.

---

1   Strictly speaking, the multiplier is different after the tax change because the coefficient b_2 is changed. But the effect of this is too small to be worth allowing for.

2   This procedure assumes that there is no switching from taxed to untaxed goods and is appropriate for an across-the-board change in indirect taxation. For an analysis of indirect tax changes involving changes in relative prices, see Hopkin and Godley, op. cit.

IV.4   Economic Forecasts

It has been suggested above that it is not satisfactory to manage the economy simply by reacting to observations of the current situation. If the government is to reduce the risk of unduly delayed, possibly destabilizing, actions it must attempt to forecast the course of domestic output and employment. The difference between the forecast path of GDP and the path required by the employment target determines the direction and extent of budgetary action.

National income forecasts are prepared in the Treasury three times a year. The timing of the three main forecasts is geared to the Budget, which is normally in the first half of April. A preliminary assessment of next year's prospects is generally made in late autumn, and this is brought up to date and extended a further six months in February and March. A third forecast is made in early summer.

From a policy point of view the most important forecast is the one made in February. This extends from the last-known figures for GDP (which relate to the third quarter of the previous year) as far as the second quarter of the following year. It covers seven quarters altogether, of which the last five quarters, from the second of this year to the third of next, are genuinely in the future. The first two quarters, from last October to March of the current year, represent a kind of no-man's land between an imperfectly known past and an unknown future. The problem here is one of piecing together bits of statistical information such as the monthly figures of exports, imports, retail sales and industrial production into a reasonably coherent picture of the base period. This is always difficult because there is very little monthly information about investment or government expenditure, and the difficulties can be made worse by apparent contradictions between the various monthly figures of production, sales and employment.

Once the base period is established, the forecast proper (i.e. the part relating to the future) can be started. The methods by which this is done need not be described in detail.[1] They have evolved steadily over a number of years and have made increasing use of econometric techniques as a result of the accumulation of economic statistics and their improvement. The forecasting model may best be thought of in terms of dependent expenditures, such as consumption, stockbuilding and imports, which are determined primarily by the current level of GDP, and autonomous expenditures, such as government purchases, fixed investment and exports, which in the short run are largely independent of GDP. In forecasting the latter a good deal of use is made of direct information from business firms and government departments. Government current expenditure and the government component of fixed investment, for example, can be predicted from information provided by government departments and the nationalized industries. The forecast of business fixed investment can be arrived at partly by reference to the sample enquiries into investment intentions conducted by the Department of Trade and Industry and the CBI. The forecast of housing and investment may be

---

1 The evolution of the Treasury's forecasting methods may be followed in A.D. Roy, 'Short-term Forecasting for Central Economic Management', in K. Hilton and D.F. Heathfield (eds.), *The Econometric Study of the United Kingdom*, Macmillan, 1970, and J.R. Shepherd, 'Short-term Forecasting for the UK Economy', in Sir Alec Cairncross (ed.), *The Managed Economy*, Blackwell, 1970. More recent accounts are J.R. Shepherd, H.P. Evans and C.J. Riley, 'The Treasury Short-term Forecasting Model', Government Economic Service Occasional Papers (HMSO) and finally in HM Treasury, *Macroeconomic Forecasting Model, Technical Manual*, HMSO, 1979. Any *NIER* will give an impression of the methods used by the National Institute of Economic and Social Research.

derived largely from figures of housing starts and an assumption about the period of housing construction. The export forecast is made on the basis of expected trends in world trade, and will also be affected by sharp changes in the competitive position. In forecasting the dependent expenditures it is possible to employ behavioural relationships of the type we have suggested in section III. There are many different ways, however, of formulating consumption and investment functions and it is not an easy matter to judge which of them is best. Thus although a large econometric model is now used by the Treasury as part of its forecasting work it may be assumed that parts of the model will be disputed by those responsible for getting the forecast right and that the model, therefore, is not likely to dictate the forecast to the exclusion of all argument and discussion. Furthermore, as every forecaster knows, there are always events which the model is not able to handle (strikes and fuel shortages, for example) and which necessitate judgmental estimation of their effects upon economic activity.

The main upshot of the government forecasting work is a table in considerable detail of the course of GDP and its components, quarter by quarter, over a period of two to three years. The published version of the forecast normally extends to the middle of the calendar year after the Budget.[1]

IV.5   Criticisms of Demand Management

It is not wholly surprising that demand management has come in for heavy criticism from journalists and economists. This is to be expected of any sphere of government policy, and especially one involving frequent changes in tax rates. In assessing these criticisms it is not always easy to distinguish criticisms of the objectives of demand management from criticisms of the way it is carried out.

The criticisms divide into four main groups: (i) that the economy has fluctuated considerably despite the advocacy of 'stable' employment in the 1944 White Paper; (ii) that the technical apparatus of demand management has been inadequate to its task; (iii) that economic policy has been in some sense destabilizing; (iv) that errors in demand management have been connected with the rapid inflation of the 1970s.

(i) On the first of these points there is no doubt that the course of the economy has been something less than stable for most of the period since demand management was inaugurated. This phenomenon (which has sometimes been labelled the 'stop-go' cycle) has been described and charted in section II of this chapter. What is not so clear, however, is the extent to which this instability implies a criticism of the aims of policy (which is largely a subjective matter) or of the technical apparatus for achieving those aims. For even an unstable and highly cyclical time path for the economy may represent a series of changes of mind by successive governments about the best level of employment at which to run the economy. The conflicts or presumed conflicts between economic objectives are sufficiently obvious to make it doubtful whether the target pressure of demand has always been the same. Indeed, in so far as the facts can be ascertained, the target appears to have fluctuated quite significantly.

Fluctuations in targets may be detected from the available information on Treasury forecasts. These forecasts, after allowance for the effects of tax changes introduced at the time, represent the increase in GDP which the government finds

---

1   These appear in the *Financial Statement and Budget Report.*

acceptable at the time they are made. As such they are tantamount to target increases in output. For the period 1955-68 these target rates of increase may be related to the level of *potential output* (the level of GDP in a specific period which could have been produced with employment at some standard percentage of the labour force). A series for the target use of potential output is given in table 1.8, and shows a fall of about 4% between 1955 and 1959, increases in 1960 and 1964, and a fairly steady target from then until 1968. Unfortunately, this procedure cannot be continued after 1968 because of the breakdown in the relationship between unemployment and vacancies (see section II). The best that can be done is to relate target changes in actual output to the growth rate of output (2.0% per annum) which would have maintained unfilled vacancies at a constant percentage of the labour force. The main feature of this series is the sharp increase in the intended pressure of demand between 1971 and 1973 and the equally sharp contraction in 1975.

(ii) As regards the technical apparatus of demand management the key question is whether, and by how much, it has failed to achieve the target levels of employment or GDP. Since the target levels of GDP are equivalent to the government forecasts after allowance has been made for the effects of each Budget, this question is essentially a matter of the accuracy of forecasts.[1] If the Treasury forecasts the increase in GDP incorrectly then it will be led into taking the wrong measures. The result will be that the target level of GDP will be missed by the same amount as the forecast is in error.

The question of the accuracy of Treasury forecasts can only be answered satisfactorily for those forecasts which have been published or described with sufficient clarity to permit comparisons with the outcome. For 1968 and after, the forecasts have been published as part of the *Financial Statement and Budget Report*. But before this date the information is not always as good, and must be assembled from official documents or even from forecasts made by other bodies at the same time. Nevertheless, the task is worth attempting even though the results (see table 1.8) cannot be sacrosanct.[2]

The main point to emerge from an assessment of Treasury forecasts over the period since 1955 is that, whilst they have not been as accurate as might have been hoped, they have led policy seriously astray on only four or five occasions. There is not much doubt that the 1959 forecast, when the error was 4%, was the worst forecast of all. It meant that an unforeseen recovery in total output was coupled with an expansionary Budget, and the result was a much higher level of employment at the end of the year than the government had actually intended. By contrast, the forecasting error in 1962 went the other way, with the result that there was a recession despite the policy aim of a roughly 4% rise in output (implying high employment). The error was put right in 1963, although the recovery went further than intended. The worst forecast of recent years appears to have been 1974, when the Treasury was much too optimistic (by 3.2% of GDP) about the economic outlook.

Taking the whole period from 1955-79, the average error in Treasury forecasts (regardless of sign) was about 1.1% of GDP. This implies an average deviation of

---

1 Forecasting accuracy is not always simple to interpret: there may be strikes or other events of an unforeseeable nature which affect the accuracy of the forecasts without necessarily discrediting the methods by which they are derived.

2 The same qualifications apply to the series for the Target Use of Potential Output.

TABLE 1.8

Short-term Targets and Forecasting Errors, UK, 1955-79

		Target use of potential output or target pressure of demand[1] %	Forecast and target change in GDP from year earlier[2] %	Actual change in GDP from year earlier[3] %	Error (forecast less actual) %
1955	(year)	99	2.9	3.8	−0.9
1956	,,	98	1.1	1.2	−0.1
1957	,,	97	1.3	1.7	−0.4
1958	,,	95	−0.4	−0.3	0.1
1959	(4th qtr)	94	2.8	6.6	−3.8
1960	,,	98	3.1	3.8	−0.7
1961	,,	94	1.8	2.0	−0.2
1962	,,	98	3.9	0.7	3.2
1963	,,	97	4.6	6.5	−1.9
1964	,,	101	5.4	3.5	1.9
1965	,,	99	2.7	2.9	−0.2
1966	,,	98	2.0	1.6	0.4
1967	,,	97	3.1	1.9	1.2
1968	(2nd half)	97	3.6	4.8	−1.2
1969	,,	98	1.9	0.1	1.8
1970	,,	99	3.6	2.2	1.4
1971	,,	97	1.1	1.3	−0.2
1972	,,	101	5.5	2.5	3.0
1973	,,	102	6.0	5.8	0.2
1974	,,	102	2.6	−0.6	3.2
1975	,,	97	0.0	−1.7	1.7
1976	,,	97	3.9	4.1	−0.2
1977	,,	97	1.5	1.4	0.1
1978	,,	98	3.0	3.1	−0.1
1979	,,	96	−0.5	0.9	−1.4
1980	,,	91	−3.1		

Notes and sources:

1   Potential output for 1955-68 is the level of GDP which is estimated to be attainable with a 1.0% rate of unemployment: source M.C. Kennedy 'Employment Policy − What Went Wrong?' in Joan Robinson (ed.), *After Keynes*. For 1968-79 the level of GDP required to maintain a constant vacancy rate is assumed to have grown at 2.0% per annum, i.e. the actual growth rate for 1969-78.

2   Kennedy, op. cit., and *Financial Statement and Budget Reports* (HMSO).

3   Average estimate of GDP, *ET(AS)*, 1980.

about 0.4% between the actual and desired unemployment rate, and is equivalent to an error between the appropriate rate of income tax and the actual rate of about 3p in the £. There is not much evidence that the forecasts have become any more accurate with the passage of time.[1]

(iii) A number of writers have sought to show or to deny that demand management has been destabilizing.[2] To do this it is necessary to make assumptions

1   For an official calculation of the average error in GDP forecasts and its breakdown by expenditure, see *ET*, November 1978.

2   For reviews of these and other studies of short-term policies, see G.D.N. Worswick, 'Fiscal Policy and Stabilization in Britain' in A.K. Cairncross (ed.), *Britain's Economic Prospects Reconsidered* and M.C. Kennedy, op. cit.

as to the target level of output and the level which output would have attained in the absence of discretionary intervention. Most writers in this field have made somewhat questionable assumptions about the targets and the instruments of intervention. Thus one has claimed that policy was destabilizing because it was demonstrable that 'policy-off' changes in GDP (i.e. after deducting the effects of changes in taxation and government spending) were less widely scattered round the average annual increase in GDP than policy-on (i.e. actual) changes in GDP.[1] It is arbitrary, however, to measure failures of policy in terms of dispersion around an average annual increase in GDP. For there is, first, no presumption that governments were aiming each year at a constant rise in GDP, and secondly, there is every reason (in times of depression or boom) to suppose that they would aim at increases above or below the average.

The stabilizing effectiveness of short-term policy has also been investigated in terms of the stability of GDP around its trend. It has been shown by Artis[2] that for the 1958-70 period the dispersion of quarterly levels of observed GDP from their time-trend was larger than the dispersion of estimated 'policy-off' GDP (i.e. after deducting the cumulative effects of all tax changes introduced after a particular base year) from their (different) time-trend. This result indicates that policy was 'destabilizing' in the sense of this particular method of measurement. But as the author made clear, there was never any presumption that the course of target GDP coincided with trend GDP. It is also questionable whether 'policy-off' GDP should be arrived at by subtracting from actual GDP the cumulative effect of measures taken over several years rather than the effect of those measures taken in the particular year.

(iv) During the period of fast inflation in the 1970s demand management came in for some further criticisms. One popular source of complaint was that the very fast expansion of demand during 1973, together with the high pressure of demand in 1974, were responsible for the acceleration in the rate of inflation. This criticism greatly overstates the case since by far the most important factor in the acceleration of inflation over this period was the massive increase in import prices (almost 100% in two years). This is not to deny, however, that the higher pressure of demand in 1973 and 1974 would have added something to the rate of inflation, or that the very fast pace of the expansion did not create its own special pressures. (The annual rate of increase in GDP between the first quarters of 1972 and 1973 was 9.3%.) But the main factor responsible for the inflation in this period was almost certainly the rise in world commodity prices and its inevitable consequence for UK material and food prices (see section V below).

It has also been suggested[3] that 'the whole intellectual basis of postwar "demand management" by government is undermined if the natural unemployment rate hypothesis is true'. The hypothesis in question postulates that there is some level of the unemployment rate, the natural rate, which is compatible with a zero rate of price inflation provided that the expected rate of price inflation is also zero. If the unemployment target is set below the natural rate then inflation will accelerate. Wage increases will generate price increases which lead to expected price increases

1   B. Hansen, *Fiscal Policy in Seven Countries, 1955-65*, OECD, Paris, 1969.

2   M.J. Artis, 'Fiscal Policy for Stabilization', in W. Beckerman (ed.), *The Labour Government's Economic Record, 1964-70*, Duckworth, 1972.

3   M. Friedman and D. Laidler, 'Unemployment *versus* Inflation', IEA, 1975 Occasional Paper 44, p. 45.

and hence to further and larger wage increases. Some of the assumptions behind
this hypothesis are rather dubious when applied to the UK economy (see section
V). But even if the assumptions were true (and variants of them in the shape of the
wage-price spiral hypothesis have been accepted for many years), there is no reason
why it should undermine the basis of demand management. Governments which
sought to avoid accelerating inflation would simply set the target rate at or above
the natural rate of employment. They would seek to achieve their target level of
unemployment by exactly the same combination of forecasts and instruments
which we have described. Far from destroying the basis of demand management,
the natural-rate hypothesis simply underlines its importance.

A more acceptable line of criticism is that the Treasury's economic forecasting
framework fails to take sufficient note of monetary variables.[1] This omission
reflects a deep-seated failure of economics, both monetarist and Keynesian, to
provide acceptable estimates of the quantitative effects of changes in the supply of
money. The omission is probably most serious in connection with the manner in
which Budget deficits are financed. The multiplier effects of tax and government
expenditure changes are normally calculated on the assumption that the money
supply is adjusted so as to maintain interest rates. But a tight control of the money
supply, or an insistence upon the financing of deficits by borrowing from the
public, could have effects on expenditure which are not taken into account.

IV.6   Demand Management and the PSBR

Demand management can, and has, been described without reference to the Budget
deficit or the public-sector-borrowing requirement (PSBR), which is the combined
deficit of the central government, local authorities and public corporations. This
was deliberate. For if tax rates are to be decided according to the government's
target level of GDP, and if the government's expenditure is set according to its
social or political objectives, then the government deficit will be a *consequence* of
demand management and not an independent target on its own. At given tax rates,
the size of the deficit will also vary with the state of the economy, since the tax
base (predominantly incomes and expenditure) will vary with the level of economic
activity and prices, as will certain transfer payments, notably unemployment
benefits.

In the 1960s the PSBR was never more than £2 billion a year but in the 1970s it
rose well above this figure, reaching £10.5 billion in 1975 and £8.4 billion in 1978
(calendar years). This was approximately 5% of GDP at market prices.

The significance of this figure needs to be examined. What it means is that the
public authorities have to borrow this sum of money from the banking system,
private residents or overseas lending. If the money is borrowed from overseas, the
interest paid will constitute a transfer of national income abroad. If it is borrowed
from the private sector, it will lead to a competition for funds and a rise in interest
rates. This will mean higher monthly payments for anyone buying their houses with
a mortgage; it also leads to falling security values, including those of ordinary
shares. Thus the only alternative is to finance the deficit by the issue of new
money, and this may be done without any undesirable effects on mortgage
payments or property values. This last course, however, is frequently resisted on

---

1 See for example D. Laidler, Minutes of Evidence, *Ninth Report from the Expenditure
Committee* (1974), HC 328.

the grounds that any increase in the money stock *necessarily* involves an increase in the level of prices. This hypothesis, which is a generalisation of the quantity theory of money to circumstances where real output is not necessarily fixed, is arguably false (see section V) but very widely held in certain quarters, particularly in the City of London. Since it implies that there is no method of financing a public-sector deficit which does not have serious economic consequences, it forms the basis of a view that the PSBR should gradually be reduced. This objective, pursued with determination, implies the end of demand management and its replacement by a target for the PSBR. It appears to be the policy of the Conservative government elected in May 1979.[1]

V.   INFLATION
V.1   Inflation and its Causes

Inflation is defined variously as *any* increase in the general level of prices or as any *sustained* increase. In this chapter we shall use the wider definition since it enables us to include short-lived increases in the general price level, such as those of 1920, 1940 and 1951-2, within the sphere of discussion without raising the further definitional question of whether they were sufficiently 'sustained' to be called inflations.

In measuring the rate of inflation we have a choice of index numbers. The appropriate index of the prices charged for all goods produced in the UK economy is the implied index number for GDP, so called because it is obtained by dividing the value of GDP at current prices by GDP at constant (1975) prices. The GDP index includes export prices. If an index is required to measure the prices of goods purchased by UK residents, the best general measure is the implied deflator for total domestic expenditure, since this is an average of the prices paid for consumption and investment goods, both privately and publicly purchased. If we are chiefly interested in the prices paid for consumer goods and services we have a choice between the implied price index for consumers' expenditure and the index of retail prices. The former, like all implicit indices, is not compiled directly from price data but is found by dividing the current value of consumers' expenditure by the volume estimate as measured at constant prices. By contrast the index of retail prices (the cost-of-living index) is compiled directly from price data. It registers the prices of a collection of goods and services entering a typical shopping basket. The composition of the basket has been revised from time to time so as to keep up with changes in the pattern of expenditure. Being a base-weighted index it gradually becomes outdated in coverage. In periods of inflation it will tend to exaggerate the increase in the cost of living because consumers will switch their expenditure patterns towards those goods which are rising less rapidly in price. Nevertheless, it is accurate enough for most purposes.

The 1970s are now well established as the most inflationary decade of the twentieth century. The index of retail prices trebled between 1970 and 1979. The average rise in retail prices was 12.7% a year in the 1970s compared with 3.3% in 1953-69, 2.1% in 1934-9 and declining prices in 1925-33.

---

1 See the budget speech, 27 March 1980, and the speech by the Financial Secretary quoted at length in the Treasury *Economic Progress Report*, March 1980.

Any general explanation of inflation in an open economy like the UK needs to take account of at least three independent types of inflationary impulse:

(i)   increases in import prices
(ii)   excess demand in the home economy
(iii) wage push.

Any economy which is engaged in overseas trade is exposed to inflationary impulses from the world outside. In the UK, where such a large part of our food and raw materials are imported from overseas, the effects of world inflation are felt primarily through higher prices paid for imported primary commodities and consequential increases in production costs and food prices. Many of our most violent changes in prices, both up and down, can be traced to changes in the world prices of primary commodities.

The second main ingredient in our theory of inflation is the pressure of demand upon productive potential and productive resources. Excess demand is a manifestation of market forces. We should expect wages and/or prices to increase whenever excess demand (i.e. demand less supply at going prices) is positive, and to fall when it is negative. In the economy as a whole we can expect positive and negative excess demands to exist simultaneously in different markets, so that there is bound to be a mixture of conflicting tendencies with some prices tending to decline as others are tending to rise. From a macroeconomic point of view we are interested in the balance of excess demands and excess supplies, and this for most periods can be measured by either the unemployment percentage or the vacancy rate, although neither measure is perfectly satisfactory (see section II). Both these measures relate to the labour market, and there are unfortunately no general statistical indicators of excess demand in the market for goods.

The third main ingredient in our model of inflation is more controversial, and is the potentially independent force of wage-pushfulness. It is necessary to include this as a separate factor because wages are widely fixed by bargaining between the representatives of powerful groups, the union and the firm or employers' federation, each of which has the ability to influence the bargain by threatening to interrupt production and employment. Whilst there are reasons to expect that the pressure of demand for labour will normally be an influence in the bargaining process, we cannot exclude the possibility that alterations in the strength of the union, in the loyalty of its members, and in its preparedness to strike, may act as an independent force (i.e. independent of market forces) in determining wage increases.

We can combine these three main initiating causes of inflation into a more complete model by relating them to wage increases, price increases and expected price increases in the manner illustrated in figure 1.5. The model assumes that the *process* by which excess demand leads to price inflation is through the rate of increase in wages. Higher wages mean higher average costs of production and these lead after a time-lag to higher prices. This will happen either because business firms tend to set prices by a constant markup over variable costs or because they seek to maximize profits. Higher prices lead, again after a time-lag, to higher wages since trade unions will tend to claim compensation for increases in the cost of living, or in other words to restore the real wages of their members. Thus the central ingredient of our model is a wage-price spiral which is superimposed upon the excess demand for labour. But besides excess demand the spiral may also be set in motion by exogenous increases in wages coming from wage-push, or by increases in import prices as a consequence of movements in world commodity prices.

A possible objection to this manner of presenting the inflationary process is that it does not appear to allow for a direct influence of excess demand upon the rate of price increase. This omission is forced upon us mainly by the dearth of statistical indicators of excess demand in the goods market and partly, too, by the fact that a number of studies have attempted to find evidence of this relationship and have not been successful.[1] However, we do not wish to pretend that there is never a direct effect of excess demand upon prices — only that the main sequence to have been identified is from excess demand to wage increases and then to prices.

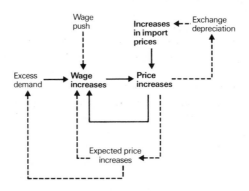

Figure 1.5   Inflationary processes

A second objection to the model might be that there is no reference to the quantity of money. This lack of an explicit reference, however, does not rule out monetary causation of inflation since additions to the quantity of money will raise prices through the medium of excess demand, and excess demand has a prominent place in the model. This amounts to saying that monetary inflation is a branch of demand-pull inflation. An increase in the money supply will act through interest-rate reductions or more directly through credit availability to increase the demand for goods and services, and hence create excess demand. There is no place in our model, or in economic theory in general, for an influence of money upon prices which is not transmitted through the medium of excess demand.

Besides excess demand and the wage-price spiral, figure 1.5 allows for two other possible interactions between wages and prices, both of them operating through the effect of rising prices upon expected future prices. The first of these is the possibility that expectations of future price changes, rather than compensation for past increases, may be a major factor in wage bargaining. It has been suggested by some writers[2] that the expectation of a price increase of, say, 10% in the next twelve months will induce trade unions and employers to settle for increases in nominal wages of as much as 10% more than would have occurred if prices had been expected to be stable. This hypothesis assumes a high degree of sophistication

1   For example L.A. Dicks-Mireaux, 'The Inter-Relationship between Cost and Price Changes, 1945-1959', *OEP* (NS), Vol. 13(3), reprinted in R.J. Ball and P. Doyle, *Inflation*, Penguin, 1969. The model of figure 1.5 is an extension of the relationships estimated by Dicks-Mireaux.

2   For example M. Friedman, 'The Role of Monetary Policy', *AER*, Vol. 58(1), pp. 1-17, and *Unemployment versus Inflation*, Institute of Economic Affairs, 1975.

upon the part of bargaining groups and may not be of great relevance to the UK economy during much of its history. Few would deny, however, that really rapid inflation will force the realization that failure to allow for future price increases can lead to a painful erosion of purchasing power between one wage settlement and the next. Thus expectational wage bargaining is a form of behaviour which is likely to evolve as a consequence of rapid inflation. It is possible that this form of behaviour has begun to emerge in the UK although it is not clear that it is widespread.

The second additional link between wages and prices runs from expectations of higher prices to the level of excess demand. As consumers become aware that prices are going to rise rapidly in the future they may seek to protect themselves from an erosion of the value of their money by switching out of money and financial assets into goods. The effects of this form of behaviour will be manifested in a tendency for the savings ratio to decline (which has not happened in the UK) and for the velocity of circulation of money to rise (which has also not happened). We have included it in the figure, along with the link between price expectations and wage bargaining, because it is a mode of behaviour which has been observed in other countries in periods of hyperinflation.[1] It is a form of behaviour which, along with expectational wage bargaining, is likely to develop as inflation gathers pace and as people learn from experience how money can lose its value. The fact that such behaviour can become general adds greatly to the danger of inflation getting out of hand and provides an extremely powerful case for stopping it as early as possible.

A third linkage in the system is that running from domestic prices to import prices. As domestic costs and prices rise, exporters have to increase their prices too. If the demand for exports is elastic this leads to a deterioration in the balance of payments which, in turn, leads to a decline in the exchange rate. When this happens the sterling price of imports increases, and domestic costs and prices rise further.

One further point which will not be clear from the scheme in figure 1.5 is that increases in the price level always tend to raise the demand for money. If the quantity of money is kept unchanged the effect will be to raise interest rates, thus lowering the levels of real output and employment, and causing a reduction in excess demand which will ultimately check the inflation. This check will be removed, however, if the central bank is aiming to maintain interest rates so as to stabilize the cost of the national debt. It will then have to *increase* the money supply as the demand for money rises. Thus although inflationary processes may be initiated by excess demand, wage push or increased import prices, they may continue only through permissive increases in the supply of money.

V.2   Imported Inflation

There is a very real sense in which the UK takes its price level from the world outside. Nearly every major increase or decrease in the price level has been associated with a major change in import prices (see table 1.9). Import prices were very volatile in the early 1920s; they rose rapidly in 1940 at the beginning of the

1   See, for example, A.J. Brown, *The Great Inflation*, London, 1955 and P. Cagan, 'The Monetary Dynamics of Hyperinflation' in M. Friedman, *Studies in the Quantity Theory of Money*, Chicago, 1956.

Second World War; and again in 1951 with the Korean War; and they rose by 87% between 1972 and 1974 as a result of a very fast rise in fuel prices (260% in the two years) together with price increases for basic materials (up 100%) and food, beverages and tobacco (70%). It was this very large rise in import prices which was mainly responsible for the protracted spiral of price and wage increases in the 1970s.

TABLE 1.9

Changes in Import and Retail Prices, UK, Selected Years

	Change in import prices (%)	Change in retail prices (%)
1920	19.0	15.8
1921	−33.3	−9.2
1922	−19.6	−19.0
1940	38.5	16.5
1951	33.0	9.1
1973	27.3	9.2
1974	55.5	16.1
1976	21.8	16.5
1977	16.0	15.8

Sources: retail prices *BLS*, *DEG*; import prices 1920-40 *LCES* (average value index for merchandise imports), 1951-77 *ET(AS)*, *AAS* (unit value index).

The main effect of a rise in import prices is to increase costs of production which, in turn, means higher final prices. Imports of goods and services comprise some 22% of TFE, so that, as a rough rule of thumb a rise of 10% in import price will lead to an initial rise in final prices of 2%; and these will be raised further by the response of wages. An additional effect occurs in the case of imports in inelastic demand such as foodstuffs and materials. Here the difficulty of substituting domestic output for imports means that the import bill rises and the exchange rate, assuming this to be flexible, declines. When this happens the sterling price of imports rises further and there is an additional increase in final prices. The average elasticity of demand for UK imports has been increasing as a result of a growing proportion of finished manufactured goods, the demand for which is relatively elastic. But even in 1979 the bulk of merchandise imports, some 62%, consisted of food, beverages, tobacco, fuel and industrial materials, the demand for which is very inelastic.

Imported inflation is not readily curable because there is not much prospect of offsetting the effect on final prices other than by inducing large reductions in total demand and employment. It is only when the balance of payments is in surplus that a rise in import prices can be offset by an appreciation of the exchange rate.

V.3　Demand-pull Inflation

Whilst external influences seem to have been responsible for the inflation of 1972-5 and for nearly all the more dramatic periods of inflation in UK history, there is no doubt that the internal pressure of excess demand exerts its own influence upon the

inflation rate. The evidence for such an influence can be found by examining rates
of wage or price inflation at differing demand pressures. Numerous studies in the
1950s and 1960s showed a strong negative relationship between the level of
unemployment (which is inversely related to excess demand) and the rate of change
of money wage rates. One of the earlier studies of this kind, and certainly the most
influential, was published in 1958 by Professor A.W. Phillips.[1] This examined the
relationship between unemployment rates for nearly a century, and on the basis of
data for 1861-1913 suggested that the relationship was negative, as expected, and
also nonlinear.[2] The wage increases to be associated with different rates of
unemployment were as follows:

Unemployment rate	1.0	2.0	3.0	4.0	5.0
% change in wage rates	8.7	2.8	1.2	0.5	0.1

The relationship became known as the *Phillips Curve* and implies a nonlinear
marginal 'trade-off' between the rate of wage increase and unemployment. Thus
the rate of wage increase declines by nearly 6% if the unemployment rate goes up
from 1.0% to 2.0%, but by only 1.6% if it goes up from 2.0% to 3.0%. The
trade-off suggested is a modest one at all but the highest pressures of demand for
labour.

One of the more remarkable features of the Phillips Curve, and one which
distinguishes it from most similar studies, was that it was found to be highly reliable
in predicting increases in wages during much later periods of time than the years
1861-1913 which had been used to derive the equation. Thus Phillips was able to
show a very close correspondence for 1948-57 between the wage changes implied
by his relationship and those that actually took place. The Phillips Curve was also
very accurate in predicting wage increases over the period 1958-66, which was after
the study had been published. During these eight years there was not a single error
in excess of 2.5% and the mean error (regardless of sign) was only 1.1%;
furthermore, the positive and negative errors tended to offset each other so that the
mean algebraic error was only 0.1% over this period. These predictive successes,
however, have to be seen in the light of what was an exceedingly stable level of
unemployment compared with the experience from which Phillips had started.
In 1861-1913 unemployment rates ranged from 1 to 11% whereas in 1948-66 they
were between 1 and 2.3%. Thus one could argue that postwar experience up to
1966 tested only a small part of the Phillips relation. Nevertheless, it passed this
test fairly well.

---

1 A.W. Phillips, 'The Relation between Unemployment and the Rate of Change of Money
   Wage Rates, 1861-1957', *Economica*, November 1958.

2 The equation for the schedule was:

$$\frac{\Delta W}{W} = -0.900 + 9.638U^{-1.394}$$

It can also be expressed in logarithmic terms as

$$\log \left\{ \frac{\Delta W}{W} + 0.9 \right\} = 0.984 - 1.394 \log U$$

where $\frac{\Delta W}{W}$ is the percentage rate of wage change and U is the unemployment rate.

(Phillips, op. cit.)

After 1966, however, the pure Phillips Curve became increasingly unreliable as a guide to the rate of wage inflation. It under-predicted by about 4.5% per annum in 1967-9, by 10-12% in 1970-3, and by more than 20% in 1974 and 1975. There is now, unlike the period 1861-1913, no recognizable relationship between statistics of the unemployment percentage and the rate of wage increase. Wage inflation and unemployment have, if anything, increased together. It is important, therefore, to ask whether the breakdown of the Phillips relationship can be explained, and here several factors come to mind.

(i)   The first is the collapse of the old relationship between unemployment and vacancies. As we saw in section II, there has been a rise since 1965 of about 4% in the unemployment percentage associated with a 1% vacancy rate. Now if the vacancy percentage can be regarded as a consistent measure of excess demand, this would help to explain part of the wage inflation which is now observed to occur with high unemployment. It can hardly explain it all, however, because the vacancy rate has not been exceptionally high.

(ii)   The second main factor is the omission from the pure Phillips equation of the causal influence of price changes. This would not have mattered so much in the early 1960s when inflation was moderate. But the omission is serious with inflation at the rates experienced in the 1970s.

(iii)   A connected factor is the probability that wage increases have become increasingly sensitive to price increases during the 1970s as a result of learning to live with inflation. This is not an easy matter to establish empirically, but it is nonetheless probable that a growing number of trade-union negotiators have insisted on full compensation for price changes whilst others have sought wage negotiation at more frequent intervals. There may also have been some tendency to follow the 'expectations-augmented Phillips curve', with expected rather than actual price changes being taken as the basis for wage demands.

(iv)   Finally, the Phillips relationship has been partly obscured by a number of fairly determined attempts in 1972-3 and 1975-8 to control wage increases by incomes policy.

Whilst these factors are the most likely explanations for the breakdown of the Phillips relationship in statistical terms, they do not, in our view, imply that the theoretical relationship underlying the Phillips curve — the link between excess demand and the rate of wage inflation — should be abandoned. What we have seen is a breakdown of the unemployment series as a measure of excess demand, together with the growth and strengthening of an omitted variable, the past or expected rate of price inflation. This judgment has to be seen in the light of what was said in section I about the falsification of economic hypotheses. The Phillips relation was for many years extremely well corroborated by the test of prediction outside its measurement period; now that it has 'failed' we can interpret the failure *either* as a case of missing variables and measurement error *or* as a breakdown of the demand-pull theory of inflation. In our view the latter interpretation is not acceptable since we should then have to re-interpret the cyclical correlation between wage increases and unemployment – observed for 100 years – in some other way. It also seems to be a matter of elementary 'commonsense' that wage awards will be higher when there is a shortage of labour.

V.4   Wage-push Inflation[1]

The question of whether wages have increased as a result of unions pushing up wages independently of market forces is controversial chiefly because of the large volume of historical evidence in favour of a demand-pull explanation. This evidence, however, need not preclude the possibility of sporadic outbursts of wage-push inflation. Nor is there any reason in principle why wage-bargaining procedures should respond precisely and consistently to the pressure of demand in the labour market.

The main evidence in favour of a wage-push contribution to recent inflation concerns the 'pay explosion' of 1970 when the rate of wage increases was about 12% faster than could be predicted by the pure Phillips Curve. It was also about 7% higher than could have been predicted from a relationship estimated by Artis in which excess demand was measured by the number of vacancies and price changes were included as an additional causal variable.[2] It can be argued that this was a consequence either of the relaxation of incomes policy in late 1969 or of direct wage-push on the part of the trade unions. The two types of explanation are not unconnected because the government was under strong pressure from the unions themselves to bring incomes policy to an end. Evidence in favour of greater union 'militancy', which we may define for our purposes as willingness to strike in order to obtain wage increases, may be seen in the very substantial increase in industrial disputes over this period. The number of days lost in industrial disputes rose very sharply (see table 1.10). They more than doubled between 1968 and 1970, whilst between the same two years the proportion of stoppages attributed to pay disputes increased from 54% to 64%. The evidence is certainly *suggestive* of a wage-push element in the 1970 pay increase and in the next year or two.

V.5   Inflation in the 1970s: a Summary

In table 1.10 we have grouped together the main factors which have been suggested as causes of or contributors to the rate of inflation. The key question is why the rate of inflation in the 1970s, which averaged 13% a year, was so much higher than in the 1960s when the annual inflation rate varied between 1 and 5%. One candidate which must be considered is the pressure of demand in the economy. But as the table shows, unemployment was very much higher in the 1970s and

---

1 See Aubrey Jones, *The New Inflation*, Penguin, 1973; D. Jackson, H.A. Turner and F. Wilkinson, *Do Trade Unions Cause Inflation?*, Cambridge University Press, 1972; P. Wiles, 'Cost Inflation and the State of Economic Theory', *EJ*, June 1973: E.H. Phelps Brown, 'The Analysis of Wage Movements under Full Employment', *SJPE*, November 1971; K. Coutts, R. Tarling and F. Wilkinson, 'Wage Bargaining and the Inflation Process', *Economic Policy Review*, No. 2, March 1976, Department of Applied Economics, University of Cambridge: M.C. Kennedy, 'Recent Inflation and the Monetarists', *Applied Economics*, June 1976.

2 M.J. Artis, 'Some Aspects of the Present Inflation', *NIER*, February 1971, reprinted in H.G. Johnson and A.R. Nobay (eds.), *The Current Inflation*, Macmillan, 1971.

TABLE 1.10

Inflation 1955-79: possible contributors

	(1) Unemployment percentage	(2) Unfilled vacancies percentage	(3) Change in wage rates (%)	(4) Change in retail prices (%)	(5) Change in import prices (%)	(6) Change in exchange rate (%)	(7) Days lost in industrial disputes (m)	(8) Change in money stock (%)
1955	1.0	1.5	6.9	4.5	3.0		3.8	
1956	1.0	1.2	8.0	2.0	1.9		2.1	
1957	1.3	0.8	5.0	3.7	0.9		8.4	
1958	1.9	0.6	3.6	3.0	-7.2		3.5	
1959	2.0	0.7	2.6	0.6	-1.0		5.3	
1960	1.5	0.9	2.6	1.0	0.0		3.0	
1961	1.3	0.9	4.2	3.4	-2.0		3.0	
1962	1.8	0.6	3.6	2.6	-1.0		5.8	
1963	2.2	0.6	3.7	2.1	4.0		1.8	
1964	1.6	0.9	4.8	3.3	3.0		2.3	5.6
1965	1.3	1.0	4.3	4.8	0.6		2.9	7.6
1966	1.4	1.1	4.6	3.9	1.5		2.4	3.4
1967	2.2	0.8	3.9	2.5	0.3		2.8	10.0
1968	2.3	0.8	6.6	4.7	12.3	-14.3	4.7	6.8
1969	2.3	0.9	5.3	5.4	3.1		6.8	2.4
1970	2.5	0.8	9.9	6.4	4.5		11.0	9.5
1971	3.3	0.6	12.9	9.4	4.7		13.6	13.9
1972	3.6	0.6	13.8	7.1	5.7	-4.8	23.9	24.5
1973	2.6	1.4	13.7	9.2	27.6	-9.3	7.2	26.3
1974	2.5	1.3	19.8	16.1	46.6	-3.1	14.8	10.2
1975	3.9	0.6	29.5	24.3	14.4	-7.7	6.0	6.6
1976	5.2	0.6	19.3	16.5	21.8	-15.3	3.3	9.5
1977	5.7	0.7	6.6	15.8	16.0	-5.0	10.1	10.0
1978	5.6	0.9	14.1	8.2	4.0	1.4	9.4	15.0
1979	5.3	1.0	14.9	13.4	10.4	7.6	29.1	12.6

Sources: (1) GB, excluding school-leavers, *BLS, DEG*. (2) *DEG*, Feb. 1976, Feb. 1980; adult vacancies. (3) Weekly rates for manual workers, all industries and services, *ETAS*, 1980. (4) *ETAS*, 1980; *DEG*, February 1980. (5) *ETAS*, 1980; *AAS*. (6) 1968, parity rate; 1971-9 effective exchange rate, *ES*. (7) *BLS, DEG*. (8) Sterling M_3, change during year: *FS*, Bank of England (not available before 1963-4).

unfilled vacancies were much the same as they had been before. Nevertheless, there were two years — 1973 and 1974 — when the vacancy rate was higher than in any year in the 1960s. It can be plausible that if the pressure of demand then had been held at, say, the 1972 level, the rate of wage increase would have been 5.7% less than it actually was whilst the rate of price increase would be less by about 4%.[1] But clearly this only accounts for a small part of the inflation actually experienced — 16% in 1979, rising to 24% in 1975 — so that the main onus of explanation must be sought elsewhere. And the relatively low vacancy rate in most of the 1970s confirms that excess demand could not have been the main factor responsible.

The factor which, in our view, made by far the largest contribution to the 1970s inflation was the quite dramatic rise in world commodity prices. This had the effect of raising UK import prices by over 100% between 1972 and 1975. With imports accounting for one-fifth of TFE, this was bound to raise final prices by about 20%. The initial effect, moreover, would have carried through into wages and back again to prices, so that the final effect would have been considerably greater.

It can, of course, be argued that some part of the increase in import prices was a consequence of our own inflation rate being faster than that of other countries, so that the exchange rate was forced downwards. Doubtless there is some element of truth in this contention although, as table 1.10 shows, the decline in the exchange rate in 1972-4 was not comparable in magnitude to the rise in import prices. It was not really until 1976 that our own relative inflation rate became the cause of the falling exchange rate.

As we have argued in section V.4 above, a further factor in the 1970s inflation may have been wage-push inflation. There was more than a suspicion of this in the 'wage explosion' of 1970, and in the figures of days lost in industrial disputes (table 1.10), to suggest that trade-union members were more prepared to go on strike for higher pay than they had been earlier. But the 1970 pay explosion could equally have been explained by the ending of incomes policy, whilst the high strike figures in the 1970s as a whole must be partly attributed to inflation itself. Thus the case for a 'wage-push' inflation is a difficult one to make although it cannot be ruled out as a possibility.

Taking these various factors together it seems possible to conclude that the initial, but least important, factor in the 1970s inflation was some element of wage-pushfulness or resistance to incomes policies. This was followed in 1972-4 by a simultaneous rise in world commodity prices and a raising of the internal pressure of demand. The high pressure of demand, however, was not sufficient to account for rates of inflation in excess of those experienced in boom years in earlier decades. Thus the single most important cause of inflation in the 1970s was the increase in import prices.

V.6   Monetary Explanations of Inflation

The increased rate of inflation in the 1970s was accompanied by markedly faster increases in the stock of money. The money supply had been rising at about 6% a

---

1 The calculation assumes that unemployment in 1972-4 has to be reduced by 1.5% in order to indicate excess demand consistently with its performance in the 1950s. This means the unemployment rates of 3.6% and 2.5% in 1972 and 1974 respectively are adjusted to become 2.1% and 1.0%. Wage-rate changes are calculated from these levels on the basis of the original Phillips equation; see footnote 2 on p. 42.

year in 1964-9 whereas in 1971-4 the rate of increase was very much faster. A number of economists, journalists and stockbrokers have interpreted the connection between the rise in the rate of monetary expansion and the faster inflation rate as cause and effect.[1] Some have attributed to money the sole blame for the inflation.

It is generally accepted in economic theory that increases in the supply of money can lead to higher real output or to higher prices. But they do so by raising the aggregate demand for goods and services, thus adding to the pressure of demand. This means that if the inflation of the 1970s had been caused by the rise in the money supply it would have been accompanied by a rise in vacancies and lower unemployment. These changes, moreover, would need to have been substantial to account for such a sharp increase in the rate of inflation. However, as we have already explained above, there was no general or sustained increase in the pressure of demand in the 1970s. Unemployment was higher than earlier, and the vacancy rate, although high in 1973 and 1974, was lower on average in the 1970s than it had been earlier. This absence of any increase, let alone any marked increase, in the pressure of demand is fairly compelling evidence against the monetarist point of view.

This conclusion, however, does not prevent us from agreeing that *if* the money supply had not been allowed to increase so fast, then inflation in the 1970s would have been less severe. If, for example, the money stock had increased at only 6% per annum during the decade instead of the recorded 14%, then it is reasonable to conjecture that interest rates would have been much higher and that expenditure would have been curtailed. Thus the pressure of demand would have been lower with a consequential lowering of the rate of wage increase. But it is difficult to believe that tighter money would have had much impact upon the rise in oil and other import prices, or their consequential effects on final prices.

V.7   Inflation and Economic Policy

In the period when inflation was merely creeping it was possible to regard it as a small price to pay for the benefit of high employment. A gently sloping trade-off between inflation and unemployment made the problem of political compromise minimal compared with the situation in the 1970s. The advocacy of an incomes policy in the 1960s was associated either with those who hoped to be able to run the economy at a pressure of demand which now seems unthinkable, or else with those who sought to use it as an instrument of income redistribution.

The arrival of fast inflation in the 1970s transformed the policy problem. It resulted in a rapid erosion of real incomes during the intervals between wage settlements, with effects that were socially divisive and disruptive. It also transformed economic behaviour. Economic units learned how to live with inflation and sought to defend their real wages either by insisting on a full

---

1   For example M. Parkin, 'Where is Britain's Inflation Rate Going?', *LBR*, July 1975, W. Rees-Mogg, *The Times*, 13 July 1976, and, for an American example, M. Friedman, *Money and Economic Development*, Praeger, 1973. The monetarist case against the Keynesians is put in D. Laidler, 'Inflation in Britain: a Monetarist Perspective', *AER*, September 1976, and the Keynesian case against the monetarists in Sir John Hicks, 'What is Wrong with Monetarism?', *LBR*, October 1975; Lord Kahn, 'Thoughts on the Behaviour of Wages and Monetarism', *LBR*, January 1976; E.H. Phelps Brown, 'A Non-Monetarist View of the Pay Explosion', *TBR*, March 1975; M.C. Kennedy, 'Recent Inflation and the Monetarists', *Applied Economics*, June 1976.

compensation for past increases in the cost of living or possibly, in a few cases, by bargaining on the basis of price forecasts. This meant that there were only two ways of bringing inflation under control. One was to deflate domestic demand to such a low pressure that the effect of unemployment upon the rate of wage increase was large enough to offset that of cost-of-living compensation and/or price expectations. Given that prices in 1975 were increasing by 24% a year, this would have necessitated either an intolerably high unemployment figure or an impossibly long period of correction. The other alternative was an incomes policy under which the rate of wage increase was subjected to firm quasi-statutory control. This was the main course adopted, although unemployment was allowed to increase as well. The incomes policy was introduced in three stages, starting in July 1975 with a maximum wage increase of £6 per week. This policy gave way to limits of £2.50-£4.00 per week in July 1976, and in July 1977 to a 10% limitation on pay increases. The winning of union agreement to the first two stages of the incomes policy was a singular act of diplomacy which may well have saved the UK economy from hyperinflation.

It was certainly the first time that an incomes policy can be said to have made a significant impact upon the rate of wage inflation. The increase in average weekly wage rates, which had been 30% in 1975, fell to 19% in 1976 and in 1977 to only 7%. But the government was not able to obtain union agreement to a continuation of incomes policy in 1978, and it was unwilling to enforce a statutory policy. Thus the rate of wage increase rose to 14% in both 1978 and the following year. The Conservative government elected in May 1979 made no attempt to revive the policy, choosing instead to enforce a severe and extended deflation of domestic demand (see section VII).

VI   ECONOMIC GROWTH
VI.1   The Growth of Productive Potential

In ordinary language it is usual enough to speak of any increase in GDP, however it comes about, as economic growth. In economic theory and applied economics it is best to reserve the term for increases in a country's productive potential. This means that demand-induced spurts of economic expansion, such as those occurring in cyclical recoveries, do not qualify as economic growth in the sense we have in mind.

TABLE 1.11

Economic Growth, UK, 1900-78

| | | Percentage increase per annum | | |
	GDP	GDP per man	Employed labour force	Capital stock excluding dwellings
1900-13	1.0	0.0	1.0	1.9
1922-38	2.3	1.1	1.2	1.1
1950-60	2.6	2.2	0.4	2.8
1960-70	2.8	2.5	0.3	4.3
1969-78	2.0	2.0	0.0	3.6

Sources: ET, October 1979; *NIBB*, 1980; *ET(AS)*; London and Cambridge Economic Service, *The British Economy, Key Statistics, 1900-1970.*

The table shows that both the growth rates of productive potential and the underlying trend in productivity have increased since the beginning of this century.

The growth rate of productive potential can only be measured satisfactorily over very long intervals of time or between periods when the utilization of resources was closely similar. Thus the periods indicated in table 1.11, which presents estimates of the growth rate in the UK, have been chosen because they begin and end with similar rates of unemployment or vacancies.

The concept of the growth rate of productive potential is not without its limitations. In the first place it says little or nothing about the causes of growth but simply describes a time-trend. An extrapolation of the growth rate for any period into the future could easily turn out wrong if the forces that determine full employment output are going to be present in different amounts or combinations from those of the past.

A second reservation concerns the interpretation of growth *rates* generally and their relation to *levels*. In calculating growth from 1969 to 1978, for example, one takes the compound rate of increase which will transform the level of GDP in 1969 into that of 1978. This does not tell us anything about the intervening years, during which the level of GDP could have been above or below the suggested time path. Thus the average *rate* of growth is, in general, no guide to the average *level* of output over the period. An allied point is that the *level of potential output* is arbitrarily defined by the unemployment (or vacancy) rate at which it is measured. This does not necessarily represent the maximum attainable level.

One of the questions which the economics of growth must try to answer is why some countries have grown so much faster than others and why, in particular, the underlying growth rate of the UK economy has been slower in the postwar period than that of most other industrial countries (see table 1.12). The answer, if it is to be found at all, must be sought under the more general heading of the causes of economic growth.

The causes of economic growth have been debated by economists since the time of Adam Smith. Growth must depend, in the first instance, upon the increase in the quantity and quality of the factors of production and the efficiency with which they are combined. These increases may be influenced, however, by factors on the side of demand such as the pressure of demand on resources and the degree to which it fluctuates.

The supply of labour depends primarily on the evolution of the population of working age, including net migration, the secular decline in hours worked, and the increase in the length of annual and national holidays. Changes in the pressure of demand, however, affect the size of the labour force and the number of hours worked, and, over the longer period, may influence migration.

The quality of labour must in large degree depend upon the facilities available for education and training, the opportunities taken of them, and the degree to which they match the changing demands for skills arising out of changes in technology and the structure of aggregate demand. Measurement of these influences, however, is difficult and there is little evidence to show which way, if at all, they have affected the international comparison in table 1.12. The mobility of labour from job to job and from area to area is probably an important factor in economic growth in so far as it reflects the degree to which the labour force can adjust to economic change. It has been argued, not without evidence, that much of the relatively fast growth of the German, Italian and French economies can be attributed to the movement of labour from the agricultural to the industrial sectors.[1] But it is still not clear how much of this mobility has been a cause and how much a consequence of the disparity in growth rates between the agricultural and industrial sectors.

One obvious influence on the growth of labour productivity is the rate of increase in the nation's stock of capital, both in quantity and in quality. Some indications of the growth of the UK capital stock are given in table 1.11, where it can be seen that the rate of increase, like that of productivity, has tended to rise during the course of this century. The stock of capital, however, is extremely difficult to measure. This is because the figures of depreciation in the national accounts are based on data collected for tax purposes and cannot serve as very precise indications of the rates of scrapping and deterioration of existing capital. Moreover, the economic value of a piece of capital equipment is an inherently subjective concept, depending on expectations of future returns and modified by problems of evaluating risk. Estimates of the capital stock, therefore, must be treated with a good deal of reserve.

TABLE 1.12

Rates of Growth, 1967-77

| | *Annual percentage rates* | |
	GDP	*GDP per capita*
Belgium	4.3	4.0
Denmark	3.4	2.9
France	9.5	3.8
Germany	3.8	3.5
Italy	3.6	3.9
Japan	7.4	6.9
Netherlands	4.2	3.2
Sweden	2.2	1.7
United Kingdom	2.1	1.9
Canada	4.7	3.3
United States	2.9	2.0

Sources: National Accounts of OECD Countries, 1952-1977.

The quality of the capital stock is, perhaps, even more important and even more difficult to measure. According to one widely accepted view the quality of capital depends, by and large, upon its age structure. This view looks upon the capital stock as a series of vintages of gross investment, each new vintage containing machines of higher quality than the previous one. Scientific and technical progress are embodied in new machines, not old ones, so that the most recent capital equipment is likely to be the most efficient. This view is the basis of the 'catching-up hypothesis' which has been advanced to explain the faster growth of some countries in the early postwar period. The argument is that those countries in which the capital stock was seriously depleted by the war were in a position to replenish it with brand-new equipment, and were thus enabled to grow faster than those

---

1   A. Maddison, *Economic Growth in the West*, Allen and Unwin, 1964.

countries where the bombing and destruction had been less severe. The embodied view of technical progress, together with the difficulties of measuring the quantity of capital, has led a number of economists[1] to emphasize gross rather than net capital formation as the better indicator of the extent to which capital resources have been enhanced. A high rate of gross investment, even if it is entirely for replacement purposes, will reduce the age of the capital stock and increase its quality.

Turning to influences on the side of demand, two aspects of the question need to be distinguished: the average pressure of demand and the size of fluctuations around the average. It can certainly be argued that a low average pressure of demand, such as obtained (to choose an extreme example) in the 1930s, is inimical to innovation and investment. It hinders investment because capital equipment is under-utilized and because its continuation for any length of time is likely to set an unfavourable climate for expectations. High demand, on the other hand, will generally have the opposite effect. It has also been argued that high demand encourages managers and workers to devise new and better ways of working with existing equipment, thereby making technical progress of a variety which is not embodied in new types of machine. This effect has sometimes been described as 'learning by doing', and it fits in with the view that the scale of production problems that have to be solved is itself a stimulus to their solution. Evidence has been produced, for example, to show how the time taken to assemble a prototype airframe has progressively diminished as the work force has gained experience of repeating the same jobs over and over again. On the other hand, it has also to be borne in mind that high demand pressure may work the other way. The presence of a sellers' market with easy profits could also diminish the incentive to innovate and even lead to lazy attitudes to production. Again, extreme pressure can promote mental and physical exhaustion. Thus for any single firm there may be some optimum pressure of demand where technical progress is maximized and beyond which the rate of progress tends to fall. For the economy as a whole the optimum pressure of demand is likely to be a rather complex average of the individual production units, and not something about which it is easy to make generalizations.

Another question is whether the amplitude of fluctuations tend to impede economic growth. It seems probable that the expectation of fluctuations will retard capital formation because profitability will be held down in periods of recession. It may also be the case that expectations of cycles lead to the installation of machinery which can be adapted to use in periods of both high and low output, whereas the prospect of steady growth could enable the introduction of machinery which would be specially designed to produce at a steadier level of sales. In this case it is likely that the extra adaptability will be achieved at some cost to the efficiency of capital, and growth will be slowed down. It may be no coincidence, therefore, that three countries with some of the lowest growth rates in the 1950s — the UK, US and Belgium — suffered sharper fluctuations in unemployment than the others.[2] (Japan was the exception to this rule.)

---

1 For example, A. Maddison, ibid.

2 On these points see A. Maddison, ibid., pp. 43-56, and R.C.O. Matthews, 'The Role of Demand Management', in Sir Alec Cairncross (ed.), *Britain's Prospects Reconsidered*, Allen and Unwin, 1970.

VI.2   Economic Growth and Policy

Governments prefer a fast rate of growth to a slow rate because it results in greater
tax revenues from a given structure of tax rates, and thus permits a larger provision
of public services (hospitals, schools and so forth) than would otherwise be possible.
Fast growth may also render a policy of income redistribution less painful to the
better off than would be so if the growth of income was slow or non-existent. Thus
it is not surprising that governments have often announced a faster growth rate as a
goal of economic policy.

What is not so clear, however, is whether the means of attaining faster growth are
sufficiently well known and understood. There is considerable controversy among
economists as to the effects on economic growth to be had from, say, a faster
growth of the capital stock and from technical progress. Many would argue that
neither are quantifiable, and that the attempts which have been made to quantify
them are suspect in a number of ways. Thus it does not seem that growth policy is
in the same category as, for example, demand-management policies, in which
moderately fine calculations can be made as to the effects of changing the
instruments of policy by known amounts. Probably all that can be hoped for
from policy to promote growth is action, or a series of actions, designed to create a
climate which is favourable to worthwhile investment, innovation and enterprise.
It seems doubtful, however, if even the most determined attempt to alter the
environment would show results within the lifetime of a single government. Nor
does it seem likely, to judge from earlier experience, that dramatic effects can be
expected from the mere announcement of a growth target. This was last done in
1965 when the government published a National Plan in which the rate of growth
of GDP was to have been 4% per annum for 1964-70. In the event the growth rate
turned out to be only 2.4%, and much of the public investment which had been
based on the 4% growth assumption proved to be excessive. It is still debatable
whether the growth rate would have been any higher if the balance of payments
had been managed more adroitly than it was.

VII   ECONOMIC PROSPECTS AND POLICIES 1980-2

In early 1980 unemployment in the UK as a whole was about 1.5 million, the
highest figure for forty years. It was, nevertheless, possible to argue that labour
shortages in particular areas or occupations were sufficiently intense to imply some
upwards pressure on wages from domestic demand. The number of unfilled
vacancies was about 0.7% of the labour force, and this was roughly comparable
with earlier years of moderate recession (e.g. 1971 or 1977). The rate of inflation
by April was more than 20% — after being only 8% some two years earlier. The
revival of inflation was chiefly attributable to an explosion of wages after the
relaxation of incomes policy in 1978. Wage rates had increased much *less* rapidly
than prices in 1978, whereas in 1979 they rose much *more* rapidly (see table 1.10).
This, along with higher import prices (up 10% in February on a year earlier), higher
oil prices and a rise in VAT in the budget of June 1979, were the chief factors in
the revival of inflation. The rise in wages was seen by many as signifying the
impossibility of designing an incomes policy which would do more than postpone
inflation.

The upsurge in the inflation rate meant that price stability became the chief aim
of government economic policy. The budget of March 1980 was unusual in that it

gave no stimulus (even a slight check) to domestic demand in spite of the forecast of a sharp recession. The principal tax changes were an improvement in income tax allowances in line with inflation and a rise in the duties on fuel, drink and tobacco. The net increase in revenue was estimated at roughly £1 billion, or 0.7% of GDP. The economic forecast[1] was for a fall in GDP of 3.2% between the second half of 1979 and the first half of 1981, with the implication of a substantial drop in the pressure of demand and a rise in unemployment to more than 2 million.

In post-Keynesian terms the 1980 budget could be seen as a forthright attempt to bring inflation under control by means of fiscal deflation. But it was doubtful whether the impending fall in demand pressure would be enough to halt inflation, or to bring it down to some tolerable figure (say 5%) in only a few years. With an uncontrolled wage-price spiral and an initial rate of inflation of 20%, it was reasonable to expect wage awards a year hence to be not less than 20%; and with wage costs amounting to about three-quarters of total variable costs, it seemed likely that the rate of inflation (in 1981) could not be less than 15% and, in 1982, perhaps 11%.[2] Much would depend on whether trade unions would accept declines in real wages in the absence of an incomes policy.

The government's approach to inflation was, however, based on rather different considerations. It seems to have assumed that a reduction of the growth rate of the money stock to some low figure would lead inexorably to the same low figure for the rate of price increase. This is the 'theory' which has become associated with influential journalists such as the editor of *The Times*, and which is loosely connected with the concepts and empirical regularities stressed by Professor Milton Friedman.[3] The approach is not based upon any integrated account of how the economy works, or of the processes of wage and price determination. The most convincing regularity is the long-term correspondence (over centuries) between price levels and the stock of money, where the direction of cause and effect is a matter of interpretation rather than fact, and where the economy can be assumed to be moving from one full-employment position to another. A second regularity which has been stressed by Friedman is that, on the average, there is a lag of 2-3 years between a change in the inflation rate and a change in the growth rate of the money stock (with output changing in the first instance). The evidence for this observation is not so good, but even if it were, it would not entitle anyone to the view that in all circumstances an $x\%$ reduction in the monetary growth rate would achieve an $x\%$ fall in the inflation rate. For the observed regularity is not necessarily causal and, being no more than an average, cannot be expected to hold when other relevant conditions (e.g. the change in import prices, the initial rate of price change) are different. In some circumstances, the whole of the reduction in the monetary growth rate might be transmitted to real output with comparatively little effect on prices. Yet the view that the inflation rate is caused and cured by a change in the growth rate of the stock of money has found a number of adherents, and it does, of course, have the merit of being easy to understand.

---

1 *Financial Statement and Budget Report 1980-1.*

2 The assumptions here are a one-year lag from price changes to wage changes and no lag between wage increases and prices. No allowance is made for the feedback from prices to the exchange rate and import costs.

3 See M. Friedman, *The Counter-Revolution in Monetary Theory*, Institute of Economic Affairs, 1970, for a statement of the 'key propositions of monetarism' and *Money and Economic Development*, Praeger, 1973 for his evidence.

It is difficult to know how much influence these ideas had on the budget speech of March 1980. But the policies which it announced were, at least in part, consistent with this kind of approach. Thus the Chancellor announced 'a medium-term financial strategy' by which the growth rate of the money stock was to be progressively reduced over a 5-year period, and this was to be achieved by a parallel reduction in the PSBR. The decline in the budget deficit was to be brought about partly by rising revenue from North Sea oil and partly by a planned decline in real government expenditure. The main figures were:

	1980-1	*1983-4*
Percentage change in money stock (£M3)	7-11	4-8
PSBR (% of GNP)	3¾	1½
General government expenditure at 1979 survey prices (£ billion)	70	67½

Source: Financial Statement and Budget Report 1980-1.

The strategy assumed no change in tax rates and a rise in GDP after 1981 at only 1% a year, which was less than the underlying growth of productivity and insufficient, therefore, to hold employment steady.

With such a novel approach to inflation and its control, it was extremely difficult in early 1980 to foresee the outlook for the economy. Clearly 1980 and 1981 were going to be years of recession, with a sharper downturn and more unemployment than in 1975. But the prospect for investment looked particularly bleak in view of high interest rates and the government's evident intention of maintaining demand well short of capacity output. If the inflation policy failed, it was possible to envisage either the restoration of incomes policy or a still stiffer dose of deflation. Thus the outlook for the economy depended not only on policy, but also on expectations of whether policy would work, and on expectations of whether it would be changed. There appeared to be no good reasons for expecting a recovery from the recession.

REFERENCES AND FURTHER READING

An elementary textbook which introduces most of the policy issues discussed in this chapter is A.K. Cairncross, *An Introduction to Economics*, 5th edition, Butterworth, 1973, whilst intermediate books are F.S. Brooman, *Macroeconomics*, 6th edition, Allen and Unwin, 1977, and D.C. Rowan, *Output, Inflation and Growth*, 2nd edition, Macmillan, 1974. A good short guide to the national accounts is S. Hays, *National Income and Expenditure in Britain and the OECD Countries*, Heinemann, 1971. Economic fluctuations in the UK are described by R.C.O. Matthews in 'Postwar Business Cycles in the UK', in M. Bronfenbrenner (ed.), *Is the Business Cycle Obsolete?*, Wiley 1969. An advanced treatment of aggregate demand theory is given in M.K. Evans, *Macroeconomic Activity*, Harper and Row, 1969, whilst M.J.C. Surrey, *The Analysis and Forecasting of the British Economy*, NIESR and Cambridge University Press, 1971, is helpful on forecasting. On economic policy there is M.J. Stewart, *The Jekyll and Hyde Years*, Dent, 1977, W. Beckerman (ed.), *The Labour Government's Economic Record 1964-70*, Duckworth, 1972, and F.T. Blackaby (ed.), *British Economic Policy 1960-74*, National Institute of Economic and Social Research and Cambridge University Press, 1978. D. Morris (ed.), *The Economic System in the UK*, Oxford University

Press, 2nd edition, 1979, gives an excellent coverage of various aspects of demand management and inflation. Two recent books on inflation are J.S. Flemming, *Inflation*, Oxford University Press, 1976, and J.A. Trevithick, *Inflation*, Penguin, 1977. On the current state of the economy the best general guide is given quarterly in the *National Institute Economic Review*, and this may be supplemented by the *Midland Bank Review*, also published quarterly, and the annual *Economic Policy Review*, Department of Applied Economics, University of Cambridge.

2

Monetary, credit and fiscal policies

N.J. Gibson

I INTRODUCTION: THE POLICY DILEMMA

The previous chapter seeks to convey an overall picture of the UK economy, paying particular attention to fluctuations in economic activity, demand management, inflation, and economic growth. This chapter concentrates on a narrower area, the monetary, credit and fiscal policies of the authorities, that is, the UK government and the Bank of England.

The term 'policy' implies the existence of goals and a strategy or instruments to achieve them. For much of the period since the Second World War the most frequently cited policy goals in the UK have been the maintenance of full employment, price stability and fixed exchange rates, the encouragement of economic growth and the achievement of a 'satisfactory' balance of payments.[1] However, since the late 1960s the emphasis on the maintenance of fixed exchange rates has all but disappeared and instead more flexible exchange rates have become the norm, though this does not mean that the balance of payments has become a matter of little concern. Furthermore, a reduction in the rate of inflation, rather than the maintenance of price stability, or full employment, has come to dominate the policy goals of the authorities.

The standard policy instruments at the disposal of the authorities are monetary, credit and fiscal. That is, by changing the rate of growth of the money supply, interest rates, the availability of credit and by altering taxes and government expenditure the authorities may hope to realize some or all of their policy goals. But in addition to the instruments mentioned, the authorities may vary exchange rates, restrict imports and impose controls on prices and incomes. They may even go beyond this and introduce rationing and other measures.

Once a set of goals is chosen a host of questions arise. Can they be defined precisely? Are they mutually compatible within the particular economic system, given the policy instruments at the disposal of the authorities? If they are not, which goals should be sacrificed or modified? Are there alternative policy instruments that might be used to achieve one or more of the policy goals? Have the authorities, or for that matter has anyone else, the necessary knowledge about the relationships between instruments and goals? Do they know exactly when and by how much to manipulate the policy instruments or even how many instruments they need?

These questions highlight what might be called the policy dilemma. It is, for instance, not at all certain that full employment and price stability can be attained simultaneously with the help of the policy instruments currently at the disposal of

---

1 See chapters 3 and 5 respectively for an extensive explanation and discussion of the balance of payments and incomes controls.

the authorities. The reason, at least in part, is that there is apparently no simple, well-understood relationship between the policy actions of the authorities and such magnitudes as full employment and price stability. The effects of monetary and fiscal policy may be apparent only after some delay and the delay itself may be variable, depending on the initial economic and other circumstances when the policy actions were first taken, as well as the events that subsequently impinge on the system, including changing expectations about the future behaviour of the system and how people react to them. Thus the problems of the policy-maker are extremely complex and remain so despite advances in macroeconomic model building.[1]

Implicit in the foregoing discussion of goals and instruments are questions concerning both value judgments and how an economic system works. Each of these questions is a recurring theme in this chapter. Section II looks briefly at the theoretical and empirical basis of monetary and fiscal policy. Section III discusses the structure of the banking and financial system, and examines some money and credit theories. The taxation system is considered in section IV which also includes a brief discussion of taxation within the EEC. Finally, in section V policy since the early 1960s is briefly surveyed, and a short discussion of the prospects and possible implications of economic and monetary union within the EEC is also included.

II SOME THEORETICAL AND EMPIRICAL BACKGROUND
II.1 Certain Keynesian and Monetarist Positions

As implied above, the use of monetary and fiscal policy presupposes some knowledge about policy instruments and goals. One view is that monetary policy is by and large ineffective and that, say, increases in the money supply and reductions in interest rates will have little or no effect as an encouragement to expenditure and hence will have little or no impact on output and employment, whereas fiscal policy in the form of changes in taxation and government expenditure will have substantial effects. Another view, but this time applied to fiscal policy, is that an increase in government expenditure will not stimulate an expansion of output and employment but will only substitute government expenditure for private expenditure — the so-called crowding-out effect. And, similarly, that a reduction in taxation will have no net expansionary effect on expenditure and hence on output and employment. In contrast, however, changes in the money supply are believed to have marked effects on an economy.

Implicit in these contrasting statements are different models of the economic system. The first, which completely discounts the importance of monetary policy, is generally associated with an extreme Keynesian viewpoint; and the second, which completely discounts the importance of fiscal policy, with an extreme monetarist position.

It has now been argued persuasively that the first viewpoint does far less than justice to Keynes himself and that it is a serious misinterpretation of his work to attribute to him the general view that 'money does not matter'.[2] On the contrary he was greatly impressed by the power of monetary policy for good or ill as regards

---

1 HM Treasury, *Macroeconomic Model Technical Manual 1979*, October 1979.

2 Axel Leijonhufvud, *On Keynesian Economics and the Economics of Keynes: A Study in Monetary Theory*, Oxford University Press, 1968.

the functioning of the economic system. In particular, and despite the experience of the great depression, he was not an adherent of what has come to be called the liquidity-trap hypothesis; that is, that the rate of interest might have a floor below which it would not fall and possibly prevent the achievement of full employment. However, he certainly envisaged this as an extreme possibility and wrote 'whilst this limiting case might become practically important in the future, I know of no example of it hitherto'.[1] At the same time, neither theoretical nor empirical work supports an extreme monetarist position, one which has perhaps been unkindly paraphrased as 'money is all that matters'.[2]

However, to contrast the Keynesian and monetarist positions in this stark way may be unnecessary and even misleading. Recent work on the US economy suggests that, 'in the "short run" both monetary and fiscal policies have powerful effects, first on real output and, more gradually, on prices, with the relative size of the two effects dependent on the degree of slack in the economy'.[3] The same study also states that, 'in the longest run the response of the economy to both monetary and fiscal policy is very much consistent with the views advanced by Friedman and the monetarists. In particular, the money supply does *not* affect real output, or real interest rates (money is neutral) but only the price level; and a change in real government expenditure, money supply (and tax rates) constant, does *not* affect real output but only its composition, as the expansion in government expenditure tends to displace an equal amount of private demand.'[4]

There are dangers in applying uncritically to another economy findings which relate to a particular economy. However, there is evidence that the effects on the UK economy of monetary and fiscal policies may not be all that different, at least qualitatively, from those found for the US economy.[5] Nevertheless, the UK economy is in many respects very different to the US economy, particularly in terms of the relative openness of the former in the sense of its much larger dependence on foreign trade. Both economies are, however, highly open ones as regards the ease with which funds can move in and out of their monetary and financial markets.

In a regime of *fixed* exchange rates with no expectation of any changes in them — or, indeed, floating rates if held within a narrow range — and highly developed international capital markets, with freedom of movement of funds between them, the ability of a single country such as the UK to maintain interest rates at levels substantially different from those in the rest of the world is very limited. This clearly affects the usefulness of monetary and credit policy as an instrument of domestic economic policy. In the extreme case the country concerned will be a price-taker as regards both interest rates and traded goods prices and the money supply will be endogenous; in the long run monetary policy or more precisely domestic credit policy will only influence the holdings of foreign exchange reserves. However, in the case of fiscal policy and fixed exchange rates,

1 J.M. Keynes, *The General Theory of Employment, Interest and Money*, Macmillan, 1936, p. 207.
2 James Tobin, 'The Monetary Interpretation of History: A Review Article', *AER*, June 1965.
3 F. Modigliani, 'The Channels of Monetary Policy in the Federal Reserve-MIT-University of Pennsylvania Econometric Model of the United States', in *Modelling the Economy*, edited by G.A. Renton, Heinemann Educational Books, 1975, p. 241.
4 Ibid.
5 See, P.M. Jackson and S.T. Cook (eds.), *Current Issues in Fiscal Policy*, Martin Robertson, 1979.

the conclusion is rather different; changes in fiscal policy may still affect domestic output and employment. For instance, an expansionary fiscal policy may in the short run tend to increase output and employment, though perhaps relatively little in a highly open economy and where the consequences of government policy are anticipated and acted upon.

With *flexible* exchange rates an economy can pursue a so-called independent monetary policy in the sense that it can in principle determine the rate of growth of its money supply. However, to the extent that this policy affects its traded goods prices relatively to those of the rest of the world, this will be reflected in the exchange rate. In particular, a relatively expansionary monetary policy will lead to a depreciation of the exchange rate.[1] In so far as the latter has been anticipated this will tend to raise in advance domestic interest rates relatively to those abroad. These consequences, however, do not preclude some short-run expansionary effects on output and employment if prices are slow to adjust. Expansionary fiscal policy with flexible exchange rates, given the domestic money supply, would on a monetarist interpretation lead to an appreciation of the exchange rate in so far as it increased real income. However, these conclusions would of course require modification depending on how the rest of the world responds to the particular policy changes.

For monetarists inflation is essentially a monetary phenomenon and in principle can be avoided by restricting the rate of growth of the money stock to a rate equal to the secular rate of growth of output, making if need be allowance for population and real income growth. Furthermore, they believe that the authorities have in principle the power to do this, though it may require the acceptance of flexible exchange rates. Monetarists go on to argue that once an inflationary process is under way, economic behaviour is strongly affected by expectations about the future levels of prices and that attempts to reduce the pace of inflation by a more restrictive monetary policy will generally bring about conditions in which output and employment may be static or declining, whilst prices continue to rise. In other words monetarists are not surprised by what has come to be called 'stagflation'. Indeed monetarists tend to believe that inflation in market-based economies cannot be cured without the cost of sluggish or even declining rates of growth of output and rising unemployment in the short run − a phenomenon which has been only too familiar in the 1970s and is clearly persisting into the 1980s.

Keynesians, and indeed others − with varying degrees of emphasis − are inclined to see inflation not primarily as a monetary phenomenon but as a consequence of a dynamic adjustment process whereby groups of workers and business interests struggle to preserve or improve, largely by wage and price fixing, their relative shares of the real national income.[2] This struggle is seen as often bringing both workers and business into conflict with government, upon which each of them may put such pressure that it feels obliged for electoral or other reasons to pursue permissive monetary and fiscal policies. These policies may seem, at least for a

---

1   In official British practice the term 'exchange rate' refers to the price of one unit of the domestic currency in terms of a foreign currency. It is frequently much more convenient to follow the opposite practice and define an exchange rate − just like any other price − in terms of the number of units of domestic currency per unit of foreign currency.

2   This is not to deny that the behaviour of import prices, and capital flows and the like, over which a particular country may have little or no control, may be a further important factor influencing domestic prices, especially under a system of fixed exchange rates. See chapter 1, section V.2.

time − which may become shorter and shorter as experience accumulates − to be consistent with the short-term wishes of both workers and business. The *apparent* logic of this approach is to institute a wages, prices and incomes policy. For it is argued that whilst restrictive monetary and fiscal policies may succeed in reducing the growth of output and increasing the level of unemployment, they will do little to come to grips with the fundamental causes of inflation.

On the face of it the so-called monetarist and Keynesian approaches to the explanation of inflation are strongly opposed. The monetarist position would seem to require that the market-based economic system is fundamentally stable and that disequilibria will be self-correcting, provided the monetary framework is controlled in a way that avoids unanticipated changes in the general price level. It is not argued that this requires a constant price level though it is generally accepted that this is probably what should be the target. To achieve this, prices and incomes policies are unnecessary, and indeed lead to misallocation of resources and inefficiency.

The Keynesian position seems to imply that conflicts over relative shares of the real national income and, in particular, relative real wages can be resolved at least temporarily through permissive monetary policies and inflation, together with a prices and incomes policy. But this is tantamount to postulating the persistence of money illusion and an inability to learn from experience, hardly a strong base on which to build a theory with such profound economic and social significance. Furthermore, it needs to be stressed that the success to date, other than in the short run, of so-called prices and incomes policies as a means of avoiding inflation and indeed 'stagflation' would seem to have been extremely limited.[1]

II.2   Views of the Bank of England

The Bank is necessarily committed to pursuing the major policy goals mentioned earlier in the introduction, though the relative emphasis placed on the individual goals may and does change through time. But, in addition, the Bank sees itself as having an overriding responsibility for the financing of the government and the management of the national debt, and a general responsibility for the efficiency and 'prudential supervision' of the major part of the financial system.[2] These latter responsibilities, as interpreted by the authorities, are fundamental to an understanding of their approach to monetary and credit policy and to the operation of the whole financial system.

The Bank would argue that its approach to policy is pragmatic and necessarily conditioned by the economic and institutional circumstances existing at any point of time, as well as the general climate of professional opinion about the power of monetary and other policies to influence the economic system. Just how important these considerations are is illustrated by the following excerpt from a lecture delivered by a Governor and referring to the period immediately following the Second World War.

---

1 For further discussion of inflation and prices and incomes policy, see chapters 1 and 5.
2 See 'Papers Submitted to the Wilson Committee', *BEQB*, vol. 18, No. 3, September 1978, pp. 379-402.

At the end of the war it was widely believed that interest rates should be kept low to finance reconstruction as well as to ease the servicing of a greatly increased national debt; and it was some while before it was universally accepted that a slump was not after all inevitable. A fairly comprehensive system of physical controls had been maintained to suppress inflation; and the doctrine of Keynes, at least as interpreted by his followers . . . had led to a totally new emphasis on fiscal policy. The active drive for cheap money was succeeded by a period in which monetary policy went into limbo. There was general scepticism about its relevance.[1]

There can be little doubt that the Bank shared this scepticism.

But towards the end of 1951 the authorities, largely in response to balance of payments problems, decided to re-activate monetary policy. This, however, did not in any sense imply that the authorities had become convinced that careful control of the money supply was the key to effective monetary policy. On the contrary, and with the possible exception of a period in the mid-1950s, monetary policy throughout the whole period up to the late 1960s placed major emphasis on influencing the cost and availability of credit to the various sectors of the economy. Much reliance was placed on hire-purchase controls, the control of bank lending through quantitative and qualitative restraints, including ceilings on advances, liquid asset ratios and special deposits. Furthermore, through time the credit controls became more specific and direct, with the authorities detailing the priorities that should be observed.

Since about 1969, however, the authorities have been more prepared to acknowledge the disadvantages of quantitative and qualitative controls and, especially during the last five years or so, to give more attention to the growth of monetary aggregates, including the money supply. More recently they have become openly critical of the very policy instruments — the reserve-assets ratio and the supplementary special-deposits scheme — they introduced in the early 1970s but are now proposing to abandon. These matters are considered further in section III.3 below.

It is only since 1976 that the Bank has been prepared to announce a target growth rate for the money supply. The present Governor has stated that:

> The most immediate benefit from publicly announced monetary targets derives from the assurance that money will not itself be a source of instability. Beyond this, monetary targets give a clear indication to those responsible for economic decisions — including those affecting the course of future costs and prices — of the limit to which the authorities are, in effect, prepared to see inflation financed in the months ahead: the implication being that inflation at a faster rate will inevitably put output and employment increasingly at risk.[2]

---

1 'Monetary Management in the United Kingdom', *BEQB*, vol. 11, no. 1, March 1971, p. 41. See also, 'The Operation of Monetary Policy since the Radcliffe Report', ibid., vol. 9, no. 4, December 1969, pp. 448-60.

2 *BEQB*, vol. 17, no. 4, December 1977, p. 461. See also ibid., vol. 18, no. 1, March 1978, 'Reflections on the Conduct of Monetary Policy', pp. 31-7.

This represents a fascinating development in official thinking and despite qualifications and certain protestations is a retreat from the Bank's extreme Keynesianism of earlier years and a movement in the direction of the monetarists. Moreover, as will be seen below, this new emphasis on the importance of the growth of the monetary aggregates calls in question the approach of the authorities to monetary policy over the last thirty years and especially in the early 1970s when they permitted massive and irregular expansion of the money supply. Indeed it is arguable that the depth and duration of the 'stagflation' of recent years is to a considerable extent a direct consequence of these policies of the early 1970s.[1]

II.3   Some Empirical Work

A great deal of the empirical work on the relative merits of monetary and fiscal policy as stabilization instruments has been carried out in relation to the US economy.[2] The evidence, as indicated above, suggests that monetary policy in terms of acceleration or deceleration of the rate of change in the money supply is important for the behaviour of both nominal and real income in the short run, though the precise effects on output and prices are not well understood. There is also evidence that fiscal policy affects output, employment and prices. Furthermore, some of the evidence also indicates that for stabilization purposes monetary policy is more powerful than fiscal policy. However, it should be stressed that these conclusions are provisional and should be treated as such. Nevertheless, there is no doubt that since the late 1960s there has been a major shift in professional opinion in the US on the importance of monetary policy as a stabilization instrument, which has frequently been coupled with a reduced emphasis on the significance of fiscal policy, which is not to say that the latter is unimportant.

As far as the UK is concerned there is perhaps rather less agreement about the relative merits of monetary and fiscal policy as stabilization instruments. However, some recent experiments with the Treasury macroeconomic model suggest that the output or multiplier effects of various fiscal policies are relatively small, of the order of 1.0 or less after the first year, and in most instances tend to diminish thereafter.[3] Moreover, and this is very important, these outcomes are without making allowance for factors which might be expected to dampen multiplier effects. These factors include, for example, feedback effects from interest rates and the price level.

As regards monetary policy and its effects on output and prices, this too remains a controversial area both with respect to the stability of the demand for money (and the indirect evidence this provides for the potential effectiveness of monetary policy), as well as the so-called direct or multiplier effects of monetary policy. However, despite the many difficulties there is evidence to support the view that

---

1 See section V of this chapter.

2 The term 'stabilization' gives rise to problems of meaning and definition, particularly when a number of different policy goals are being pursued simultaneously. In the rest of this section it is assumed that the primary stabilization objectives are the rate of growth of real and nominal gross domestic product.

3 G.R. Lewis and P.A. Ormerod, 'Policy Simulations and Model Characteristics' in P.M. Jackson and S.T. Cook (eds.), *Current Issues in Fiscal Policy*, Martin Robertson, 1979.

monetary policy has some effects on output and prices in the short run but with the price effects dominating in the long run.[1]

The absence of widespread consensus about the merits of monetary and fiscal policy in the UK context makes it difficult, as will be seen below, to give a confident assessment of the merits of the policies pursued by successive governments. However, it seems fair to say that much professional opinion in the UK, whilst it may not have moved as much as in the US, is less sceptical about the relevance of monetary policy, in terms of control of the money supply as an instrument for economic management, than it was a few years ago. This is not to say that professional opinion has seriously downgraded fiscal policy. Many British economists view it as an important macro-policy instrument. But there is one thing on which there is more professional agreement and that is that neither monetary nor fiscal policy can, in the present state of knowledge, be used with confidence for 'fine tuning' or, alternatively, sensitive, short-run control of the economic system; and some would add that the attempt to do so may increase uncertainty and exacerbate the situation.[2] Others would go further and argue that the theoretical case for macroeconomic intervention is seriously weakened if individuals in the system respond to changes in the light of all the information available and in that sense behave rationally. In short, the balance of professional opinion in Britain would seem to be shifting and becoming more sympathetic to the monetarist notion that monetary and fiscal policy should be carried on in a way which helps to provide a stable framework for economic decision-making, in particular a stable price level, and that the adherence to appropriate target rates of growth of the money supply may be crucially important to this end. There are, however, notable exceptions to this viewpoint. However, it is of major interest that the government is now committed to this position with the announcement in its 1980 budget of a 'medium-term financial strategy' to bring down over the next four years to progressively lower levels the rate of growth of the money supply.[3]

III   THE BANKING AND FINANCIAL STRUCTURE AND MONEY AND CREDIT CONTROL
III.1   The UK Banking Sector

The UK banking sector consists of the UK offices of all those banks, including the National Girobank since September 1978, which observe the uniform reserve ratio introduced in September 1971 and, in addition, the Banking Department of the Bank of England and the discount market. The banks which observe the uniform reserve ratio are known as listed banks and are classified into three main groups, British, Overseas and Consortium banks. The British banks include the London clearing banks, the Scottish clearing banks, the Northern Ireland banks, Accepting houses and other British banks. The Overseas banks are made up of three main groups, American banks, Japanese banks and other overseas banks. Consortium banks are banks which are owned by other banks but in which no single bank holds

---

1   Alan Budd, 'Economic Viewpoint: Monetary Targets and a Financial Plan' in *Economic Outlook 1979-1983*, Vol. 4, no. 2, November 1979, London Business School Centre for Economic Forecasting.

2   For a contrary view, see 'Committee on Policy Optimisation' (Ball Report), Cmnd. 7148, HMSO, 1978.

3   For further discussion see section V.1 below.

more than 50% of the share capital and where at least one of the participating banks is an overseas bank.

Perhaps the most notable feature of the UK banking sector in recent years is its remarkable rate of expansion in terms of the number of banks involved and in the growth of deposits. The growth in numbers has been concentrated amongst other British banks, Overseas banks and Consortium banks. At the end of 1979 some 370 institutions were covered by the official UK banking-sector tables published by the authorities. Ten or so years ago the figure was perhaps one-third of this number.

Because of the growing number of banks which get incorporated in the statistics there are difficulties in determining precisely the growth of deposit liabilities in the UK. However, bearing this in mind, at the end of 1970 total deposits of the UK banking sector were about £32,000m, whilst by the end of 1979 they had reached about £190,000m, a compound rate of growth of some 22% p.a. Of these totals, over £16,000m and £49,000m respectively were sterling deposits and the rest were denominated in other currencies. Thus sterling deposits grew at about 13% p.a. These developments have the most profound significance for the operation and control of the monetary and financial system of the UK. This point is returned to below in discussing the major categories of banks included in the UK banking sector.

III.2   The Bank of England

The Bank of England acts as banker to the government and plays a basic role in smoothing government cash transactions and in administering and managing the national debt — broadly speaking, the debt liabilities of the State to its nationals, to its own agencies and to overseas holders. As agent of the government the Bank helps to regulate and control foreign exchange transactions and manages the Exchange Equalization Account, which holds the official gold, foreign exchange reserves and SDRs of the UK.[1]

The Bank is divided into two parts for accounting purposes; it produces two balance sheets, one for the Issue Department and one for the Banking Department. The origin of the double-balance-sheet system is to be found in monetary controversies during the first half of the nineteenth century and was introduced under the Bank Charter Act, 1844, separating the note-issue function from all other functions of the Bank. But the two balance sheets still retain a certain, if somewhat artificial, significance in that the Issue Department is classified in the national accounts of the UK as belonging to the public or government sector, whilst, as already mentioned, the Banking Department is classified for banking purposes with the banking sector. The position of the Issue Department in December 1979 is shown in table 2.1.

The notes in circulation are necessarily held by persons, companies and financial institutions. Notes in the Banking Department would, of course, disappear from the accounts if the two balance sheets were amalgamated. The assets of the Issue Department, except for some commercial bills, local authority debt and some holdings of company securities, such as British Petroleum ordinary stock, under the heading of 'other securities', are classified as government securities but also include

---

1   See 'The Exchange Equalisation Account: Its Origins and Development', *BEQB*, vol. 8, no. 4, December 1968.

TABLE 2.1

Issue Department (selected items), 12 December 1979 (£m)

Liabilities		*Assets*	
Notes:			
In circulation	10,089	Government securities	8,635
In Banking Dept.	11	Other securities	1,465
	10,100		10,100

Source: FS.

government-guaranteed securities, Treasury bills and Ways and Means Advances to the National Loans Fund. Any increase in the note issue generally implies an equal addition to holdings of government securities. In other words, when the Issue Department supplies additional notes, which it does via the Banking Department, it obtains interest-earning government securities in exchange. Indeed the note issue may be looked upon as a means by which the government helps to finance its expenditure.

The assets of the Issue Department are a means of helping the government to organize its finances in another way. The government is continuously concerned with the issue and redemption of the national debt; it may need to borrow new funds or pay off maturing obligations. The Issue Department underwrites all new issues of government stock, taking up any that is not bought by the public on the day of issue and subsequently selling it as demand appears. Similarly, the Issue Department purchases stocks nearing redemption, avoiding large cash payments to the public when the actual redemption date arrives. The Issue Department may in fact be in the market as a buyer or seller of government securities, or both, almost continuously. That is, it engages extensively in open-market operations.

The balance sheet of the Banking Department is shown in table 2.2

TABLE 2.2

Banking Department (selected items), 12 December 1979 (£m)

Liabilities		*Assets*	
Deposits:			
Public	20	Government securities	1,462
Bankers	462	Advances and other accounts	161
Reserves and other		Premises, equipment and other	
accounts	697	securities	365
Special deposits	806	Notes and coins	12
	1,985		2,000

Source: FS.
Note: The balance sheet does not exactly balance because certain subsidiary items have been omitted. This is also true of other balance sheets summarized in this chapter.

Public deposits are all government balances. They include those of the Exchequer, the National Loans Fund, HM Paymaster General, the National Debt Commissioners and Dividend Accounts. The total amount involved is relatively small by comparison with bankers' deposits despite the enormous scale of government transactions. The main reason for this is that government attempts to keep these balances as low as possible consistently with carrying out its operations. Any so-called surplus balances are used to retire government debt in an attempt to keep down costs. Net payments from the government to the community will have an immediate effect on bankers' deposits, increasing the cash holdings of the banking system. The reverse is also true and smoothing-out movements of funds between public and bankers' deposits is a major preoccupation of the Bank day to day.

Bankers' deposits belong to the London and Scottish clearing banks, other British banks including the National Girobank, Northern Ireland banks, Overseas and Consortium banks and the discount houses. As bankers' deposits necessarily appear as assets in the balance sheets of these financial institutions and will therefore be discussed later, nothing more is said about them at this point.[1]

Reserves and other accounts include balances of overseas central banks, certain dividend accounts, local authorities and public corporation accounts, as well as unallocated profits of the Banking Department. The accounts of the Bank's remaining private customers are also included here. These accounts are not without importance but they are not central to this chapter and so are not discussed further.

Special deposits were a new category of deposit, first introduced in April 1960, that the London clearing banks and Scottish clearing banks were from time to time obliged to transfer to the Bank in support of its monetary and credit policy. This scheme came to an end on 15 September 1971 when all outstanding special deposits were repaid. Since then two new schemes have been introduced, the first on 16 September 1971 for special deposits on which the authorities pay interest, and the second on 17 December 1973 for supplementary special deposits on which no interest is paid.[2] Both are discussed below.

Government securities introduce the assets of the Banking Department and include Treasury bills and longer-dated government securities and Ways and Means Advances to the Exchequer.[3] These advances occur if the Exchequer finds itself short of funds at the end of the day and wishes to make up its balance; the advances are generally only overnight loans, being repaid the following day.

The Banking Department, through sales and purchases of government securities, affects the volume of bankers' deposits and hence the cash holdings of the banking system. In general, government securities in the Banking Department can be used in much the same way as those in the Issue Department to facilitate debt management and monetary policy. However, the assets at the disposal of the Banking Department are much smaller than those available to the Issue Department.

Advances and other accounts are of three main types: advances to the discount market, loans to the remaining private customers of the Bank and what are called

---

1　See below, p. 78.

2　The rate paid on interest-bearing special deposits is adjusted weekly to the nearest 1/16% per annum to the average rate of discount for Treasury bills issued at the latest weekly tender.

3　A 'bill' in the sense used here is a piece of paper which is evidence of indebtedness on the part of the person or body on whom it is drawn. The bill is said to be 'discounted' when it is purchased at a price below its value on maturity. Hence Treasury bills are evidence of indebtedness of the Treasury. These bills have usually ninety days to run to maturity and might be acquired by the discount houses at, say, £97.50 per £100, which would represent a discount of approximately 10% per annum on the value at maturity.

support loans to deposit-taking institutions. The first are the most important to the operation of the monetary and financial system, and attention is concentrated entirely on them. They are discussed in the section dealing with the discount market.

Premises, equipment and other securities and notes and coins can be dealt with briefly. Other securities are non-government securities and include bills purchased by the Bank in order to keep a watch on the quality of the bills circulating in the London market. The Bank will not purchase bills of which they disapprove and this acts as a deterrent to their circulation. Other securities also include some holdings of equity share capital of other companies. Notes are the counterpart of the item in the Issue Department and some coin is held for ordinary business purposes.

III.3   The Authorities and Monetary and Credit Control

It was indicated above (p. 61) that in the late 1960s the Bank became increasingly concerned that its use of quantitative and qualitative controls for the purposes of monetary and credit policy adversely affected the efficiency and operation of the banking and financial system. After careful study it issued in May 1971 a consultative document entitled 'Competition and Credit Control', setting out proposals which purported to have 'the objective of combining an effective measure of control over credit conditions with greater scope for competition and innovation'.[1]

The main proposals in the document were:

(i)   to introduce right across the banking system a uniform minimum reserve assets ratio fixed at 12.5% of its sterling deposit liabilities;

(ii)   to extend the special deposits scheme to all banks, enabling the Bank to call for additional deposits to be made with it; and

(iii)   that the London and Scottish clearing banks should abandon their cartel arrangements for the fixing of interest rates.

The foregoing proposals, after discussions with the interested institutions, became effective from 16 September 1971. Separate proposals were put before the discount houses and finance houses; these are considered later.

The detailed definition of sterling deposit liabilities or what are now called *eligible liabilities* of the banks gives rise in practice to certain difficulties about what their precise composition should be. Eligible liabilities are defined broadly as follows: sterling deposit liabilities excluding deposits, except certificates of deposit, having an original maturity of over two years, since these are considered to be more akin to loan capital; and sterling resources arising from switching foreign currencies into sterling. Interbank transactions, including sterling certificates of deposit, and transactions with the discount market (except for reserve assets) are counted on a net basis. Transit items both within individual banks and between banks are dealt with in special ways in order to eliminate double counting.

The assets which are eligible for inclusion as reserve assets are also carefully defined. They 'comprise balances with the Bank of England (other than special and

---

1   *BEQB*, vol. 11, no. 2, June 1971, p. 189.

supplementary deposits); money at call (secured and immediately callable) with the listed discount market institutions . . . and with listed brokers; British government and Northern Ireland government Treasury bills; UK local authority bills eligible for rediscount at the Bank of England; commercial bills eligible for rediscount at the Bank of England – up to a maximum of 2% of eligible liabilities . . ., and British government stocks and stocks of nationalized industries guaranteed by the Government with one year or less to final maturity.'[1] In addition, the London clearing banks have to maintain on average over each banking month as part of their minimum reserve ratio the equivalent of 1.5% of their eligible liabilities in balances at the head office of the Bank of England and described as the cash requirement. Till-money is not eligible for inclusion as reserve assets.

At the same time as the authorities announced their minimum reserve assets ratio they amended and extended the coverage of their interest-bearing special-deposits scheme. The initial version of the scheme required that each bank should be prepared to deposit with the Bank of England a uniform percentage of its eligible liabilities. The Bank intimated, however, that in the future it might want to call for special deposits at different percentage rates on domestic and overseas deposits.[2] Subsequently the Bank announced a revised scheme.

Under the revised scheme the Bank may as before decide to operate a uniform rate of call for special deposits applied to *all* eligible liabilities or – and this was new – a variable rate of call. The variability may be achieved in a number of ways. First, eligible overseas liabilities may be subject to a lower rate of call or be exempted from a particular call. Alternatively, the Bank may call for special deposits in relation to the *increase*, if any, in eligible overseas liabilities over a specified time period. The call may be in addition to or separate from a call applied to the *total* of each bank's eligible liabilities. The revised scheme clearly gives the Bank considerable flexibility in differentiating between domestic and overseas deposits in making calls for special deposits.

In December 1973, some two years after the introduction of the initial proposals, the Bank announced a non-interest-bearing special-deposits scheme as a supplement to the existing scheme. The supplementary special-deposits scheme was designed to curtail the growth or rate of growth of the banks' *interest-bearing* deposits and worked as follows – it has been discontinued from June 1980.

The Bank specified for a given time period a maximum or target rate of growth above the average level in a defined base period for interest-bearing eligible liabilities, and any growth in excess of this was subject to progressively higher rates of call for supplementary special deposits. Before the scheme was abolished the final rates of call for growth of interest-bearing eligible liabilities in excess of the permitted maximum were, for an excess of up to 3%, a rate of call of 5% of the excess, for an excess of more than 3%, and up to 5%, a rate of call of 25%, and thereafter the rate of call was 50%.

In presenting their Competition and Credit Control proposals the Bank of England claimed to be shifting their 'emphasis towards the broader monetary

1 Additional notes to table 4, *BEQB*, vol. 20, no. 1, March 1980. The listed discount-market institutions are the discount houses, two discount brokers and the money trading departments of certain listed banks – there are five of the latter. Listed brokers comprise money brokers and jobbers on the stock exchange. Eligible commercial bills are bills which are payable in the UK and have been accepted by certain approved banks (ibid.).

2 'Competition and Credit Control: Further Developments', *BEQB*, vol. 13, no. 1, March 1973, pp. 51-5. (Neither the special-deposits scheme nor the supplementary special-deposits scheme, which is described below, has been applied to the Northern Ireland banks.)

aggregates . . . (including) . . . the money supply under one or more of its many definitions . . . (and) . . . domestic credit expansion'.[1] More recently it has been stated that in 1971 'the arrangements for credit control were modified, with the broader aim of regulating the growth of the money supply principally by variations in interest rates'.[2] However, it would be a mistake to suggest that controlling the money supply took precedence as a policy objective over the authorities' preoccupation with the behaviour of interest rates in the short end of the market. Indeed the then Governor of the Bank stated that 'It is not expected that the mechanism of the minimum asset ratio and Special Deposits can be used to achieve some precise multiple contraction or expansion of bank assets. Rather the intention is to use our control over liquidity, which these instruments will reinforce, to influence the structure of interest rates. The resulting changes in relative rates of return will then reduce shifts in the asset portfolios of both the public and the banks'.[3]

The preceding discussion suggests that there was (and the Green Paper discussed below, that there still is) a certain ambivalence, or at least a lack of precision, in specifying the objectives of monetary and credit policy. On the one hand some emphasis is placed on the control of the money supply, but on the other interest rates, particularly in the short end of the market, seem also to be an objective in their own right, presumably because of the importance attached to interest-rate behaviour for government debt management. However, the authorities cannot have it both ways; if they are serious about controlling the money supply, then ultimately in a market situation they must accept interest rates consistent with that policy.

It will be seen later (in section V.1 below) that throughout the 1970s the growth of the money supply has been highly irregular and extremely rapid in comparison with previous experience. Furthermore, whatever may have been true of the achievements of the authorities in dampening down fluctuations in short-term interest rates over brief time periods, by the end of the 1970s interest rates in the short end of the market had never been higher in nominal terms in the almost 300-year history of the Bank of England. However, the failure to realize their policy objectives cannot be legitimately blamed by the authorities on the policy instruments which they introduced and had at their disposal, unsatisfactory though those instruments turned out to be.

The authorities in a recent Green Paper have explored at some length the problems of monetary control and the efficacy of different policy instruments. They take the view that monetary control in the medium term can be accomplished by appropriate fiscal and interest-rate policies and especially through a tightly controlled PSBR. In other words they are stressing, surely correctly, that if the growth of the money supply is to be controlled in the medium term it is essential *not* to rely on the banking system as a residual source of finance for budget deficits. For to do so is almost bound to subordinate the growth of the money supply to the importunate demands of government.

---

1 'Key Issues in Monetary and Credit Policy', *BEQB*, vol. 11, no. 2, June 1971, p. 165 (parentheses added).

2 'The Gilt-edged Market', *BEQB*, vol. 19, no. 2, June 1979, p. 138.

3 'Key Issues in Monetary and Credit Policy', ibid., p. 197.

4 *Monetary Control*, Cmnd. 7858, HMSO, March 1980.

Putting aside the question of medium-term control of the money supply, the Green Paper concentrates on its short-term control and the instruments that might help to achieve that end. The authorities are clearly far from satisfied with how the reserve-assets ratio and supplementary special-deposit schemes have worked though they seem to be more satisfied with the special-deposits scheme which they plan to retain. There is reason to believe that the composition of the reserve-assets ratio with its high concentration directly and indirectly on government debt has distorted 'the yield relationship between short-term assets qualifying as reserve assets and others; and that this distortion is a factor inhibiting the development of a broader market in short-term public sector debt which might otherwise be helpful to shorter-run control of the monetary aggregates.'[1]

In the light of this and because the cash requirement of the London clearing banks, that is, the 1½% of their eligible liabilities which they hold as balances with the Bank of England, has become the effective 'fulcrum on which the Bank of England works when it seeks to affect short-term interest rates through its money market operations', the authorities have decided to abolish the reserve-assets ratio. However, they propose to specify for the banking system primary liquidity norms to fulfil what they consider to be prudential needs; 'primary liquidity would be provided by cash, and by those assets which the Bank of England is customarily prepared to buy in its open market operations, or which represent claims on institutions in the money market having access to lender of last resort facilities'.[2] The cash requirement is to be replaced 'by one whereby all banks and licensed deposit-taking institutions above a minimum size would be required to hold cash balances with the Bank'.[3] Thus the system would seem formally to be returning to a cash requirement basis.

As already mentioned, the supplementary special-deposits scheme, commonly known as the 'corset', has been abolished. It introduced major distortions into the banking system. It encouraged, for instance, the banks to sell short-term public-sector debt to, say, the company sector which had the effect of reducing eligible liabilities but had little effect on the liquidity of the economy since there is practically no difference for a company holding a Treasury bill rather than a certificate of deposit with the Treasury bill held by a bank.

There is also evidence that the banks have attempted to ameliorate the effects of the corset by increasing the volume of their acceptances.[4] That is, instead of granting advances or overdrafts which might lead to or be a consequence of increased eligible liabilities, and give rise to penalties under the corset, the banks would encourage customers to issue commercial bills to the non-bank private sector and guarantee these bills by accepting them, that is, the individual bank would attach its name to them. 'To the holder such bills are no less liquid than a certificate of deposit of comparable term, and to the borrower they are a very close substitute for bank credit.'[5]

---

1 *Monetary Control*, ibid., p. 7.

2 ibid., p. 19.

3 ibid., p. 7.

4 Between June 1978 and December 1979 sterling acceptances of banks in the UK increased from £2,255m to £5,670m, an increase of 151%, whilst interest-bearing eligible liabilities increased from £29,718m to £33,609m, an increase of 13%.

5 *Monetary Control*, ibid., p. 5.

This type of diversion of funds in response to restrictions or controls is known as disintermediation, and ordinarily gives rise to resource costs and loss of efficiency. It also, of course, distorts statistical data and generally encourages the movement of funds into uncontrolled or less-controlled areas. The inference that should probably be drawn from this and similar experience is that in controlling or influencing the monetary system it is of fundamental importance to rely upon and operate through the voluntary behavioural practices of competitive monetary and financial institutions. It is not at all clear that the authorities accept this inference and one of its major requirements, which is the widespread availability of frequent and accurate information about the asset and liability structures of the banking and financial system.

The Green Paper went on to consider further instruments of monetary control, including monetary base systems and what it called indicator systems. By a monetary base system is meant one in which the banks hold, either because it is mandatory or for prudential reasons, base money which is generally defined to include bankers' deposits with the central bank and may also include their holdings of central-bank notes and official coin as well as those held by the public. Thus in the widest sense base money constitutes deposit and note liabilities of the central bank plus official coinage. In principle this base money is under the control of the authorities, and by regulating its supply they can, on certain conditions, control or at any rate influence the volume of deposits of the banking system and more generally the supply of money.

The most widely understood monetary base system is probably the textbook mandatory one where the banks are required to hold base money in a fixed proportion to deposits. The simplest is where the proportion relates to deposits and base money on the same date – known as current accounting – but it is possible to envisage a lagged accounting system where 'current base requirements are fixed by reference to deposits in a previous period . . . (or) lead accounting where the holding of base assets would put a limit on deposits for some future date'.[1]

Alternatively a monetary base system might be non-mandatory or voluntary where the banking system finds it desirable to maintain a fairly systematic relationship through time between its deposit liabilities and base money.

The authorities are sceptical about both types of monetary base system, though the writer remains unconvinced by their arguments in the Green Paper and, in particular, their opposition to a non-mandatory or voluntary monetary base system which is the direction in which they are of necessity pushed by their proper concern over disintermediation.

By an indicator system is meant one where divergences between the mandatory monetary base and its officially desired level would 'trigger changes in the Bank of England's lending rate and so other interest rates'.[2] The advantage claimed for this approach over current methods of adjusting the Bank's lending rate 'is that it could reduce what may be a bias towards delay'.[3]

What precise monetary control system will emerge from these deliberations remains at the time of writing (April 1980) unknown. However, it is clear that the authorities have learned, especially from the experience of the 1970s, that arbitrary interference with a highly developed banking and financial system, which no longer

---

1 *Monetary Control*, ibid., p. 10.

2 ibid., p. 12.

3 ibid., p. 13.

can be thought of as domestic but is international in its coverage, gives rise to serious problems of disintermediation. What is less clear is that the authorities are prepared to fashion instruments of control which would minimize such tendencies by operating on the voluntary behaviour of the banking system, supplemented by an extensive and frequent balance-sheet information system.

III.4   The Discount Market

The discount market is officially described as being made up of eleven discount houses, two discount brokers and the money trading departments of five listed banks which all carry on essentially the same type of business. The discount houses are a special type of bank which borrows a substantial proportion of its funds in the inter-bank market — from the clearing banks, accepting houses, other British banks and overseas banks. Most of these funds are at call or on overnight loan — some 82% on 12 December 1979 — and hence lenders may demand their repayment immediately or subject to very short notice. The discount houses use these borrowed funds to acquire both sterling and other currency assets. The assets include short-dated British government securities, Treasury bills, commercial bills, local authority bills and securities and certificates of deposit. Under the new credit control arrangements the discount houses were first obliged to hold a minimum of 50% of their eligible borrowed funds in 'British government and Northern Ireland government Treasury bills, local bills and bonds and British government-guaranteed and local authority stocks with not more than five years to run to maturity'.[1]

In practice, however, the Bank found that the operation of the compulsory minimum public-sector-debt ratio had many disadvantages. In particular, it produced interest-rate distortions in short-term money markets and complicated 'the Bank's task of securing adequate influence over credit extended by the discount market'.[2]   The distortions arose primarily when a house or houses were operating near to the limit of their public-sector-debt ratio. In these circumstances if a house wished to acquire other assets it could only do so by simultaneously purchasing public-sector assets. This had the effect of pushing rates on the latter to relatively low levels in comparison with rates on other assets. Similar problems arose when the Bank attempted to give help to the market through the purchase of public-sector assets.

For reasons such as these the Bank abolished the public-sector-debt ratio and replaced it from 19 July 1973 with a new form of control. This limits for each member of the discount market its aggregate holdings of what are clumsily called 'undefined assets' — largely private-sector assets — to a maximum of twenty times its capital and reserves.[3]   The actual ratio these undefined assets bear to capital and

1 'Competition and Credit Control: the Discount Market', *BEQB*, vol. 11, no. 3, September 1971, p. 314. Company tax reserve certificates were also eligible for inclusion in the public-sector-lending ratio.

2 'Competition and Credit Control: Modified Arrangements for the Discount Market', *BEQB*, vol. 13, no. 3, September 1973, pp. 306-7.

3 Undefined assets are all assets other than the following: balances at the Bank of England; UK and NI Treasury bills, British government and local authority stocks with not more than five years to final maturity; local authority and other public boards' bills eligible at the Bank; local authority negotiable bonds; and bank bills drawn by nationalized industries under specific government guarantee. *Source: Financial Statistics: Explanatory Handbook*, April 1979, p. 66.

reserves is known as the 'undefined assets multiple'. The new control avoids at least some of the major distortions that arose from the use of the former public-sector-debt ratio. Nevertheless it still discriminates in favour of the public sector and could clearly give rise to difficulties for members experiencing a loss of reserves and thus inhibit their ability to expand. The capital resources base for the calculation of the multiple was £164m for 1979; it is calculated as a three-year moving average of the end-of-December figure of the net worth of each member. If the clearing banks or other lenders demand repayment of their loans and the discount market cannot borrow elsewhere or otherwise obtain funds, the members turn to the Bank of England, which makes funds available to them against suitable collateral which, except for eligible bank bills, consists of the public-sector assets formerly included in the public-sector-debt ratio. Furthermore, the collateral must include a minimum proportion of Treasury bills. The members of the discount market are the only financial institutions which have automatic access to the Bank in this way. This privilege was extended to the discount houses on the understanding that they apply each week for the full amount of the Treasury-bill issue. Each house submits a bid of a size at or above a minimum agreed with the Bank of England and at prices of its own choosing.

TABLE 2.3

Discount Market (selected items), 12 December 1979 (£m)

Borrowed funds		*Assets*	
Sterling: Bank of England	–	Sterling: UK and NI	
Other UK banking sector	4,228	Treasury bills	709
Other UK	275	Local Authority and	
Overseas	65	Other public sector bills	142
Other currencies:		Other bills	2,496
UK banking sector	85	Certificates of deposit	84
Other UK	19	Other funds lent	196
Overseas	32	British government stocks	764
		Other investments	397
		Other currencies:	
		Certificates of deposit	109
		Other assets	22
	4,704		4,919

Source: FS.
Note: Total undefined assets £2,977m; undefined assets multiple 18.2.

The traditional practice was that the Bank acted as lender of last resort to the monetary and financial system, through the intermediation of the discount houses, by lending to them at or above a rate called Bank rate. But with the increased flexibility of short-term rates following the introduction of the new credit control arrangements in September 1971, the significance of Bank rate, which had formerly been a major reference point for other rates, declined. By September 1972 the rate on Treasury bills which historically had always been below Bank rate jumped to almost 1% above it. With the approval of the Chancellor of the Exchequer the Bank published 'new arrangements for determining and announcing their minimum rate for lending to the (discount) market. From 13 October 1972, the lending rate was to be ½% above the average rate of discount for Treasury bills at the most recent tender, rounded to the nearest ¼% above'.[1] The Bank, however, retained the right to depart from these arrangements and if need be announce independently of them a change in the *minimum lending rate* — the title which has superseded Bank rate. The Bank did in fact depart from the minimum-lending-rate formula on 13 November 1973 when it raised the rate from 11¼ to 13%. The operation of the formula was restored when market rates adjusted to the new rate. And on 11 March 1977 a further modification was made; 'where the operation of the formula would have brought about a reduction in the rate, the Bank reserved the right, exceptionally, either to leave the rate unchanged, or to change it by less than would result from the operation of the formula'.[2] On 25 May 1978 it was announced that in future minimum lending rate would be determined by administrative decision and any change would normally be announced at 12.30 p.m. on a Thursday, with the new rate becoming effective immediately.

Traditionally, Bank rate was described as a penal rate, as it was generally at a level in excess of what were called 'market rates' — the rates ruling in the market for Treasury bills and prime bank bills. The theory was that if the discount houses were borrowing at Bank rate they were therefore making losses and would hasten to pay off their debts to the Bank, with a consequential reduction in the cash base of the banking system. However, there were periods when public-sector debt of the kind held by the discount houses yielded more than Bank rate. Thus the penal-rate argument would not be valid for borrowings from the Bank against these securities, and a similar argument holds as regards the minimum lending rate. Moreover, it is conceivable that if the discount houses were expecting a reduction in interest rates they might be prepared to borrow for a time at the so-called penal rates to take advantage of capital appreciation and high running yields on some or all of their asset holdings. The Bank, of course, has the option, which it may or may not use, to charge more than the minimum lending rate or to raise it. However, it is clear that the penal-rate argument is not totally convincing, though the Bank is now in such a powerful position in relation to the very existence of the market that it is almost inconceivable that it would flout the wishes of the authorities.

For many years, however, the Bank has helped to relieve cash shortages in the money market by purchasing bills from the members at market rates, as well as providing funds at Bank rate (or, now, minimum lending rate) or above, depending on which the Bank felt was more appropriate in the light of monetary and economic conditions. Furthermore, in June 1966 the Bank introduced an important modification in its method of lending. Previously *loans* to the discount houses had usually been for a minimum period of seven days and charged at Bank rate or occasionally above. But since then the Bank is prepared to lend overnight and generally at market rates.

Thus the Bank now exercises great flexibility in the supply of funds to the discount market. The Bank is also prepared to absorb, by sales of bills to the discount houses, surplus funds that they cannot otherwise conveniently employ. The Bank is therefore in a commanding position to influence day-to-day rates in this money market.

The discount houses occupy a very special position in the market for Treasury bills. Before the introduction of the new credit control arrangements the discount

1 'Commentary', *BEQB*, vol. 12, no. 4, December 1972, p. 443.
2 *Financial Statistics: Explanatory Handbook*, April 1979, p. 44.

houses tendered as a syndicate at a single rate for the whole weekly issue of Treasury bills. Under the new arrangements and with the encouragement of the authorities they still tender for the whole issue but no longer at an agreed rate.

Covering the tender has the merit from the point of view of the Treasury that it 'guarantees' them the funds and helps the authorities to influence Treasury bill and other short-term rates. However, from another point of view the procedure is an odd one. For in the final analysis the discount houses are able to tender for the whole Treasury bill issue because, as already explained, the Bank stands ready to support them. Moreover, they would presumably become concerned if they could only cover the tender over a sustained period by borrowing at minimum lending rate. To avoid this the Bank may, as has been shown, supply the discount houses with funds at market rates. The discount houses then use the funds to acquire the new Treasury bills. But this is tantamount to the Bank lending directly to the Treasury and so increasing the cash base of the banking system, as the Treasury spends the funds, unless the whole process is offset in some other way, such as by the Bank selling securities to the non-bank public.

There may be, in fact, an element of charade about the whole procedure of the discount houses tendering for the full Treasury bill issue. The danger is that the charade hides what is really happening – the financing of the Treasury by borrowing from the central bank. This may tend to subordinate monetary policy to the exigencies of government financial needs; and there is a lot of evidence to suggest that the consequences of this are inflationary. Moreover, the procedure, and indeed the whole treatment of the discount market, is inconsistent with the competitive determination of interest rates by market processes, emphasized by the Bank in introducing the new credit control arrangements.

III.5   The London Clearing Banks[1]

The London clearing banks are so named because they are all members of the Committee of London Clearing Bankers. Up to 1968 there were eleven clearing banks, although not all of them were independent. But with the mergers of 1968 and 1970 only six clearing banks remain and these also are not all independent. The banks are dominated by the big four, Barclays, National Westminster, Lloyds and Midland, who between them control over 95% of total deposits and have a network of some 12,000 branches. The clearing banks' primary function is the management of the payments system in England and Wales, although they necessarily carry out all the usual commercial banking functions and, since the introduction of the new credit control arrangements and the greater freedom that has gone with them, have shown themselves increasingly willing to broaden their activities and now claim that they offer all the services usually associated with the accepting houses and the other leading merchant banks.[2]

For many years the clearing banks acted as a cartel in fixing the interest rates they paid on deposits and charged on advances. These practices had come in for

---

1 Limitations on space do not permit discussion of the Scottish clearing banks and the Northern Ireland banks, which carry on very similar activities in Scotland and Northern Ireland respectively.

2 *The London Clearing Banks*, Evidence by the Committee of London Clearing Bankers to the Committee to Review the Functions of Financial Institutions, November 1977, pp. 29-30.

increasing criticism because of the encouragement they undoubtedly gave to uneconomic non-price competition, especially in the form of branch extension, and the general lack of dynamism they had imparted to the whole system. It would, however, be false to argue that the banks had totally stood aside from competing in terms of price for deposits and in granting credit. For many of them had done so through subsidiaries and associated companies such as finance houses (described below) and other financial institutions. To be unduly critical of the banks may be unjustified as it is highly likely that the authorities, with their predilection for short-run stability of nominal interest rates, condoned the existence of the cartel arrangements and would not have welcomed interest-rate competition by the banks for deposits and advances.

Sight deposits and time deposits are the main liabilities of the London clearing banks. Sight deposits, which may or may not be interest-bearing, are withdrawable on demand and transferable by cheque; they are the most important means of payment in the economy. Until the introduction of the new credit control arrangements in September 1971 time deposits were interest-bearing and subject to notice of withdrawal, generally seven days, and not ordinarily transferable by cheque. However, these conditions could be waived, though usually with some loss of interest. Since September 1971, however, the London clearing banks have in addition to these time deposits been prepared to take what are called fixed-term deposits; that is, deposits for fixed periods which may be far in excess of seven days; these deposits are sometimes referred to as wholesale deposits, because of their size and because they mainly involve financial institutions and large corporations. Deposits and other items of the balance sheet of the London clearing banks for December 1979 may be seen in table 2.4.

Closely related to the fixed-term deposits, though with at least one fundamental difference because of their negotiability, are negotiable certificates of deposit. These too have only appeared in the balance sheets of the London clearing banks since September 1971. The certificates are generally denominated in either sterling or US dollars. In the words of the Bank of England: 'A sterling certificate of deposit is a document, issued by a UK office of a British or foreign bank, certifying that a sterling deposit has been made with that bank which is repayable to the bearer upon the surrender of the certificate at maturity'.[1] The definition of a dollar certificate of deposit is analogous.

A sterling certificate of deposit is generally for a minimum amount of £50,000 and normally a maximum of £500,000 'with a term to maturity of not less than three months and not longer than five years'.[2] Certificates of deposit have advantages for both the issuers and the holders. Issuing banks have found them to be a useful means of raising large amounts for strictly fixed periods – unlike the so-called fixed-term deposit where payment may be requested, and be hard to refuse, before maturity. And holders have found them highly convenient as they can sell them in the secondary market if they need liquid funds. The discount houses are the major operators in the secondary market. Certificates of deposit first made their appearance in the UK in May 1966 with the introduction of

---

1 'Sterling Certificates on Deposit', *BEQB*, vol. 12, no. 4. December 1972, p. 487. See also 'Sterling Certificates of Deposit and the Inter-Bank Market', *BEQB*, vol. 13, no. 3, September 1973, pp. 308-14; and the 'London Dollar Certificate of Deposit', *BEQB*, vol. 13, no. 4, December 1973, pp. 446-52.

2 *BEQB*, vol. 12, p. 487.

certificates denominated in dollars. Sterling certificates did not appear until October 1968.

Turning to the assets part of the balance sheet, it may be seen that these consist of notes and coin, the various kinds of reserve assets, special and supplementary special deposits, different types of market loans and advances, British government stocks of more than one year to maturity, and certain miscellaneous assets. Some of these items require further discussion.

TABLE 2.4

London Clearing Banks, 12 December 1979 (£m)

	Sterling[1]	Other Currencies[2]	Total[3]
(i) *Liabilities*			
Sight and time deposits:			
UK banking sector	3,174	1,923	5,097
Other UK	30,703	743	31,446
Overseas	2,273	5,327	7,600
Certificates of deposit	1,292	353	1,645
Capital and other liabilities	–	–	8,534
	37,443	8,346	54,323

	Sterling	Other Currencies[2]	Total
(ii) *Assets*			
Notes and coin	937	–	937
Reserve assets: Balance with			
Bank of England	437	–	437
Money at call	1,828	–	1,828
UK and NI treasury bills	474	–	474
Other bills	674	–	674
British government stocks up to 1 year	306	–	306
Special and supplementary deposits	393	–	393
Market loans and advances (other than reserve assets):			
Banks in UK and discount market	7,034	3,111	10,145
Certificates of deposit	408	46	454
UK public sector	619	505	1,124
UK private sector	20,449	727	21,176
Overseas	3,110	3,986	7,096
Other UK	9	–	9
British government stocks over 1 year and undated	1,310	–	1,310
Other investments	1,432	434	1,866
Bills	72	16	88
Sterling and other currencies miscellaneous assets	–	–	6,007
	39,492	8,825	54,324

Source: FS.
Notes: Eligible liabilities £28,971m. Reserve assets £3,719m. Ratio 12.8%.

1 Of total sterling deposits of £37,443m, sight deposits amounted to £17,251m.

2 The figures are affected by changes in exchange rates and the totals have been rounded.

3 Total liabilities is the sum of the sterling and other currencies totals plus capital and other liabilities. Total assets is the sum of the sterling and other currencies totals plus miscellaneous assets.

Notes and coin are used by the banks for their day-to-day business. The reserve assets include balances with the Bank of England which the banks use to settle their inter-bank indebtedness and to make payments to the authorities. If for some reason a bank, or the London clearing banks as a whole, find that their cash holdings are tending to fall below some desired ratio to deposits, they can through time rectify the position in a number of ways. It may be possible for them to sell or exchange some of their assets for cash, draw on their funds with other UK banks, sell stocks or negotiate repayment of advances or recall some of their money at call – another reserve asset – from the discount market. If the latter happens the discount market may, as already explained, have to turn for assistance to the Bank of England. This will generally happen if the banking system as a whole is short of cash. If the Bank does not wish to lend at its minimum lending rate, perhaps because it is anxious to keep interest rates from rising, then it will normally enter the open market and purchase securities at market rates, paying for them with cheques drawn on the Bank and so relieving the cash shortage. However, if the Bank wishes to see some upward pressure on interest rates it may wait for the discount houses to come to the Bank and only make cash available at the minimum lending rate or even possibly above.

In so far as the Bank is not prepared to make a permanent net addition to the stock of cash available and ruling out a surplus of cash in the rest of the banking system, then, unless there is an inflow of funds from abroad and which the authorities do not neutralize, some reduction in deposits of the London clearing banks or in the deposits of the banking sector as a whole may be expected. One of the consequences of this is likely to be upward pressure on interest rates.

Of the remaining reserve assets shown in table 2.4, money at call includes not only funds lent to the discount houses but also funds lent for periods not exceeding one month to money brokers on the stock exchange, discount brokers, jobbers and stockbrokers, and bullion brokers. Treasury bills and other bills have been described previously. The London clearing banks, by an understanding with the discount houses and the Bank of England, do not generally bid for Treasury bills at the weekly tender, at least not for themselves, though they may do so on behalf of clients. Bills bought on their own account by the clearing banks are usually held to maturity, though they are, on occasion, sold to the Bank if the latter is looking for maturities that are no longer held by the discount houses. The purchase of bills by the Bank from the clearing banks is one of the ways by which the Bank may relieve pressure on the discount houses and obviate their need to borrow at minimum lending rate or above. This is described as 'indirect help' to the discount houses as opposed to 'direct help' by means of purchases from the houses themselves.

Special and supplementary special deposits which were discussed earlier are not considered further. Market loans and advances include a wide range of assets some of which are indicated in table 2.4. Loans to the discount market refer to funds which are not immediately callable and are unsecured in contrast with the money at call included in reserve assets. Loans and advances in sterling to the UK private sector are quantitatively of major importance and comprise more than 50 per cent of total sterling assets. Advances are of two main types, loans and overdrafts. With the loan, the customer's account is credited with the amount, whereas the overdraft is literally an overdrawing of a current account which is debited accordingly. Loans include contractual-term loans which have developed since the early 1970s and with a duration up to five or seven years not uncommon. Advances are generally assumed to be the most lucrative of the banks' assets. Until the introduction of the new credit control arrangements by the London clearing banks, rates on advances were tied to Bank rate under their cartel agreements on interest rates. Each bank now fixes what it calls a *base* rate for advances. The base rate may and does differ between the banks but is generally close to the minimum lending rate of the Bank of England. The actual rates charged for advances varies with the nature and status of the customer but most rates are between 1% and 5% higher than the base rate. The London clearing banks do, however, have uniform rates for nationalized industries borrowing under Treasury guarantee and for certain other government-supported borrowing.

The London clearing banks have responded to the increased flexibility provided by the new competition and credit control arrangements by competing more strongly amongst themselves and with other financial institutions. This is indicated by the marked change in their balance sheets in recent years, both in terms of their rate of growth and of the structure of their liabilities and assets. They are now much more actively involved in what has been called the parallel money markets, such as the market for negotiable certificates of deposit, the inter-bank sterling deposits market — both as borrowers and lenders — and similarly in the euro-dollar market; that is, the market or markets for US dollars held outside the US. In each of these ways the London clearing banks have diversified their activities and in so doing have narrowed some of the differences between themselves and other types of bank. However, the London clearing banks, like their Scottish and Northern Ireland counterparts, have a predominant proportion of their assets and liabilities in sterling and remain largely responsible for the day-to-day payments system; other types of bank, as will be seen in the next section, tend to concentrate their activities in other currencies.

III.6 Accepting Houses, Other British Banks, Overseas Banks and Consortium Banks

The business of this group of banks varies substantially amongst themselves, although they have enough in common to allow them to be discussed together. Since about 1957-8, when exchange control restrictions were substantially relaxed and funds could begin to move more freely between international financial centres, the accepting houses, other British banks, overseas banks and, more recently, consortium banks, have greatly expanded, and at a much more rapid rate than the clearing banks. Moreover, these banks have been active participants in the development of new and important money markets.

The term 'accepting house' arose because of the important role the houses played and still play in 'accepting' bills of exchange, the commercial or financial bill already encountered in the discussion of the discount houses and the clearing banks. A bill is accepted by signing it and in so doing the acceptor becomes liable for payment of the bill on maturity. The accepting houses accept bills on behalf of clients and in this way earn commissions.

Accepting houses are also known as merchant banks since the banking side of their activities generally emerged as a consequence of their business as merchants, particularly in overseas trade. The activities of the accepting houses are excitingly diverse. The individual houses engage in one or more of the following activities: the gold and silver bullion markets; the foreign exchange market; the foreign currency deposit business — including certificates of deposit — in the making of new issues of both domestic and overseas securities; advising on mergers and takeovers; managing investments on behalf of clients; participating in equity investment in business and industry; and acting as trustees.

Other British banks refers to banks with majority UK ownership, leaving aside consortium banks which have foreign participation. The group also includes the offices in GB of the NI banks and also branches of their subsidiaries. The composition of the group is very diverse; it now consists of over seventy members, some of whom were formerly classified as finance houses as well as highly specialized banks in the fields of investment and international finance.

The overseas banks are banks which maintain branches or subsidiaries in London but whose main business is overseas. There are now about 200 of these compared with around 80 in the early 1960s; they play a major part in the movement of funds into and out of London and in the finance of international trade. Of the 200, over 60 are branches and subsidiaries of American banks and some 20 of Japanese banks.

Consortium banks are 'banks which are owned by other banks but in which no one bank has a direct shareholding of more than 50 per cent, and in which at least one shareholder is an overseas bank'.[1] There are almost 30 of them and they are predominantly concerned with international finance and the management of foreign currency deposits.

In terms of total deposits, this group of banks far exceeds in size the London clearing banks. In mid-December 1979 the former had deposits totalling some £194,000m whilst the latter had some £46,000m. These are, however, gross figures and include inter-bank transactions as well as some internal accounts. This element of double counting inflates the figures of the other types of bank to a proportionately greater extent than it does those of the London clearing banks. Nevertheless, with the growth of these banks in the last twenty years or so there has been a radical restructuring of the banking system in the UK. The scale of the change can perhaps be appreciated when it is recalled that their deposits totalled less than £1,000m in the late 1950s.

It might, however, be argued that to contrast the total deposits of this group of banks with those of the London clearing banks is to exaggerate the significance of the growth of the former since so much of that growth has taken the form of foreign currency deposits, or what is widely called euro-currency business, as may be seen in table 2.5. It should be noticed that the foreign currency deposits are roughly matched by foreign currency assets. To the extent that this is the case they do not directly affect the UK gold and foreign currency reserves. However, there may be indirect effects, both on the foreign currency reserves and on the management of monetary and credit policy generally, through the earnings of the banks and through effects on interest rates, which will necessarily have repercussions on the highly integrated London money markets.

But even in terms of sterling deposits this group of banks has come to rival the London clearing banks in terms of size, with liabilities of some £34,000m and £37,000m respectively in mid-December 1979. However, for the purposes of monetary and credit control the eligible liabilities of this group of banks of around £18,000m in mid-December 1979 remain somewhat less than the nearly £29,000m of the London clearing banks. But there can be no doubting the dramatic changes that have taken place in the UK banking system and there is good reason to believe

---

1 *Financial Statistics: Explanatory Handbook*, April 1979, p. 64.

TABLE 2.5

Accepting Houses, Other UK Banks, Overseas Banks and Consortium Banks, 12 December 1979 (£m)

	Sterling[1]	Other Currencies[2]	Total[3]
(i) *Liabilities*			
Deposits:			
UK banking sector	15,488	34,305	49,793
Other UK	11,287	4,098	15,385
Overseas	5,097	102,315	107,412
Certificates of deposit	2,406	19,302	21,708
Capital and other liabilities	—	—	7,371
	34,278	160,020	201,669
	Sterling	**Other Currencies[2]**	**Total**
(ii) *Assets*			
Notes and coin	45	—	45
Reserve assets: balances with			
Bank of England	11	—	11
Money at call	1,578	—	1,578
UK and NI Treasury bills	452	—	452
Other bills	329	—	329
British government stocks up to 1 year	195	—	195
Special and supplementary deposits	355	—	355
Market loans and advances (other than reserve assets):			
Banks in UK and discount market	12,476	32,525	45,001
Certificates of deposit	2,417	2,229	4,646
UK public sector	3,497	1,826	5,323
UK private sector	13,527	7,169	20,696
Overseas	1,321	114,393	115,714
Other UK	785	—	785
British government stocks over 1 year and undated	718	—	718
Other investments	857	1,903	2,760
Bills	394	396	790
Sterling and other currencies miscellaneous assets	—	—	2,260
	38,957	160,441	201,658

Source: BEQB.
Notes: Eligible liabilities £18,386m. Reserve assets £2,265m. Ratio 14.0%.

1 Of total sterling deposits of £34,278m, sight deposits amounted to £7,268m.

2 The figures are affected by changes in exchange rates.

3 Total liabilities is the sum of the sterling and other currencies totals plus capital and other liabilities. Total assets is the sum of the sterling and other currencies totals plus miscellaneous assets.

that those changes accelerated in the 1970s, in part under the influence of the new competition and credit control arrangements.

Furthermore, it is widely held that the reserve-assets ratio introduced under those arrangements, and subsequently the supplementary special-deposits scheme, as a means of influencing the activities of the banking sector, have not been entirely successful. As already indicated, the authorities are reconsidering their whole approach to influencing the monetary aggregates, though the very definition of these becomes more problematical in a world of currency substitution and off-shore banking.

III.7   Finance Houses and Other Consumer Credit Companies

A finance house is an institution which specializes in the financing of hire purchase, credit sales and other forms of instalment credit.[1] There are many companies involved in this business but the bulk of it is carried on by a small number of large firms. Hire purchase and credit sale, though legally distinct, generally take the form of a down-payment by the purchaser with the rest of the debt being paid off by instalments over a specified period. The period varies with the type of product, and may be as little as six months for some household goods or as much as five years for industrial machinery; the period for cars — the most important type of hire-purchase debt — may be up to three years.[2] The finance houses and consumer-credit companies attempt to organize their contracts so that the debt outstanding at any time on the transaction is less than the value of the product being acquired; this gives them some security and indicates why they concentrate on financing the purchase of durable or semi-durable goods rather than perishable goods. In practice hire-purchase debt is frequently paid off well in advance of the terminal period. This is important in assessing the liquidity of their assets.

Deposits are the single most important liability of the finance houses and consumer-credit companies, and are of two main kinds: fixed-term deposits, usually for three or six months, and deposits subject to notice of withdrawal, again normally for three to six months. Deposits may, however, be for as long as twelve months or even longer. The deposits earn interest at rates which are greatly influenced by those ruling in the money markets, especially the inter-bank deposits market and the market for sterling certificates of deposit. The chief depositors are the banking sector, industrial and commercial companies, other financial institutions and other residents, as well as a small amount of funds from overseas residents. Current accounts are not unknown amongst the finance houses but do not appear to be a significant part of their business. The banking sector provides most of the remaining funds to the finance houses by means of discounting bills and by advances. Capital reserves are also important.

Hire purchase and instalment credit generally accounts for the greater part of their assets with most of the remainder made up of other advances and loans, leased assets and, as regards the finance houses, reserve assets under the new credit control arrangements. Not all the hire purchase and instalment credit outstanding is owed directly to the finance houses; part of it arises from the purchase by the latter of debt from retailers and is known as 'block discounts'. Retailers do of course retain some hire-purchase debt, but the finance houses own the bulk of it. Other advances and loans include loans to garages (to finance stocks of vehicles) and to property companies and short-term loans to industrial and commercial companies. Until the

---

1   See R.M. Goode 'Reflections on Credit Law', *The Three Banks Review*, March 1978, pp. 26-42.

2   These periods are subject to control by the authorities.

introduction of the new credit-control arrangements, the finance houses held very few assets in liquid form, relying on their ability to attract additional deposits, on their borrowing powers and on the speedy repayment of their assets to meet any liquidity requirements.

The new credit-control arrangements for the finance houses which come under the scheme are very similar to those applied to the banks. (Companies with eligible liabilities of less than £10m are exempt so long as they remain below this limit.) The minimum reserve-assets ratio for those within the scheme is 10% compared with 12.5% for the banks. The main reason indicated by the Bank for the difference is that the imposition of the reserve-assets ratio was more of a burden on the finance houses than on the banks since the former in the ordinary way did not hold any eligible assets.

In December 1979 the eligible liabilities of the finance houses totalled only £460m and their holdings of reserve assets were £48.0m, giving them a ratio of 10.4%. Like the banks, the finance houses are subject to calls for both special deposits and supplementary special deposits. As regards calls for special deposits, the Bank has stated that they 'will normally be at the same rate as calls on the banks, but the Bank will have the right in certain defined circumstances to call special deposits from the finance houses at a higher rate. In no circumstances, however, will the total of reserve assets and special deposits represent a higher proportion of eligible liabilities for the finance houses than for the banks.'[1] Only eight finance houses now come under the new credit-control arrangements since a number of former finance houses have found it preferable to acquire the status of banks for purposes of the scheme.

It is clear that the introduction of a minimum reserve-assets ratio for the finance houses imposed on them a significant burden, especially as the return on reserve assets tend to be below their cost of borrowing. Furthermore, the banking sector as a whole now offers the finance houses much more competition than before the advent of the new competition and credit control arrangements. In terms of size the finance houses and other consumer-credit companies, excluding those which are now classified as banks, are very small in relation to the banking sector.

To their cost, the finance houses have for many years – with some intermissions – been subject to the special attention of the authorities. From time to time they have stipulated some of the terms on which instalment credit may be granted; in particular the minimum down-payments that must be made on different products by borrowers and the maximum repayment periods. These kinds of restrictions have come in for much criticism because of their arbitrariness and selectivity, and the – at any rate short-run – disruptive effects they can have on the production and sales of certain consumer-durable industries, especially the car industry. The Crowther Committee on consumer credit gave great impetus to criticisms such as these, recommending the abolition of terms control and credit ceilings and the encouragement generally of equal competition amongst credit institutions.[1] The new credit-control arrangements as applied to the finance houses initially went some way in this direction, but since December 1973 there have again been regulations governing the terms on which instalment credit, other than industrial instalment credit, may be offered.

---

1 'Reserve Ratios and Special Deposits', *BEQB*, Supplement, vol. 11, no. 3, September 1971.

1 *Report of the Committee on Consumer Credit*, Cmnd. 4596, HMSO, March 1971.

III.8   Building Societies

Building societies are mutual or non-profit-making bodies which specialize in the provision of finance for the purchase of both new and secondhand houses. There are some 300 building societies, less than one-seventh of the number some eighty years ago. The individual societies differ greatly in size, from some very large ones with a national network of branches to those with only one office.

Over 90% of the liabilities of the building societies are shares and deposits. Both are essentially deposits, so that the term 'share' is something of a misnomer. However, the shareholder is a member of the society whereas the depositor is not, and the latter has a prior right of liquidation over the shareholder. Deposits earn a slightly lower rate of interest than shares. Shares and deposits are subject to notice of withdrawal, though in practice both are paid on demand or on very short notice, except for fixed-term deposits. The interest rates on shares and deposits are quoted *net* of income tax, which is paid by the societies at an average or composite rate and is less than the basic rate of tax. In early 1980 the interest rates recommended by the Building Societies Association were 10.5% on paid-up shares and 10.25% on deposits. These rates are net of tax and are equivalent approximately to 15.0% and 14.64% respectively before deduction of basic tax, and these latter rates, much to the concern of the London clearing banks, are generally in excess of the rates they offer on ordinary deposit accounts. Furthermore, the rate of growth of the shares and deposits of the building societies has been so rapid in recent years that with a total of some £45,000m at the end of 1979 they are now considerably in excess of the total sterling deposits of the London clearing banks at £37,000m.

Mortgages usually account for about 80% of the assets of building societies and are predominantly for private house purchase. Most mortgages are for between twenty and thirty years with continuous repayment by instalments. The average life is generally about ten years, making the assets of building societies much shorter-lived than might appear. The recommended interest rate on new mortgages to owner occupiers was 15.0% in early 1980. But this is the gross rate, as interest payments on a housing loan – up to £25,000 for a principal residence – are allowable against income-tax assessments: if allowance is made for income-tax relief at the basic rate, the interest rate is reduced to 10.5% net. For those who pay less than the basic rate of tax, or no tax at all, there is an option mortgage scheme, supported by the government, which reduces the cost.

All the other assets, except such things as office premises, are classified as liquid assets by the societies. Liquid assets must be at least 7.5% of total assets, and both the type of asset and the maturity distribution are regulated by the Registrar of Building Societies. At the end of 1979 the actual liquid-assets ratio was 18.0% of total assets. Cash holdings and balances with banks are relatively small and vary a lot seasonally.

The building societies dominate the market providing finance for home purchase and they are therefore relevant, directly and indirectly, to the activity of the house-building industry. The societies cannot for long expand the supply of finance to borrowers unless there is a corresponding net inflow of funds from new shares and deposits; otherwise they would deplete their liquid assets and in time risk upsetting public confidence in their management. The interest rates the societies pay and the relationship they bear to the competing rates would appear to be a major determinant of the net inflow of funds to the societies.

III.9 Other Financial Institutions

The United Kingdom is particularly rich in the variety and number of its financial institutions. The term 'rich' is used advisedly, for financial institutions that are able to mediate freely between borrowers and lenders facilitate the achievement by both parties of a preferred distribution of their assets and liabilities and help to make the allocation of scarce resources more efficient. However, limitations on space prevent more than a brief mention of some of the remaining major financial institutions.

National Savings Bank and Trustee Savings Banks: The organization of, and services offered by, the National Savings Bank, formerly the Post Office Savings Bank, and Trustee Savings Banks have altered considerably over the last ten years. The National Savings Bank, which is distinct from the National Girobank – the latter, as already mentioned, being part of the banking sector is not discussed further here – has two types of account, ordinary and investment. The ordinary account pays 5% per year and the first £70 of interest is free of all United Kingdom income tax. The maximum amount allowed on ordinary account for a single-depositor is £10,000. Funds in ordinary accounts are channelled directly to, and classified as part of, the public sector. Investment accounts in March 1980 were paying 15% a year before tax and a maximum holding of £50,000 is permitted. One month's notice of withdrawal is required. At the end of 1979 total deposits on investment account were some £1,530m. The corresponding investments are all public-sector investments.

The Trustee Savings Banks have been reduced in number since 1976 from 72 to 19. In the same year the current accounts of the ordinary department were combined with the former special investment department to form what is called the New department. And in November 1979 the ordinary deposits, which had hitherto been classified as part of the public sector, were also added to the New department and the separate titles were discontinued. At 12 December 1979 the Trustee Savings Banks had sight and time deposits totalling £5,304m. The corresponding assets were nearly all public-sector debt but included advances to customers of £190m.

Insurance Companies: There are some 800 insurance companies engaged in business in the UK, but by far the greater part of British business is carried on by the members of the British Insurance Association, which has less than three hundred members. The fundamental purpose of insurance is to facilitate the spread of risk between persons and bodies and through time.

Insurance falls into two main categories: life assurance, and a catch-all, general insurance, which includes fire, marine, motor and other accident insurance. The insurance companies also operate the pension schemes of many industrial and commercial companies. Life assurance for the most part gives rise to long-term liabilities which the companies must be in a position to meet. This gives them an interest in long-term investments and in assets that may be expected to increase in capital value over the years. General insurance, on the other hand, is carried on much more on a year-to-year basis, ideally with premiums for the year being sufficient to cover the risks underwritten and to allow for expenses and the accumulation of limited reserves. So the disposition of funds arising from general insurance is largely governed by short-term considerations; assets must be quickly realizable without undue fear of capital loss.

The insurance companies, with total investments at the end of 1979 of over £50,000m, are of great importance in the UK's capital markets. They are large holders of both government and company securities.

Investment Trusts: Investment trusts are limited companies which specialize in the investment of funds provided by their shareholders or borrowed from debenture holders or other lenders. Despite the term 'trust' they do not operate, as do the unit trusts, under trust deeds which specify the terms and conditions governing the management of investment funds, but are, in fact, limited companies whose assets consist mainly of company securities and who are not allowed by their articles of association to distribute capital gains as dividends. In addition to investment trusts there are private investment companies and investment holding companies which often perform similar functions. But these are not considered to be investment trusts in the sense used here and are not discussed in this chapter. Attention is concentrated on the group of about 200 investment trusts that are recognized as such for tax purposes by the Inland Revenue.

Investment trusts expand by raising funds from new capital issues, borrowing in the form of loan capital and by retaining some of the income and capital profits from previous investments. But once again it is the asset side of the balance sheets that is of chief interest. At the end of 1979 the total market value of investments of recognized investment trusts was almost £5,600m. Most of this was invested in company securities, practically all ordinary shares. Some 34% of the company securities were those of overseas companies.

This extremely heavy concentration of investment in ordinary shares is a postwar phenomenon. Before the war investment trusts had substantial holdings of fixed-interest securities. But the fear of inflation eroding the real value of fixed-interest investments has encouraged the investment trusts to rearrange drastically the distribution of their assets. The size of the investment trusts makes them important operators in the ordinary share market. They also fulfil a useful function in helping to finance small companies by holding their unquoted securities. Their ability to invest overseas has from time to time been seriously affected by government restrictions and tax measures, but the former is now virtually non-existent since the abolition of exchange controls in 1979.

Unit Trusts: Unit trusts perform a similar function to investment trusts. But unlike the latter they do operate under trust deeds and have trustees, often a bank or insurance company. The unit trusts are authorized by the Department of Trade and are run by managers who are quite distinct from the trustees. Returns are currently collected from some 305 unit trusts; in 1960 the figure was fifty-one.

Unit trusts do not issue share capital and are not limited companies, but they issue units which give the owners the right to participate in the beneficial ownership of the trusts' assets. The units are highly marketable as they can always be bought from or sold to the managers at prices which reflect the market value of the underlying assets. As more units are demanded the managers provide more; for this reason they are sometimes called 'open-end' trusts, as opposed to 'closed-end' trusts such as the investment trusts which do not expand in this way.

Like the investment trusts the assets of the unit trusts are almost entirely company securities, made up of ordinary shares. But in contrast to the investment trusts most of the assets are UK securities, mostly of companies. At the end of 1979 the total holdings of British government and company securities of the unit trusts were £3,300m. Their rate of growth has been rapid; in 1960 their total assets were only £190m. Their growth may be an attempt by small investors and others to protect themselves against inflation by participating indirectly in ordinary share investment.

The Stock Exchange: The Stock Exchange is not strictly a financial institution but an association of stockjobbers and stockbrokers which provides a market for variable-price securities, both government and company securities. Without this market where securities may readily be bought and sold, the whole business of raising funds through outside sources would tend to be more expensive and less efficient. Since March 1973 the Stock Exchange comprises the Stock Exchange of the UK and the Republic of Ireland. Before that date, though with close links, they were distinct organizations.

A feature of the Stock Exchange is the jobbing system. Jobbers are traders in securities; they act as principals, buying and selling on their own account and making their profits on the difference between their buying and selling prices, which they generally stand ready to quote for the securities in which they specialize. This function can be extremely important in giving stability to the market which might otherwise be much more volatile and possibly mislead investors.

Brokers generally act as agents for customers, buying and selling on their behalf, usually but not always through jobbers.

Speculation is a term frequently associated with the Stock Exchange and nearly always carries overtones of abuse and criticism. To some degree this may reflect ignorance of the functions of the Stock Exchange, though this is not to imply that speculation is always economically and socially beneficial. But the speculator at his best, if he is doing his job properly, will be helping to keep the price of shares in touch with economic realities, damping down the effects of irrelevant rumours and false information; he will, in fact, be improving one part of the communications network of the economic system and contributing to an 'efficient' capital market. However, the economic, social and moral implications of speculation are much wider and more far-reaching than can be dealt with here.

Traditionally the terms 'bulls' and 'bears' have been applied to particular types of speculation, though they are now used more generally to refer respectively to markets tending to rise and fall in price. But traditionally a 'bull' was someone who bought securities on a rising market hoping he would be able to sell them at a profit before he had to pay for his purchase. The 'bear' sold the shares that he had not got, on a falling market, in the hope that he would be able subsequently to buy and deliver them at a lower price.

An idea of the scale of Stock Exchange activities can be obtained from the figures on turnover; that is, sales and purchases. The total turnover during 1979 was about £169,000m, a relatively good year. Turnover of British government securities was some £129,000m. Clearly the Stock Exchange is of major importance to the financial activities of both the public and private sectors of the economy.

IV   THE TAXATION SYSTEM
IV.1   Introduction

Taxation and the role of government in society are necessarily closely linked and discussion of the one involves some consideration of the other. It is often said that taxation in a market economy has three main functions: (1) to provide or encourage the provision of goods and services that are not easily or adequately supplied by the market if left to itself, and also to discourage the provision of those goods and services that are considered to have harmful effects on society — and perhaps the reverse for those goods and services which are considered beneficial to society; (2) to redistribute income and wealth; and (3) to facilitate the exercise of fiscal policy as a means of economic stabilization.

The first may be approached by making a distinction between so-called private and public goods, and noting a possible discrepancy between private and public costs and benefits — what has come to be called the externalities problem. Private goods refers to those goods where the utility a person gets from their consumption depends on how much of them he has and at the same time the more he has the less anyone else gets. Public goods on the other hand are such that, once the goods are produced, their consumption by one person does not diminish the amount available to others. Any kind of food is an example of a private good and some forms of national defence are an example of public goods. The market system can by and large handle the problem of producing and pricing private goods but not public goods, since the price system cannot operate effectively to determine an appropriate amount to produce, nor determine its distribution. It needs to be stressed immediately that pure private goods and pure public goods are extreme cases and that, in general, elements of both may be combined in the same good.

Externalities are said to arise when the costs and benefits are not internalized to the individual producer or consumer. A typical example is what has been called the 'smoke nuisance', when a producer engages in a productive activity that gives off smoke and spreads grime and dirt in the immediate neighbourhood and possibly causes chemical erosion of buildings in the surrounding area. The costs of these nuisances are generally not voluntarily paid for by the producer and reflected in the quantity produced and price of his product. This kind of example could be greatly extended, as could similar examples on the benefits side. Indeed, in so far as a so-called public good was provided privately, it would be an example of external benefits being conferred widely throughout a community. Clearly, externalities pose a fundamental problem for society, and in particular suggest that where they are present in a market-based economy, the market if left to itself will produce too much of a good which imposes external costs on the society and too little of a good which confers external benefits on it. In such circumstances there seems to be no simple answer to the question, on the one hand, of the appropriate domain of market processes and, on the other, of the role of government. These are difficult and far-reaching issues in political economy.

The second function of taxation — the redistribution of income and wealth — is closely related to the matters just discussed. Because there is no self-evident reason why a competitive market economy should lead to an optimum distribution of income and wealth — however difficult that may be to define — so governments have come to use taxation and the revenue raised thereby to bring about some redistribution. It should perhaps be said that there is also no obvious reason why government redistribution policies will be optimal, since the distribution and exercise of political power in society also begs some fundamental and intractable questions. Indeed, government interest and the public interest, in so far as these can be assessed, may by no means coincide.

The third function of taxation as an aspect of fiscal stabilization policy is already familiar from earlier discussion in this chapter and the preceding one.

IV.2   The Size of Government

It is well known that in this century governments have become, in terms of their own activities, far more important in relation to the economic life of the community. Nevertheless, it is by no means straightforward to measure the size of government economic activity relatively to the rest of the economic system. Perhaps the best that can be done is to take a number of different measures.[1]

One of these is the direct claims the general government makes in any time period on the volume of goods and services available to the community from its own economic activity. In this context 'general government' includes central and local government, but excludes such things as the nationalized industries or, more generally, public corporations. Table 2.6 shows that government expenditure claimed about 22% of the gross national product in the late 1960s, then gradually increased to almost 27% by 1975, but had fallen to 23% by 1978.

TABLE 2.6

General Government: Total Expenditure on Goods and Services as a Percentage of GNP at Market Prices, 1968-78

Year	1968	1969	1970	1971	1972	1973	1974	1975
%	22.5	21.8	22.2	22.2	22.6	23.0	25.0	26.8

Year	1976	1977	1978
%	25.8	23.9	22.9

Source: NIBB, 1979 edition.

It is arguable that the foregoing understates the 'size' of government. For instance, it takes no account of subsidies, grants and debt interest paid by the government and ignores its net lending. The reason for this is that these are mainly classified as transfer payments. That is, the government raises the necessary funds by taxation and borrowing, and transfers them back to the community and overseas. Thus the government does not buy goods and services directly as far as this type of expenditure is concerned. But there is no doubt that these transfers are extremely important in relation to taxation and government borrowing, and greatly influence the economic system. When they are included in government expenditure then the previous percentages are markedly increased. Table 2.7 shows that for the second half of the 1960s the percentage is raised to over 40% of gross national product and that a marked jump occurred in the mid 1970s to a peak of over 49% in 1975. Since then the percentage has fallen to 44% in 1978. Clearly, grants, subsidies, debt interest and net lending have been of major importance in recent years as a component of government expenditure and, as will be seen, the financing of total government expenditure has posed formidable problems for government and the monetary authorities.

---

1 See A.R. Prest and N.A. Barr, *Public Finance in Theory and Practice*, 6th edition, Weidenfeld and Nicolson, 1979, for a discussion of some of the latest issues involved.

TABLE 2.7

General Government: Total Government Expenditure as a Percentage of GNP at Market Prices, 1968-78

Year	1968	1969	1970	1971	1972	1973	1974	1975
%	41.8	40.3	40.5	40.6	41.2	41.2	46.6	49.3

Year	1976	1977	1978
%	46.8	43.4	44.1

Source: NIBB, 1979 edition.

IV.3   The Budget and Borrowing Requirements

The Budget is traditionally the annual financial statement which the Chancellor of the Exchequer makes in the House of Commons either in late March or early April around the end of each financial year. The statement includes an account of the revenue and expenditure for the previous financial year and forecasts for the year ahead. In the ordinary way there is only one budget, but in times of crisis one or more supplementary budgets may be introduced to give the Chancellor the opportunity to modify his earlier policies by altering taxation and expenditure. Tables 2.8, 2.9 and 2.10 bring together in an aggregated form the main features of the 1980-1 budget accounts.

The receipts of the Consolidated Fund cover 'all government revenue, other than borrowing and sums received by government departments in the course of their normal activities (known as appropriations in aid)',[1] and are shown in table 2.8. They fall under four main headings: inland revenue, customs and excise (including EEC own resources), vehicle excise duties and miscellaneous receipts. The first two refer to the great revenue-collecting departments of state and the major taxes and duties collected by these are discussed below.[2] Vehicle excise duties are collected by the Department of the Environment. Miscellaneous receipts include interest and dividends, broadcast-receiving licences and certain other receipts.

The two main categories of expenditure shown in table 2.9 are supply services and consolidated fund standing services. The first is voted annually by Parliament; the second is a standing charge against revenue.

The National Loans Fund was set up in April 1968. Broadly speaking it is intended to carry further the separation of current and capital items in the accounts. Most of the domestic lending of the government and all transactions relating to the National Debt, including its creation, the repayment of loans from the Fund and interest payments thereon, now appear in the National Loans Fund. Table 2.10 shows just how important the central government is as a source of capital funds for the nationalized industries, other public corporations, and local

---

1 *Financial Statistics: Explanatory Handbook*, 2nd edition, HMSO, April 1979, p. 36.

2 EEC own resources include revenue from the Common External Tariff, agricultural levies and sugar levies that, under the EEC Treaty and subsidiary legislation, are considered as belonging to the European Community and available for its Budgetary purposes. See *Official Journal of the European Communities*, 94 of 28 April 1970.

authorities. The government must raise these funds either through taxation or by
borrowing. In these accounts there is a substantial deficit forecast for the
consolidated fund, a large net borrowing of £10,665m by the National Loans

TABLE 2.8

Central Government Revenue, 1980-1 (Forecast) (£m)

Inland Revenue		
Income tax	23,830	
Surtax	8	
Corporation tax	4,860	
Petroleum revenue tax	2,560	
Capital gains tax	490	
Development land tax	25	
Estate duty	17	
Capital transfer tax	400	
Stamp duties	670	
Total Inland Revenue		32,860
Customs and Excise		
Value added tax	12,450	
Spirits, beer, wine, cider and perry	2,825	
Oil	3,650	
Tobacco	2,775	
Betting and gaming	475	
Car tax	575	
Other excise duties	10	
EEC own resources		
Protective duties	950	
Agricultural levies	290	
Total Customs and Excise		24,000
Vehicle excise duties		1,411
National insurance surcharge		3,509
Total Taxation		61,780
Miscellaneous receipts		3,635
Grand Total		65,415

Source: Financial Statement and Budget Report 1980-1.

Fund and a central government borrowing requirement of £9,313m (the latter is
not shown in Tables 2.8 to 2.10).

The net borrowing by the National Loans Fund, the 'central government
borrowing requirement' and the 'public sector borrowing requirement' (PSBR) are
closely inter-related. To get from the net borrowing by the National Loans Fund to
the central government borrowing requirement it is necessary to take into account
the central government's net indebtedness to various official funds, which are
distinct from the Consolidated Fund, namely the National Insurance Fund, certain
departmental balances and miscellaneous items, and Northern Ireland central
government debt. The position for the financial year 1978-9 (the latest financial
year for which complete data are available) is shown overleaf:

TABLE 2.9

Central Government Supply Services and Consolidated Fund Standing Services, 1980-1 (Forecast) (£m)

Supply Services

I	Defence	10,668	
II	Overseas Services	1,391	
III	Agriculture, Fisheries & Forestry	725	
IV	Trade, Industry, Energy and Employment	4,150	
V	Government Investment in Nationalized Industries	648	
VI	Roads and Transport	1,700	
VII	Housing	3,422	
VIII	Other Environmental Services	465	
IX	Law, Order and Protective Services	1,988	
X	Education and Libraries, Science and Arts	2,656	
XI	Health and Personal Social Services	10,582	
XII	Social Security	7,276	
XIII	Other Public Services	1,676	
XIIIA	House of Commons Administration	11	
XIV	Common Services	1,530	
XV	Northern Ireland	982	
XVII	Rate Support Grant, Financial Transactions, etc.	14,742	
	Total Supply[1]		64,612
	Revised and supplementary provision (net)		153
	Total Supply Services		64,765

Consolidated Fund Standing Services

Payment to the National Loans Fund for service of the National Debt	4,950	
Northern Ireland – share of taxes, etc.	1,136	
Payments to the European Community, etc.	2,301	
Other Services	23	
Total Consolidated Fund Standing Services		8,410
Total		73,175
Consolidated Fund Deficit		−7,760
Grand Total		65,415

Source: Financial Statement and Budget Report 1980-1.
Note: 1   At 1980-1 Estimate prices.

		£m
	Borrowing required by National Loans Fund	8,597
less	Surplus of National Insurance Fund	341
less	Surplus of departmental balances, etc.	235
plus	N.I. central government debt	63
	Central government borrowing requirement	8,084

The PSBR is the amount the public sector borrows from the other sectors of the economy and from overseas. It includes the central government borrowing requirement and in addition the borrowing of local authorities and public

corporations from outside the public sector. For the financial year 1978-9 the
figures were as follows:

		£m
	Central government borrowing requirement	8,084
plus	Local authorities net borrowing from other sources	952
plus	Public corporations net borrowing from other sources	247
	Public sector borrowing requirement	9,283

The authorities were able to finance this PSBR by borrowing £9,788m from the
non-bank private sector and £952m from the overseas sector; they actually reduced
their indebtedness to the banking sector by £1,457m. The borrowing took a
number of forms such as notes and coin, national savings, Treasury bills,
government securities and other specialized forms of debt.

As regards the overseas sector it should be noted that a fall in the foreign
exchange reserves because of an external deficit brings an inflow of sterling to the
public sector and so helps to finance the public sector borrowing requirement; it is
in effect a selling of an asset — foreign exchange reserves — for sterling. The
opposite is, of course, true for an external surplus.

To the extent that the PSBR is financed from the banking sector it can add
directly to the money supply and, in so far as the reserve asset base of the banks is
increased, lead to further expansion of the money supply unless offsetting action is
taken by the authorities. However, it should be stressed that there is no simple
automatic relationship between the PSBR and changes in the money supply. But
clearly the budgetary and monetary and financial systems are highly
interdependent, and so are fiscal, monetary and credit policy and exchange rate
policy.[1]

The annual budget as an instrument of fiscal policy has frequently been
criticized because of its inflexibility. In the ordinary way the major taxes such as
income tax and corporation tax cannot be varied between Finance Acts.[2] Thus
though it might be thought desirable, because of changed economic conditions, to
alter these taxes more frequently, this cannot be done without all the inconvenience
of a supplementary budget. However, the authorities have more leeway over some
other sources of revenue. From the point of view of flexibility one of the most
important has been the power, first granted in the Finance Act 1961, to vary the
rates of nearly all customs and excise duties and formerly purchase tax by at most
10%, and known as the regulator. This kind of power was retained with the introduction of value added tax in 1973 though the regulator may be used to vary this tax
by as much as 25%.[3] Thus there are now substantial powers to vary taxes between
budgets. This, of course, leaves other crucially important problems, such as the
timing and scale of tax changes and their anticipation by the public, but these are
taken up later.

---

1 All statistics in the text are from *FS*, February 1980. For further discussion of the public
   sector borrowing requirement, see section V below.

2 The Finance Act puts into law the budget proposals, subject to the Provisional Collection of
   Taxes Act which allows certain tax changes to take effect immediately and in advance of the
   enactment of the Finance Bill which is subject to any amendments made to it by the House
   of Commons.

3 Thus if the customs or excise rate of duty was 10% it might be varied between 9% and 11%,
   and as regards a VAT rate of 15% between 11¼% and 18¾%.

Alterations in government expenditure are also, in principle, a possible way of making fiscal policy more flexible. But government expenditure may be planned years in advance of its formal inclusion in the budget estimates and periodic modifications of the plans may give rise to problems, since much of the expenditure is on a continuing basis and cannot be easily varied. Furthermore, it may be extremely costly to slow down or postpone some kinds of expenditure, particularly investment expenditure. Hence frequent variation of government expenditure is not an ideal instrument of fiscal policy.

The budget accounts, as already indicated, are incomplete in a number of ways. They deal, for example, only peripherally with local government finances and the national insurance funds.[1] But if general government is considered, it is found that for 1979-80 estimated taxes on income and expenditure, plus national insurance and similar contributions and taxes on capital, totalled over £72,000m or almost 40% of GNP at factor cost. This is a further indication of the scale of government in the UK economy.

TABLE 2.10

National Loans Fund, 1980-1 (Forecast) (£m)

(i) *Payments*

Interest, management and expenses of national debt		10,000
Consolidated Fund Deficit		7,760
Loans (net)		
To nationalized industries	800	
Other public corporations	1,044	
Local and harbour authorities	915	
Private sector	−3	
Within central government	149	
Total		2,905
Grand Total		20,665

(ii) *Receipts*

Interest on loans, profits of the Issue Department of the Bank of England, etc.	5,050	
Service of the National Debt – balance met from Consolidated Fund	4,950	
Total		10,000
Net Borrowing by the National Loans Fund		10,665
Grand Total		20,665

Source: Financial Statement and Budget Report 1980-1.

IV.4   Income Taxation

Up to April 1973 individuals were subject to income tax and surtax, with the latter chargeable in addition to income tax on incomes in excess of a certain level. From

---

1 National insurance is discussed further in chapter 5.

that date, apart from certain residual matters, the existing income tax and surtax were replaced by a single graduated personal tax, known as unified tax. The main aims of unified tax were to simplify the tax structure, permit a smoother graduation in tax rates as income rises and simplify the administration of the whole system. The unified tax is constructed on the concept of earned income and so manages to dispense with the calculation of earned income relief, which was required under the previous system since it was constructed in terms of investment income. As well as earned income and investment income a further concept requires to be mentioned, that is chargeable income. Chargeable income is the income which remains from all sources after deduction of personal, family and certain other allowances.

The main personal allowances have since an amendment to the 1977 Finance Act been linked to the retail price index − an example of indexation − and for 1980-1 are as follows: for single persons £1,375 and for married couples £2,145. The age allowances for the elderly are £1,820 for a single person and £2,895 for a married couple. The allowances which had formerly existed for children resident in the UK were finally phased out under the 1979 Finance Act and have been replaced by tax-free child benefit; and the same is due to happen for overseas children.

Once taxable income has been determined, the various tax rates come into operation. For 1980-1 the tax bands, or ranges of earned income in relation to each tax rate, are as follows:

£	%
0-11,250	30
11,251-13,250	40
13,251-16,750	45
16,751-22,250	50
22,251-27,750	55
Over 27,750	60

The unified tax retains the former distinction between earned and investment income but has been modified in an important way. The first £5,500 or less of investment income is treated in exactly the same way as earned income but, above this, carries a surcharge of 15%, thus making a maximum rate of 75%.

It is evident from the foregoing discussion that one of the main features of income taxation is its progressiveness. This is, of course, by design. It can be traced to notions of ability to pay. It is assumed that those with larger incomes are or should be able to pay proportionately more of them in taxation. In addition, progressive taxation lends itself to income redistribution, to the extent that government expenditure benefits the less well-off in the community; and some would argue that greater equality of income is important to the maintenance of a politically stable society. But progressive taxation also diminishes the direct reward for extra work as income increases and may act as a disincentive to more effort.

It has also been suggested that steeply progressive taxation is a disincentive to movement from one job to another; it may be difficult to get a sufficiently large income after tax to compensate for the costs of upheaval and change. If this is correct then the tax system may misallocate resources and be a drag on economic efficiency and growth. There is also no doubt that highly progressive taxation stimulates tax avoidance − the search for loopholes in the law permitting a reduced tax bill − and indeed tax evasion which is, of course, illegal. If it is possible to

spend less than a pound on advice to save a pound in tax then clearly this is a
powerful incentive. The energies and resources of lawyers, accountants and tax
experts generally may thus be diverted into socially costly tasks.

To the extent that some or all of these problems arise, the community may have
to make difficult choices between more redistribution and a smaller total income,
or somewhat less redistribution and a larger total income, with each choice
associated with varying degrees of social and political conflict. Once more there
would seem to be no escape from the difficult problems which arise in sustaining
the on-going life of a complex and diverse society.

It has long been a goal of taxation policy that the system of taxation should be
easy to understand, equitable and cheap to administer. How far this continues to
be true of the system in the UK is open to question. Concern has been expressed
about the distortions and inefficiencies generated by the complex interdependencies
of the whole system of taxation and the social security system.[1]   In particular,
there is concern about what has come to be called the 'poverty-trap', that is where
people under the current system who are in low-paid jobs or unemployed may find
that the effective marginal tax on their additional earnings may be extremely
high — it has been in excess of 100% in some circumstances — when both taxation
and loss of social security benefits are taken into consideration. The introduction
of tax-free child benefit should help to alleviate this problem.

There are, however, various proposals for dealing more radically with these and
related problems by, in effect, integrating to some degree the direct taxation and
social security systems. One proposal is known as 'the negative income tax', which
ideally is designed to permit a single assessment of income and provide either for
calculating the tax due if income is above a certain level or for a transfer to be paid
if it is below that level. The particular scheme that has received most official
attention in the UK is known as a 'tax credit system'.[2]   There seems to be little
doubt that a tax-credit scheme such as that proposed could achieve some
simplification and economies over present arrangements for taxation and in the
administration of at least some social security benefits. However, it would be a
mistake to assume that it offers a simple panacea to the problem of all those with
low incomes.

IV.5   Capital Gains Taxation and Development Land Tax

Until the Finance Act of 1971 there were two capital gains taxes, the short-term
and the long-term tax, but under this Act the former was abolished, leaving what is
called capital gains tax. Under this tax gains are taxable on the disposal of most
assets. Important exemptions are principal private residence, private motor cars,
National Savings securities, most life assurance policies and betting winnings, gifts
to charities and British government and government-guaranteed securities. In
addition, the first £3,000 of net annual gains of individuals are exempt but
thereafter the tax rate is 30%. Since 1971 all gains at death are exempt; and there
are various special provisions for gains on gifts. There are provisions generally
allowing the offset of losses against gains on those assets that are subject to tax.
Gains realized by companies are ordinarily chargeable to corporation tax, which for
the year 1980-1 is at 52%. However, from 1973 the effective rate of tax on

---

1   See *The Structure and Reform of Direct Taxation*, Report of a Committee chaired by
    Professor J.E. Meade, The Institute for Fiscal Studies, Allen and Unwin, 1978.

2   See *Proposals for a Tax-Credit System*, Cmnd. 5116, HMSO, 1972.

company gains has been only 30% − achieved by the expedient of leaving out of account a fraction of the gain. Authorized unit trusts and approved investment trusts are exempt from capital gains tax.

The major justification put forward for the introduction of capital gains taxation is on grounds of equity. The argument, ignoring dividends, is roughly as follows. An individual may purchase £100 worth of securities in 1978 and − if he is lucky − find that in 1979 they were worth £200. If he sold the securities and if there were no capital gains tax, he could maintain his capital intact and still have £100 to spend, therefore his £100 is essentially income and should be taxed as such. But is this really equitable with progressive income-tax rates? It might be that if the £100 were spread over a number of years a lower tax charge would arise. Does this mean that gains should be averaged over a number of years, or would a compromise solution be to charge rates somewhat less than income-tax rates? The UK capital gains tax seems to favour the latter.

In discussing the £100 gain above, nothing was said about prices. But if prices have risen by 20% over the period then £120 would be required to maintain his capital intact in real terms, leaving £80 in current prices as the income he might spend without eroding the former; in effect, inflation is a form of tax and indeed may be said to be levied without Parliamentary approval. The question arises − is it legitimate to tax nominal gains as opposed to real gains? The answer would seem to be no. Thus the equity argument is by no means as straightforward as it might seem; and a really comprehensive discussion of the matter would have to consider the wider issues of the distribution of income and wealth generally in relation to the operation of the social and political system and the problems of indexation in a period of inflation.

Capital gains taxation is, of course, important for other reasons besides those of equity. It may affect investment and saving and the functioning of the capital markets, and pose difficult problems of administration. To the extent that the return on investment takes the form of capital gains − especially the return on risky investment − taxing them may discourage such investment. This discouragement may, however, be mitigated to some extent, since the tax is postponable and payable only on realized capital gains. The allowance of losses as an offset to taxable capital gains also works in the same direction. Nevertheless, the effect may well be to depress investment.

The effects on saving are perhaps even more problematical but may also be adverse, as may the effects on the operation of the capital markets. Since the tax is on realized gains this encourages the retention of the same securities as, of course, the holder has the income on the tax that would otherwise have to be paid if the securities were realized. There is therefore a discouragement to switching between securities which reduces the flexibility of the market and perhaps makes the raising of capital more costly. A possible offset to these effects is the realization of capital losses since these are allowable for tax purposes against corresponding capital gains.

The administrative problems are particularly great where problems of valuation arise. This is especially true of changes in the value of assets which do not ordinarily have a market value; an example is unquoted securities. The problem of valuation may become less acute as time proceeds and the community gets accustomed to the tax.[1]

---

1 For further discussion of all of these issues, see Prest and Barr, *Public Finance in Theory and Practice*, op. cit., pp. 333-44.

The Development Land Tax of 1976 makes realizations of development value from land subject to a special development tax but there is no liability to income tax, corporation tax or capital gains tax on gains subject to development land tax. The term 'development value' refers to the difference between the base value of the land and its disposal value for development purposes. The base value 'is the highest of: (1) cost of acquisition plus the cost of "relevant improvements", plus any increase in current use value since the date of acquisition; or (2) current use value at the date of disposal, plus 15%; or (3) acquisition cost of the land, including all improvements, plus 15%'.[1] The first £50,000 of realized development value in any financial year after 1 April 1980 is exempt from tax. The standard rate thereafter is 60% of realized development value.

Various people and bodies are exempt from development land tax, including the main residence of owner-occupiers for land up to one acre, and certain co-operative housing associations provided that if they dispose of dwellings or land they do so to 'a housing association registered with the Housing Corporation or to the Housing Corporation itself'.[2] Disposals to other purchasers are liable to development land tax.

No doubt the development land tax is an attempt by the state to appropriate what it considers to be inequitable capital gains from certain forms of land development. However, it is difficult to see how it can fail to raise the costs of new housing and in so doing confer actual or potential capital gains to owners of existing houses.

IV.6   Corporation Tax, Depreciation and Other Allowances and Petroleum Revenue Tax

Corporation tax draws a strong distinction between the company and the shareholder, taxing each as separate entities. A basic argument used in favour of corporation tax is the opportunity it gives the authorities to distinguish between the personal and company sectors for policy purposes. They may wish, for instance, to curtail consumption expenditure with as little adverse effect as possible on investment expenditure. An increase in income tax, leaving corporation tax unchanged, may tend to have the desired effect and may even encourage smaller dividend distributions, leaving more funds available to companies for investment purposes.

The foregoing analysis begs, however, a number of important questions. Among these are the following. Should future consumption be preferred to present consumption, in so far as larger current investment makes possible a larger future income and so consumption? Are the companies with retained profits the ones which should grow? This is not at all self-evident. It means that companies avoid the discipline of having to raise funds in the market and probably favours the larger established company at the expense of the smaller or newer company. Furthermore, greater encouragement of profit retention tends to reduce the flow of funds through the capital market to the detriment of companies dependent on it. The corporation tax also tends to distort the operation of the capital market by

---

1 *The British System of Taxation*, HMSO, 1977, p. 24.

2 Ibid.

encouraging firms to rely more on loan or debenture capital at the expense of ordinary or other forms of share capital, since the interest on the former is allowed as a cost in the calculation of profits and hence liability for tax, whereas this is not true of the latter. It may, of course, be argued that the gains from introducing corporation tax outweigh all the disadvantages. However, the Chancellor in his 1980 budget announced that the government would publish later in the year a consultative Green Paper reviewing the present corporation-tax system.

This system, known as the *imputation system*, was introduced from April 1973. Under it, all profits, whether distributed or not, are subject to the same corporation-tax rate, but part of the tax is imputed to shareholders, and collected from the company at the time of payment of dividends. If, for instance, the corporation-tax rate is 52% and the basic income-tax rate is 30%, then a company whose activities are entirely within the UK and which had profits of 100 would have a corporation-tax liability of 52. If during a year it paid a dividend of 21 to its shareholders, it would be treated as a gross dividend of 30 from which income tax of 30% had been deducted. The company would pay the 9 to the Inland Revenue and this, which is called advance payment of corporation tax (ACT), would be credited against the company's corporation-tax liability of 52. Shareholders subject to basic-rate income tax would be deemed to have discharged their tax liabilities; only in the case of those exempt or subject to higher rates would a refund or additional charge be necessary. Small companies whose annual profits do not exceed £70,000 are subject to a reduced rate of corporation tax (40% for the year to March 1980) with the scale of reduction tapering off for companies with profits up to £130,000.

The imputation form of corporation tax has certain advantages over the two-rate system when it comes to negotiating double-taxation agreements with other countries; and should facilitate the movement towards tax harmonization within the European Community, as it puts Britain broadly in line with French and German company taxation and with recent proposals by the Commission.

In assessing liability to corporation tax, allowance is made, broadly speaking, for all the costs incurred by the company, including the wear and tear of physical capital and, as mentioned above, interest on loans and debentures but not dividends paid on shares. However, depreciation is not allowed on all physical assets; there are no allowances on such things as retail shops, showrooms and offices, except in Enterprise Zones where there are 100% capital allowances for commercial and industrial buildings.

In addition to depreciation allowances for wear and tear successive governments have attempted to stimulate investment by various kinds of incentive. Two main kinds are operative in the UK: initial allowances, and investment or cash grants. Initial allowances, introduced in 1945, are permitted in the first year in addition to the ordinary depreciation allowances and the two together are known as first-year allowances. In other words the rate at which depreciation may be written off is accelerated; the total amount of depreciation permitted remains 100%.

Investment or cash grants are now largely confined to what are called the assisted areas and are known generally as regional development grants. There are three main types of assisted areas: special development areas, development areas and intermediate areas. In 1979 the areas covered some 40% of the employed population of Britain but during that year it was announced that over the next three years this would be reduced to 25%. Special investment grants are also payable to the shipbuilding and computer industries.

The position since the 1972 budget is that all capital expenditure throughout the UK on machinery and plant, excluding passenger cars, is subject to a first-year allowance of 100%, often called free depreciation; and the initial allowance on new industrial buildings is 50% plus an annual allowance of 4% on the construction cost. However, small industrial buildings of 2,500 square feet or less erected between 27 March 1980 and 26 March 1983 qualify for 100% initial allowance. Thus as far as these allowances are concerned no distinction is made between the assisted areas and the rest of the country. However, as already indicated, the assisted areas do receive special treatment. In addition to the allowances mentioned the special development areas and the development areas receive regional development grants of 22% and 15% respectively of qualifying capital expenditure on new plant and machinery and buildings. An important feature of the system of regional development grants is that they do not affect the recipient's entitlement to the first-year or initial allowances on the *full* amount of the capital investment.

With the rapid rise in prices in the last few years many companies found themselves subject to heavy taxation on the increase in the value of their stocks. In November 1974 the government introduced measures giving special tax relief on such increases and these have subsequently been extended. This is an important innovation as it is tantamount to an acceptance, at least in part, of inflation accounting. In the 1980 budget stock relief was further extended to allow in certain circumstances postponement, for one year, of tax otherwise recoverable as stocks fell.

The whole system of allowances and grants thus gives rise to many complicated issues, only a few of which can be touched on here. First, should depreciation allowances be on an original or a replacement-cost basis? This question would be of little or no significance if prices were generally stable. But in periods of rising prices it would seem that if the community is to preserve intact its physical stock of capital, it is preferable to have allowances based on a replacement-cost basis. However, if the problem is approached in a different way the argument may not be so clear-cut. Suppose a firm purchases a piece of equipment and thereafter prices rise, including the price of the equipment, then the capital value of the old equipment also rises, giving a capital gain to the firm. If allowances are permitted on a replacement-cost basis the firm is, in fact, receiving untaxed capital gains. Is this equitable in relation to other sections of the community or is it a useful compromise to allow only original costs in calculating depreciation, so that the apparent capital gains are subject to corporation and income tax as, until the modification relating to the increase in the value of stocks, was the practice in the UK? The answer is far from obvious but clearly the issues become more acute in periods of rapid inflation.[1]

Initial allowances and investment grants should act as a stimulus to investment. The first may be regarded as reducing the amount of tax payable on a profitable investment. The second is, of course, a direct subsidy to investment and the benefits do not depend upon the availability of profits. It is not at all self-evident that the subsidy is to be preferred, as it may mean that investment takes place in forms of dubious profitability — there is therefore the likelihood of misallocation of resources, at least as determined in relation to market prices.

---

1 See Prest and Barr, *Public Finance in Theory and Practice*, Chapter 16, for further discussion.

A major feature of investment grants and regional development grants is the extent to which they are discriminatory. They make investments in certain places more profitable than in others and some types of investment more profitable than other types. This, of course, is by design and is intended to stimulate investment in the places and in the forms the government desires. The basis for this intervention hinges on the conviction that the market, reflecting the interacting decisions of consumers, savers and investors, if left to itself will lead to misallocation of investment and to underinvestment, and to regional imbalance in the levels of employment and economic activity. However, as far as regional employment is concerned, it is not at all obvious that this form of capital subsidization, which cheapens capital relatively to labour, with the latter generally in excess supply, is the best way to proceed.[1] But the issues that regional development grants and investment incentives generally raise are extremely complex. Some of the issues, such as the distribution of income and wealth in society and stabilization policy, were referred to in the introduction to this section but cannot be explored further here, except to say that the empirical evidence, such as it is, suggests that investment incentives have not been very effective in stimulating capital growth in the country as a whole — though they certainly seem to have stimulated growth in the assisted areas — since the overall growth rate has for many years lagged behind that of the US and most western European countries. Moreover, their use as stabilization instruments depends crucially on the timing and actual variation in the grants and allowances. It may be doubted that government or anyone else has the knowledge to manipulate these successfully.

The Petroleum revenue tax (PRT) system has become increasingly important in recent years as a consequence of exploitable North Sea oil and gas discoveries, and is likely to be even more important in the next few years with government revenue estimated to reach some £4,000m in 1980-1 and over three times this amount by the mid-1980s.

The tax system has three main components. The first is a royalty of 12½% of the wellhead value, though this can be refunded in whole or in part to encourage a licensee to develop or continue production from a commercially marginal field. The second is PRT, which is chargeable on each field separately at 70% since 31 December 1979 on net income, defined as receipts from oil sales less royalties and operating costs (excluding interest payments) and less certain reliefs. The main reliefs are as follows: 135% from 1 January 1979 of capital expenditure on exploration and development, including such expenditure on abortive or abandoned fields in the rest of the North Sea; a relief in terms of money value of ½ million metric tonnes per year up to a maximum of 5 million tonnes per field but without any carry forward or backward of this relief; finally as a safeguard against rising costs or falling oil prices there is a provision restricting PRT to not more than 80% of the amount by which the net income on a field exceeds 30% of the capital expenditure to date. If the net income is 30% or less of capital expenditure, no charge arises. The third component of the tax system is corporation tax which is levied at 52% on net income after deducting royalties and PRT.

---

1 See chapter 4, section VI.3.

IV.7   Value Added Tax

Value added tax (VAT), as its name implies, taxes value added at each stage of the productive process with the final selling price to the consumer being made up of the cost of production plus the rate of tax. An example may help to make the matter clearer. Suppose the value added tax rate is 10% – the standard rate for 1980-1 is 15% – and that a manufacturer buys all his raw materials at a cost of 110 including tax. The 10 is known as input tax. The manufacturer processes the raw materials and sells the final product to a retailer for 220 including tax. The 20 is known as output tax and the manufacturer pays the difference between the output tax and the input tax to Customs and Excise, namely 10. The retailer may be supposed to sell the product to the consumer for 330 including tax. Thus the output tax of the retailer is 30 and the input tax is 20, so he also pays 10 to Customs and Excise.

Thus the tax, as it were, comes to rest with the consumer, and this is why VAT is frequently described as an indirect tax on consumer expenditure. It should be stressed, however, that the foregoing is intended only as a simple arithmetical explanation of the VAT method and should not be interpreted as implying that the tax is necessarily wholly passed on to the final consumer. The problems of tax incidence are extremely complex and, in principle, require to be examined within the framework of a dynamically adjusting process. And even then most economists would be far from confident that they understood the intricacies of tax incidence. Notwithstanding the difficulties surrounding tax incidence, the matter is returned to briefly below in relation to the form of VAT in the UK.

The government has given many reasons for substituting VAT for the previous purchase tax and selective employment tax.[1] The latter taxes were felt to be over-discriminatory in their effects on the prices of goods and services, and they needed to be replaced by a more broadly based indirect tax, causing less distortion of consumer choice and so allowing a more efficient allocation of resources. It was also argued that VAT would benefit the balance of payments as it is more easily remitted on exports than purchase tax – imports are liable for VAT. Finally, VAT has either been adopted by the actual members or is in process of being adopted by the prospective members of the European Economic Community – as a step towards harmonization – and so the UK had little or no alternative but to move in the same direction.

There can be little doubt that the way purchase tax and selective employment tax were levied certainly distorted relative prices and that difficulties would arise in trying to levy them in a way that minimized this kind of distortion. Thus value added tax may well be superior on the basis of this criterion. However, in solving one problem another one may be created in that it can be argued that a general tax on consumer expenditure is regressive and discriminates against those on lower incomes. Successive governments have attempted, and it would seem with some success, at least as far as short-run consequences are concerned, to get round this criticism by what is called zero-rating most food, coal, gas, electricity, the construction of buildings, public transport fares, and drugs and medicines supplied on prescription. Zero-rating means that the trader does not have to charge tax on his sales and, in addition, he can claim a refund of any tax he may have paid to his suppliers because of tax paid on inputs entering into the final product.

---

1   See Green Paper, *Value Added Tax*, Cmnd. 4621, 1971; and *Value Added Tax*, Cmnd. 4929, 1972.

The balance-of-payments argument in favour of value added tax is superficially persuasive, at least in the short term, in that imports bear the tax whereas exports are zero-rated. However, it is not at all clear what are the long-term implications for the balance of payments.

Certain other features of value added tax deserve to be mentioned. As well as a zero-rated category of goods there is also an exempted category. For exempted goods the trader does not have to charge tax on his sales but he cannot claim a refund for any tax included in the price of his purchases. Exempted goods and services include land, insurance, postal services provided by the PO, betting and gaming (which already carry excise duty), finance, education and health services. Small traders with a business turnover of less than £13,500 a year in taxable goods and services are exempt from the tax.

IV.8   Excise Duties and Protective Duties

Until recently the practice in the UK has been to distinguish between customs duties which were imposed on imports and excise duties which were levied on home-produced goods and services. External duties had two functions; one, to raise revenue in a similar way to excise duties and two, to give protection to British-produced goods or preference to goods from specified countries. However, the accession of the UK to the European Communities obliged her to bring (by the end of the transition period, namely 1 January 1978) her practices into line with the rest of the Community. Thus duties for revenue purposes are now known as excise duties and are levied on both home-produced goods and similar imported goods. Protective duties refer to what was formerly the protective part of customs duties and these have been generally brought into line with the Common Customs Tariff of the European Community. This means that the UK, like other members of the Community, now operates a common tariff on imports from non-members, whilst trade between the member countries is free of customs duty. As may be seen from table 2.8, the large revenue yielders are tobacco, oil and alcohol with a total estimated yield of £9,250m in 1980-1, or almost 15% of total revenue from taxation. Moreover, this does not take account of VAT on these products.

An outstanding feature of the duties and taxes on tobacco, oil and alcohol is their scale, the large proportion that they represent of the purchase price. Ordinarily it might be expected that something which has the effect of substantially increasing the price of a product would lead to less of it, perhaps much less of it, being bought. By and large this does not seem to have happened with these three products – their demands are said to be inelastic with respect to price. However, some doubts are beginning to be expressed about the buoyancy of the revenue from tobacco, though this may be due to other causes besides the scale of taxation. The inelasticity of demand with respect to price implies that these duties and taxes may have little direct effect on the allocation of resources. But there will be an indirect effect because the funds withdrawn by taxes from consumers will scarcely be spent by the state in the same way as if they had been in the hands of the former.

It is often argued that indirect taxes are to be preferred because they are less of a disincentive to the supply of labour than direct taxes. This is an extremely difficult issue and depends on many factors, such as the scale of duties and taxes to be substituted, say, for a reduction in direct taxes or for forgoing an increase, the type and range of the goods involved and, in particular, whether they are considered as substitutes or complements for leisure. For an individual, in choosing between additional work or leisure, may well consider not only the direct tax on extra earnings but also the type of goods and services that can be bought with additional income either now or in the future and either by himself or those who may inherit from him.[1]

It is also arguable that on equity grounds indirect taxes are regressive in that they fall more heavily on the relatively low-income groups. There would seem to be some truth in this as far as tobacco and beer are concerned, but possibly to a lesser extent for petrol, given that bus fares are largely insulated from increases in oil duties. On the other hand the relatively less well-off seem to obtain benefits from government welfare and other services. But if the community opts for extensive government expenditure on welfare services and education it seems unavoidable that one way or another a large proportion of the tax revenue must be raised from the mass of taxpayers. If at the same time the latter are important beneficiaries from government expenditure then they are indirectly paying for perhaps all of or a major part of these benefits. This is in no way to deny, however, the power of taxation, or at least certain forms of it, to redistribute income and wealth.

IV.9   Capital Transfer Tax and Wealth Tax

Capital transfer tax was introduced under the first Finance Act 1975 at the same time as estate duty was abolished. The tax, often called a gifts tax, applies, subject to certain exemptions, to gifts made during life and to transfers on death. Transfers of what is called settled property or property held in trust are also subject to the tax. The tax is chargeable as the gifts or transfers occur and is cumulative. That is, in calculating the tax due on successive gifts or transfers the previous ones are taken into account and progressively higher rates of tax apply. The rates of tax on what are known as lifetime transfers are lower than for transfers on death. The tax is in general payable by the donor but may be recovered from the beneficiary.

The main exemptions are transfers between husband and wife both in life and on death; transfers in any one year of up to £2,000 plus any unused part of the previous year's exemption; outright gifts to any one person during the tax year up to a value of £250; and transfers made out of income after tax as part of normal expenditure which leave the donor sufficient income to maintain his usual standard of living. Marriage gifts are given special treatment; transfers by a parent up to £5,000 are exempt and up to £2,500 by any other ancestor and £1,000 by anyone else. Business owners and working farmers also get special relief; for purposes of the tax, value transferred is reduced by 50%. Transfers to charities or political parties are completely exempt if made more than a year before death. There are also special provisions relating to the exemption of gifts of works of art and historic buildings made during the individual's lifetime.

The first £50,000 of transfers, after taking into consideration all exemptions, is tax-free whether made during lifetime or on death. The rates for lifetime transfers then rise from 15% on the next £10,000 — for transfers on death the rate is 30% — by gradual steps to 75% on both lifetime transfers and transfers on death of over £2.01m. Transfers made within three years of death are subject to the rates applicable on death.

---

1   See *The Structure and Reform of Direct Taxation*, op. cit.

The intention of the capital transfer tax and indeed the wealth tax to be discussed below is to reduce the inequality of wealth distribution. It should clearly be more effective in achieving this than the estate duty which it replaced, since the latter was avoidable if gifts were made during lifetime and outside the *inter-vivos* period. However, it is arguable that an accessions tax, that is a tax on recipients rather than on donors, would have been more effective as a means of achieving greater wealth equality. For an accessions tax would encourage a spreading of gifts between recipients in a way that would reduce tax liability; this is not true of the capital transfer tax.

The precise form of the capital transfer tax and the exemptions it incorporates make it extremely important for individuals with even quite modest capital assets to plan their affairs carefully if they wish to minimize their tax liability. This too could be a source of inequity, depending on the foresight and luck of donors. Finally, like all such taxes it may encourage increased consumption expenditure and perhaps expenditure on education, travel and the like.

The then Chancellor announced in his 1974 budget that the government intended to introduce an annual wealth tax. Subsequently a Green Paper was published outlining the proposals the government had in mind.[1] In a foreword to the Green Paper the Chancellor stated that 'income by itself is not an adequate measure of taxable capacity. The ownership of wealth, whether it produces income or not, adds to the economic resources of a taxpayer so that the person who has wealth as well as income of a given size necessarily has a greater taxable capacity than one who has only income of that size.'[2] It is not clear what precise form the wealth tax might ultimately take, as it has run into much criticism both in and outside Parliament. A Select Committee of the House of Commons established to examine a wealth tax did not find it possible to present an agreed report and for the present, especially since the change of government in 1979, the matter would seem to be in abeyance.

IV.10   Taxation and the European Community[3]

It is evident from the preceding discussion that some of the recent tax reforms of the UK are designed to bring its taxes, or at any rate some of them, more closely into line with those of the European Community. Members are obliged under the Treaty of Rome and subsequent directives to harmonize their tax legislation as regards turnover taxes, excise duties and other forms of indirect taxation. In particular, the Community has adopted value added taxation as its main general indirect tax and this is binding on all members, though there remains considerable variety in the number and scale of rates levied. Contributions to the Community budget are in part calculated on the basis of value added tax.

The Community intends to harmonize the main excise duties on tobacco, oil and alcohol. As far as the UK is concerned this may eventually mean a reduction in the duties on tobacco and alcohol since these are much higher than in most of the countries of the present Community. Corporation-tax harmonization is still under consideration within the Community but it seems likely that the credit or

---

1   *Wealth Tax*, Cmnd. 5704, 1974.

2   Ibid., p. 111.

3   See chapter 4, section III.2 on the Common Agricultural Policy.

imputation system will be adopted and, as was seen earlier, the UK has anticipated this eventuality. The Community does not require harmonization of direct personal taxation.

The fundamental justification for tax harmonization within the Community stems from the very concept of the Community as, amongst other things, a common, unified competitive market. This requires, it is argued, the disappearance of all artificial barriers to trade and capital flows between the member countries, including those that might be created by different tax systems. On the basis of this approach the impetus towards uniformity or harmonization of taxation is immense. This is especially clear in the case of value added tax and excise duties and is becoming more so, as far as corporation tax is concerned, with the increasing importance of international companies and the mobility of capital, which the Community is determined to foster among its members. The need to harmonize personal direct taxation is not felt to arise as it is believed that mobility of labour is not greatly affected by differences between member countries in this type of tax.[1]

The whole process of tax harmonization carries important consequences for both the Community and its member countries. By implication it places great stress on the efficient allocation of resources as indicated by the static competitive model. By the same token it neglects, or at least puts on one side, the fundamental questions of externalities and of income and wealth distribution, except to the extent that these will be dealt with by harmonization of social security arrangements and with the help of the Community budget, and by regional policy measures. Up to the present none of these areas is well developed, though some progress has been made in each of them. Finally, harmonization is relevant to the whole issue of stabilization policy. It remains to be seen to what extent it will be possible for individual members to vary indirect taxes such as value added tax as an instrument of fiscal policy. This could obviously pose serious problems for member countries and, not least, the relative fiscal power of the Community vis-a-vis its individual members. These matters have, as yet, had little public discussion in the UK.

V   POLICY IN RETROSPECT AND PROSPECT
V.1   The 1960s and 1970s

In the brief review of policy below attention is concentrated on the record of the authorities in the pursuit of their major policy goals. For most of the 1960s the authorities were preoccupied with the achievement of full employment, price stability, economic growth, stability of exchange rates and a 'satisfactory' balance of payments. But in the late 1960s the commitment to fixed exchange rates became less strong and was abandoned in the early 1970s; and in the last couple of years a reduction in the rate of inflation rather than price stability has come to dominate the other policy goals including full employment and economic growth. Indeed the authorities now see the curtailment of the pace of inflation as a necessary means to achieving more employment and faster economic growth.

---

1 However, the Community intends to harmonize such matters relating to direct taxation as tax deduction of dividends at source.

During the 1960s unemployment in Great Britain averaged less than 2%, though from 1967 onwards it was in excess of this figure. But for the 1970s it has averaged 4.0% with the trend ominously rising and in early 1980 was in excess of 5.5%. Thus the policy goal of full employment, if some 2% to 3% unemployment is taken as the norm, is far from being currently achieved and this has also been true of the last few years. However, it may well be that the unemployment norm should now be taken as substantially greater than these figures.

Retail prices rose over the 1960s at a compound rate of some 3.8% a year, with the rate of increase accelerating in the later years to around 5%. However, even this latter rate seems low in comparison with the rates experienced since then. Over the nine years 1970 to 1979 the annual rate has been over 13%, which implies that during the period prices have risen by more than 200%. But even 13% is relatively mild in comparison with a rate of 24% between 1974 and 1975 and the rate of around 19% being experienced in early 1980. Thus there has been a complete failure to achieve price stability, as measured by retail prices, and the degree of failure has increased dramatically during the 1970s.

If economic growth is measured in terms of gross domestic product then this grew at a compound rate of around 2.8% a year during the 1960s, though by no means regularly, and just about 1.9% a year between 1970 and 1979. Between 1973 and 1975 gross domestic product declined by about 3% but had grown by over 6% between 1972 and 1973. Thus whilst economic growth has indeed taken place it has been far from regular and has been low by international standards for developed countries.

For the first half or more of the 1960s fixed exchange rates were a major goal of economic policy. But in the year or two leading up to the devaluation of sterling in November 1967 this policy came increasingly under question and by 1972 the Chancellor of the Exchequer was prepared to say in his budget speech that 'the lesson of the international balance of payments upsets of the last few years is that it is neither necessary nor desirable to distort domestic economies . . . in order to maintain unrealistic exchange rates, whether they were too high or too low'. In the light of the exchange-rate fluctuations in recent years and their repercussions on international monetary and economic co-operation, it seems doubtful that such a cavalier statement would be made now, though this is not to say that fixed exchange rates have once more become a widely accepted policy goal in the UK.

Whatever may be true of the official attitude to exchange rates and whether it is to be regarded as a goal or an instrument of policy, there is no doubt about the authorities' concern over the balance of payments. For most of the 1960s and in the 1970s the balance of payments has been a matter of grave concern to the authorities and time and time again they have felt constrained to take drastic action to improve the position. For example, the period 1964-8 was one of sustained crisis for sterling and the balance of payments. In the five years ending in December 1968 the cumulative current-balance deficit was £874m and the balance for official financing, which includes the current balance, investment and other capital flows, the EEA loss on forwards and the balancing item, was the enormous sum of £3,676m. Arithmetically this was mainly financed by borrowing on a large scale from the IMF and other overseas monetary authorities.[1]

---

1 See chapter 3 for further discussion.

For the next four years, from 1969 to 1972 inclusive, the current balance was in surplus and considerable amounts of foreign debt had been repaid. By early 1972 the current balance was beginning to deteriorate, and during the five years 1973 to 1977 inclusive the cumulative current-balance deficit was £7,673m, almost half of which occurred in 1974. Putting aside official finance this large sum was mostly counterbalanced by investment and other capital inflows and by a substantial positive balancing item. Borrowing from the IMF and foreign-currency borrowing enabled the official reserves to increase markedly.

Over this period, or more precisely since June 1972, the exchange rate of sterling had been allowed to float, though by no means free from official intervention. During 1973 it averaged about $2.45 to the pound, falling to $1.75 in 1977. However, since the US dollar has itself experienced variations in its exchange rate during this time, a better indicator for sterling is what is called the 'sterling effective exchange rate' which is a weighted index of movements against a basket of other currencies. From 1973 to 1977 the rate declined from 86.3 to 62.1, a depreciation of 28%.

The current balance improved in 1978 with a surplus of £932m but went into substantial deficit in 1979 and is provisionally estimated at £2,437m. However, at the end of 1979 the official reserves were over £10,000m, having been helped to the extent of £1,500m by a recent revaluation of their gold component. Between 1977 and 1979 the effective exchange rate increased from 62.1 to 67.8, a rise of over 9%.

Thus during the 1970s the UK, like much of the rest of the world, has experienced relatively variable exchange rates. The responsibility for this cannot be laid solely upon the UK authorities since exchange rates are by definition the rate at which one currency exchanges for another and so the authorities of more than one country are necessarily involved. But clearly the UK authorities must be held accountable, at least in part, for the outcome. Fundamental to that outcome is the behaviour of the domestic price level and the monetary approach to exchange-rate behaviour suggests that a basic influence on the domestic price level are the monetary aggregates.[1] But as already indicated it was not until as recently as 1976 that the monetary aggregates began to figure prominently as a feature of monetary policy.

From 1963 I to 1966 I, (where I refers to the first quarter) M_1, which may roughly be thought of as transactions balances, grew at a relatively stable rate of about 5.4% a year. For the next four years to 1970 I the compound rate of growth was irregular, being negative over a number of quarters between 1966 and 1967 and again between 1968 and 1969, but averaged about 2.4% a year over the four years. The contrast with the next three years to 1973 I is striking, when the rate of growth was some 12% a year. It then dropped to just over 3% during the year to 1974 I, rose to some 16.5% in the year 1975 I, and in the five years from 1974 IV to 1979 IV has grown at a compound rate of over 15% a year, including, for the year ending 1977 IV, an extremely rapid rate of 21.8%.

---

1 Three definitions of the money stock are used in the text: M_1, sterling M_3, and M_3. M_1 consists of notes and coin in circulation with the public and UK private-sector sterling sight deposits. Sterling M_3 equals M_1 plus private-sector sterling time deposits (including certificates of deposit) and public-sector sight and time sterling deposits. M_3 equals sterling M_3 plus UK residents' deposits in other currencies (including certificates of deposit). Each definition is corrected for items in transit and each series is available in two forms, one adjusted for seasonal variation and the other unadjusted. In the discussion of the trend of the money stock in the text above, seasonally adjusted data are used. See Statistical Appendix, A-5, for an unadjusted series.

From 1963 I to 1970 I sterling M_3 and M_3 followed a similar growth pattern to that of M_1 but at a rather faster rate at just over 6% a year in each case. However from 1970 I to 1973 I the annual compound rate of growth of each was almost 18%, some 50% faster than the growth of M_1 over the same period. For the year to 1974 I, sterling M_3 and M_3 grew at approximately 24% and 25% respectively, in strong contrast with the 3% for M_1. During the five years ending 1979 IV, sterling M_3 and M_3 each grew at some 11% a year, rather less than M_1 at 15% a year.

Any economist — not necessarily an extreme monetarist — who suspects that a relatively stable and low growth of the monetary aggregates, perhaps of the order of 4% to 5% a year, would be conducive to overall economic stability, cannot but be dismayed by rates of growth in the monetary aggregates greatly in excess of these figures. It may have seemed to the authorities that they had good reasons for permitting these large rates of growth and for allowing them to be highly variable, but that, in so doing, they contributed to inflation, economic uncertainty and stagflation — namely low or negative rates of growth of output and high unemployment — seems to be increasingly evident, though this remains a controversial judgment. Moreover, it is in no way to deny the importance of the many forces affecting the UK economy in recent years and the difficulties that arise in trying to counteract them, including the increases in oil prices, the impact of rising import prices and the problems of controlling the monetary aggregates in an open economy, subject to large foreign movements of funds and an exchange-rate regime of, for the most part, controlled floating. Nor is it being implied that it would be advisable to take whatever measures were required to reduce forthwith the growth of the monetary aggregates to low and stable rates. Such a policy would probably be highly disruptive of economic activity and very costly in economic and social terms. A move to lower and more stable rates of growth of the monetary aggregates would seem to be best approached gradually over a period of years. Indeed this approach has been accepted by the Chancellor in his 1980 budget. This matter is taken up again below.

A credit aggregate which has occurred frequently in recent discussions of monetary policy is 'domestic credit creation' (DCE). In the words of the Bank of England, 'It is a measure of domestically generated credit in a form which leads directly to monetary expansion'.[1] It may be looked upon as consisting of three main items, 'that part of the public sector borrowing requirement which is not offset by purchases of public sector debt by the UK private sector other than banks . . ., the increase in bank lending (in sterling) to the UK private sector . . . (and) . . . the net increase in the banks' sterling lending to overseas residents'.[2] The reason for including the latter in *domestic* credit expansion is that 'such lending is largely connected with the finance of UK exports and has, therefore, much the same effect on a domestic liquidity as direct bank lending to a UK exporter'.[3]

---

1 'DCE and the Money Supply — a Statistical Note', *BEQB*, vol. 17, No. 1, March 1977, p. 39.

2 Ibid., pp. 39-40 (words in parentheses added).

3 Ibid., p. 40.

The outcome for DCE for the financial year 1978-9 was as follows:

		£m
	Public sector borrowing requirement	9,283
less	Purchases of public sector debt by non-bank private sector	8,513
plus	Sterling lending by banking sector to the private sector[1]	6,285
plus	Banks' lending in sterling to overseas sector	334
	Domestic Credit expansion	7,389

DCE came into renewed prominence in December 1976 when the Chancellor of the Exchequer undertook to keep it within certain levels in his negotiations with the IMF for support for sterling. However, the foregoing accounting identity indicates that there is no simple relationship between PSBR and DCE, though this should not be taken as implying that the former is unimportant for monetary and credit conditions.

DCE and hence PSBR may also be related to changes in sterling M_3 in a way which highlights the importance of the overseas sector. The position for the financial year 1978-9 is shown below:

		£m
	Domestic credit expansion	7,389
less	External and foreign currency finance of the public sector	624
less	the increase in overseas sterling deposits	619
less	the net increase in the Banks' foreign currency deposits[2]	−142
less	the increase in the banks' non-deposit liabilities[3]	1,003
	Change in sterling M_3	5,285

Very broadly speaking the first three items deducted from DCE are 'the counterpart in the balance of payments accounts, of the current account . . . deficit plus any capital flows . . . from the UK private sector (including the balancing item)'.[4] Alternatively DCE may be looked upon as roughly the change in sterling M_3 plus the external deficit in the sense just defined.[5]

The importance attached to DCE seems to vary with the state of the balance of payments, with rather less attention being given to it when the latter is in surplus than when it is in deficit. The reason for this would seem to be that when there is a deficit in the balance of payments, a target for DCE necessarily makes the money stock target correspondingly less and clearly has an appeal to international creditors such as the IMF. Indeed at its simplest and in a regime of fixed exchange rates, a

---

1 Includes Bank of England Issue Department purchases of commercial bills.

2 'Net' refers to change in deposit liabilities (£20,526m) less change in lending (£20,668m).

3 The non-deposit liabilities (net) include the capital and internal funds and reserves of the banking sector less their investments in UK banks and other non-financial assets plus certain residual errors.

4 'DCE and the Money Supply − a Statistical Note', op. cit., p. 41.

5 It may be helpful in understanding this to consider a highly simplified and aggregated banking system where the money stock M would equal domestic credit DC plus foreign exchange reserves R. Hence $\Delta M = \Delta DC + \Delta R$ and $\Delta DC = \Delta M − \Delta R$, that is, ΔDC is the change in M less the change in R where $−\Delta R$ is the counterpart of the deficit in the balance of payments.

small open economy which wishes to improve its balance-of-payments position should restrict DCE, or more specifically bank lending, to the private sector and the PSBR.

As regards fiscal policy, difficulties arise in trying to determine whether it is in some sense expansionary, contractionary or neutral. For instance, it is argued that the actual budget balance for some period of time may be a misleading guide to what is called 'fiscal stance' and that a better one would be to assess what the budget balance would be if there were full employment or some other standardized level of economic activity with unchanged taxation and expenditure policies. In particular, with given tax rates, unemployment and social security benefit rates, the budget deficit will be markedly less or the surplus greater at 'high' levels of employment and economic activity than at low levels and so it is this kind of 'standardized budget balance' that is a better indicator of fiscal stance.[1]

But this approach, like others, gives rise to difficulties. What precisely is meant by a standardized level of economic activity? It may be difficult to get other than a more or less arbitrary working definition of this term. Furthermore, it would seem that the budget balance should be indexed to allow for inflation. Again, a deficit or surplus may be more or less inflationary or deflationary respectively, depending on how it is financed or managed. The effects of, say, a deficit being financed through a net increase in the rate of growth of the money stock, as opposed to the sale of government debt to the non-bank private sector, will generally be very different. This might suggest that in assessing the effects of a change in the budget balance it is desirable to hold monetary policy constant in some sense, perhaps in terms of a constant rate of growth of the money stock. Similar questions arise in relation to exchange-rate policy; a constant policy might be to hold exchange rates fixed or at the other extreme to allow them to float, depending on the current policy. All of these points need to be held in mind as a qualification to the following discussion which concentrates on the planned budget deficits or surpluses at the time of the actual budgets and broadly contrasts them with the immediately preceding budgetary stance.

The budgets of the late 1960s were designed to be contractionary in that they aimed for growing surpluses and had as a major objective an improvement in the balance-of-payments position.[2] A marked improvement did take place in 1969 and the budget for 1970 would seem to have maintained a roughly neutral stance aiming at much the same surplus as in the previous year.

The budgets between 1970 and 1980 varied considerably in their policy stances and were constructed from 1971 onwards against a background of turbulent world economic conditions in terms of exchange-rate movements, raw material prices and, of course, oil price crises beginning in late 1973. Like its two predecessors the 1971 budget planned for a substantial surplus, though somewhat less than that of the 1970 budget, and a *negative* borrowing requirement, thus envisaging a net repayment of debt. During 1971, as for some years previously, the growth of output was sluggish and unemployment began to rise, whilst the balance of payments on current account was strongly in surplus, as it had been for the past two years.

---

1   See T.S. Ward and R.R. Neild, *The Measurement and Reform of Budgetary Policy*, IFS/Heinemann, 1978.

2   The budgets referred to are the annual budgets at the beginning of each financial year. However, the authorities have often found it necessary to introduce supplementary budgets.

It was against this background that the budget of 1972 was designed. It was highly expansionary. It planned for a very small surplus and net borrowing of £2,667m, representing a ratio of some 4% of GDP at market prices. It was not until 1973 that the economy showed much evidence of a response to this large fiscal stimulus. During 1972 the overall balance of payments was showing signs of serious weakness. Despite the latter, the 1973 budget carried the expansionary process even further with an anticipated deficit of almost £1,200m, over twice the realized deficit for 1972-3, and net borrowing of some £3,650m, and was accompanied by, as mentioned earlier, massive expansion of some of the monetary aggregates – excesses for which the UK economy can be said to have paid dearly.

As has already been seen, output grew rapidly during 1973, as did prices, and unemployment fell, whilst the current-account deficit on the balance of payments got markedly worse. Predictably the 1974 budget had to try and rectify the position. It planned to turn a provisional deficit for 1973-4 of some £1,700m into a surplus of about £980m, and provisional net borrowing of £3,100m into a surplus of around £600m. These were dramatic and large changes in relation to overall budgetary figures, and though in the event they were not realized, taken in conjunction with monetary and other measures they probably helped to improve the balance-of-payments position, though necessarily at the expense of the rate of growth of output and increased unemployment.

The 1975 budget was prepared against a background of world recession, rapidly rising prices at home with unemployment tending to increase and a massive deficit in the current balance of payments for 1974. The consolidated fund surplus of some £980m expected twelve months earlier had become a deficit of over £3,200m and net borrowing had turned out to be almost £6,000m instead of £3,100m. Despite some increases in taxation the Chancellor planned for a deficit for 1975-6 on the consolidated fund of over £2,700m and net borrowing of some £4,600m. As in the previous year these figures were far from being realized. The 1975-6 deficit on the consolidated fund was actually over £6,600, well over twice what had been planned a year earlier, and net borrowing became £8,750m, some 8% of GDP at market prices.

By the time of the 1976 budget it was evident that during 1975 there had been a useful improvement in the balance of payments though it still had a substantial deficit, and the pace of inflation was slowing down but was still large by the standards of other developed countries. However, unemployment had increased markedly. In these circumstances the budget was designed to be more or less neutral and the government showed its determination to control public expenditure by putting a strict limit – known as cash limits – on the actual amount of cash that might be spent on a wide range of public services. In the event the deficit for 1976-7 on the consolidated fund turned out to be some £1,100m less than forecast and net borrowing was some £4,100m less than planned.

However, the year 1976-7 was a very difficult one for the UK economy, with sterling under strong downward pressure in the exchange markets, output sluggish, prices continuing to rise rapidly, unemployment increasing and a substantial rise in official borrowing from abroad. Against this background the 1977 budget planned for a deficit on the consolidated fund of some £5,700m and net borrowing by the National Loans Fund of some £7,600m, each of which was around £1,000m in excess of the pre-budget forecast for 1977-8 and probably implied that in real terms the Budget was expansionary. Monetary policy also turned out to be expansionary with a growth in sterling M_3 to mid-April 1978 of 16¼%, against a target range of 9% to 13% for the financial year.

The forecast for 1978-9 was that the consolidated fund deficit would be about £8,600m and net borrowing by the National Loans Fund almost £9,900m. Once receipts from other departmental funds were taken into account, the central government borrowing requirement became some £7,900m. Each of these figures was about £2,000m greater than the pre-budget forecast for 1978-9 and on the face of it represent a considerable fiscal stimulus for the economy, though the Chancellor also announced tighter monetary targets and, in the event, the actual growth of sterling M_3 to April 1979 was less than in the previous financial year.

The next two budgets in 1979 and 1980 were the responsibility of a new government elected in May 1979. The first of these provided for a substantial shift from direct to indirect taxation and reductions in previously planned government expenditure. However, the forecast deficit on the consolidated fund for 1979-80 was to be some £500m less than before the budget changes and the central government borrowing requirement about £1,350m less. Thus in real terms the budget should be considered contractionary and the target range for sterling M_3 was reduced from an annual 8%-12% range to 7%-11%.

The 1980 budget purports to be a major departure from its predecessors in that it inaugurates a 'medium-term financial strategy' designed to bring down the rate of inflation — prices being 19.1% higher in February 1980 than a year earlier — through progressive reductions in the growth of the money supply. The target range for sterling M_3 is to fall by 1% a year from 7%-11% for 1980-1 to 4%-8% for 1983-4. Moreover, the government has stated categorically that 'Public expenditure plans and tax policies and interest rates will be adjusted as necessary in order to achieve the (monetary) objective'.[1] It visualises the PSBR falling as a percentage of GDP from 3¾% in 1980-1 to 1½% in 1983-4.

The whole strategy is, of course, highly controversial but for what it is worth it seems to this author to be potentially of fundamental importance for the control of inflation and the long-term growth of the economy. It remains to be seen, however, if the government will be able to persist with this strategy. Clearly the pressures to depart from it will be great in face of a projected 2½% fall in GDP in 1980, rising unemployment and price increases still in double figures well into 1981 and perhaps beyond.

V.2   Policy and the European Community

Whatever may be the merits or demerits of past monetary and fiscal policy there is no doubt the UK is and has been affected by the moves to establish economic and monetary union amongst the members of the European Community. Some eight years ago this was envisaged as involving absolutely fixed exchange rates between members' currencies, free from any exchange-rate margins, or, alternatively and preferably, a single Community currency; the establishment of a Community system for the central banks, possibly along the lines of the Federal Reserve System of the United States and with analogous powers; the harmonized management of national budgets under a Community decision-making body which would have authority to influence member countries' levels of revenue and expenditure, as well as the methods of financing the deficits and the disposal of surpluses.[2]

1 *Financial Statement and Budget Report 1980-1*, p. 16 (parentheses added).

2 *Report* to the Council and the Commission on the Realization by Stages of Economic and Monetary Union in the Community, Werner Report, Supplement to Bulletin 11 – 1970 of the European Communities.

However, these far-reaching proposals received a cool response from member countries and little progress was made towards implementing them. But more recently the matter was again taken up by the Community, particularly by Mr Roy Jenkins when President of the Commission of the European Communities, and is reflected in the establishment of the EMS.[1]

The EMS came into operation on 13 March 1979, and is designed in the words of the European Council 'to establish a greater measure of monetary stability in the Community'.[2] One of the basic features of the EMS is the agreement between the fully participating members to maintain their exchange rates, except for Italy, within ± 2¼% of agreed central rates. Italy was allowed a margin of ± 6% because its currency was floating at the time. The UK decided, at least for the time being, not to participate in the exchange-rate arrangements, but is a party to other aspects of the scheme.

During 1979 there were two realignments of exchange rates, one in September when the Deutschmark was revalued by 2% and the Danish krone devalued by 3% against the other member currencies, and the second in November when the Danish krone was again devalued, by 4.7% against the other currencies. Despite these realignments it is claimed, probably fairly, that the new arrangements did help to stabilize exchange rates between the members during at any rate the first year of operation of the EMS.

One of the implications of a strictly fixed exchange-rate relationship between currencies, according to the monetary approach to exchange-rate behaviour, is the need to ensure that monetary and credit policies are consistent with its maintenance. This requires, in particular, that the money supply of the subordinate or satellite currencies should become endogenous and other policies, including credit and fiscal policies, be subordinated to this end. Ideally this would be carried out by careful co-ordination of policies between the members and this would certainly seem to be what the Community has in mind. For the European Council has stated that 'The European Monetary System will facilitate the convergence of economic development and give fresh impetus to the process of European Union'.[3] It remains to be seen if the Community will be able to achieve the kind of co-ordination required and if the UK will become a full participant.

V.3   Conclusions

The policy record of the UK for the period since the 1960s has been extremely disappointing. The simultaneous achievement of the various goals over a sustained period has continuously eluded the authorities. This failure or relative failure raises far-reaching questions about the choice of policy goals, the nature and adequacy of the policy instruments at the disposal of the authorities, and the limitations on our knowledge of the detailed and interdependent relationships between goals, instruments and targets. Moreover, these questions ultimately go far beyond the realm of the economic. For if a choice has to be made between the different goals in terms of the degree to which they can be achieved then serious

---

1   See Roy Jenkins, 'Europe's Present Challenge and Future Opportunity', Jean Monnet Lecture, European Institute, Florence, 27 October 1977, and reprinted in *Lloyds Bank Review*, January 1978, No. 127, pp. 1-14.

2   *European Economy*, Commission of the European Communities, No. 2, March, 1979, p. 7.

3   *European Economy*, ibid.

political problems may arise. If, for instance, price inflation can only be reduced at the expense of substantial unemployment and sluggish economic growth then the very political institutions of the society may come under strain. However, the last few years suggest that these strains have been carried more easily than might have been expected.

Furthermore, the discussion in V.1 suggests that policy errors and misjudgments have contributed significantly to the economic problems of recent years. In particular, both monetary and fiscal policy have from time to time been used in ways which could only be expected to give rise to future economic problems. In the recent past the monetary and budgetary policies of 1972 and 1973 clearly come to mind and, to a lesser extent, the policies pursued in 1977 and 1978. However, there seems to be a greater acceptance across a wide range of political opinion that rapid and variable inflation imposes serious costs on the community, putting at risk both employment and living standards; and that both monetary and budgetary policy must be managed in ways that contribute to its curtailment. These developments, if they persist, as must be hoped, augur well, as far as domestic measures are concerned, for the recovery of the UK economy over the next several years, though this is in no way to imply that sound monetary and budgetary policies are a sufficient condition for that recovery; but the efficiency of industry and the functioning or malfunctioning of labour and other markets — broadly the supply side of the economy — is the concern of other chapters.

REFERENCES AND FURTHER READING

Bank of England Quarterly Bulletin

F.T. Blackaby (ed.), *British Economic Policy 1960-74: Demand Management*, NIESR Students' Edition, Cambridge University Press, 1979.

The British System of Taxation, Central Office of Information Reference Pamphlet 112, HMSO, 1977.

K.A. Chrystal, *Controversies in British Macroeconomics*, Philip Allan, 1979.

H.G. Johnson et al., *Readings in British Monetary Economics*, Oxford University Press, 1972.

M.A. King and J.A. Kay, *The British Tax System*, Oxford University Press, 1978.

The London Clearing Banks, Evidence by the Committee of London Clearing Bankers to the Committee to Review the Functioning of Financial Institutions, Longman Group, 1978.

A.T. Peacock and G.K. Shaw, *The Economic Theory of Fiscal Policy*, 2nd edition, Allen and Unwin, 1976.

Michael Posner (ed.), *Demand Management*, NIESR Economic Policy Papers I, Heinemann Educational Books, 1978.

A.R. Prest and N.A. Barr, *Public Finance in Theory and Practice*, 6th edition, Weidenfeld and Nicolson, 1979.

Robin Pringle, *Banking in Britain*, Methuen, 1975.

Jack Revell, *The British Financial System*, Macmillan, 1973.

The Structure and Reform of Direct Taxation, Report of a Committee chaired by Professor J.E. Meade, Allen and Unwin, 1978.

D. Swann, *The Common Market*, 4th edition, Penguin Books, 1978.

3

Foreign trade and the balance of payments

J.S. Metcalfe

I   THE UK BALANCE OF PAYMENTS
I.1   Introduction

The importance to the UK of foreign trade, foreign investment and the balance of
international payments will be obvious to anyone who has followed the course of
events since 1960. The growth of the UK economy, the level of employment and
real wages, and the standard of living have been, and will continue to be, greatly
influenced by external economic events. It is the purpose of this chapter to outline
the main features of the external relationships of the UK and to discuss economic
policies adopted to manipulate these external relationships, with the primary focus
of attention being on the years since 1960.[1]

To begin with, it is often said that the UK is a highly 'open' economy, and some
indication of the meaning of this is given by the fact that in 1979, exports of goods
and services were 34.0% of GNP, and imports of goods and services were 34.1% of GNP,
both figures being greater than the corresponding figures for the mid-1960s and
substantially greater than those for 1938.[2] A high degree of openness implies that
the structure of production and employment is greatly influenced by international
specialization. For the UK it also means that about half the foodstuffs and the bulk
of raw materials necessary to provide inputs for industry have to be imported. In
the sense defined, the UK is a more open economy than some industrial nations like
West Germany and France, but less open than others such as Belgium.

I.2   The Concept of the Balance of Payments

The concept of the balance of payments is central to a study of the external
monetary relationships of a country but, as with any unifying concept, it is not
free from ambiguities of definition and of interpretation. Such ambiguities stem
from at least two sources, viz.: the different uses to which the concept may be
put – either as a tool for economic analysis, or as a guide to the need for and
effectiveness of external policy changes; and the different ways in which we may
approach the concept – either as a system of accounts or as a measure of
transactions in the foreign exchange market.

From an accounting viewpoint, we may define the balance of payments as a
systematic record, over a given period of time, of all transactions between domestic
residents and residents of foreign nations. In this context, residents are defined as
those individuals living in the UK for one year or more, together with corporate

---

1   Earlier editions of this volume contain a discussion of external developments between 1945
     and 1960. See, e.g., the 5th edition (1974).

2   In 1938 the export: GNP ratio stood at 14% and the import: GNP ratio at 19%.

bodies located in the UK, and UK government agencies and military forces located abroad. Ideally, the transactions involved should be recorded at the time of the change of ownership of commodities and assets, or at the time specific services are performed. In practice, trade flows are recorded on a shipments basis, at the time when the exports documents are lodged with the Customs and Excise, and at the time when imports are cleared through customs. The problem with this method is that the time of shipment need bear no close or stable relationship to the time of payment for the goods concerned, and it is this latter which is relevant to the state of the foreign exchange market, although over a year the discrepancies between the two methods are likely to be small. All transactions are recorded as sterling money flows, and when transactions are invoiced in foreign currencies their values are converted into sterling at the appropriate exchange rate. Because sterling is a 'key' or 'vehicle' currency, it is used as an international medium of exchange, and it transpires that 70% of UK exports and roughly 15% UK imports are invoiced directly in sterling.

Like all systems of income and expenditure accounts, the balance of payments accounts are an ex-post record, constructed on the principle of double-entry book-keeping. Thus each external transaction is effectively entered twice, once to indicate the original transaction, say the import of a given commodity, and again to indicate the manner in which that transaction was financed. The convention is that credit items which increase net money claims on foreign residents, e.g. exports of goods and services and foreign investment in the UK, are entered with a positive sign, and that debit items which increase net money liabilities of domestic residents, e.g. imports of goods and services and profits earned by foreign-owned firms operating in the UK, are entered with a minus sign. It follows that, in sum, the balance of payments accounts always balance and that the interpretation to be read into the accounts depends on the prior selection of a particular sub-set of transactions. It will be clear, therefore, that there can be no unique picture of a country's external relationships which may be drawn from the accounts.

When analysing the balance of payments it can be useful to make a distinction between autonomous external transactions, transactions undertaken for private gain or international political obligation, and accommodating external transactions, transactions undertaken or induced specifically to finance a gap between autonomous credits and autonomous debits. This distinction is by no means watertight, as we shall see subsequently, but it provides a useful starting point when structuring the accounts and when trying to formulate notions of balance of payments equilibrium.

The Structure of the External Accounts of the UK: It is current practice to divide the external accounts of the UK into three sets of items: (i) current-account items, (ii) capital-account items, and (iii) official financing items. Current-account items and all, or part (depending on taste), of capital-account items can as a first approximation be treated as if they correspond to autonomous external transactions, while official financing items may be treated as corresponding to accommodating transactions. The structure of the external accounts and figures for 1975-9 are shown in table 3.1.[1]

---

1   For further details the reader may consult the *UK Balance of Payments 1979*, HMSO, 1979. This annual publication is known as the *Pink Book*.

TABLE 3.1

UK Summary Balance of Payments, 1975-9 (£m)

		1975	1976	1977	1978	1979
Current account (credit +/debit−)						
Exports (fob) (+)		19,330	25,193	31,734	35,071	40,689
Imports (fob) (−)		22,663	29,104	33,973	36,564	44,001
Visible trade balance		−3,333	−3,911	−2,239	−1,493	−3,312
Government services and transfers (net)		−937	−1,451	−1,833	−2,392	−2,861
Other invisibles and transfers (net)		+2,538	+4,160	+3,848	+4,817	+3,736
Invisible trade balance		+1,601	+2,709	+2,015	+2,425	+875
Current balance	1	−1,732	−1,202	−224	+932	−2,437
Capital transfers	2	–	–	–	–	–
Investment and other capital flows						
Official long-term capital	3	−291	−165	−319	−336	−401
Overseas investment in UK public sector[1]	4	+43	+203	+2,182	−80	+943
Overseas investment in UK private sector	5	+1,699	+2,070	+3,067	+2,678	+3,305
UK private investment overseas	6	−1,290	−2,232	−2,222	−4,268	−5,038
Overseas currency borrowing (net) by UK banks:						
To finance UK investment abroad	7	+320	+165	+520	+835	−445
Other borrowing	8	−85	−271	−136	−1,354	+1,903
Exchange reserves in sterling:						
British government stocks	9	+7	+14	+5	−115	+247
Banking and money market liabilities	10	−624	−1,421	−24	−4	+488
Other external banking and money market liabilities in sterling	11	+550	+255	+1,481	+301	+2,602
Import credit	12	+82	+76	+351	+243	−19
Export credit	13	−570	−1,100	−613	−685	−281
Other short term flows	14	+285	−610	+114	−414	+221
Total investment and other capital flows	15	+126	−3,016	+4,406	−3,199	+3,525
Balancing item	16	+141	+589	+3,179	+1,141	+623
Balance for official financing	17	−1,465	−3,629	+7,361	−1,126	+1,711
Allocation of special drawing rights	18	–	–	–	–	+195
Gold subscription to IMF	19	–	–	–	–	–
Total lines 17-19	20	−1,465	−3,629	+7,361	−1,126	+1,906
Official financing						
Net transactions with IMF	21	–	+1,018	+1,113	−1,016	−596
Net transactions with overseas monetary authorities plus foreign currency borrowing by HM Government[2]	22	+810	+1,758	+1,114	−187	−251
Drawings on (+)/additions to (−) official reserves	23	+655	+853	−9,588	+2,329	−1,059
Total official financing	24	+1,465	+3,629	−7,361	+1,126	−1,906

Source: ET, March 1980.
Notes: 1 Excludes foreign currency borrowing by the public sector under the exchange cover scheme.

2 Including the foreign currency borrowing by the public sector under the exchange cover scheme.

Current-account items consist of exports and imports of commodities (visibles) and invisibles which include services (e.g., insurance, shipping, tourist and banking transactions), profit and interest payments received from abroad, less similar payments made abroad, certain governments transactions, e.g. maintenance of armed forces overseas, and specified transfer payments, e.g. immigrants' remittances and foreign aid granted by the UK government. The rationale for collecting these items together is that the majority of them are directly related to flows of national income and expenditure, whether public or private. In particular, visible and invisible trade flows are closely related to movements in foreign and domestic incomes, the division of these incomes between expenditure and saving, and the division of expenditure between outlays on foreign goods and services and outlays on domestic goods and services. It should be remembered, however, that trade flows may change not because of changes in incomes, but because of spending out of past saving (dishoarding) or because of the need to build up inventories of means of production, changes which correspond to variations in holdings of assets. Profit and interest flows are classified in the current account because they correspond directly to international flows of income.

Capital-account items can be arranged in several ways. One may distinguish official capital flows (line 3) from private capital flows (e.g. lines 5 and 6). Alternatively, one may classify by the maturity date of the assets involved and distinguish long-term capital flows (e.g. lines 3-6 inclusive) from short-term capital flows (e.g. lines 11-14 inclusive). Equally one could, in principle, distinguish capital flows according to the implicit time horizon of the investor undertaking the appropriate decisions. The inevitable limitations of alternative classificatory schemes should not be allowed to hide one basic point, that all capital flows correspond to changes in the stocks of foreign assets and liabilities of the UK, although not necessarily to changes in the net external wealth of the UK. As such, these capital flows are motivated primarily by the relative rates of return on domestic and foreign assets after due allowance is made for the effects of risk and taxation. Flows of direct and portfolio investment in productive capital assets (lines 5 and 6) thus depend on prospective rates of profit in the UK compared to those abroad, and changes in holdings of financial assets depend on relative domestic and foreign interest-rate structures. A relative increase in UK profit and interest rates will normally stimulate a larger net capital inflow or a smaller net capital outflow, and vice versa for a relative fall in UK profit and interest rates. One important factor, which should not be overlooked here, is the influence of anticipated exchange-rate changes upon the capital gains and losses accruing to holdings of assets denominated in different currencies. If a sterling depreciation is anticipated, for example, this will provide a powerful incentive for wealth holders to switch any sterling denominated assets they hold into foreign currency denominated assets, in order to avoid the expected capital losses on holdings of sterling assets.[1] The 'capital value' effect is particularly important in inducing changes in the flow of short-term capital. It is worth commenting at this stage upon lines 9, 10 and 11, which correspond to changes in sterling balances. Sterling balances arose out of the key currency role of sterling, which led to private traders and foreign banks holding working balances in sterling and which also led governments to hold part of their official exchange reserves in sterling. This latter

---

1 Subject to the possibility that forward exchange cover may have been taken (cf, section III.6 below).

aspect was particularly important for the overseas sterling area (OSA) countries who traditionally maintained their domestic currencies rigidly tied to sterling, maintained the bulk of their foreign exchange reserves in sterling, and pooled any earnings of gold and non-sterling currencies in London in exchange for sterling balances. Furthermore, between 1940 and 1958, OSA countries were linked to the UK through a tightly knit system of exchange controls which discriminated against transactions with non-sterling area (NSA) countries, and especially those in the dollar area. The sterling area was effectively a currency union which allowed members to economize on their total holdings of gold and non-sterling currency reserves. One important consequence of this was that the sterling-area system created substantial holdings of UK liabilities to foreigners which had no maturity date and which could be liquidated at a moment's notice, so forming a permanent fund of contingent claims on the UK gold and foreign currency reserves. OSA countries could acquire sterling balances in the following three ways: by having a current-account surplus with the UK; as the result of a net inflow of foreign investment from the UK; and from pooling in the UK any gold and foreign currency earned from transactions with NSA countries.[1]

At the beginning of World War II the total of sterling balances stood at approximately £500m; by the end of the war they had risen to £3,7bn, around which figure they fluctuated between 1945 and 1966. In contrast to the stability in the total quantity of sterling balances, there were marked changes in the country composition; some countries, e.g. India and Pakistan, ran down their wartime accumulation of balances, while other countries, e.g. some Middle East countries, acquired new holdings of sterling balances.[2] The continued existence of the sterling-area financial arrangements depended upon two conditions being satisfied. Firstly the OSA must have a high proportion of their transations with each other and with the UK. Secondly, there must be a continued confidence in the ability of the UK, in its role of banker to the OSA, to match short-term sterling liabilities with an equivalent volume of official reserves or other short-term assets. From 1958 onwards neither of these conditions were satisfied. The OSA countries began to transact more intensively with NSA countries and the UK moved into a position of seemingly permanent deficit on her basic balance, thus increasing short-term liabilities relative to official reserves and other short-term assets and creating the conditions for the sterling crises which became frequent in the 1960s.[3] It was not unexpected, therefore, when the sterling area effectively ceased to exist in June

---

1   Ignoring reserve diversification activities, the flow increment of sterling balances was equal to the OSA basic balance surplus with the UK, plus the fraction of the OSA basic balance surplus with NSA countries pooled in the UK. The change in UK official reserves, exclusive of any change in official foreign borrowing, less the change in sterling balances (the change in the UK's short-term liquidity position, one might say) was equal to the basic balance of the UK. These relations held only as approximations; changes in trade credit, for example, would have to be zero for them to hold exactly. The concept of the basic balance is defined below in section. 1.3.

2   Detailed information on this may be found in Susan Strange, *Sterling and British Policy*, Oxford, 1971, chapters 2 and 3.

3   If official short-term and medium-term foreign borrowing by the UK government is subtracted from the official exchange reserves, this gives a measure of 'cover' for the sterling liabilities. In 1962 the ratio of 'cover' to total sterling liabilities was 51%. By end 1967 the 'cover' had disappeared entirely, outstanding official borrowing exceeding the official reserves by £3.8bn.

1972.[1] Recent developments with respect to sterling balances are treated in section III.6 below.

We come next to the balancing item (line 16), which is a statistical item to compensate for the total of measurement errors and omissions in the accounts, arising from, for example, the under-recording of exports and the reliance upon survey data for certain items such as foreign investment and tourist expenditures. A positive balancing item can reflect an unrecorded net export, an unrecorded net capital inflow, or some combination of the two. The major source of changes in the balancing item is likely to be unrecorded changes in net trade credit, reflecting discrepancies between the time when goods are shipped and the time when the associated payments are made across the exchanges. As can be seen from table 3.1, the balancing item is very volatile and can on occasions, e.g. 1977, be of a magnitude comparable to or greater than the surplus or deficit on current account. The total of investment and other capital flows together with the balancing item is known as the balance for official financing (BOF, line 17), which can, in principle, be treated as the net balance of autonomous transactions.[2] Before we come to accommodating transactions, two adjustments to the BOF have to be made, both of which relate to the UK's membership of the IMF. First, we have the allocation of special drawing rights (SDRs) (line 18), which is treated as a credit item since it effectively adds to the official reserves of the UK (line 23). Secondly we have the UK's reserve tranche subscription to the IMF. When the UK's IMF general quota is increased, the UK is obliged to subscribe 25% of the increase to the IMF in the form of SDRs or other convertible foreign exchange (up to April 1978 this subscription was paid in gold and the reserve tranche was known as the gold tranche) and the official reserves fall by the corresponding amount. Any entry in line 19 is the requisite double entry to balance the accounts and may be treated as the acquisition of assets at the IMF.

The total of lines 17-19, the *adjusted balance for official financing* (line 20), has to be matched by an equal amount of official financing. If, for any year, line 20 has a negative sign then the authorities must reduce the official external assets or increase the official external liabilities of the UK, undertaking the reverse operations if line 20 is positive in sign. There are three ways in which the necessary adjustments can be made. First, the UK may draw upon or add to the official gold and currency reserves (line 23). Over the period 1970-6 the average annual value of the UK's gross reserves was £2,42bn, but since then they have increased almost four-fold with an average value for 1977-9 of £9.51bn. During the period the composition of the reserves has also altered considerably. At end 1970 the reserves consisted of 48% gold, 43% convertible currencies and 9% SDRs, but by March 1979 the gold portion had fallen to 6% and the convertible currency position risen to 89%. At that time the basis on which the gold and SDR portions of the reserves are to be valued was changed to a market-price-related basis. Gold is to be valued at the average free-market gold price of the three months to end-March less a 25% discount, a change which immediately increased the gold component of the reserves

---

2 Prior to 1972, the OSA consisted of the Commonwealth, except Canada, South Africa, Iceland, Ireland, Kuwait, Jordan and some others. Before June 1972 these countries were known as the scheduled territories, but after June 1972 only Ireland and Gibraltar remained in this category. The demise of exchange control in October 1979 formally ended the OSA/NSA distinction.

3 Prior to 1976 this measure of external transactions was known as the total currency flow.

to 19% of the total.[1] Similarly SDRs are now valued at their average dollar exchange rate in the three months to end-March. Both these valuation rules are subject to annual revision. At end-1979 SDRs accounted for only 5% of UK reserves. Over the period 1970-9 the UK reserves averaged 20% of annual visible imports and 13% of total imports. As a second line of defence, the UK can borrow foreign currencies from the IMF. An amount equal to 25% of the UK's quota may be borrowed automatically, the so-called reserve tranche position which is classed as part of the official reserves.[2] The UK has further access to four credit tranches, each of which corresponds to 25% of quota,[3] but access is dependent upon the UK government adopting economic policies which meet with the approval of the IMF, this being particularly so for drawings beyond the first credit tranche. The maximum amount the UK could borrow at year-end 1979, including the reserve tranche position, stood at SDR 2,925m. The points to remember about IMF finance are that it is temporary (borrowings have to be repaid within 3-5 years), conditional, and cheap (4%-6%), relative to current commercial rates of interest. Finally, the UK has access to a considerable network of borrowing facilities built up with foreign central banks in the 1960s, primarily as a short-term defence against speculative capital flows. These have proved to be of considerable value to the UK, and have been supplemented since 1973 by direct government borrowing, mostly from the euro-dollar market.

It may already be apparent that the distinction between autonomous and accommodating transactions, upon which this discussion is based, is not entirely satisfactory. For example, by manipulating UK interest rates the government can create an inflow of short-term capital to accommodate a given current-account deficit, even though from the point of view of individuals or banks buying and selling the assets, the transactions are autonomous. Similarly, autonomous government items such as foreign aid may be deliberately adjusted to accommodate a deficit elsewhere in the accounts. At a more general level, whenever the government adopts policies to change the balance of payments, the effects of these policies will influence the totals of autonomous transactions so that they cease to be independent of the underlying state of the balance of payments. Despite these difficulties the autonomous-accommodating distinction provides a useful starting point for any arrangement of the external accounts.

So far we have examined the external accounts in isolation but they may equally be examined as an integral part of the national income and expenditure accounts.

From this viewpoint, the balance of payments deficit (surplus) on current account is identically equal to the excess (shortfall) of national expenditure over national income and hence to the reduction (increase) in the net external assets owned by UK residents.[4] It follows that the UK can only add to its external net assets to the extent that it has an equivalent current account surplus.

---

1 In April 1980 the formula was altered to read 'or 75% of the final fixing price on 31 March, whichever is the less'.

2 Automatic borrowing can exceed the reserve tranche position to the extent that the total IMF holding of sterling falls below 75% of the UK quota.

3 Between March 1976 and March 1978 the credit tranches were temporarily raised to 36.5% of quota, prior to the implementation of the sixth general review of quotas. See section III.9 below.

4 Cf. J. Hicks, *Social Framework*, OUP, 1971, chapters 8 and 21.

Finally, we should note that, although the accounts separate current-account items from capital-account items, there are several important links between the two sub-sets of transactions. We have already pointed out that a non-zero current account results in changes in the net external assets of the UK. As these assets and liabilities have profit and interest flows attached to them, any change in the total of external net assets will lead to changes in the interest, profit and dividend flows which appear in the current account. Furthermore, because they also result in equivalent changes in national income they will affect the current account indirectly through any effects on national expenditure and the demand for imports. Similarly, within the context of a given current-account position, capital flows which change the composition of external net assets will change the average rate of return on these assets and so react back on the current account. These are perhaps the more straightforward links, but others exist, for example, between trade flows and the balance of export and import credit, and between trade and investment flows and changes in total sterling balances. As has often been said, the balance of payments is akin to a seamless web and it can be grossly misleading to treat individual items in isolation from the rest of the accounts.

I.3   Equilibrium and Disequilibrium in the Balance of Payments

It is obviously important, both for purposes of economic policy and historical analysis, to have clear definitions of balance of payments equilibrium and disequilibrium. However, the formulation of such definitions is not easy. As a first approximation, we could define balance of payments equilibrium as a situation in which, at the existing exchange rate, autonomous credits are equal to autonomous debits and no official financing transactions are required. This definition raises three problems. First, that of the time span over which equilibrium is defined. Clearly, a daily or even monthly span of time would be of little value, and it is generally accepted that a sufficient span of years should be allowed so that the effects of cyclical fluctuations in income will have no appreciable net impact on external transactions. Secondly, if the exchange rate is allowed to fluctuate freely to equate the demand with the supply of foreign exchange, then equilibrium is always attained automatically, and any notion of payments disequilibrium becomes redundant. Thirdly, and in contrast, if the exchange rate is managed in some way to make it partially or completely independent of market forces, we must then accept that policies can be adopted to manipulate autonomous transactions in such a way as to make them balance. However, the problem which this raises is that the attainment of external equilibrium at a given exchange rate may involve unacceptable levels of employment or inflation, an interest-rate structure which is counter to economic-growth objectives and a trade policy inconsistent with international obligations. To take account of these issues we can formulate the following definition of equilibrium. The balance of payments is in equilibrium when, at the existing exchange rate, autonomous credits are equal to autonomous debits over a period of good and bad years, without involving: (i) departures from full employment or price stability; (ii) departures from the desired rate of economic growth; and (iii) adoption of tariffs or subsidies inconsistent with accepted international obligations.

The question now arises of the sets of autonomous transactions to be used in this definition of equilibrium. One possibility is to consider current-account transactions alone, but equilibrium would then involve a constant level of net external wealth and there is no particular merit in this, particularly for a growing economy. As far as the UK is concerned, two sets of autonomous transactions have been used in discussions of balance of payments performance, the basic balance and the balance for official financing.

The basic balance, defined as the sum of the current account and the net flow of long-term capital, attracts attention on several grounds, not least as one indicator of secular trends in external transactions. If the basic balance is in equilibrium, any net outflow (inflow) of long-term capital results in an equivalent increase in the stock of external assets (liabilities) of the UK. Furthermore, all net flows of short-term capital must be matched by equivalent, offsetting changes in official financing. Thus the basic balance puts below the line all capital flows essentially related to the role of the UK as an international banking and financial centre; capital flows which may be particularly sensitive to accommodating monetary manipulation.

Since 1969, however, the UK authorities have preferred to utilize the BOF as the appropriate indicator of external performance. In contrast to the basic balance, this places all short-term capital flows above the line, so that a zero BOF corresponds to a situation of no changes in the total of officially held external net assets. There are several arguments in favour of the switch to the BOF, viz.: (i) many short-term capital flows are linked to items in the trade balance, e.g. trade credit, or to the financing of long-term investment, and cannot sensibly be separated from items on the basic balance; (ii) short-term capital flow are inherently volatile, therefore they provide poor accommodation and should not be used for the purpose; and (iii) the BOF avoids the problem of separating the balancing item from the basic balance with the attendant danger of a misleading treatment of any errors and omissions. In the short term, of course, the BOF is more volatile than the basic balance, but over the longer run the two measures should coincide, provided that short-term flows net out to zero. A further advantage of the BOF is that it shows the potential increase (decrease) in the UK money supply as a result of a surplus (deficit) in the aggregate of autonomous balance of payments transactions.

I.4   The Balance of Payments, 1961-79

We shall now use our concepts of equilibrium to assess the balance of payments performance of the UK since 1961. To assist in this, table 3.2 contains average annual figures for selected items in the balance of payments in the periods 1961-4, 1965-7, 1968-71, 1972-6 and 1977-9. The first sub-period covers a complete short cycle ending in a boom year, while the remaining four are somewhat arbitrary and are separated by the 1967 devaluation, the floating of sterling in June 1972, and the sharp break in the trend in the sterling exchange rate which occurred at end-1976. The averages of course hide substantial annual variations but they will suffice for present purposes.

In the *Brookings Report*, R. Cooper suggested that the UK balance of payments position, at least up to 1966, could be summarized in terms of four propositions: (i) the UK is normally a net exporter of long-term capital, with a surplus on the current account; (ii) the visible trade balance is normally in deficit, but the invisible balance shows a surplus more than sufficient to offset this; (iii) the role of the UK as banker to the OSA gives volatile short-term capital flows an important position in the balance of payments; and finally, (iv) the trading, investing and international financial activities of the UK are carried out with a very inadequate underpinning of

TABLE 3.2

Trends in the UK Balance of Payments, Annual Averages for Selected Periods (£m) and Average Growth Rates for UK GDP and World Exports of Manufactures

	1961-4	1965-7	1968-71	1972-6	1977-9
1 Visible balance	−210	−292	−191	−3,188	−2,348
2 Government services and transfers (net)	−377	−459	−485	−911	−754
3 Private invisibles (net)	+569	+676	+1,189	+2,642	+2,526
4 Invisible balance	+192	+217	+705	+1,731	+1,772
5 Current account balance	−18	−76	+514	−1,457	−576
6 Balancing item	−25	+19	+126	+93	+1,648
7 Balance of long-term capital	−139	−137	−117	+48	−163
8 Balance of long-term and other capital flows[1]	−183	−467	+288	−364	+1,577
9 Basic balance (5+7)	−157	−215	+397	−1,409	−739
10 Basic balance plus balancing item (9+6)	−182	−196	+523	−1,316	+909
11 Balance for official financing	−225	−524	+927	−1,755	+2,649
12 Gold subs., IMF and SDRs	−	−15	+65	+21	+65
13 Total lines 11 and 12. Adjusted balance for official financing	−225	−539	+992	−1,734	+2,714
14 Net foreign currency borrowing by HM government (inc. IMF)	+143	+421	−595	+1,357	+59
15 Transfer $ portfolio to reserves	−	+173	−	−	−
16 Drawing on (+) or additions to (−) official reserves	+82	−55	−398	+373	−2,773
17 Total official financing	+225	+539	−992	+1,730	−2,714
18 Average annual growth real GDP (1975 prices) %	3.2	2.3	2.6	2.0	2.1
19 Average annual growth volume of world export manufactures %	8.3	8.1	11.1	7.4	5.1

Sources: UK *Balance of Payments 1979* and *ET*, March 1980. World exports from various issues of *NIER*.
Note: 1 Excludes Capital Transfers in 1973 and 1974 and EEA losses on forwards 1967 and 1968.

foreign exchange reserves.[1] Certainly the years 1956-60 fit into this pattern with an average annual long-term capital outflow of £189 million offset by a current-account surplus of £136m per annum and a net short-term capital inflow of £53m per annum. After taking account of the balancing item and other factors, the UK was able to add to its reserves at an annual rate of £79m. From this 'traditional' UK payments position the first two sub-periods of table 3.2 show unmistakable signs of a slide into fundamental disequilibrium. The trade balance continued to deteriorate throughout the two periods, despite a sustained growth of world trade, and so did the current account, which moved into increasing deficit. A successful attempt by the government to restrict the growth of overseas public expenditure in 1965-7 only prevented the deficit from being worse than it would otherwise have been. To some extent a reduction in the net outflow of long-term capital helped reduce the deficit on the basic balance, but the improvement here was more than offset by massive short-term outflows induced by the sterling crises

---

1 R. Caves (ed.), *Britain's Economic Prospects*, Allen and Unwin, 1968, chapter 3.

of 1961, 1964 and each of the three following years. It was, of course, the
weakness in the current account and basic balance, and the perpetual fear of a
sterling devaluation which were crucial here. An important consequence of this lack
of confidence in sterling was the need to incur substantial foreign debts and to
liquidate the government's portfolio of dollar securities, in order to maintain the
parity of sterling.

The inevitable devaluation, which took place in November 1967, was followed
by a substantial turn-around in the external payments position, although it is not
completely clear to what extent this was attributable to the devaluation, to the
acceleration in the growth of world trade, or to measures to restrict demand
growth and DCE after 1968 (between 1969 and 1971 the average rate of growth of
real GDP fell to 1.75%). The visible deficit was reduced and an increase in the
invisible surplus resulted in the current account moving back into surplus. When
combined with a reduction in the net outflow of long-term capital this created a
very strong position in the basic balance, especially when account is taken of the
balancing item. Apart from this, confidence in sterling returned after 1968, no
doubt helped by the Basle arrangements of that year, and short-term capital
flowed back into the UK at an identified annual average rate of £405m. So strong
was the improvement in the payments position, that the UK was able to repay a
substantial part of the debts raised in defence of sterling in the previous two periods
and, at the same time, add to the official reserves. It cannot be claimed that this
period saw a return to equilibrium in the external accounts simply because of the
severe restraint on domestic growth which took place. However, it can at least be
argued that the foundations were then laid for a return to equilibrium once the
foreign debts had been repaid.

That the return to equilibrium has not been achieved is clear from the figures for
1972-9. The most important point about this period is that it was one of substantial
disruption to the international trading system. The rise in the relative price of
primary commodities and oil, together with the associated slackening in the growth
of world trade, created a sharp deterioration in the UK balance of trade during this
period which was reinforced, in the short-run, by the depreciation of sterling
between June 1972 and November 1976. Over the period 1972-6 the current
account moved into deficit at an annual average rate of £1,457m. Between 1977
and 1978 there was remarkable recovery with an average current-account surplus of
£354m, but 1979 saw the return to the substantial deficit shown in table 3.1, to
give an average deficit for 1977-9 of £576m. To a considerable degree, however,
the 1979 figures were distorted by labour disputes and the loss of markets in Iran
which created a visible trade deficit in the first quarter some three times greater
than might otherwise have been expected. Temporary distortions apart, the three
years to 1979 undoubtedly marked an improvement in the current-account
situation. A major factor in this turn-around was the coming on stream of North
Sea oil, the deficit on trade in petroleum and related products falling from one of
£3.95bn in 1976 to one of £0.8bn in 1979. Unfortunately 1979 also saw a
substantial reduction in the invisible surplus which fell by 64% from the 1978 level.
This was largely due to increased contributions to the EEC budget, the remission of
overseas profits associated with the NS oil programme, and increased interest
payments on overseas debt.

Between 1972 and 1976 two factors helped to cushion the effect of the trade
deficit on the basic balance, an improvement in the net inflow of profits, interest
and dividends, and a reversal of the traditional UK position as a net exporter of

long-term capital: – a change which was largely the result of foreign investment to exploit NS oil resources. The average basic-balance deficit over this period of £1,409m was financed in two principal ways: (i) a net inflow of short-term capital, as oil-producing countries allocated part of their surplus revenues to sterling assets; and (ii) resort to substantial foreign currency borrowing by the government and public-sector bodies, supplemented by drawing upon the official reserves. This policy of 'financing' the deficit has not been without its problems. As the events of 1976 and 1977 demonstrated, short-term capital can flow out of the UK as quickly as it may flow in, placing substantial pressures on the exchange rate and the official reserves. Indeed the UK reserves fell from $7.02bn at end-February 1976 to a low of $4.13bn at the end of 1976 and were rebuilt even more rapidly to a figure of $20.5bn at end-1977. The policy of official borrowing added $17.7bn to outstanding short-term and medium-term overseas public-sector debts between end-1972 and end-1977. The strengthening of the UK payments position after 1976 brought substantial inflows of short-term capital back into the UK and the consequent growth in the reserves, and the appreciation of sterling, has allowed the UK government to accelerate repayment of some of the debts incurred after 1972 and to restructure the remaining burden of the debt. Even so, a total of $11.2bn remains to be repaid before end-1984 and the interest burden on the post-1972 borrowing is likely to come to $1.7bn in 1980 alone.[1]

There can be no doubt that the period 1972-9 was again one of fundamental disequilibrium in the UK balance of payments. The basic-balance deficits of 1972-6 were incurred at a time of deepening domestic recession, with the unemployment percentage rising from 2.3% at end-1973 to 5.5% at the beginning of 1977, and with an average growth rate of real GDP well below the level of the previous ten years. The subsequent improvement in the basic balance has occurred without any substantial reduction of the unemployment rate or any sustained increase in real GDP growth.

To summarize experience over the period 1961 to 1979, the one crucial factor appears to be the persistent weakness of the visible trade account, which more than offsets the steady improvement in the invisible trade surplus. The resulting current-account deficits combined with the propensity to export long-term capital, progressively undermined the ability of the UK to act as an international financial centre by borrowing short and lending long. The principal result of this has been the termination of the UK's role as banker to the overseas sterling area and the persistence of disruptive changes of international confidence in the external value of sterling.

North Sea Oil and Gas: Much recent economic policy discussion in the UK has been concerned with the economic effects of the exploitation of oil and gas resources in the North Sea, the production of NS oil first becoming substantial in 1976. It is generally argued that the effect on GDP will be relatively small, effectively offsetting the loss of real income imposed on the UK by the increase in

---

1 See *BEQB*, December 1979, Appendix table 18, and the article 'UK Official Short and Medium Term Borrowing from Abroad', *BEQB*, March 1976, pp. 78-81. Approximately $10.4bn represented borrowing by the public sector, nationalized industries and local authorities, the bulk of which is covered by the exchange cover scheme reintroduced in 1973. A further $4.2bn represented official borrowing from IMF under the oil facility, and the standby arrangements negotiated at the beginning of 1977.

the relative price of oil since 1973,[1] and the direct effects on employment negligible. However the effects on the balance of payments and public-sector revenue are substantial. The major effect will therefore be to alter the environment in which economic policy is formulated and to open up prospects of substantial real growth, unimpeded by trade-balance constraints, over the next decade. Section III.5 discusses some of the policy options opened up by NS oil; in this section we briefly outline some calculations of the likely magnitude of NS oil effects on the balance of payments and the difficulties surrounding such calculations.

The major difficulties relate to important areas of uncertainty, e.g. with respect to oil yields, trends in exploitation and development costs, the share of extractive equipment provided by UK firms and, most importantly, in the sterling price of oil. This latter element will depend jointly on the ability of the OPEC cartel to determine the future real increase in the dollar price of oil, a decision over which the UK as a minor world producer will have no influence, and upon the policies which the UK government adopts with respect to the exchange rate. Other aspects of government policy, as yet uncertain, will be of equal importance. In particular, the production and depletion policy adopted, whether it matches production to domestic demand or allows net exports of crude oil, and the levels of royalty and petroleum revenue tax charged, which will determine the proportion of profits left to the oil producers for potential remission overseas. One further obvious difficulty is that the total benefits from NS oil to the balance of payments will not be independent of how the government feels able to exploit these benefits for domestic purposes.[2]

When calculating the direct impact of NS oil and gas on the UK balance of payments, account has to be taken of the following items. First, the net effect on the balance of trade in oil and gas as home output is exported or substituted for imports. Second, the net trade in equipment and technical services to discover and extract the oil and gas. Third, the inflows of foreign capital to finance extraction and development, and, finally, the net flows of interest, profits and dividends, remitted overseas by the foreign-owned firms operating in the North Sea. It is worth remembering that the balance of payments effects of these operations started well before the flow of NS oil began. Thus in the years 1972-6 total net imports of equipment and services amounted to £1.84bn, an amount which was almost covered by a cumulative net capital inflow of £1.34bn. During 1979 the net contribution to the balance of official financing was made up as follows, balance of trade effects + £8.4bn, net IPD due overseas − £1.1bn, and net capital inflow + £1bn, to give a total effect on the BOF of + £8.2bn. The most recent calculations of the effect on the BOF in 1985 suggest a net oil and gas related contribution of +£8.7, though this figure is subject to all the previously noted uncertainties.[3]

---

1 At 1978 prices, NS oil and gas will contribute some 7.3% extra to GDP in 1980, perhaps rising to 9.6% GDP in 1985. *TER*, No. 112, August 1979.

2 In particular, the exchange-rate policy adopted to accommodate to NS oil is an important determinant of the total economic effect on government revenue and the balance of payments. For a useful account of the effect of different exchange-rate assumptions, see S.A.B. Page, 'The Value and Distribution of the Benefits of NS Oil and Gas, 1970-1985', *NIER*, No. 82, 1977, pp. 41-58.

3 Derived from *TER*, No. 112, August 1979. The figures are at constant 1978 prices and are not directly comparable with other estimates, e.g. by the National Institute. See Page, op. cit., p. 53, for a comment on this.

TABLE 3.3

Area Composition of UK Merchandise Trade, 1955-79 (percentages)

	Imports (c.i.f.) 1955	1965	1975	1979	Gm 1970-9	Exports (f.o.b.) 1955	1965	1975	1979	Gx 1970-9
Western Europe	25.7	35.8	51.0	59.8	23.2	28.9	41.8	49.0	58.2	23.0
EEC[1]	12.6	23.6	36.3	43.1	26.8	15.0	26.3	32.2	41.8	24.8
North America	19.5	19.6	13.3	12.8	14.2	12.0	14.8	11.1	11.3	16.3
USA	10.9	11.7	9.6	10.2	17.3	7.1	10.6	8.9	9.5	17.5
Other Developed[2]	14.2	11.9	7.9	6.1	14.3	20.5	14.8	9.4	5.8	11.1
Japan	0.6	1.4	2.8	3.1	44.8	0.6	1.1	1.6	1.4	17.0
Total Developed Countries	59.4	67.4	72.2	78.7	21.6	61.4	71.4	70.3	75.3	20.6
Centrally Planned Economies	2.7	4.4	3.0	3.2	16.5	1.7	2.9	3.3	2.8	16.2
Oil Exporting Countries[3]	9.2	9.8	13.5	7.0	16.8	5.1	5.6	11.4	8.9	26.1
Other Developing Countries	28.7	18.4	11.3	11.1	16.3	31.8	20.1	15.0	12.8	16.8
Total	100.0	100.0	100.0	100.0	20.3	100.0	100.0	100.0	100.0	20.2

Gm   Average annual compound growth in the value of imports.
Gx   Average annual compound growth in the value of exports.

1   The nine Community members as of 1980.
2   Japan, plus Australia, New Zealand and South Africa.
3   Small discrepancies exist between the countries listed for 1955 and those for subsequent years.

Sources: AAS, various. *TI*, 16 March 1972 and 16 March 1979; *BB*, 14 March 1980.

II FOREIGN TRADE OF THE UK
II.1 Structure and Trends, 1955-79

In this section we shall examine the major structural features and trends in the foreign trade of the UK between 1955 and 1979.[1] In focusing attention upon certain longer-term trends, we will find evidence of a marked decline in the international competitive performance of UK manufacturing industry; a decline which, it may reasonably be claimed, is the proximate source of the unsatisfactory behaviour of the balance of payments noted in the previous section.

Geographical and Commodity Trade Structure: The traditional picture of UK foreign trade was one in which manufactures were exchanged for imports of foodstuffs and raw materials, with the bulk of the trade being carried out with the Commonwealth and overseas sterling area countries. That this picture is now completely out of date is shown in tables 3.3, 3.4 and 3.5, which illustrate the radical changes in trading structure which have occurred in the quarter century since 1955. To some small extent these changes reflect the relaxation of wartime import restrictions and the general postwar movement toward free-er trade that resulted from the several rounds of GATT tariff reductions. But, in general, they are the outcome of more deepseated changes in competitive forces.

TABLE 3.4

Commodity Composition of UK Imports, Selected Years 1955-79 (percentages)

SITC Group	Description	1955	1965	1975	1979
0, 1	Food, Beverages, Tobacco	36.2	29.7	17.7	13.4
3	Fuel	10.4	10.6	17.7	11.9
2, 4, 5, 6	Industrial Materials and Semi-Manufactures	47.9	43.0	34.1	36.8
7, 8	Finished Manufactures	5.2	15.3	28.3	36.2
9	Unclassified	0.3	1.4	2.2	1.7
	Total	100.0	100.0	100.0	100.0

Sources: TI, 16 March 1972 and 16 March 1979; *BB*, 14 March 1980.
Note: Imports are measured on an overseas trade statistics basis and are valued c.i.f.

The major changes in the geographic composition of UK trade are shown in table 3.3. Several general trends are immediately apparent. Compared to 1955, the following years show an increased dependence on trade with developed countries, a trend which has been primarily at the expense of trade with the less developed

---

1 Since, over the period, some 65-70% of total exports and imports reflected commodity transactions, we here concentrate solely on commodity trade. For a treatment of invisible items in the current account, see P. Phillips, 'A Forecasting Model for the United Kingdom Invisible Account', *NIER*, No. 69, 1974. Interest, profit and dividend flows are discussed in section III.7 below. For further details on invisibles, consult the COI pamphlet, *Britain's Invisible Exports*, HMSO, 1970.

members of the OSA.[1] An interesting development since 1975 is the increased importance, for obvious reasons, of the oil-exporting countries as a market for UK exports. The decline in their importance as a source of UK imports between 1975 and 1979 is the direct result of the exploitation of the UK's NS oil resources. As far as trade with the developed nations is concerned, the most striking trend is the increasing importance of trade with the EEC. In 1972, the year prior to UK entry, the current nine EEC members accounted for approximately 30% of UK exports and imports, but by 1979 the export share had risen to 41.8% and the import share to 43.1%. As table 3.3 indicates, this development has been largely to the detriment of trade with the more advanced former members of the OSA. The growing importance of Japan as a source of UK imports may also be noted.

TABLE 3.5

Commodity Composition of UK Exports, Selected Years 1955-79 (percentages)

Description	1955	1965	1975	1979
Engineering Products[1]	36.5	43.5	44.3	37.2
Machinery	21.1	26.6	28.6	22.9
Road Motor Vehicles	8.7	11.6	9.2	7.3
Other Transport Equipment	5.7	3.3	3.9	4.2
Scientific Instruments	1.2	2.1	2.6	2.8
Semi-Manufactures[2]	29.7	26.8	23.4	23.0
Chemicals	7.8	9.2	10.6	11.5
Textiles	10.1	5.8	3.6	3.1
Metals	11.8	11.8	9.2	8.4
Other Semi-Manufactures and Manufactures[3]	12.6	13.2	14.6	17.1
Non-Manufactures[4]	21.2	16.4	17.8	22.7
Food, Beverages, Tobacco	6.5	6.6	7.1	6.9
Basic Materials	5.6	4.0	2.8	2.9
Fuels	4.6	2.7	4.1	10.1
Other	4.5	3.0	3.8	2.8
Total	100.0	100.0	100.0	100.0

SITC Groups: 1   7, 86, 87.
             2   5, 65, 67-9.
             3   Remainder of 6 and 8.
             4   0, 1, 2, 3, 4 and 9.

Sources: AAS, various, *TI*, 16 March 1972 and 16 March 1979; *BB*, 14 March 1980.

Exports are measured on an overseas trade statistics basis and valued f.o.b.

The switch toward a greater trade dependence on the industrialized, urbanized, high per-capita-income countries of Western Europe, Japan and North America has been matched, not unexpectedly, by significant changes in the commodity structure of UK trade, particularly in respect of imports. The changing structure of UK import trade is shown in table 3.4. Most important here is the increase in the

---

1 In 1955 these countries provided 22.8% of UK imports and absorbed 21.6% of UK exports; the corresponding figures for 1977 were 6.3% and 9.4%.

proportion of imports of finished manufactures, the share of which increased seven-fold between 1955 and 1979, and the decline in the proportion accounted for by foodstuffs, beverages and tobacco. Imports of finished and semi-manufactures now account for some 65% of total UK imports. This same trend has also been experienced by other EEC countries although it remains the case that the UK is more dependent upon imports of non-manufactures than are, for example, France or West Germany.[1] On the export side, table 3.5 indicates that changes in the structure of UK trade are less noticeable. Indeed comparing 1955 with 1979 the only major differences are in the areas of semi-manufactures and fuels. The decline in the share of engineering products between 1975 and 1979 is a cause for some concern to which we return below. Looking to the future, the possibility of substantial net exports of North Sea oil over the next ten years is likely to raise substantially the share of fuels in total exports and to diminish the share of fuels in total imports, over and above the changes that have already taken place between 1975 and 1979.

It will be apparent from this that UK trade is increasingly dominated by an exchange of manufactures for manufactures with the advanced industrialized nations. These structural changes would imply that UK manufacturing industry has experienced and will continue to experience greater foreign competition in home and export markets. They also help to explain the disintegration in the sterling area system which occurred after 1964.

Perhaps one of the more striking indicators of UK trade performance during the 1970s is provided by the comparative figures on the growth in trade in finished manufactures. Between 1970 and 1979 the import volume of finished manufactures increased at an annual rate of 13.2%, while the corresponding volume of exports of finished manufactures only grew at 3.9% per annum. This important difference can easily be overlooked by concentrating attention on the overall figures for exports and imports, which in both volume and value terms increased at not too dissimilar rates.

II.2   The Decline in Competitive Performance

The trend toward increasing trade deficits which became evident in the early 1960s, coming as it did after a relaxation in trade and currency restrictions, has rightly been taken as indicative of a widespread lack of competitive edge in UK industry relative to foreign industry. Evidence to support this view is provided by the progressive decline of the UK's share of world exports of manufactures[2] and by evidence of the increased import penetration of the UK market by foreign competitors. The net effect of these trends is to substantially limit the scope for the UK to grow without coming up against a balance of trade constraint. Thus, for example, the well-known study by Houthakker and Magee found a UK income elasticity of demand for imports of 1.66, double the corresponding world income elasticity of demand for UK exports of 0.86. Starting from balanced trade, these figures would suggest that the UK can only grow at half the world average rate if

---

1   M. Panic, 'Why the UK's Propensity to Import is High', *LBR*, No. 115, 1975.

2   'World', in this context, means W. Germany, France, Italy, Netherlands, Belgium, Luxemburg, Canada, Japan, Sweden, Switzerland, USA and UK. In 1977 they accounted for 75% of manufactured exports from all industrial nations. See *TI*, 7 June 1978, p. 22.

balanced trade is to be maintained.[1] Some further indication of the problem may be gained by the fact that between 1970 and 1979, when UK manufacturing production grew at an average annual rate of 0.7%, the volume of exports of all manufactures increased by an average of 4.5% per annum, but the volume of imports of all manufactures increased at an average annual rate of 10.2%. A growth of imports of this magnitude, in the industries in which the UK's traditional comparative advantage is thought to lie, is obviously a serious matter. Indeed it has prompted widespread fears of the imminent de-industrialization of the UK, with the manufacturing base so eroded by foreign competition that full employment and payments equilibrium cannot be achieved without a substantial reduction in real income.[2]

The statistics of the decline in the UK share of world exports of manufactures are dramatic and indicate that the share fell from 20.4% in 1954 to 17.7% in 1959, 11.9% in 1967 and a low of 8.8% in 1974. Rough calculations for this period would suggest that a 10% increase in world exports of manufactures was associated with a 5% to 6% increase in UK exports of manufactures.[3] Since 1974, however, the position has changed substantially, indeed despite a 30% increase in world trade in manufactures between 1975 and 1979 the UK share appears to have stabilized at an average figure of 9.4%.[4]

Of itself, the decline in export share need not give rise to concern, since it may simply reflect a decline in the UK share of world manufacturing production, the natural result, say, of her early industrial start. (In 1899 the UK accounted for 32.5% of world exports of manufactures.) However, this is far too complacent a view. Once it is recognized that between 1959 and 1973 the volume of world trade in manufactures grew at historically unprecedented rates of between 7-13% per annum, and that the UK was alone among the major industrial countries in experiencing a substantial drop in export share, there are grounds for disquiet. Furthermore, the decline in the UK's share in world manufacturing production may itself reflect the same factors which hinder UK trade performance. In this respect it is worth noting that during the long industrial boom of the 1960s and early 1970s, the UK share of OECD manufacturing output fell from 9.6% in 1960 to 5.8% in 1973.

On the import side the evidence for a loss of competitive edge is equally disturbing. Even though all the major industrialized nations have experienced a rising import share since 1955, the UK seems to be relatively more import prone than her competitors and to have a relatively high income elasticity of demand for

---

1   H.S. Houthakker and S.P. Magee, 'Income and Price Elasticities in World Trade', *REST*, Vol. 51, pp. 111-25. This study covered the period 1951-66. For a critique, see A.D. Morgan, 'Income and Price Elasticities in World Trade: A Comment', *MS*, Vol. 38, 1970, pp. 303-14.

2   Cf., the various contributions to F. Blackaby (ed.), *De-Industrialization*, Heinemann, 1979.

3   *NIER*, No. 73, 1975, p. 12.

4   The decline in the UK manufactured-exports share has also been matched by a similar fall in her share of world invisible exports, from 20.9% in 1960 to 12.5% in 1976. Unlike manufactures, however, the UK share of world invisible imports has fallen along with the share in invisible exports. Cf., J.R. Sargent, 'UK Performance in Services', in F. Blackaby (ed.), op. cit.

imports.[1]   Recent calculations show that over the period 1968-79 the ratio of imports of manufactures to the value of domestic absorption of manufactures increased from 17% to 25%. This trend appears to be widespread across manufacturing industry and is particularly significant in certain sectors, e.g. motor vehicles, office equipment, construction equipment and miscellaneous metal goods.[2] Some care, however, is required in interpreting these figures since they reflect to some extent the increasing division of labour in the international economy which has occurred particularly since 1958. Similar calculations on the export side indeed show a corresponding trend increase in the proportion of UK output which is exported, with the average ratio of UK manufacturing exports to manufacturing production increasing from 17.6% in 1968 to 24.5% at end 1979. [3]

To explain these developments in any precise sense is not easy, since several interrelated factors are involved and the relative weight to be attached to each is difficult to establish and may vary over time. At the most general level, and since it is trade in manufactures which is crucial, there would seem to be two potential sources of the poor UK trade performance: an increasing lack of price competitiveness; and a failure to produce and market commodities of the right quality, in the face of rapidly changing technologies and world demand structures. Certainly in the period up to 1967 the movement of UK export prices relative to the export prices of her major trade competitors can explain some of the loss of export share. Averaged over the period 1959-67, UK dollar export prices rose at an annual average rate of 2%, compared to 1.3% for the other major industrial nations.[4] It follows that the relative price of UK manufactures rose by some 6.4% over this period and, assuming an export price elasticity of -2, this could account

1   A.D. Morgan, 'Imports of Manufactures into the UK and other Industrial Countries 1955-69', *NIER*, No. 56, 1971; M. Panic, op. cit.; L.F. Campbell-Boross and A.D. Morgan, 'Net Trade: A Note on Measuring Changes in the Competitiveness of British Industry in Foreign Trade', *NIER*, No. 68, 1974, suggest that from 1963, UK manufacturing industry had never been sufficiently competitive to restore the country's trade situation to the position held in that year. The evidence for 1970-8 would suggest that each 1% increase in real GDP in the UK has associated with a 3.8% increase in the volume of manufactured imports and a 1.8% increase in the volume of total imports.

2   J.J. Hughes and A.P. Thirlwall, 'Trends and Cycles in Import Penetration in the UK', *Oxford Bulletin of Economics and Statistics*, Vol. 39, 1977, pp. 301-17. See also *TI*, 16 February 1979, p. 312.

3   It may be noted that the sectors experiencing the greatest improvement in export performance, e.g. chemicals, electrical engineering, mechanical engineering and scientific instruments are also the sectors which perform two-thirds of the non-aerospace research and development carried out in UK manufacturing industry. See 'The Home and Export Performance of UK Manufacturing Industry', *ET*, No. 286, August 1977. Import penetration ratios and export: sales ratios are now published on a monthly basis in *MDS*. A useful account of some of the pitfalls in interpreting movements in these ratios, pitfalls which arise out of the foreign trade multiplier links between exports, imports and home output, is contained in C. Kennedy and A.P. Thirlwall, 'Import Penetration, Export Performance and Harrod's Trade Multiplier', *OEP*, July 1979, pp. 303-23.

4   Figures calculated from *NIER* Appendix tables, which also provide a valuable summary of international trends in labour productivity, unit costs and industrial output.

for 39% of the decline in UK export share between the two dates.[1] The problem with this line of argument is in applying it to developments since 1967. Between then and 1974, UK relative export prices fell by 12% and yet the UK export share still declined by 26%. If we maintain an assumed export price elasticity of -2, this would suggest that other factors would, in the absence of the improvement in competitiveness, have resulted in a decline in the UK share of world trade to 6.7% in 1974! It seems rather more plausible to argue that structural factors, as yet unspecified, have resulted in a reduction in the price elasticity of demand for UK exports. The case for a structural break in the UK export environment is reinforced by considering the period 1974-9. During this period, world exports of manufactures increased at an annual compound rate of 4.5%, and UK export price competitiveness declined by 22%. On past performance both factors should have reduced the UK share of world exports but, as we have seen, the share appears to have stabilized. This combination of circumstances lends weight to the view that non-price factors have come to play the dominant role in UK export performance.[2] On the import side there is strong evidence that the ratio of imports of manufactures to domestic demand has increased due to the decline in the competitiveness of UK manufactures. Independently of this, however, there is also a well-defined trend increase in the degree of import penetration of about 2% per annum,[3] which again suggests an important role for non-price factors. We have already noted the progressive shift in the pattern of UK trade toward exchanges of manufactures with the advanced industrial nations. It seems plausible to argue that the oligopolistic conditions found in such markets are bound to increase the importance of non-price factors in competitive performance and to reduce the price elasticities of demand for traded goods.[4] The type and quality of manufactures produced, delivery lags and after-sales service, and the general quality of marketing

---

1   An elasticity of -3 would account for 59% of the loss in export share. R. Batchelor and C. Bowe, 'Forecasting UK International Trade: A General Equilibrium Approach', *Applied Economics*, Vol. 6, 1974, estimate price elasticities for UK export volume of between -1.13 and -2.80. One difficulty with any elasticity estimates is in evaluating the length of time it takes for the effects of price changes to be fully reflected in volume changes. Some estimates suggest up to five years as being the appropriate time-lag. See, e.g., H. Junz, and R. Rhomberg, 'Price Competitiveness in Export Trade Among Industrial Countries', *AER*, May 1973, pp. 413-18.

2   Other econometric research suggests that relative price movements can only account for one-half at most of the UK's loss of export share between 1956 and 1976, and one-fifth of the loss between 1970 and 1976. See M. Fetherstone, B. Moore and J. Rhodes, 'Manufacturing, Export Shares and Cost Competitiveness of Advanced Industrial Countries', *Economic Policy Review No 3*, Dept. of Applied Economics, Cambridge 1977. More recent research suggests a representative price elasticity for UK manufactured exports, for the period 1967 to 1975, of -1.4, while for the period 1967 to 1977 (2nd quarter) the representative elasticity is reduced to -1. Cf. C.A. Enoch, 'Measures of Competitiveness in International Trade', *BEQB*, June 1978. This article also contains a useful review of alternative measures of price competitiveness.

3   C.A. Enoch, op. cit., who finds an import penetration price elasticity of -0.4 for 1967 to 1977 (2nd quarter).

4   Recent evidence suggests that in 1977 three-quarters of UK exports were accounted for by 189 enterprises and that 30% of UK exports came from foreign-owned UK firms. See Business Statistics Office, *Business Monitor MA4: Overseas Transactions 1977*, HMSO, 1979.

effort, it is frequently claimed, play a significant part in explaining the relatively poor UK trade performance.[1]

Unfortunately, the precise role of these factors has proved impossible, as yet, to determine, although it is interesting to note that similar explanations of poor British competitive performance were employed at the end of the nineteenth century.[2] However, to the extent that non-price factors are important, one would expect that an ability to innovate and market in response to rapidly changing market conditions would be an important factor in trade performance. There is evidence to show that export success in the advanced industrialized nations is positively related to the resources devoted to Research and Development (R and D) and to measures of success in inventive activity, e.g. patenting.[3] Here it is important to remember that some 50% of UK exports in 1979 were in the R and D intensive areas of engineering and chemicals. Moreover there is also evidence to suggest that the quality of UK mechanical engineering exports, as measured by the value per ton of metal processed, has been growing progressively inferior to the quality of the same exports from France and Germany, and this may be related to the stagnation in the volume of UK engineering exports since 1975.[4] It is not difficult to link together the relative contributions of price and non-price factors, at least in theory if not in practice. The central point is that we have a sequence of interacting, and mutually reinforcing, proximate sources of the trend deterioration in UK trade performance. A convenient place to begin is with the well-documented fact that since 1950 the rates of growth of output and labour productivity in the UK have been inferior to those of the other major industrial nations.[5] A relatively slow growth rate of productivity implies a trend reduction in the relative level of UK industrial efficiency, which contributes to an increasing lack of price competitiveness for UK manufactures and a relative shortage of resources for investment in capacity expansion and marketing and innovative activities. A low rate of export growth, combined with rising import penetration and a low rate of industrial investment feed back to reinforce the relatively slow growth of output. In turn, a low rate of output growth reduces the scope for the UK to exploit static and dynamic economies of scale, and scarcely provides a climate conducive to risk-taking and successful innovative activity. Consequently the growth of productivity and quality change is held back and we come full circle back to the initial source of the poor UK trade performance. A country such as the UK has no option but to maintain its technological level close to 'world best practice', if it is to maintain its historically

1   *NEDO, Imported Manufactures*, HMSO, 1965 and NEDO, *International Price Competitiveness, Non-Price Factors and Export Performance*, HMSO, 1977. See also, Report of the Committee of Enquiry into the Engineering Profession, *Engineering Our Future*, Cmnd. 7794, January 1980, Ch. 1.

2   R. Hoffman, *Great Britain and the German Trade Rivalry, 1875-1914*, Pennsylvania University Press, 1933, pp. 21-80.

3   For a review see the valuable paper by C. Freeman, 'Technical Innovation and British Trade Performance,' in F. Blackaby (ed.), op. cit. See also K. Pavitt, 'Technical Innovation and Industrial Development', *Futures*, Vol. 11, December 1979.

4   Cf., e.g., Cmnd. 7794, pp. 15-16, and the paper by D.K. Stout in F. Blackaby (ed.), op. cit. Also table 3.5 above.

5   See e.g. E.H. Phelps Brown, 'Labour Policies', in A. Cairncross (ed.), *Britain's Economic Prospects Reconsidered*, Allen and Unwin, 1971, and D.T. Jones, 'Output, Employment and Labour Productivity in Europe since 1955', *NIER*, No. 77, 1976.

high standards of living. As technologies mature, the centre of comparative advantage inevitably moves to low-real-wage countries, so an advanced country can only maintain its living standards by shifting its resources into new areas opened up by technological advance. Like the Red Queen, the UK has to run to stand still, and if it fails it will enter the ranks of the underdeveloped nations from the wrong direction. Not only does the above account apply to the long-run trend of trade performance, it also relates to an inflexibility in the UK economic structure which makes the degree of import penetration and the volume of exports particularly sensitive to fluctuations in the pressure of aggregate demand.[1] Boom periods, it is argued, come up against constraints of available production capacity and available labour supply, diverting exports to the home market and raising the volume of imports above trend, with the possibility that a ratchet effect is involved, i.e., markets once lost to foreign goods are not readily recovered when the pressure of domestic demand slackens.

The coming on stream of NS oil raises the interesting possibility that the temporary balance of payments respite it will provide may be used to break out of the circle of cumulative competitive decline. We comment on this in section III.5 below.

Other Factors: While it is the inadequate industrial growth performance which is chiefly responsible for the poor UK trade performance, several additional factors should not be ignored. On the export side, it is possible that an undue concentration on the supply of relatively slow-growing markets, and on the production of commodities for which world demand was growing relatively slowly, could explain the decline in export share. Appealing though this hypothesis is, evidence does not support the view that the structure of UK trade is responsible for poor export performance. A recent NEDO study finds no evidence in support of the view that the UK export structure is biased adversely toward the slower growing commodities in world trade.[2] Furthermore, a study by R.L. Major has shown that only 9% of the total loss in UK manufacturing exports between 1954 and 1966 can be attributed to exporting to relatively slow-growing markets.[3]

It may also have been the case that preferential trading arrangements have changed to the disadvantage of UK exporters. Isolated examples of this can be found, for example, in the relaxation by certain Commonwealth countries of import quota restrictions, which led to substantial export gains for Japan and the USA at the expense of UK producers. To set against this, an EFTA study concluded that UK exports in 1965 were 2% higher than they would otherwise have been in the absence of EFTA, although there appeared to be no noticeable effects on UK imports.[4] Of much greater importance has been the formation of the EEC.

---

1 Econometric work in this field is fraught with difficulties both of formulation and execution. For evidence on the demand-pressure/supply-bottleneck hypothesis, see e.g. J. Artus, 'The Short-Run Effects of Domestic Demand Pressure on UK Export Performance', *Staff Papers*, IMF, Vol. 17, 1970, pp. 247-67, J.J. Hughes and A.P. Thirlwall, op. cit., and C.A. Enoch, op. cit.

2 M. Panic and A.H. Rajan, *Product Changes in Industrial Countries Trade 1955-68*, NEDO Monograph No. 2, 1971.

3 R.L. Major, 'Note on Britain's Share in World Trade in Manufactures 1954-66', *NIER*, No. 44, 1968.

4 EFTA Secretariat, *The Effects of EFTA on the Economies of Member States*, Geneva, 1969, p. 162. On the loss of export share in former Commonwealth markets, see the article 'Export Performance, No Room for Complacency', *TI*, 1 September 1978.

Although UK exports to the EEC have clearly benefited it also seems likely that the effects of selling to a large and rapidly expanding market have been more than offset by reductions in UK exports to non-EEC countries, possibly due to the adverse effects of discrimination against the UK. Equally, EEC entry has clearly contributed to the recent rapid growth of imports.[1]

One final factor which may be important in explaining the rising share of imports into the UK is the substantial reduction in tariff and other import restrictions which occurred after 1945. Between 1947 and 1959 the war-time restrictions on imports were virtually eliminated,[2] and from 1955 onwards the UK tariff was progressively reduced in line with agreements concluded through GATT. The UK tariff, introduced in 1932, had developed as a two-part structure with many imports from Commonwealth producers entering the UK duty-free, and imports from the rest of the world being subject to duties which, in the case of manufactures, ranged from 10% to 33%.[3] Between 1959 and 1975 the average UK tariff on semi-manufactures fell from 16.2% to 10.5% and that on finished manufactures from 21.4% to 12%. Despite the magnitude of these changes a recent study suggests that their overall effect has proved to be relatively small, increasing the import values for semi-manufactures by 13% and that of finished manufactures by 9% relative to the values they would otherwise have had in 1971.[4]

III   ECONOMIC POLICY AND THE BALANCE OF PAYMENTS
III.1   Introduction

The coverage of this section is limited in two ways. First, pressure of space precludes more than a passing reference to events and policies prior to the floating of sterling in June 1972. Second, the concept of economic policy is limited to government intervention where the prime concern was to produce alterations in flows immediately affecting the balance of payments. It may be argued that *all* economic policy affects the balance of payments since any non-trivial intervention in the economy is likely to produce at least minor alterations in the balance of

---

1   UK membership of the EEC is treated in section III.8 below. See also M. Fetherston, B. Moore and J. Rhodes, 'EEC membership and UK trade in manufactures', *Cambridge Journal of Economics*, December 1979, where it is suggested that the net (trade-creation minus trade-diversion) effect of EEC membership between 1973 and 1977 was to reduce average UK exports by £152m and to increase average UK imports by £994m per annum at 1970 prices.

2   For details see M.F.W. Hemmings, C.M. Miles and G.F. Ray, 'A Statistical Summary of the Extent of Import Control in the UK since the War', *RES*, Vol. 26, pp. 75-109.

3   In 1957 the average margin of preference on dutiable Commonwealth imports was 9%. See PEP, *Commonwealth Preference in the UK*, 1960. The swing in UK trade toward manufactures and the advanced industrialized nations progressively made this degree of preference less important.

4   A.D. Morgan and A. Martin, 'Tariff Reductions and UK Imports of Manufactures 1955-71', *NIER*, No. 72, May 1975. It is possible that this study understates the true reduction in protection afforded to UK manufacturing industry because it deals only with nominal tariff rates and not effective tariff rates — the effective rate taking into account the impact of tariff changes on the cost of imported means of production. Recent calculations for the period 1968-72 show that while the nominal rate on manufactures fell by 36%, the effective rate fell by 46%. M. Oulton, 'Tariffs, Taxes and Trade in the UK: The Effective Protection Approach', *Government Economic Service Occasional Papers No. 6*, 1973, p. 9.

forces affecting trade and payments flows. Some policies may well have major implications for trade but, for present purposes, are not regarded as balance of payments policies. Thus, attempts to control inflation or to stimulate efficiency and growth are likely, if successful, to have substantial impacts on trade flows, but these problems are discussed elsewhere in this book and, in any case, may be judged desirable for reasons other than those concerned with the balance of payments. Equally, policies which are directed explicitly at trade flows may involve related adjustments in 'domestic' policy, as we shall see below in the discussion of exchange-rate management. Manipulation of tariff and other barriers to trade is a legitimate branch of balance of payments policy, but, in practice, government action of this nature is circumscribed by international agreements, and again pressure of space precludes more than a cursory discussion of what might be done within these constraints. Entry to the EEC is obviously a policy decision of incalculable magnitude affecting all aspects of economic behaviour but this section will confine itself to some balance of payments implications of that decision. The influence of the international monetary system for UK policy is so important that we conclude the section by looking at recent developments in that field.

When interpreting the following discussion it is important to remember that the conduct of balance of payments policy, or for that matter of economic policy in general, is not a matter of 'fine tuning'. In part this reflects the fact that UK balance of payments performance is as much determined by the economic policies adopted in other countries as it is by policies adopted in the UK. On top of this, familiar problems of forecasting the direction and rate of change of economic variables, political and other limitations on the values of policy variables, and conflict between different policy objectives, taken together, mean that practical policy-making is more an art than a science.

III.2 The Exchange Market Framework

It is a familiar proposition that modern industrial economies have evolved by means of a progressive division of labour and that one important condition for this is the adoption of a single internal currency, to act as an intermediary in all economic transactions. The international division of labour has so far, however, proceeded without this advantage. Since nations continue to maintain separate currencies for internal use, it follows that international transactions must proceed with the simultaneous exchange of national currencies, apart, that is, from those transactions conducted in key currencies. This exchange of currencies takes place in the foreign exchange market and it is there that the relative prices of different national currencies, exchange rates, are established.

An important policy issue which faces the government of any country is, therefore, that of the degree of restraint which it wished to place on the exchange of its own currency with the currencies of other nations. Not only will the chosen restraints limit the type and geographical direction of transaction which domestic residents may make with foreigners, but they will also have an important bearing upon the conduct of policy to achieve internal objectives such as full employment and price stability. Successive UK governments have exercised their options in two ways: by adopting particular forms of exchange-rate policy, and by placing restrictions upon the currencies against which sterling may be exchanged for the pursuit of specified transactions, i.e., by exchange control.

Between 1945 and June 1972 the UK operated the foreign exchange market for sterling in accordance with the rules of the par-value system.[1] This required the official adoption of a par value for sterling to be expressed in terms of gold or the US dollar of 1944 fineness together with the acceptance of a band of fluctuation of the spot rate around the par value.[2]

Provided the spot rate[3] for sterling, as determined by market forces, lay within the permitted band, the UK exchange authorities did not need to take any action. However, should the exchange rate be under pressure to stray outside this permitted band then the exchange authorities were obliged to intervene in the foreign exchange market, selling foreign exchange from the reserves when sterling was at its lower limit and purchasing foreign exchange to add to the reserves when sterling was at its upper limit. Thus the par-value system allowed some degree of variability in the foreign exchange rate but required that the UK keep a buffer stock of foreign exchange reserves, which it could use to maintain the exchange rate within the specified bounds.

It must be noted that the par value of a currency was not fixed for all time once a country decided to abide by this system. On the contrary, a country could, when its balance of payments was in 'fundamental disequilibrium' and after consultation with the IMF, change its par value. This UK governments did twice, devaluing sterling in 1949 and again in 1967.

In contrast to what is required in the market for spot exchange, IMF rules placed no formal restrictions on the movements of forward exchange rates for a currency. Nor were any necessary. In normal circumstances, the forward exchange rate will stand in a simple relationship[4] to the spot exchange rate, reflecting the role of the forward market in providing cover for the exchange risks inherent in spot market transactions.

A major change in UK policy occurred in June 1972, when the par-value system was 'temporarily' abandoned and sterling allowed to take whatever values the balance of demand and supply for foreign exchange might dictate. However, a policy of allowing sterling to float has not meant that the exchange market ceases to be an object of policy concern. The government still has to decide to what extent sterling will float freely, without official constraint, and thus to what extent it is going to manage the exchange rate. Recent UK experience suggests a

---

1 This is the name given to the exchange-rate system adopted by the majority of Western nations after the Second World War. The central body of the system is the International Monetary Fund (IMF).

2 Until December 1971 the permitted band of fluctuation was 1% on either side of par. Under the Smithsonian reforms of that time the band was widened to 2¼% on either side of par. The gold par values of different currencies determined their par exchange rates.

3 A distinction must be made between the spot-market and the forward-market exchange rates for a currency. The spot exchange rate is the price of foreign currency for immediate delivery, that is, at the time the rate for the transaction is agreed. A forward exchange rate is the price of foreign currency for delivery at a specified date in the future.

4 This is the interest parity relationship. Provided interest arbitrage funds are in perfectly elastic supply then the percentage difference between spot and forward exchange rates for any pair of currencies will equal the interest differential on assets of the appropriate maturities denominated in those currencies. However, with arbitrage funds not in infinitely elastic supply, the forward rate will deviate from the interest parity value. In the limit, when the supply of speculative funds to the forward market is infinitely elastic, the forward rate will equal the value of the spot rate expected to hold at the time forward contacts mature.

considerable degree of exchange management to iron out potentially violent fluctuations in the spot rate without, if possible, influencing its longer-term trend.

The second important aspect of UK exchange policy is that of exchange control, and here 1979 saw some important changes when, in October, the exchange control restrictions which had been built up since 1945 were abolished. Exchange control is a complex issue with a detailed history of evolution, so that space precludes more than the most general remarks.[1] The legal basis of exchange control is contained in the Exchange Control Act of 1947, which assigns to the Treasury the authority to formulate exchange-control policy. The day-to-day responsibility for implementing the exchange-control provisions is delegated to the Bank of England, while, in turn, the daily volume of foreign currency transactions is handled by authorized exchange dealers, i.e. the commercial banks. The Exchange Equalization Account acts only as a residual purchaser or seller of foreign exchange in order to support a given exchange rate. As far as UK residents were concerned, practice after 1960 was to allow complete freedom for current transactions[2] but to restrict transactions on capital account in various ways. Exchange control in the UK was greatly complicated by the international-reserve and medium-of-exchange functions of sterling, which result in foreigners holding sterling balances. After 1958 a distinction was maintained between two such categories of sterling, external-account sterling and resident sterling. External-account sterling consisted of sterling balances held by non-sterling-area residents. This was freely convertible into any currency for current and capital transactions. Resident sterling consisted of sterling balances held by residents of the UK and, of the overseas sterling areas, who were treated in the same fashion as UK residents, i.e. allowed full convertibility on current account but restricted convertibility for capital transactions to non-sterling-area countries.

From 1958 UK exchange-control regulations stayed broadly unchanged. However, with the float of sterling in 1972 several modifications were required, which essentially involved giving the former sterling-area countries external-account status. By October 1979 the sterling area, for exchange-control purposes, consisted only of a handful of countries.[3] The major implications of the abandonment of exchange controls relate to capital-account transactions and these are discussed in more detail in sections III.6 and III.7.

III.3   External Economic Policy with a Floating Exchange Rate

In June 1972 the UK abandoned its commitment to the par-value system and sterling began to float relative to other currencies. By the middle of 1973 sterling had been joined in this respect by all other major currencies, so that for the advanced industrial nations as a whole the par-value system had been abandoned. With sterling only one of many currencies engaged in a simultaneous float, there is no simple index of movements in the international value of sterling. Sterling may

---

1   A useful historical account of UK exchange control will be found in B. Tew, *International Monetary Co-operation 1945-1970.* Hutchinson, 1970, The interested reader may also consult the IMF *Annual Reports on Exchange Restrictions.*

2   Apart, that is, from certain restrictions on the availability of exchange for foreign travel and for the making of gifts and other transfers to non-sterling area residents.

3   See footnote 1 on page 121 above.

appreciate in terms of some currencies while, at the same time, it depreciates in terms of others. Current practice is to rely upon the, so-called, 'effective exchange rate', which is a suitably weighted average of the movements of sterling compared to the currencies of those countries which are most important in UK trade.[1]

The movement in the effective exchange rate since June 1972 can be divided conveniently into three phases. The first, to November 1976, was one of almost continual depreciation, with the movement being particularly rapid after February 1976. In the last quarter of that year, the effective rate averaged 59.6 compared to an average of 72.0 in the first quarter and an average of 95.2 in 1972. Between the end of 1976 and the end of 1978 the effective rate was remarkably stable, rarely deviating more than 2% points either side of an average quarterly value of 62.6. The final phase, from January 1979, has been one of steady appreciation, the effective rate ending the year at 70.2. The movement of sterling relative to individual currencies, in particular the dollar, has been much more volatile although the broad trends have mirrored that of the effective exchange rate. Before we analyse the causes of these movements it will prove useful to outline some of the more important economic implications of floating exchange rates.

Floating Rates and Economic Policy: The case for floating exchange rates rests, in large part, upon the alleged simplicity and automaticity of the free-market mechanism in re-allocating resources in response to changing circumstances. In a dynamic world in which comparative advantages change rapidly and national inflation rates differ, changes in exchange rates are necessary if widespread under-utilization of productive resources is to be avoided. The advantage of floating rates, it is argued, is that the necessary changes can occur progressively at a pace dictated by the costs and profitability of resource allocation, and not, as with the par-value system, by sudden, discrete jumps dictated by speculative pressure and political expediency. The resource-allocation advantages are only one aspect of the benefits derivable from the adoption of a floating exchange rate. More important for present purposes are the implications for the conduct of macroeconomic policy. For it seems clear that with a more flexible exchange-rate policy the UK could have avoided most of the policy dilemmas of the period 1960-71, and that the period since 1971 would have generated impossible policy contradictions had the UK adhered to the par-value system.

There is, first, the minor point that the government no longer has to decide what constitutes an equilibrium exchange rate; to a large extent, this will be decided automatically within the foreign exchange market. One cannot go from this, however, to suggest that the conduct of domestic economic policy can proceed independently of developments in the foreign exchange market. The correct management of domestic demand is just as important with a floating exchange rate as it is with a fixed exchange rate. Balance of payments problems do not disappear with the adoption of a floating exchange rate, they are simply manifested in different forms. Developments that would lead to a loss of reserves with a fixed exchange rate, lead to a depreciation in the foreign exchange value of the currency if the exchange rate is allowed to float. In the first case, the loss of reserves will result, unless it is a once-and-for-all loss, in a policy-induced contraction in domestic income, while with a floating rate, the loss in real domestic purchasing

---

1   For details see *ET*, June 1974, *BEQB*, March 1977 and *TER*, March 1977.

power occurs automatically as the prices of tradeable commodities rise with the currency depreciation.

The main advantage of a floating rate is that it allows a greater independence of domestic economic policy-making. In particular, full-employment objectives may be more consistently pursued; there being some value of the exchange rate which will give exactly a zero currency flow at any, non-inflationary, level of employment. Furthermore, since a floating rate provides the minimum of linkage between the circular income of different trading nations, it follows that a floating exchange rate will isolate the level of demand for UK goods from changes in foreign incomes and preferences for UK goods. An increase in foreign demand which, under a fixed rate, would generate a multiple expansion in UK incomes, now generates an appreciation of the sterling rate of exchange, such that the final increase in the value of UK exports is exactly matched by an appreciation-induced increase in the value of UK imports, i.e. in domestic expenditure on foreign goods. The total demand for UK goods, and therefore UK incomes, will remain unchanged.[1] The isolation of domestic incomes from external changes in demand has, of course, as counterpart the proposition that the level of domestic income is more sensitive to changes in the level of *domestic* money expenditure. In this respect, an economy with a floating exchange rate will behave in the same manner as a closed economy; the effects of changes in foreign trade upon the circular flow of income are completely negated. The policy consequence of this is that the multiplier repercussions of monetary and fiscal policy will be greater in an economy with a floating exchange rate than in the same economy with a fixed exchange rate.[2] Correspondingly, the cost of mistakes in demand management will be increased with a floating rate and so policy must be conducted with greater attention to underlying economic circumstances.

Other Implications of Floating Rates: The relative merits of fixed and floating exchange rates are matters of considerable controversy among economists. Some of the alleged advantages of flexible exchange rates have already been mentioned. The object of the present section is to deal with two less clearcut aspects of the controversy. In particular, the view that private speculation will convert floating exchange rates into wildly fluctuating rates, and the view that a floating rate increases the uncertainty faced by international traders and investors to the detriment of the international division of labour.

The case for and against floating rates depends essentially on the view taken of the effects of speculation in the operation of free markets. If these markets are to be cleared continuously, without undue fluctuations in the exchange rate, it is essential that speculators take over the role of the monetary authorities and operate in a stabilizing manner, selling sterling when the rate is temporarily 'too high' and buying sterling when the rate is temporarily 'too low'. Temporary fluctuations in the exchange rate follow, in part, because daily imbalances in the demand and

---

1 A more detailed discussion would have to modify this argument, in respect of any change in the aggregate savings ratio which followed the exchange appreciation and the possible effects on demand of any changes in international interest-rate levels.

2 Again this is subject to qualifications, depending upon the sensitivity of international capital movements to policy-induced changes in interest rates and the time span considered for analysis. With floating rates a greater degree of interest sensitivity of capital flows enhances the potency of monetary policy and limits the potency of fiscal policy for the management of aggregate demand.

supply for foreign exchange will result from random and seasonal factors, even if the balance of payments is basically in equilibrium over a longer time span, and because short-period trading adjustments to relative price changes are likely to be inelastic. The proponents of floating exchange rates argue that speculative activity will be stabilizing and that speculators will be able to predict the trend value of the exchange rate so as to ensure minimal variation in the actual exchange rate around the trend value. Opponents fear that this will not be the case and the exchange market will be dominated by too much uncertainty for speculators to recognize the appropriate trend. Successive waves of optimism and pessimism will follow the frequent revision of expectations, and generate substantial movements in exchange rates, out of all proportion to the volume of trading.

The difficulty with the above arguments is that we have little factual evidence to decide either way. Certainly the period with floating rates has witnessed some sudden, sharp movements in exchange rates out of step with underlying economic circumstances. Thus, for example, between end-September and end-October 1979 sterling depreciated by 6.0% against the dollar; it then appreciated to completely reverse this movement by end-November. On the other hand, the average daily movement of the sterling-dollar rate over the period 1976-8 comes to 0.03 percentage points, which is not excessive and is well within the limits permissible under the par-value system. However, should private speculation prove to be less stabilizing than is thought desirable, there is no reason why the authorities should not engage in 'official' speculation, if necessary at the expense of private operators. Indeed this is precisely what the authorities have undertaken when supporting the sterling par-value against speculative pressure and when managing the exchange rate over various periods since June 1972. The implication is, of course, that even with a floating exchange rate the authorities must maintain a stock of exchange reserves. Widespread adoption of exchange-management practices would also require the institution of international co-ordination and surveillance of exchange-rate practices — this appears neither impossible nor undesirable within the framework of an existing body such as the IMF (see section III.9 below). Finally, it must not be overlooked that destabilizing speculation can disrupt any exchange-rate framework and clearly did so with the par-value system. One of the major drawbacks of the par-value system was that it gave a one-way option to currency speculators. A currency under pressure would be pushed to one of the official intervention limits. This immediately signalled the possibility of a change in par value in a direction in which no one could have any doubt. Naturally, a large and cumulative movement of funds across the exchanges was therefore encouraged. A likely advantage of floating exchange rates is that the problem of a one-way speculative option will be much reduced.

The view taken of the effects of speculation determines the importance of the arguments on uncertainty and the inhibition of trade and investment. Provided that floating rates do not fluctuate wildly there is no reason why the bulk of trade and investment should be seriously affected. After all, exchange risks can always be covered with simultaneous deals in spot and forward markets. For sterling transactions involving the major currencies, the foreign exchange market currently provides active dealings for contracts up to one year in duration. Since some 92% of UK exports are financed on credit terms of less than six months' duration,[1] with,

---

1   See Business Statistics Office, *Business Monitor MA4: Overseas Transactions 1977*, HMSO, 1979.

no doubt, a similar proportion for imports, there should be no difficulty in traders covering their exchange risks. Longer-term trade contracts and international investment projects will face problems but then, in an uncertain world, they always will. In addition it is argued that, should the forward premium on sterling exceed the appropriate interest differential, then traders will have to face extra costs of finance. There are two counter-arguments to this. First, the difference between forward premia and interest differentials will be smaller, the greater is the response of international capital flows to arbitrage possibilities. Particularly now that UK exchange controls have been relaxed, there is no reason to expect the costs of forward cover to be prohibitive. Secondly, suppose it could be demonstrated convincingly that additional exchange-rate uncertainty had reduced trade and investment. This could still not constitute an argument against floating rates, until the claimed costs could be shown to be greater than the employment and resource mis-allocation costs imposed under a par-value system.

III.4   The Exchange Rate and the Balance of Payments, 1972-9

In section I.3 we have outlined the rapid changes in the UK's external position in the 1970s, showing that from an initial surplus the current account moved into substantial deficit during 1973-6 and then recovered until 1979. On the domestic front, as other chapters show, this period saw very rapid and variable inflation rates, high and variable interest rates and the emergence of substantial unemployment. The purpose of this section is to outline some of the major factors leading to the changes in the current account and the exchange rate during the period and their relation to domestic and international events. The first point to be clear upon when interpreting the events of the period is that the exchange rate for sterling has not been allowed to float freely, rather it has been managed quite actively, and this policy has produced economic effects which are a mixture of those occurring under the extremes of fixed and freely floating rates. Since the equilibrium exchange rate at any point in time reflects the balance of demand and supply of foreign exchange, it is useful to begin with an outline of the major forces affecting the volume of autonomous external transactions.

Purchasing-Power Parity: A convenient place to begin is the theory which relates the values taken by a currency's exchange rate to its purchasing-power parity. Broadly speaking, this means that the equilibrium exchange rate between the currencies of two countries is proportional to the ratio of the price levels of the respective countries. Moreover, providing this factor of proportionality remains constant, the proportionate rate of change of the exchange rate will be approximately equal to the difference between the inflation rates in the two countries.[1] The proximate source of the depreciation of sterling between 1972 and

---

1 Probably the clearest statement of the purchasing-power parity theory is still contained in J.M. Keynes, *A Tract on Monetary Reform*, Macmillan, 1923, pp. 87-106. For a recent survey, see L.H. Officer, 'The Purchasing Power Parity Theory of Exchange Rates: A Review Article', *IMF Staff Papers*, Vol. 23, 1976. The exact formula for the percentage change in purchasing-power parity between two dates is $(P'-P)/(1+P)$, where P and P' are the proportionate changes in the domestic and foreign price levels.

end-1976 can then be found in the excess of the UK rate of inflation over a suitably weighted average of the inflation rates in her major trading partners, it being a matter of indifference what the source of this inflation differential may be, whether it be related to excessive monetary expansion in the UK or to excessive wage push by UK trade unions. To investigate this further we may compare the movement in the UK's effective exchange rate, in the computation of which the OECD countries have a weight of 89%, with the movements in the consumer price indices in the UK and the combined OECD countries. Between end-1972 and end-1976, the ratio of the OECD to the UK price levels fell by 19%, while the effective rate for sterling fell by 32%. Clearly sterling depreciated more quickly than purchasing-power parity changes alone would suggest, particularly during 1976, and ended the period 16% points below purchasing-power parity. Between end-1976 and end-1978 the effective rate for sterling remained constant. However, the appreciation of sterling in 1979, combined with a further decline in purchasing-power parity, meant that sterling ended 1979 with an effective rate 4% points above purchasing-power parity. This catching-up of the exchange rate fits in well with industrialist's concern during 1979, that an overvalued exchange rate was adversely affecting UK exports. Of course, these calculations are rather rough and ready and depend crucially upon an assumption, not unwarranted, that sterling was at purchasing-power parity in 1972. Nevertheless, they are sufficiently robust to serve as a basis for discussion.

The first question is why sterling depreciated more quickly than purchasing-power parity between 1972 and 1976. An important factor here is that the purchasing-power parity theory only holds true if economic structure remains constant during the comparisons. In a full analysis it is important to take account of cyclical fluctuations in output, of differences in productivity growth and the quality dimensions of international competition, of changes in domestic and foreign profit and interest rates, and of changes in tariff structure and geographic trading patterns, for example through the effects of UK membership of the EEC. (See section II.) Furthermore, account would have to be taken, in so far as they affect short-term capital flows, of exchange-rate expectations. For example, fears of an acceleration in the future rate of UK inflation may well have created the sharp depreciation of sterling during 1976 in anticipation of a future decline in purchasing-power parity. On this view it is the somewhat tenuous state of inflation expectations which governs the short-run relation between the exchange rate and actual purchasing-power parity. Of much greater importance, however, has been the change in the terms of trade since 1972 and the progress of the UK towards self-sufficiency in oil. These important changes in economic structure were bound to make the effective exchange rate deviate from purchasing-power parity. The primary element here was the increase in the foreign currency prices of imported materials, foodstuffs and oil. Between 1972 and 1974 the average SDR price of primary commodities, excluding oil, increased by 107%. From this peak prices subsequently fell, the 1976 index indicating an 84% increase over 1972, but with a rising trend from then on they ended 1979 120% above the 1972 level. Relative to the prices of world exports of manufactures, however, 1976 saw primary commodity prices only 20% more expensive compared to 1972, and 1979 (3rd quarter) saw them only 17% more expensive. Indeed apart from 1974 and 1977, the terms of trade between primary products and manufactures have rarely varied more than 20% from the 1972 norm. Without question, the most significant price change was that relating to the quadrupling of the posted price of oil by the OPEC nations at the end of 1973, which increased the cif price of oil to the UK from $3.45 per barrel to $11.58 per barrel.[1] The implications of this development were considerable and worldwide, affecting not only individual economies but also the stability of the international monetary system. Some of the wider issues are treated in section III.9 below. Between 1975 and 1978 the price of oil relative to world manufactured exports remained constant at roughly 168% of the 1972-3 level. However, the increase in the oil price from June 1979 takes the 1980 price to $20.5 per barrel, with a forecast price for 1985 of $40 per barrel, representing an estimated increase in the real price of oil of 72% above the 1978 level. The effects of these price changes on the UK current account after 1973 were indeed dramatic, and it is interesting to note that relative price changes rather than quantity changes have been the major influence on the current account; the exact reverse of the situation in the 1960s. Thus between 1972 and 1976 relative price changes worsened the non-oil balance of trade by an average of £248m per annum and the oil balance by an average of £925m per annum, and these effects are far greater than the contemporaneous quantity effects on the trade balance.[2] It is not surprising, with the current-account deficits experienced between 1972 and 1976, that the effective exchange rate for sterling would have fallen more quickly than purchasing-power parity would indicate. The rapid slide of sterling also contributed to the deterioration of the UK terms of trade over this period. In 1976 the terms of trade were 19% below their 1972 level, a deterioration which may be decomposed into a 111% increase in sterling export prices, a 79% increase in foreign currency import prices and a 31.3% depreciation in the effective exchange rate.

As the short-run elasticity of demand for oil and commodity imports does not differ appreciably from zero, the impact effect of the oil and other price increases was simultaneously to worsen the trade balance and to generate deflationary pressure in the UK economy. It is as if the UK government had raised indirect taxes, so cutting the demand for UK output, and had then transferred the tax proceeds to the oil-producing and primary-commodity-producing nations. In addition, the similar effects on other industrial economies produced cuts in the demand for UK exports and so provided a further deflationary stimulus: while very little help could be expected in the short run from the spending of OPEC funds on UK-produced goods.

Several options were open to the government to deal with this situation. It could have attempted to eliminate the current-account deficit either by a severe policy-induced cut in aggregate demand, or by allowing the exchange rate to depreciate sufficiently to improve the non-oil trade balance of the UK at the expense of the other industrialized countries. Neither option has proved to be feasible or otherwise desirable. The only effective policy proved to be that of substantial foreign borrowing, combined with a broadly neutral stance toward domestic aggregate demand.[3] Over the period 1972-6 the net outcome for the UK

---

1 The posted price should not be confused with the market price of oil. The posted price is the administrative price from which the OPEC countries assess the royalty payments and tax payments due from the oil-extracting companies.

2 See the article, 'The Terms of Trade', *BEQB*, September 1978.

3 Although the March 1975 budget was intended to produce substantial cuts in the government borrowing requirement, it can be argued that their net effect on the aggregate demand was negligible. See *NIER*, May 1975, p. 11. A more deflationary stance was adopted in 1976 and 1977 announcing further reductions in future public expenditure. Calculations suggest, however, that over the period 1975/7 the net stance of fiscal policy had a small stimulating effect on the economy. See the article, 'Why is Britain in Recession', *BEQB*, March 1978.

was therefore one of rising external indebtedness, combined with falling domestic production as the deflationary effects of the change in the terms of trade worked through to expenditure and demand.

Foreign borrowing has taken place under three separate headings. Prior to 1973, the OPEC oil-producers traditionally received about 25% of their oil revenue in sterling and normally deposited this as sterling balances in London. With the increase in oil revenues following the Tehran agreement, the immediate response was to place much of the surplus in London. In 1974 some 37% of surplus oil funds, a total of $21 billion, was placed in London. In the subsequent years the total amount of short-term finance made available in this way declined considerably in the face of falling surplus oil revenues and an increasing unwillingness to deposit funds in a depreciating currency. In fact, between 1975-7 only $4bn to $4.5bn flowed into the UK, on an annual basis, representing 12%-14% of surplus oil funds. The second important source of finance has been nationalized-industry and local-authority borrowing under the Treasury exchange cover scheme. Much of this has been in the form of OPEC funds taken out of the euro-dollar market in the form of medium-term (3-7 year) loans. Some $3.4bn was raised in this way in the two years to the end of 1975 and a further $3.6bn to the end of 1977. Finally, the UK government has itself engaged in substantial borrowing. Most important here have been the $2.5bn and $1.5bn loans raised from the euro-dollar market in 1974 and 1977, the $2bn borrowed from the IMF at the end of 1975 – 60% of which represented a drawing on the specially created oil facility – and the stand-by agreement with the IMF agreed at the end of 1976 under which the UK could draw $3.9bn from its remaining credit tranches, $1.2bn being taken in January 1977.

While the policy of foreign borrowing allowed the UK to accommodate its payments deficit in anticipation of the benefits of NS oil, it also clearly prevented the exchange rate from dropping even further below purchasing-power parity than it did. As pointed out in section I.4, this increased external debt and has created an interest and amortization burden which implies the need for a substantial UK current-account surplus in the 1980s. The major change relevant to the 1977-9 period is the growth in production from the NS oil fields, which has turned the current account towards a surplus and effectively insulated the terms of trade from future variations in the relative price of oil. The appreciation of sterling during 1979 and its catching-up with purchasing-power parity has been almost entirely due to the direct effects of NS oil on the current account, together with the indirect effects on confidence which encouraged substantial capital inflows into the UK during 1979. With the expected gains in the relative price of oil in the early 1980s it is anticipated that sterling investments will continue to provide an attractive haven for future surplus OPEC oil revenues. Over the period 1977-9 the sterling effective exchange rate rose by 14% and this was associated with an improvement in the terms of trade of 6%, with sterling export prices increasing by 21% and foreign currency import prices rising by 30%. The net outcome of this discussion is that while the effective exchange rate for sterling has been influenced by changes in purchasing-power parity, changes in real forces and in particular relative primary commodity and energy prices have also been an important underlying factor behind changes in the effective exchange rate during the 1970s. Furthermore, the short-run movement of the exchange rate has been influenced at times by substantial short-term capital flows and by the official policy, up to 1978, of supporting the exchange rate through foreign borrowing.

III.5   Management of the Exchange Rate

In the previous section we have seen how the sterling exchange rate has been heavily managed at times during the period since 1972, the primary weapons in this management being foreign currency borrowing and changes in the stock of UK foreign exchange reserves.

There are several important reasons why a government may wish to manage the exchange rate. In the first instance it may view changes in the demand and supply of foreign exchange as temporary and so act as a speculator to prevent such temporary changes in the balance of autonomous transactions from influencing the exchange rate. Such a policy could be justified as a way to minimize the disruptive effects of temporary exchange-rate variations on trade and investment. As a second example, the government may take a view that the balance of autonomous transactions has shifted permanently but at the same time considers that an immediate full adjustment of the exchange rate would be too disruptive to patterns of employment and resource allocation. The exchange rate could then be actively managed toward its new long-run level at a pace which allows the pattern of resource allocation to change smoothly. The problem with this line of argument is, of course, the familiar one — how does the government know the exchange rate appropriate to different sets of internal and external circumstances? Too easily a policy of 'leaning into the wind' may become a policy of manipulation of the exchange rate to satisfy other objectives.

One very important such objective in the UK context could be that of engineering a depreciation of sterling to maintain or increase the competitiveness of UK manufacturing exports and import substitutes. This policy could be justified in terms of offsetting the medium-term effects on the sterling exchange rate of NS oil which, if left unchecked, could undermine the competitiveness of UK industry and leave the country with greatly diminished foreign exchange earning power when the NS oil resources are exhausted. The appreciation of sterling during 1979 brought this problem to the forefront of discussion, with increasing concern about the de-industrialization of the non-oil sector of UK industry. The mechanism of a managed depreciation would be as follows. The impact effect would be to change relative prices. The relative prices of tradeable commodities, exports, imports and their close substitutes will increase and, depending on the pricing policies of domestic and foreign firms,[1] the terms of trade will typically deteriorate as sterling import prices rise relative to sterling export prices. The changes in relative prices then induce substitutions in patterns of production and consumption which, though they may at first be negligible, grow in magnitude as contracts are re-negotiated and as new plant and equipment is installed to take advantage of changed profit opportunities. Available evidence would suggest that the magnitudes of these quantitative responses do produce a long-run improvement in the trade

---

1   On the pricing policies of UK firms following the 1967 devaluation, see P.B. Rosendale, 'The Short-Run Pricing Policies of Some British Engineering Exporters', *NIER*, No. 65, 1973, and the valuable study by D.C. Hague, E. Oakeshott and A. Strain, *Devaluation and Pricing Decisions*, Allen and Unwin, 1974. Professor Cooper has suggested that foreign suppliers cut their foreign currency prices on average by 4%. See A.K. Cairncross (ed.), *Britain's Economic Prospects Reconsidered*, Allen and Unwin, 1971, p. 181.

balance.[1] There may, however, be an initial deterioration as a result of the adverse terms of trade effect, the so-called 'J' curve response to depreciation, as the immediate effects on relative prices precede the longer-term quantitative responses of trade flows.

Even if the elasticities of foreign and domestic demand and supply are of the right magnitude the effects do not stop there. To the extent that the trade balance improves in terms of home currency, the aggregate demand for UK goods will have increased and this, via the multiplier effects on income, will create subsequent and partially offsetting increases in the demand for imports. Furthermore, if the economy is at or near to full employment, the devaluation-induced expansion of aggregate demand will have inflationary implications which can only be prevented by reducing domestic expenditure to make room for the improvement of the trade balance. Finally, account must be taken of the import content of domestic production, and the effect of the devaluation in raising domestic costs of production and of its effects in creating pressure for higher money wages.[2] This latter qualification is of prime importance, for unless the depreciation is associated with a reduction in real wages then the only effect of a real depreciation of sterling will be to lower the long-run profitability of UK manufacturing industry. Furthermore, if domestic firms follow pricing policies to maintain rates of return on capital then the effects of the depreciation will be purely nominal and there will not be any long-run effect on flows of exports and imports. The conclusion to be drawn from this is that powerful forces are at work to offset the initial effects of a managed depreciation on the balance of trade. Indeed recent calculations show that the effects of a hypothetical depreciation in sterling are largely transitory with respect to the level of output and the current balance of payments, and that after six years a devaluation of 5% would produce a 4% increase in the UK's retail price index. These calculations also make clear that the effects of a devaluation depend on the fiscal policies and other policies to control money incomes which accompany the depreciation.[3] Certainly the depreciation of sterling in 1976 only produced a temporary increase in the international competitiveness of UK goods which had been entirely eroded by the beginning of 1979. Discussion of the inflationary effects of an exchange depreciation raises another reason why a government may wish to actively manage the exchange rate. Some of the arguments here were stimulated by the sharp depreciation of sterling in 1976, which accelerated the rate of inflation after a period in which domestic incomes restraint had reduced the rate of increase of unit labour costs in the UK from 30% in 1975 to 11% in 1976. It has been suggested, therefore, that a managed appreciation of sterling would help to combat domestic inflation. The argument is simply that the rate of inflation is influenced by the pressure of demand in the

---

1 In the special case in which there is initial balanced trade and supply elasticities of traded goods are infinite, then the depreciation improves the trade balance provided that the sum of the foreign and domestic elasticities of demand for imported goods exceeds unity. For a more general statement see C.P. Kindleberger and P.H. Lindert, *International Economics*, Irwin, 1978, chapter 15 and Appendix H. Evidence suggests that this so-called 'Marshall-Lerner' condition would be satisfied for the UK.

2 The average import content of UK manufacturing output is currently 21%.

3 Cf. *TER*, March 1978, No. 96. It is particularly important that the money supply is not allowed to expand and negate the effects of depreciation in reducing real money balances and absorption.

labour market and expectations of inflation, so that a currency appreciation reduces inflation on three fronts. It directly lowers domestic production costs, it reduces the pressure of demand for labour by its adverse effects on the demand for UK output, and by reducing inflation in this direct fashion it has the indirect effect of lowering the anticipated rate of inflation, thus moderating money wage demands and possibly increasing the viability of attempts to directly influence money wages. The effectiveness of such a policy must, however, be questioned, not least because of the ambiguity over whether any persistent change in the exchange rate is a cause of, or an implication of, domestically generated inflation. Indeed if it were the case that inflation expectations were formed, for example, from a knowledge of rates of growth of UK monetary aggregates, then the exchange rate would also reflect this information and its movements should not have any independent influence on the UK inflation rate. On more practical grounds since imports currently represent only 18%-19% of total UK expenditure, it would seem that the impact effect of, say, a 5% appreciation would at most lower the GDP deflator by 1%. Furthermore, to have any direct effect on the rate of inflation it would require a sustained appreciation of sterling not a once-for-all change in its value. It will be interesting to see whether the appreciation of sterling during 1979 is reflected in lower wage claims in 1980. It will also be clear that the claims made by 'competitiveness' and 'inflation control' upon exchange-rate policy are conflicting, and at the present time, it would appear that the anti-inflation motives for exchange-rate policy have the upper hand.

So far we have taken for granted the view that the exchange rate can be managed to achieve either balance of payments or inflation-rate effects. Such a view may prove excessively optimistic outside the short period. First, one has to recognize that in a world where all the major currencies are floating, governments may follow mutually inconsistent exchange-rate targets and find themselves in a situation of competitive exchange-rate management in which one country's policies are nullified by the action of others. Secondly, experience gained with sterling and other currencies during the 1960s and the 1970s showed that it becomes increasingly difficult for the authorities to maintain an exchange rate substantially different from its equilibrium value without inducing disruptive flows of speculative short-term capital which ultimately force a change in policy. This happened to the UK as recently as October 1977, when the government was forced to abandon its attempts to hold sterling down in the face of substantial capital inflows. Thirdly, and more fundamentally, there are strong arguments to suggest that any attempt to maintain an exchange rate other than that dictated by purchasing-power parity must be a failure in the long run. This argument simply takes account of the fact that any artificial, disequilibrium exchange rate will in general be associated with a non-zero Balance for Official Financing and thus with changes in the stock of foreign exchange reserves and the domestic money supply.[1] If the exchange rate is depreciated, for example, it is argued that this will reduce the real value of monetary assets and induce a temporary trade surplus as agents attempt to restore real asset holdings to their equilibrium levels. This surplus will expand the reserves and the money supply until balance sheets are returned to equilibrium and the pre-devaluation structure of relative prices is regained. The only permanent effect

---

1 For useful accounts of the links between external transactions and the domestic money supply see 'Of DCE, M_3 and Similar Mysteries', *MBR*, February 1977, and 'External and foreign currency flows and the money supply', *BEQB*, December 1978.

of the devaluation will be an equal proportionate increase in the price level and an increase in the stock of foreign exchange reserves. It must be stressed that this is a long-run argument, and that the links between changes in the reserves and the domestic money supply can be offset by domestic monetary policy. However, despite these qualifications it throws into perspective the point that management of the exchange rate is only likely to prove successful in the short run.

Unresolved Issues: Two major issues are likely to dominate future discussion of exchange-rate management in the UK, the uses of the NS oil benefit and the question of a return to full employment in an economy which, as section II.2 discussed, faces a severe balance of payments constraint on its long-term rate of growth.

We have already described the way in which NS oil will temporarily relax the balance of payments constraint imposed on the UK by the 1973 oil price increase and the growing uncompetitiveness of its manufacturing industry. Several options now face the government. One flows from arguing, correctly, that the UK has already had some of this benefit in advance by maintaining output and real incomes above the levels consistent with external balance, and that it was foreign borrowing during 1976 and 1977 which made this possible. The first charge on NS oil revenues is therefore to repay some of the accumulated foreign debt. However, with the OPEC surpluses likely to be greatly increased in the early 1980s it is neither necessary nor desirable to make the repayment of debt the primary use for NS oil revenues. The chief alternative option is to use the oil revenues to stimulate the economy and run a greater import bill. Here several strategies are available. One would be to allow sterling to appreciate and let the stimulus to consumption provided by higher real wages and a lower inflation rate reduce domestic unemployment. The obvious objections to this policy lie in its adverse effects on exports and import penetration and in its failure directly to promote the creation of productive capital assets in the UK. Indeed it is the latter policy – use of the NS oil revenues to reconstruct the UK's industrial base for when the oil benefits are exhausted in the 1990s – which seems to command most attention at the moment.[1] Greater public and private investment in infrastructure, alternative energy sources and industrial plant and equipment will, it is argued, create more employment and raise productivity so that the decline in the UK's industrial competitiveness will be reversed. A further alternative would be to encourage the transfer of the oil revenues into productive foreign assets and this may have been one factor behind the relaxation of exchange controls in October 1979.

The second related issue is that of persistent unemployment in the UK, currently well above the average levels of the 1960s, and the view that in order to eliminate this and at the same time revive UK industry some substantial protection in the form of import restrictions will be required. The argument here is complex and hotly debated but the broad issues are clear enough. To the extent that unemployment in the UK is a reflection of the general world recession induced by the past and expected oil price increases, then there is little to commend import restrictions. To adopt such a policy would be in the worst traditions of beggar-thy-neighbour diplomacy. However, to the extent that the UK's unemployment and lack of competitive edge in world markets reflect structural problems unique to UK

---

1 Cf., *The Challenge of NS Oil*, Cmnd. 7143, HMSO, 1978.

industry, then general import restrictions, provided they are linked to a policy of investment and industrial reconstruction, merit at least a hearing if only because the alternative policy of a sterling depreciation may not prove viable for the reasons outlined above.[1] In response to the argument that foreign retaliation will be provoked it should be remembered that any policy which improves the UK's trade balance and competitive strength, whether it be import restriction, export subsidy or devaluation, must 'harm the foreigner' so that the precise way this is achieved should be a relatively minor matter dictated by the net advantages of each policy for the UK. It should also be remembered that the purpose of such a policy is primarily to stimulate the demand for UK output so that its final effect on UK imports would be smaller than its impact effect, the difference reflecting the induced increase in imports as domestic incomes and employment increase. Indeed as the economy grows the volume of imports can also be allowed to grow in step. Practical objections to such a policy are essentially twofold. First, there are the immediate political difficulties of obtaining EEC and IMF approval, especially as any sensible policy of import restrictions would have to last for fifteen years or so, and would have to be implemented when the favourable balance of payments effects of NS oil are at their height. Second, and more fundamentally, there is no guarantee that higher levels of output and employment will lead to more productive investment, more flexible working practices and a willingness to take innovative risks. If they do not, the import restrictions could prove a recipe for stagnation rather than industrial regeneration.[2] The diagnosis then is quite simple: without a significant increase in the competitive ability of UK industry the long-term prospects for employment and living standards in the UK are quite grim. It is the nature of the medicine which is unknown, and while import controls may be a necessary part of any cure they will certainly not be sufficient of themselves to regenerate the UK industrial structure.

III.6   Short-Term Capital Flows and Balance of Payments Policy

In this section and the next we shall investigate the relationship between capital movements, the balance of payments and the exchange rate. As we have pointed out in section I.2, the distinction between short-term and long-term capital flows is to a considerable extent arbitrary, and the distinctions drawn here reflect matters of convenience alone. By short-term capital movements we shall mean transactions between UK and overseas residents, in currency, bank deposits and securities, transactions which are typically related to the finance of foreign trade or the optimal allocation of stocks of wealth between assets denominated in different currencies. In the next section, on long-term capital flows, we shall be concerned with the international direct investment operations of companies and public-sector bodies.

Short-term capital movements have traditionally played an important role in the overall UK balance of payments situation. Their importance is the joint result of

---

1 The most persistent advocates of this view have been the Cambridge Economic Policy Group, see e.g. their, *Economic Policy Review*, No. 4, March 1978, and the contribution of R. Neild to the book by R.L. Major cited at the end of this chapter.

2 The 7th edition of this volume contains a brief account of the temporary import restrictions employed by the UK in the 1960s.

the position of London as an international financial centre and of the historical role of sterling as an international reserve asset and medium of exchange. Thus some short-term capital movements reflect changes in the sterling balances which foreign governments and individuals have acquired as matters of commercial and financial convenience. The remainder reflect the role of London as the major centre for the Eurocurrency, Eurobond and other international financial markets, with banks in the UK lending and borrowing extensively in dollars and other currencies. The development of the Eurocurrency and related markets since 1958 has meant the increasing integration of European and American capital and money markets.[1] The degree of integration has increased particularly quickly in the 1970s with the rapid growth of the Eurocurrency market, with net deposits of $85bn in 1971 increasing to $480bn in 1978. The volume of deposits and the ease with which they may be switched between currencies has important implications for the stability of exchange rates and for the conduct of national monetary policies.

The significance of short-term capital flows for the conduct of UK policy arises from their magnitude relative to the official reserves and from their volatility. It is convenient to divide the capital flows which influence the UK balance of payments into two broad classes, speculative and non-speculative. The motive behind speculative capital flows is one of making a capital gain from anticipated movements in spot exchange rates. A currency speculator would be indifferent between holding sterling or dollar denominated assets, for example, if the interest rate on sterling assets equalled the interest rate on dollar assets plus the anticipated depreciation of sterling relative to the dollar. If the anticipated sterling devaluation exceeds the sterling interest advantage, holders of sterling assets will switch their assets into dollars, while UK importers will accelerate (lead) dollar payments for imports and UK exporters will try to delay (lag) dollar payments due from foreigners. Non-speculative activities are undertaken to avoid capital gains or losses associated with exchange-rate movements, and involve simultaneous transactions in both spot and forward currency markets so that the risks associated with currency transactions may be shifted onto speculators.[2] In sum, short-term capital movements depend on a complex set of interactions between national interest rates, spot and forward exchange rates and expectations of future changes in spot rates. Not surprisingly, with expectations such an important factor, short-term capital flows are highly volatile and not necessarily responsive to official attempts at their control. During periods of rapidly diverging national rates of inflation, such as experienced since 1972, interest differentials between different countries and expectations of exchange-rate changes will be greatly influenced by expectations of differences in national inflation rates. In a world of high capital mobility, the short-term capital flows induced by the expectation of divergent national inflation rates can exert a dominant influence on the actual movement of the exchange rate, as the depreciation of sterling during 1976 illustrated so graphically. Similarly, the

---

1 Eurocurrency deposits are bank deposits in currencies other than that of the country in which the banks in question are located. For the working and development of the Eurocurrency markets, consult G.W. McKenzie, *The Economics of the Eurocurrency System*, Macmillan, 1976.

2 See the 6th edition of this volume for a discussion of forward market transactions. More detailed treatments will be found in Grubel, *International Economics*, Irwin, chapter 12, and Kindleberger and Lindert, op. cit., chapter 13.

appreciation of sterling during 1979, was no doubt partially influenced by the expectation of a reduction in the UK inflation rate following the firm official commitments to reduce the rate of growth of the UK money supply. Even so, inflation expectations were not the only factors at work. The emergence of the UK as a net oil-exporter has made sterling an attractive currency to hold, particularly given expectations of further increases in the relative price of oil.

The implications of short-term capital flows for external and internal policy depend upon the exchange-market framework in operation. Under the par-value system the first impact of a short-term capital outflow fell upon the exchange reserves, and thus on the monetary base of the banking system, this being true of both speculative and non-speculative flows. Given the poor reserve/short-term liability situation of the UK, any such loss of reserves, if heavy, almost invariably provoked a change in demand management policy. A 'run on sterling' was normally followed by a policy to contract domestic demand and restore 'confidence', frequently in conjunction with foreign borrowing by the government. With a freely floating exchange rate, however, the impact effect of a net capital flow falls not upon the reserves but upon the exchange rate and, in general, will not affect the money supply.[1] A capital outflow will now work to depreciate sterling and an inflow to appreciate sterling. However, any such change in the exchange rate acts upon the current account in the same way as a policy-induced parity change. Hence, a capital outflow has effects akin to those of a devaluation, encouraging exports, discouraging imports and increasing the rate of circular flow of income. It will be clear that large and sudden capital flows can provide difficult policy problems for fully employed economies operating with floating exchange rates.

In the light of this it is relevant to enquire if the UK authorities can exert any substantial influence over short-term capital flows. In the first instance some restraint on UK residents can be obtained via exchange-control provisions which until October 1979 were a major element in UK policy to influence short-term capital flows. Under these provisions UK residents were denied the opportunity to purchase foreign currency except for authorized purposes, and direct limits were placed on the net foreign exchange positions which banks and other exchange dealers could undertaken in the course of their business.[2] A particularly important dimension of exchange control was that limiting purchase of overseas securities by UK residents. From 1947 onwards, purchases of securities issued in non-sterling-area countries could not be financed with official foreign exchange, nor could the proceeds of the liquidation of such investments be converted back into sterling at the official exchange rate. Instead, all such transactions had to pass through the investment currency market at a separate exchange rate which balanced the desire to purchase foreign currency securities with the desire to liquidate existing holdings of NSA assets. Typically the investment currency rate stood at a premium relative to the official exchange rate, the magnitude of the premium providing some indication of the degree of the restriction on potential capital outflows. Between 1950 and 1962 the premium rarely exceeded 10% and was normally less than 5%.

---

1 For a statement of the exceptions to the general rule, see the article, 'External and Foreign Currency Flows and the Money Supply', *BEQB*, December 1978.

2 For details see the article, 'Limits on UK banks' foreign exchange positions', *BEQB*, December 1975. One of the last exchange-control restrictions to be introduced was that of November 1976, forbidding UK banks to finance trade between third countries in sterling. The once-for-all gain to the reserves from this order is estimated to have been £1bn.

However, from 1962 onwards the premium increased substantially, and during the years 1975-8 it varied between a high of 81% (May 1975) and a low of 24% (August 1977) with an average level of 47%.[1] In April 1965 the controls were tightened with the introduction of a 25% surrender rule, under which 25% of the foreign currency proceeds of security sales had to be converted back into sterling at the official exchange rate, a 'tax' which is estimated to have yielded £1.07bn to the reserves between 1965 and end-1977. Further changes occurred in June 1972 when investment in OSA countries was included in the investment currency provisions, and in March 1974 when the surrender rule became applicable to OSA investments. Entry into the EEC however meant that the UK had to abide by the Community directives freeing capital movements within the Community from exchange restriction. To comply with EEC regulations, the surrender rule was abolished in January 1978 though the remaining network of controls was maintained under the escape clause, Article 108 of the Treaty of Rome, of balance of payments protection. The strength of sterling during 1979 and the prospective benefits of NS oil rendered the balance of payments argument for controls nugatory and they were partially relaxed in June 1979 and finally abolished in October 1979. From this date the capital and money markets of the UK became fully integrated with those of the rest of the world. Even so it should be pointed out that the exchange restrictions applied only to UK residents and left untouched the activities of non-resident holders of sterling who since 1958 have been free to switch between sterling and other currencies. The effects of the relaxation of exchange controls should not therefore be overemphasized. Indeed the major impact is likely to be felt through greater competition in capital and money markets rather than in any change in the net flows of capital across the exchanges. Exchange controls apart, two alternative means of inducing capital flows may be employed. Manipulation of domestic interest rates is a powerful weapon in current circumstances, given the increasing integration of financial markets. Its use is subject to two limiting provisos: international retaliation and conflict with the level of interest rates needed to attain internal objectives. The remaining policy option is official manipulation of the forward exchange rate, which would allow the authorities to create for the UK a risk-free interest-rate advantage on short-term investments, as circumstances dictate. Between 1962 and 1967 the UK achieved some success with this policy, effectively counteracting pressure on the reserves on several occasions. Although such a policy may be run at a modest profit for the UK authorities, technical losses arise if the spot rate is changed while official forward contracts are outstanding. This occurred with the 1967 devaluation, when the sum of £366 million had to be paid out to foreigners who at the time held forward contracts to sell sterling. Since that episode, there has been little indication of official forward activity.

The sterling balances, sterling held by non-residents of the UK, have always been of prime importance in the UK payments situation, indeed, to a considerable degree, changes in overseas holdings of sterling, or even the threat of changes, dominated the external economic policy of the UK between 1960 and 1976. During the period 1960-8 the reserve function of sterling placed the UK in the position of an international banker with its gold and currency reserves as backing

---

1 The premium was the percentage difference between the investment currency rate and the spot exchange rate. See the article, 'The Investment Currency Market', *BEQB*, September 1976. The market ceased to exist in October 1979 with the ending of exchange control.

for the short-term external liabilities. As pointed out in section I, the UK's external problems in the 1960s stemmed partly from a grossly inadequate ratio of official reserves to sterling liabilities. The result was a general lack of confidence in the ability of the UK to maintain its banking role, which grew particularly sharp whenever the reserves were used, or threatened to be used, to fulfil their function of financing a deficit. The confidence problem came to a head following the devaluation of 1967 when fears of a second devaluation resulted in many OSA governments liquidating their sterling balances in a policy of reserve diversification. For the OSA countries this simply reflected a rational response to their weakening economic links with the UK. For the UK, however, it represented the demise of a basic ground-rule of the sterling payments system, viz., that OSA countries pool their official holdings of gold and foreign currency in London in exchange for sterling balances. Naturally, this development caused much official concern in the UK and inspired negotiations to obtain international support for sterling, the upshot of which were the Basle arrangements of September 1968. Under the Basle arrangements twelve central banks, together with the Bank for International Settlements, extended a credit of $2bn to the UK, the facility to have a life of ten years. The finance was provided on several conditions, the most important of which was the provision by the UK of a guarantee of the dollar value of each country's official sterling-reserve holding in excess of 10% of its total reserves.[1] An important outcome of these guarantee arrangements, which were terminated at the end of 1974, was that they increased the attractiveness of sterling as a reserve asset. Following the increases in oil prices, commodity prices and the incomes of the primary producing nations in the years 1972-4, the total of official, reserve sterling balances increased to £4.1bn at end-1975 of which 70% was held by oil-exporting nations. At this time 56% of total sterling balances were held as exchange reserves compared with a figure of 35% at end-1968. Though the 1968 Basle arrangements served to perpetuate the reserve role of sterling from a UK viewpoint, from an international perspective the reserve role of sterling declined continually during the years 1970-6. Thus in 1970 sterling holdings accounted for 8.6% of world foreign exchange reserves while by 1976 this proportion had fallen to 1.7%, the former position of sterling being taken over by the deutschmark and the yen.

The precarious nature of the UK's position over the sterling balances became abundantly clear during 1976. In March 1976 the sterling exchange rate against the dollar began a rapid slide from approximately $2.00 to a low of $1.59 reached at the end of October. In the absence of the guarantee arrangements on sterling balances, official holders, and in particular the oil producers, began to diversify out of sterling on a large scale, the total of official balances falling by 38% between the end of March and the end of October to a value of £2.84bn. This reduction occurred despite the fact that the Treasury bill rate in the UK rose over the same period from 8.6% to 14.9%, and at a time when non-official sterling balances actually increased. Faced with this drain upon its foreign exchange reserves the UK government was obliged to seek a new Basle facility in which eleven central banks provided a two-year standby facility of $3bn to cover any withdrawal of official sterling balances below a value of £2.16bn, subject to the proviso that UK official

---

1   See the 7th edition of the volume for a more detailed discussion of the Basle arrangements and their subsequent renegotiation and modification.

reserves be not greater than $6.75bn. As part of the agreement the UK was to 'fund' part of the official sterling balances by offering their holders medium-term bonds in exchange for their sterling holdings.[1] In the event the arrangements proved to be superfluous. The prospect of a strengthening UK payments position, as NS oil began to flow and as the UK inflation rate declined, relative to the weakening US payments position, greatly increased the attractiveness of sterling relative to the dollar. The associated increase in UK reserves and the keeping of official sterling balances above the £2.16bn mark has meant that the 1976 Basle arrangement has never been activated. Indeed by 1979 the total of reserve sterling balances had increased by 26% on their end-1978 value, an increase largely associated with a switch out of dollars by oil-exporting countries.

One of the most interesting developments since 1975 has been the steady growth of sterling balances held by private individuals and organizations. Between end-1975 and end-1979, privately-held sterling balances increased by 143% to a total of £7.80bn. This total represents 70% of total sterling balances, the comparable figure for 1967 being 32%. Despite the growth in sterling balances since 1975 UK gold and currency reserves have increased even faster, with a ratio of reserves to total sterling balances of 36% at end-1975 and 90% at end-1979. It remains to be seen whether the improvement in the reserve/sterling-balance ratio will also be associated with a reduction in the volatility of sterling balances. If not, the problems for exchange-rate management in an era free from exchange controls could be formidable.

There have been several occasions since 1975 when, in the face of substantial short-term capital movements, the UK authorities have sought to hold the exchange rate against sustained external pressures. Three notable occasions when this occurred were between February and April 1976, when the reserves fell by 31%, between June and October 1977, when the reserves increased by 75%, and between March and June 1978, when they again fell by 19%. The normal justification for intervention on this scale is to prevent a movement in the exchange rate leading to too rapid or unnecessary reallocations of resources. On each occasion, however, the authorities were ultimately forced to abandon their interventionist stance and let the exchange rate adjust. The experience of these periods has heightened awareness of the potential conflicts between monetary targets and exchange-rate targets. Certainly the appreciation of sterling during the second half of 1979 took place without more than temporary intervention, since a sustained attempt to hold down sterling would have ignored the real, oil-induced shift in the UK payments position and would have also conflicted with the policy of reducing the rate of growth of the monetary aggregates.

The relaxation of exchange controls could be interpreted as one way of limiting the appreciation of sterling and reducing the associated adverse effects on exports, import penetration and domestic employment. Following the abandonment of exchange controls, UK residents have increased their net holdings of foreign currency assets, largely to adjust asset portfolios, and there may be a more sustained outflow as a larger fraction of the annual flow of UK savings is invested overseas.

---

1 Arrangements for the sale of the bonds were completed by April 1977, with 15 countries taking up bonds to the value of £394m. A choice of bonds was offered with a denomination in terms of four 'hard' currencies with maturities between 5 and 10 years and carrying interest rates between 5 7/8 and 8 7/8%. The bonds did not carry an exchange guarantee.

The future of exchange-rate policy thus seems nicely poised between two possibilities. If a sustained capital inflow into the UK continues then a resort to controls on capital inflows may be forced on the authorities, as with recent experience in Germany and Switzerland. Conversely if confidence in sterling should evaporate, then the possibility of massive speculative outflows may force an early re-imposition of exchange controls on UK residents.

III.7   Long-Term Capital Flows and Balance of Payments Policy

The purpose of this section is to discuss the balance of payments and other consequences of direct investment overseas and to outline the various measures adopted to control overseas investment flows.

Any additional flow of overseas investment by the UK will have immediate and continuing implications for the current and capital accounts of the UK balance of payments. With a fixed or managed exchange rate the impact effect is to reduce foreign exchange reserves, as UK investors acquire the foreign exchange needed for their overseas investment. If we consider direct investment, it is likely that the construction of new capital equipment overseas will involve some increased demand for UK exports of goods and services so that the UK current balance will improve and the charge on the official reserves be reduced accordingly. Should the new flow of foreign investment be associated with a reduction in UK home investment there will be a fall in the level of economic activity in the UK, and activity will increase abroad if the foreign investment leads to additional investment there. There will then be further repercussions on the UK current balance which stem from the multiplier process at home and abroad and the linkage between changes in activity and imports. In practice, the linkage between the capital-account and current-account transactions is likely to be such that the current account improves but not by a sufficient amount to finance the capital outflow without loss of reserves.[1] The total increase in net external assets is therefore smaller than the direct investment outflow. If the capital outflow takes the form of portfolio investment, the impact on the current account is likely to be negligible and such investment will be matched by an equivalent reduction in other net overseas assets.

In addition to the linkages between the trade balance and the flow of direct foreign investment, account must also be taken of the return flow of profit and interest income from overseas investment. In the simplest case of a steady compound growth in the stock of overseas assets in which the assets are acquired without direct resort to foreign borrowing, the return profit inflow will exceed or fall short of the capital outflow according as the rate of return on the foreign investments exceeds or falls short of the percentage rate of growth in the stock of

---

1   The theoretical mechanism which underlies this argument is known as the transfer mechanism and explanations of it may be found in standard textbooks of international economics.

overseas assets. It is not necessarily the case, therefore, that the investment outflow produces a deterioration in the overall balance of payments position, even when we ignore trade linkage effects.[1]

As long as the government aims to maintain a fixed exchange rate, the case for and against control of foreign investment involves balancing the short-term gain to the official reserves from limiting the capital outflow, against the cumulative loss through time of the forgone income from the foreign investment. When a floating exchange rate is adopted this particular problem ceases to be relevant. Any short-term cost to the reserves may be eliminated by an appropriate depreciation of the currency, and this will increase net exports so that the capital outflow may be transferred in real rather than in monetary terms. If full employment is to be maintained by government policy the final increase in net exports will have to be matched by a reduction in domestic investment or consumption. It is then possible to evaluate the costs and benefits of alternative levels of foreign investment by direct comparison of the estimated yields of the foreign investment flows with the forgone yields as resources are moved out of alternative home uses so as to accommodate the real transfer.

This last argument is subject to the qualification that interest and profits earned overseas generate tax revenues that accrue to overseas governments, whereas home investment generates tax revenues for the UK government.[2]

A country may wish to influence the inflow and outflow of long-term capital for a variety of reasons, not least among which relate to the resource-allocation effects of foreign investment and the political and economic implications of an increase in the proportion of domestic capital controlled by foreign residents. In the UK the dominant motives for restrictions on overseas investment have been protection of the exchange reserves and improvement of the balance of payments: motives which were approved under the IMF par-value rules. Policy therefore aimed at encouraging the finance of overseas investment by foreign borrowing and the plough-back of profit earned in existing foreign operations.

The salient features of UK restrictions on UK direct investment overseas can be quickly outlined. As far as investment in the OSA was concerned, direct investment, like portfolio investment, was free from exchange restrictions. This freedom was the *quid pro quo* for the unwritten obligation of OSA countries to

---

1 For a quantitative investigation of the balance of payments effects of UK direct investment overseas see W.B. Reddaway and Associates, *Effects of UK Direct Investment Overseas: Interim Report*, 1967 and *Final Report*, 1968, Cambridge University Press. For every £100 of foreign assets acquired, it was found that the current account improves by £11 in the first year (extra exports) and by £4 in every subsequent year (comprising extra exports and profit receipts, net of foreign taxation and interest payments on accommodating foreign borrowing). These figures suggest that it would take roughly 22 years before a steady capital outflow of £100 per annum becomes self-financing. With 40% foreign borrowing, the time period is reduced to 12 years. These figures well illustrate the short/long-run dilemma with respect to direct investment and the desire of the UK authorities to encourage the finance of investment by foreign borrowing. The Reddaway examples were based on a constant annual foreign investment outflow, not on an outflow growing at a constant rate.

2 A further qualification is that any depreciation designed to accommodate an additional flow of foreign investment will probably involve the UK in a worsening of its net barter terms of trade which raises the opportunity costs of that investment. Against this, however, must be set any future appreciation of the currency which follows from the return inflow of profits and interest.

pool their foreign exchange reserves in London. The balance of payments problems of the 1960s, however, resulted in the adoption of a policy of voluntary restraint on UK investment in the more advanced OSA countries. This policy lasted from April 1966 until March 1972 but the respite proved to be short-lived. The floating of sterling in June 1972 resulted in the majority of OSA countries being assigned external account status, thereby becoming subject to the same limitations as applied to investment in NSA countries. It is worth noting that this change, together with the application of the portfolio surrender rule to OSA securities, meant the end of all elements of discrimination in favour of investment in the OSA and hence the effective termination of the special economic relationship between the UK and OSA countries. From 1961 onwards, the method of restricting direct investment in the NSA took the form of treating proposed investments in terms of three categories. The least restricted category consisted of so-called 'super-criterion' projects, which were expected to bring matching returns to the balance of payments within eighteen months and which could be financed with official foreign exchange up to an effective limit of £50,000. All other projects had to be financed through the investment currency market or by overseas borrowing.[1] Although the framework remained unchanged until 1979, the criteria were alternatively strengthened and relaxed according to the underlying state of the basic balance. The most important developments in the 1970s followed from entry into the EEC. As noted in section III.6 the UK managed to stall the relaxation of exchange controls by involving a balance of payments escape clause. In December 1977, however, restrictions on direct investment in the EEC was relaxed with the foreign exchange limit for super-criterion projects raised to £0.5bn and the maximum payback period increased to three years. The more important pressure for change, however, came with the strengthening of sterling in 1979 and the prospect of net exports of NS oil. Fears that this would affect the competitiveness of the rest of UK manufacturing led to the search for ways of increasing the demand for official foreign exchange by UK residents, and financing the acquisition of overseas assets through the spot exchange market was an obvious candidate. Thus in July 1979 all limitations on the financing of direct investment overseas were abolished, as was the rule requiring that UK-controlled companies operating overseas remit to the UK two-thirds of post-tax earnings.

At present the UK places no legal restrictions upon inward investment, apart from those contained in the 1947 Exchange Control Act which apply to all UK residents. However, inward direct investment is subject to Treasury approval and the criteria upon which permission is granted are aimed at maximizing the contribution which the investment inflow makes to the reserves.[2]

It is difficult to know whether restrictions have had any significant impact on the total outflow of direct investment from the UK. The most important effect of the restrictions has been to save foreign exchange. Over the period 1965-71, for example, foreign borrowing financed 56% and internally generated profits financed 47% of all UK private investment in the NSA, so leaving a small balance to be added

---

1 For further details see the COI pamphlet, *Britain's International Investment Position*, HMSO, 1971.

2 M.D. Steuer *et al.*, *The Impact of Foreign Direct Investment on the UK*, HMSO, 1973, chapter 9. Since 1972, this constraint has been waived for EEC companies and investors.

to the exchange reserves.[1] Similarly between 1972 and 1978 48% of UK private direct investment overseas was financed out of retained profits. Quite how the relaxation of exchange controls will affect the financing of foreign investment it is too early to say. Certainly the propensity of modern corporations to finance investment from retained profits and a wish to minimize exchange risks by matching new foreign assets with additional foreign currency liabilities may mean that any induced depreciation of sterling will be slight.

Entry into the EEC as yet seems to have had a negligible effect on the pattern of the UK's overseas investment. During the 1970s roughly equal amounts, 30%, were directed to North America and Western Europe, with the EEC accounting for 22%. Of the total stock of UK direct-investment assets in the mid-1970s, 28% were located in Western Europe and 23% in North America, compared to figures of 13% and 23% in 1962.[2] This change in the share located in Western Europe is, of course, closely related to the change in the UK trade structure noted in section II.1. At the same time it is interesting to note that 90% of the UK's foreign direct-investment liabilities are owned by firms originating from Western Europe and North America.

From a balance of payments perspective it is the net balance of foreign direct investment which is significant and here we see from tables 3.1 and 3.2 how the 1970s marked a reversal of the UK's traditional role as a net exporter of private long-term capital. During the years 1970-7 the average net annual inflow of foreign capital amounted to £220m, and only in 1978 and 1979 did the traditional picture reappear. It should be realized that the net import of capital did not mean that the UK reduced its outflow of direct foreign investment; on the contrary, apart from 1974, 1975 and 1977 the outflow of UK capital increased in every year, reaching £4.4bn in 1979. Rather, the important change was the greatly increased long-term capital inflow into the UK. The chief sources of this were capital inflows associated with the NS oil programme, which accounted for 47% of the capital inflow between 1972 and 1978, and greatly increased borrowing by UK public-sector bodies, a disproportionate amount of which occurred in 1977.

Associated with the stocks of foreign assets and liabilities are return flows of interest, profits and dividends (IPD) which appear in the current account. For the UK roughly 53% of the IPD credits are related to past direct investments by UK manufacturing firms, and 7% are derived from portfolio investments. It is worth noting that, throughout the period since 1960, the outflow of foreign investment from the UK has been smaller than the return flow of IPD credits on the existing stocks of assets. While the net flow of IPD into the current account is positive, from year to year, the net receipts of foreign income are now less than 1% of GDP.

III.8   The UK and the European Economic Community

The question of UK membership of the EEC has always been controversial and the controversy has shown little tendency to abate since the UK became a full member in January 1973. On gaining office the Labour government of 1974 declared its

---

1 For further discussion see A.K. Cairncross, *Control of International Long-Term Capital Movements*, Brookings Institution, 1973, pp. 68-77.

2 For further details see J.H. Dunning, 'The UK's International Direct Investment Position in the Mid-1970s', *LBR*, April 1979.

firm intention to renegotiate the original terms of entry,[1] completed the re-negotiations in March 1975[2] and then settled the question in favour of membership with a referendum in July 1975. In this section we shall only comment upon the balance of payments implications of membership, other implications are treated in chapters 2 and 4 of this volume.

It was apparent at the time of the pre-entry negotiations that the full effect of entry into the EEC would imply a deterioration in the current account and possibly a deterioration in the long-term capital account of the balance of payments. To offset this, the UK would have to depreciate the exchange rate or employ direct policies of expenditure reduction in order to achieve the cut in real income and expenditure necessary to eliminate the adverse balance of payments effects of entry. Against this 'real resource cost' could be set the dynamic, long-run benefit of selling in a greatly enlarged market, a benefit which, it was argued, would result from greater economies of scale in production and which would be manifested in an increase in the UK growth rate.[3] Improved growth performance, it was thought, would possibly yield some offsetting dynamic gains to the basic balance, provided that productivity in the UK grew faster than the Community average. Unfortunately, while it proved possible to provide plausible estimates of the balance of payments cost, measurement of the potential dynamic gains has so far eluded any precise assessment. Certainly membership of the EEC has not reversed the relative economic decline of the UK, indeed between 1972 and 1979 per capita GNP in the UK fell from 85% to 78% of the EEC average. Optimists may argue that there has been some convergence of the UK growth rate toward the EEC average[4] but to what extent this can be attributed to UK membership it is impossible to say. At the time of writing any belief in the benefits of entry remains a matter of faith.

The effects on the UK current account can in principle be discussed under three headings: changes in the pattern of trade in manufactures, adoption of the common agricultural policy, and contributions to the Community budget.

The main implications for trade in manufactures follow from the customs union aspects of the Community, all tariffs on trade between the UK and other members having been reduced to zero in 1977 when the UK adopted the final stages of the common external tariff (CET) on trade with non-Community countries.[5]

---

1 *Renegotiation of the Terms of Entry into the European Economic Community*, Cmnd. 5593, April 1974.

2 *Membership of the European Community: Report on Renegotiation*, Cmnd. 6003, March 1975.

3 *Britain and the European Communities: An Economic Assessment*, Cmnd. 4289, February 1970.

4 Over the period 1958-72 the growth rate of per capita GNP in the UK was 61% of the nine-member Community average, the corresponding figure for 1972-8 being 75%. Calculated from EEC Commission of the European Communities, *European Economy*, November 1979.

5 The necessary tariff changes were to be achieved in stages, for details see *The United Kingdom and the European Communities*, Cmnd. 4715, July 1971. Following the completion of the Tokyo Round of multilateral tariff reductions in 1979, the average CET on industrial products will fall from 9.8% to 7.5% over an eight-year period.

It is impossible to say as yet what the final effects on the UK's pattern of trade will be. Adjustment to the tariff changes will not be immediate and we must also take into account the discrimination which is now imposed against former Commonwealth countries (excluding signatories of the Lomé convention) and the associated loss of UK export preferences in the same countries. We have already shown, in section II.1, that the direction of UK trade in the 1950s and 1960s swung progressively toward Western Europe and away from the traditional markets in North America and the OSA. It is clear that entry into the EEC has accelerated this trend. Over the years 1970 to 1973 UK exports to the EEC increased at a compound annual rate of 19.5%, while imports from the EEC increased at an average rate of 28.6%. Between 1973 and 1979 the export growth rate accelerated to 27.8%, whilst the import growth rate decelerated to 25.7%, though remaining well above the comparable growth rate for total imports at 20.2%.[1] However, it remains the case that the UK trades with the EEC less intensively than do her fellow members of the Community. Thus, in 1979 roughly 42% of UK exports and imports were exchanged with EEC countries, compared to an average intra-trade of the whole Community of 52%. This divergence of trading patterns is an important factor behind the adverse net budgetary position of the UK which emerged in 1979.

Assessments of the balance of payments cost of entry for the UK have tended to concentrate upon the effects of adopting the CAP system of agricultural support in place of the deficiency payments method formerly used by the UK. Under the deficiency payments method the UK imported foodstuffs at world prices free of any import duty. Under the CAP the UK is obliged to import all foodstuffs at the common EEC prices and to impose import levies on imports from non-EEC sources to bring their prices up to EEC levels. At the time of negotiation for entry it was estimated that EEC prices were between 18-26% higher than world market prices and that, given an inelastic demand for imports of foodstuffs, the UK import bill would be increased accordingly.

Finally, the UK is obliged to contribute to the budget of the Community and this involves a transfer of funds across the foreign exchanges, the gross contribution of the UK being assessed with reference to the share of the UK in the total GNP of the Community. The net contribution is smaller than the gross contribution to the extent that the UK receives reverse transfers from the EEC, for example, in the form of regional aid, industrial development aid and agricultural support.[2]

Estimates of the static balance of payment cost of entry produced widely varying results, although most suggested a substantial balance of payments burden[3] and thus an implicit real resource cost of UK entry to be imposed by a devaluation or other means. It was in the light of the assumed adverse balance of payments implications that the UK government renegotiated the original terms of entry. The most concrete results of the renegotiation were the creation of a mechanism for

---

1 For a more detailed analysis of the increasing intensity of the UK-EEC trade see A.E. Daly, 'UK Visible Trade and the Common Market', *NIER*, No. 86, November 1978.

2 Cf. Cmnd. 4715, paras. 91-6 and Annex A.

3 The 1970 White Paper, Cmnd. 4289, suggested a balance of payments cost ranging between £100m to £1.1bn per annum. For a comparison with other, less extreme, estimates see J. Pinder (ed.), *The Economics of Europe*, Charles Knight, 1971, chapter 6, by M. Miller. For a more optimistic assessment, see R.L. Major and S. Hays, 'Another Look at the Common Market', *NIER*, November 1970.

reducing the gross budgetary contribution of the UK in line with the UK's share in the total GNP of the Community, and the guarantee of continued access to the Community for sugar and dairy products from New Zealand.[1]

It is remarkable how inaccurate the initial estimates of the balance of payments cost have proved to be. Three factors are relevant here. First, and most important, the food-related balance of payments cost depends on the gap between EEC prices and world market prices for foodstuffs and this gap varies over time, narrowing at times of world economic expansion and widening during periods of world economic contraction. Thus the increase in world prices between 1971 and 1974 substantially reduced the import cost of the CAP system. Subsequently, however, world prices have fallen below EEC levels and the anticipated world recession during 1980-1 must increase this gap and raise again a potentially formidable burden of UK membership.[2]

The second difficulty arises from the complexities of the CAP pricing system. First, the intervention prices are not only set above world market levels but they are also set at levels which have encouraged substantial production surpluses for many commodities. Handling these surpluses either involves expenditure on storage, or subsidies to farmers to enable the surplus output to be exported to world markets. Clearly it is in the UK's interest to press for more realistic food-pricing policies and to try and ensure that EEC prices fall in line with productivity gains in the more advanced farming units. Additional difficulties have arisen because EEC food prices are set in terms of units of account and then translated into the respective member currencies at representative exchange rates, the so-called 'green' currencies, fixed by administrative decision. Now as long as the ratio between any two green currency rates is equal to the spot market exchange rate between the corresponding national currencies, the system works as intended, in that any agricultural commodity will sell at a common price throughout the EEC. Unfortunately, following the collapse of the Bretton Woods exchange-rate system in 1971 spot market rates for several EEC currencies have diverged substantially from the green currency rates. In particular, the steady depreciation of sterling after June 1972 left the spot rate for sterling below the green pound rate, the percentage gap on some occasions reaching as much as 20%, despite frequent devaluations of the green pound.[3] The consequences of divergences between green and market exchange rates are extremely disruptive to agricultural trade and production in the EEC, since they undermine the principle of common prices for foodstuffs and create profitable opportunities for arbitrage between commodities and EEC currencies. To prevent this, border taxes and subsidies have to be levied on agricultural trade between EEC countries, the total amounts of subsidy involved being known as monetary

---

1 Cmnd. 6003. For additional details of the convention which grants tariff preferences on exports to the EEC of industrial products, and some agricultural products from signatory developing countries, see P.L. Coffey, 'The Lomé Agreement and the EEC: Implications and Problems', *TBR*, No. 108, December 1975.

2 For further discussion see R. Bacon *et al.*, 'The Direct Costs to Britain of Belonging to the EEC', *Economic Policy Review*, 1978, Dept. Applied Economics, Cambridge.

3 For further discussion consult R.W. Irving and H.A. Fern, *Green Money and the Common Agricultural Policy*, Wye College, Occasional Paper No. 2, 1975, and C. Mackel, 'Green Money and the Common Agricultural Policy', *NWBR*, February 1978. The values for the green currencies are published monthly in *Bulletin of the European Communities*, Secretariat General, Brussels. The latest in the series of green pound devaluations (5%) was announced in December 1979, this being the third 5% devaluation to be negotiated during 1979.

compensation amounts (MCAs). As a substantial net importer of foodstuffs the UK has been a major beneficiary from the MCA system, and even though MCAs are now paid to the exporting country the amounts can still be viewed as a corresponding subsidy to UK consumers and treated as a notional net UK budgetary receipt. During 1978 MCAs paid on UK food imports came to £479m, which if treated as a budget receipt reduces the UK net budgetary contribution for the year from £752 to £273. Unfortunately for the UK; the appreciation of sterling during 1979 eliminated the need to pay MCA subsidies on UK food imports and thus any potential contribution to the net budgetary position. Indeed, by April 1980 the prospect of a reverse flow of MCA payments seemed imminent. There can be little doubt that the MCA system is in need of reform. While it began as a temporary measure to maintain a common market in foodstuffs following the currency disruptions of 1972-3, it has developed into a permanent feature of the CAP. However, reform will require that green currencies are linked to currency exchange rates and unless market rates are stabilized this will raise formidable administrative difficulties for the CAP. It is easy to see how the establishment of a stable European currency area would provide a convenient means for shoring up the CAP.

The third area of difficulty when estimating the balance of payments cost of entry relates to calculation of the net budgetary contribution. This question received a great deal of attention during 1979 because in 1980 the UK was due to bear, for the first time, the full budgetary cost of entry. The EEC budget is financed from the 'own resources' of the Community which consist of all import duties and agricultural levies on trade from non-EEC sources[1] plus a proportion of VAT revenue which does not exceed 1% of the proceeds of a VAT levied on a uniform basis in the Community. On this basis the gross UK contribution in 1980 was expected to be of the order of 20% of total own resources even though the UK accounts for only 16% of Community GNP. The real problem for the UK, however, lies with the net contribution. After allowing for grants and loans, the UK was anticipated to receive only 10% of the Community's expenditure leaving a net UK budgetary contribution variously estimated to lie between £1.2bn and £1.5bn during 1980. This net contribution for one year may be compared with the cumulative gross contribution of £3.19bn over the calendar years 1973 to 1978, and a cumulative net contribution over the same period of £1.34bn.[2] The estimated net contribution represents a substantial transfer across the exchanges and, not surprisingly, the UK government has sought ways of reducing this burden. Scope for action with the current EEC rules is however limited to two possibilities. First, a reimbursement mechanism, relating the gross contribution to the UK share of Community GNP, can be brought into operation, but the most that the UK can achieve from this is limited to a refund of 250m units of account, or £160m at current exchange rates.[3] Second, the UK net contribution is to a considerable degree dependent on structural features of the UK economy which cannot be changed quickly. The fact that the UK is still heavily dependent on imports from non-EEC sources enhances her gross contribution, while the small size and

---

1 Less 10%, to cover costs of collection and administration.

2 At current prices. See *The Government's Expenditure Plans 1979-80 to 1982-3*. Cmnd. 7439, January 1979. A more recent expenditure paper, Cmnd. 7746, gives an estimated net contribution at 1979 survey prices of £1bn; but see Postscript on p. 179 below.

3 For details of the reimbursement mechanism see Cmnd. 6003, paragraphs 39-42.

efficiency of her agricultural sector mean that receipts from the agricultural funds are small.[1] At the root of this budgetary problem lies the continued growth in the amount of EEC expenditure devoted to the CAP, currently about 70%, which leaves relatively small amounts for the regional, social and other programmes from which the UK would be a major beneficiary. From the UK viewpoint reform will therefore involve either a trimming of the CAP system, which appears unlikely given the imminent prospect of Spain, Portugal and Greece becoming Community members, or a more fundamental reform of the budgetary mechanism, the more likely outcome given the fact that planned expenditure on the CAP is expected to exceed the 'own resources' of the Community in 1980-1.

Although the CAP and budgetary contribution questions have tended to dominate practical discussion on EEC membership, it is important to recognize that the issue of monetary unification is potentially of greater significance to the UK. In 1971 the European Commission, following guidelines laid down in the Werner Report of 1970, adopted the goal of full monetary union to be achieved by 1980. In its fullest form this would involve the irrevocable fixing of the parities of EEC currencies one to another, full currency convertibility for current- and capital-account transactions and the creation of a Community central bank with full powers to determine monetary policy in each region of the EEC. In many respects the case for monetary union is an integral part of the case for a common market in commodities. Creation of a single currency (de facto, by fixing exchange rates, or by the adoption of a new currency unit) reduces transactions costs and promotes exchange and the division of labour which, it could be argued, is necessary if the dynamic gains from membership are to be maximized. Furthermore, it can be argued that once the members of the EEC develop intensive trade and investment links with one another then adoption of a fixed pattern of exchange rates is the only foreign exchange market policy consistent with price stability. Stable EEC parities are, of course, a very necessary part of the operation of CAP and other Community-wide policies. Whatever the merits of these arguments it should be realized that the costs of monetary unification are considerable.[2] As part of a monetary union the UK would abandon the right to change its parity unilaterally against other currencies, having already surrendered the ability to impose import restrictions and export subsidies for balance of payments purposes by adopting the CET. Expenditure-switching instruments would therefore be eliminated from the armoury of feasible economic policies. Adjustment to payments deficits must then be by domestic deflation and the creation of unemployment, with the harmful and ultimately self-defeating implications noted in section II.2 above. At best, a high degree of labour mobility to the other EEC countries may mitigate the effects on unemployment while it is possible that sustained financial support from other Community members may ease, but not eliminate, the burden of adjustment. Equally, the commitment to capital-market integration would rule out restrictions on capital transactions in order to improve the basic balance.

---

1   During 1980 the UK was expected to benefit from only 6% of farm price support expenditure but to contribute 27% of customs duty revenue and 19% of agricultural levy revenue in the EEC.

2   The interested reader may consult Y. Ishiyama, 'The Theory of Optimum Currency Areas: A Survey', *IMF Staff Papers*, Vol. 22, 1975, pp. 344-83. For a discussion of the monetary union between the UK and Eire see Whitaker, 'Monetary Integration: Reflections on Irish Experience', *Moorgate and Wall St*, Autumn 1973.

An important step toward the objectives of monetary integration was taken in March 1979 with the formal adoption of the European Monetary System (EMS), the objective of which is the creation of a zone of monetary stability in Europe, and the return of the Community to the exchange-rate certainties of its first ten years of existence. The EMS consists of two principle components, an exchange-rate structure and intervention mechanism, and a system of credits for financing payments imbalances between members. It is planned that by 1981 the credit system will have evolved into a European Monetary Fund on the lines of the IMF.[1] The exchange-rate mechanism is a logical development of the European snake. Following the collapse of the IMF adjustable-peg mechanism in 1971, the first concrete steps toward the creation of a European Monetary system were taken in April 1972 with the agreement to limit the margins of fluctuation between EEC currencies to 2.25% either side of parity rates.[2] The system proved to be ill-fated. Sterling defected in June 1972, the Lira in February 1973 and the French Franc was forced out of the snake twice, the most recent of the departures being in March 1976. Despite these set-backs, the pressures toward currency stability have proved powerful and the EMS exchange-rate system is founded on a revitalized snake or currency grid. Within this grid each European currency is assigned a central rate against the other EEC currencies, together with a permitted band of fluctuation of 2.25% either side of this central rate. An exception is made for countries when they join the system, who may initially adopt margins of 6% around central rates. Central banks are obliged to keep their currencies within the margins of fluctuation but, as became clear with the snake, this creates an asymmetric burden of obligation. The weak-currency country loses reserves and is always under pressure to adjust its internal policies to a greater extent than is the strong-currency country. In the EMS an ingenious mechanism has been introduced to try and eliminate the asymmetries of adjustment and to enhance the convergence of exchange-rate and economic policies. The key to this is the new European currency unit (ECU), which is a basket of the nine currencies, initially, but not irrevocably, of the same composition as the European unit of account. The ECU acts as numeraire for the exchange-rate mechanism and, using the currency grid exchange rates, each currency is assigned its central value in terms of ECU together with a maximum range of divergence around this central value.[3] From this basis a

---

1 Full details of the EMS mechanisms are given in Commission of the European Communities, *European Economy*, July 1979. A brief but useful summary is given in the article, 'Britain and the European Monetary System', *MBR*, Winter 1979. The arguments for monetary integration are set out by the President of the European Commission, R. Jenkins, in 'European Monetary Union', *LBR*, No. 127, January 1978. See also 'Intervention Arrangements in the European Monetary System', *BEQB*, June 1979 and P. Coffey, 'The European Monetary System – Six Months Later', *TBR*, December 1979.

2 This scheme was known as the 'snake in the tunnel', the 'snake' representing the closely linked EEC currencies which, under the pressure of market forces, was free to move up and down relative to the dollar in the 'tunnel' defined by the Smithsonian exchange-rate limits. (See section III.9.) The 'tunnel' disappeared in March 1973 when the EEC currencies engaged in a joint float against the dollar.

3 The maximum range of divergence for each currency is less than $\pm 2.25\%$ and is determined by the formula $\pm 2.25 (1-w_i)\%$, where w_i is the weight of that currency in the value of the ECU basket. The notional weight for sterling at end-September 1979 was 13.6%, giving a notional divergence range of $\pm 1.94\%$ for sterling against ECU. The divergence threshold for sterling is 75% of this, i.e. $\pm 1.45\%$.

divergence threshold is defined whereby a currency may not diverge from its central ECU rate by more than three-quarters of its divergence range. The point of these restrictions is that, in general, a currency will reach its divergence threshold before it reaches any of the bilateral intervention limits defined by the currency grid, and, once this occurs, there is a presumption that consultation will be initiated with all Community members to decide upon intervention policy, possible changes in central parities and any necessary internal policy measures. In this way it is hoped that burdens of adjustment will be more equally shared within the Community and the asymmetries of bilateral intervention avoided.

Besides acting as numeraire in the EMS, the ECU has an important role as an instrument of settlement between Community central banks and ultimately as the planned reserve asset of the Community. Member countries deposit 20% of their gold and gross dollar reserves with the European Monetary Co-operation Fund on a three-month renegotiable basis, and in return have access to a variety of credit facilities with a total value of 25bn ECU, to finance payments imbalances within the Community and to support the currency grid.[1] Of this total, 14bn ECU has been allocated to short-term monetary support and the remainder to medium-term credit facilities. Although the UK participated fully in the setting up of the EMS, and contributes to the ECU credit arrangements, it has firmly declined to join the exchange-rate system, on the grounds that the disparities of economic performance within the Community make it unwise to fix parities within the narrow limits set by the currency grid and divergence indicators.[2] This position is surely sound. The EEC countries have widely different inflation rates and rates of monetary expansion, the budgetary mechanisms of the Community affect their current-payments accounts in different ways and they differ considerably with respect to the effect of oil-price changes upon their respective basic balances. To fix parities in such circumstances is clearly folly, unless a common monetary and fiscal policy can be worked out and applied for the whole Community. But such far-reaching changes are a long way off, indeed any fiscal and monetary unification proposals are likely to run foul of strong pressures to maintain national sovereignty in the formulation and implementation of economic policy. Some indication of the difficulties ahead for the EMS was perhaps given by the inability to work out a Community approach to the decline of the dollar during 1979. Failure to adopt a common approach led in September to the first changes of the parity grid, with the German mark revalued by 2% and the Danish krone devalued by 3%. Co-ordination of policy seems to remain an ideal rather than a reality of Community affairs.

III.9   The Reform of the International Monetary System

If the quarter century from 1945 had one dominant characteristic in the international economic arena it was the integration of national commodity and capital markets into a unified and rapidly growing system of world trade and

---

1   The gold contribution is valued at the average London fixing price during the six months prior to valuation, and the dollar portion is valued at the market rate of the two working days prior to valuation. The increase in the dollar price of gold during 1979 greatly inflated the dollar value of ECU reserves, from $23bn at the beginning of 1979 to over $40bn at the end.

2   Cf. *The European Monetary System*, Cmnd. 7405, November 1978.

investment. A key role in this process was played by the international financial rules established at the Bretton Woods conference of 1944, the supervisory institution of which is the International Monetary Fund (IMF).[1] The principal features of the Bretton Woods system were, in brief, its emphasis on mutual international co-operation and its creation of a system of fixed but, in principle, adjustable exchange rates, the par-value system, together with the provision of temporary and conditional balance of payments finance by the IMF to supplement reserve media in the form of gold and foreign exchange.

Throughout the 1960s it became clear that the IMF system suffered from potentially lethal inconsistencies and that, in particular, it placed the United States in an economic position which the European industrial nations became increasingly unable to accept. The first weakness was the general unwillingness of the main industrial countries to adjust par values in the face of obvious fundamental disequilibria until the force of events, aided by currency speculation, forced governments into belated action. The case of sterling in the mid-1960s and of Germany and Japan in the late 1960s are obvious examples of this failure to use the par-value adjustment mechanism in the way originally intended by the architects of Bretton Woods. Not unrelated to this was the asymmetry between deficit and surplus countries, in that the pressure of reserve losses bore far more heavily on the deficit countries than did the converse phenomena of reserve gains on the surplus countries. In practice the 'scarce currency' provisions of Article 7 of the IMF Agreement, which were meant to act as a sanction against persistent surplus countries, were never invoked.

The second weakness involved the supply of global reserve media, which under the IMF system consisted mainly of gold and foreign exchange holdings, and in particular, of course, US dollars. The problem was that the supply of monetary gold depended on the vagaries of mining and speculative activity, and the supply of foreign exchange depended upon the balance of payments deficits of the US, which could prove to be temporary and, more important, unrelated to global reserve needs. In the light of this there was considerable discussion in the 1960s of the alleged inadequacy of world reserves which took as its basis the observed decline in the ratio of world reserves to world imports, from a value of 68% in 1951 to one of 30% in 1969; the latter being less than the equivalent ratio for the depressed years of the 1930s. A difficulty with this type of discussion was that it failed to make clear that the demand for foreign exchange reserves is a demand to finance balance of payments *disequilibria*, not a demand to finance the volume of trade. It failed, therefore, to recognize that the demand for reserve media will be smaller the more frequently exchange rates are adjusted in line with economic pressure, the more co-ordinated are national policies of demand management, and the greater the willingness of national governments and private capital markets to engage in mutual international borrowing and lending to finance payments imbalances. In the limit, for example, with a perfectly freely floating system of exchange rates, the demand for official reserves would be zero.

Finally, there was the so-called 'confidence' problem, which followed from the increasing degree of dependence of world reserve growth on foreign exchange in the form of the dollar and to a lesser extent sterling. The problem was simply that by 1964 the total of outstanding dollar liabilities exceeded the gold reserves of the

---

1 Cf., R.N. Cooper, *The Economics of Interdependence*, McGraw-Hill, 1968.

United States and from then on this disparity between dollar liabilities and gold 'cover' increased. By December 1971 the US gold stock amounted to only 16% of the total of US short-term dollar liabilities held by overseas monetary authorities. *De facto* this meant that the dollar was no longer convertible into primary reserve assets and so the willingness to hold dollars in official reserves decreased and the danger of a dollar crisis increased. As R. Triffin pointed out in 1958, the gold-exchange standard contained an automatic self-destruct mechanism,[1] with the potential risk of a severe liquidity crisis in which dollar and sterling reserves were liquidated and destroyed, while a given total of gold reserves was redistributed between countries. It is important, when trying to understand recent events, to realize that the Bretton Woods system had the effect of placing the United States and the dollar in a unique position in the international monetary system. Opponents of the United States have argued that the reserve-currency status of the dollar enabled the United States to conduct internal policies independently of its balance of payments position and to finance an outflow of direct overseas investment on advantageous terms. In contrast, it has been argued that the USA had no choice but to adopt a passive balance of payments policy and run a payments deficit of sufficient magnitude to satisfy the global demand for dollars as an international reserve asset. Whatever the merits of these viewpoints, two aspects of the situation are clear. First, because the dollar was extensively used as the intervention currency for stabilizing exchange rates, the USA had no need to concern itself with supporting the external value of the dollar. Secondly, the one option open to the USA to cure its deficit, namely a devaluation of the dollar relative to gold and therefore relative to other currencies, was steadfastly ruled out on political grounds until the events of December 1971.

Throughout the 1960s the strains inherent to the system manifested themselves in a variety of ways. Most significant, perhaps, were the *ad hoc* measures taken by the industrial countries to supplement the existing sources of balance of payments finance. At one level were the General Arrangements to Borrow, organized in October 1962, in which the Group of Ten countries (UK, France, Germany, Belgium, Netherlands, Italy, US, Canada, Sweden and Japan) agreed to lend their currencies to the IMF should the latter run short of one of their respective currencies. These arrangements have been renegotiated on several occasions, most recently in October 1975, and the amount of support now totals SDR 6.8bn. Recent years have seen increasing use of the GAB, indeed 76% of the finance for the standby arrangements negotiated by the UK in 1976 come from eight of the GAB countries. In addition to this there are the currency swap arrangements between the US and the central banks of other countries, whereby each agrees to lend or acquire currency balances for an agreed time period. Several such arrangements exist between the US and other countries, and currently total $20bn. The UK has benefited considerably from the availability of this short-term financial aid, the UK-US swap facility being increased to $3bn in March 1974. The UK has also been able to draw upon credits provided by European central banks from 1961 onwards. A second important manifestation of strain related to the official price of gold and the clear possibility that its price might have to be increased to boost world reserves and improve the asset:liability ratio of the US. Attempts to stabilize the free-market

---

1 R. Triffin, 'Gold and the Dollar Crisis', Yale, 1958, and R. Triffin, 'Gold and the Dollar Crisis: Yesterday and Tomorrow', *Essays in International Finance*, No. 132, Princeton, December 1978.

price of gold by the major central banks which had begun in 1961 had to be abandoned in March 1968 following the loss of $3bn in monetary gold stocks, sold in an attempt to hold down the free-market price during the previous five months. The Washington agreement of that time created a two-tier market for gold and effectively prevented national monetary authorities from using monetary gold stocks to finance payments disequilibria in the face of an ever-widening differential between the free-market and the official price of gold. This two-tier system was abandoned in November 1973.

The final, and some would say most significant, manifestation of strain was the increasing volume of speculative capital flows which from 1967 onwards repeatedly disrupted the working of foreign exchange markets and threatened the parities of the deutschmark, the yen and the dollar. It became increasingly clear that the par-value system could not survive unless more effective methods for adjusting exchange rates in line with changing economic circumstances could be devised, and unless some means could be found for absorbing the increasing volume of short-term capital flows made possible by the growth of the euro-dollar market.

Not surprisingly, in the face of such obvious strains, many proposals for reforming the system were put forward during the 1960s. On the fundamental question of the adjustment mechanism, proposals ranged from the adoption of freely floating exchange rates, to mechanisms for ensuring the gradual and automatic adjustment of par-values to payments disturbances, the crawling-peg proposal. However, the response of the IMF to such proposals was lukewarm, a study by the executive directors concluding by reaffirming faith in the viability of the par-value system, with the only concessions to flexibility being the suggestion of wider margins of fluctuation around par values and the temporary abrogation of par-value obligations.[1]

By far the most important development of the 1960s was international agreement on the creation of a new reserve asset, the Special Drawing Right. The outcome of several years of discussion, this scheme came into operation in 1970.

Special Drawing Rights: SDRs are book entries in the Special Drawing Account of the IMF by means of which countries can give and receive credit on a multilateral basis to finance balance of payments deficits. At the moment, SDRs are held only by those national monetary authorities which participate in the IMF arrangements and which agree to accept the provisions of the SDR scheme. The total of SDRs is agreed collectively by the members of the IMF, so that the supply of this new reserve asset is agreed by international decision; the basis for their creation being the provision of an adequate, but not inflationary, long-term rate of growth of world reserves. SDRs are thus superior to gold and foreign exchange in that their supply is not arbitrary but is, in principle, the outcome of rational discussion. The total of SDRs is revised on a five-year basis with the first allocation of $9.3 billion being made in three stages between 1970 and 1972.[2] Each country is assigned a net cumulative allocation of SDRs, in proportion to its quota in the general account of

---

1 *The Role of Exchange Rates in the Adjustment of International Payments: A Report by the Executive Directors*, IMF, 1970.

2 The revised Articles of Agreement to incorporate SDRs may be found in the IMF *Annual Report* for 1968 or in the book by F. Machlup listed at the end of this chapter. These Articles were revised under the Second Amendment (see below).

the IMF, and can treat this allocation as 'owned reserves' to finance payments imbalances. A country in deficit, for example, may use its SDR quota to purchase needed foreign exchange from other countries. One of the most ingenious features of the scheme is that utilization of a country's SDR quota is subject to the supervision of the IMF, the object being to ensure a balanced and widespread activation of the SDR facility. Use of SDRs was initially subject to three provisions: (i) they must be used for legitimate balance of payments purposes and not, for example, to diversify exchange reserve portfolios; (ii) a country need not accept SDRs in excess of twice its net cumulative allocation; and (iii) a country's average holding over a period of five years must not fall below 30% of its net cumulative allocation – essentially to prevent the persistent, as distinct from temporary, financing of a deficit with SDRs. To give effect to these provisions two types of transactions in SDRs are allowed, designated transactions and transactions by agreement. With designated transactions, the IMF decides the countries that will add to their SDR holdings and so provide the currencies required by the country running down its SDR holdings, the choice of countries for designation being decided on the basis of their balance of payments strength and the adequacy of their reserve holdings. In contrast, transactions by agreement involve the transfer of SDRs between countries without recourse to the IMF where the usual objective is to redeem the currency liabilities of the transferor.

The SDR was devised as a response to the experience of the 1960s. Unfortunately, it came into existence at a time when the ground-rules of the Bretton Woods system were about to become void. The collapse of 1971 and the responses to it are treated further below, but here it will prove convenient to trace the evolution of the SDR in the rapidly changing world monetary environment of the 1970s.

The fundamental question surrounding the SDR has always been that of whether SDRs simply co-exist with other reserve assets or whether they are destined to replace gold or foreign exchange, or both, as the reserve base of the system.

In the initial arrangements SDRs were effectively a gold substitute, they had a gold guarantee and carried a low rate of interest on net holdings of 1½%. On the understanding that the dollar was not devalued relative to gold, then SDRs were inferior to the dollar as a reserve asset because of their lower interest yield and lesser convenience of usage. However, the dollar devaluations of 1971 and 1973 upset this situation as did the resort to a general floating of the important currencies relative to gold during 1973. In response to these changed circumstances the IMF announced, on 1 July 1974, that the value of the SDR would be computed as a weighted average of sixteen currencies, that the link with gold would be terminated, and that the interest rate on net balances of SDRs would in future be related to an average of short-term interest rates in the financial centres of the five countries with the largest SDR allocations.[1] Since 1974 steady progress has been made to increase the attractions of SDRs relative to the dollar and other reserve currencies, and to develop the SDR as the logical, principal reserve asset of the

---

1 For details see the article, 'The New Method of Valuing Special Drawing Rights', *BEQB*, September 1974. The composition of the SDR basket was changed in July 1978, see 'Supplement on the Fund', *IMF Survey*, September 1979. For further analysis of the issues discussed below, see F. Hirsch, 'An SDR Standard: Impetus, Elements and Impediments', *Essays in International Finance*, No. 99, Princeton, 1975, and K.A. Chrystal, 'International Money and the Future of the SDR', ibid., No. 128, December 1978.

international monetary system. The most important changes came with the adoption of the Second Amendment to the IMF Articles of Agreement in April 1978 (see below) – changes which greatly extended the range of transactions for which SDRs may be employed by mutual agreement between countries without Fund authority, and which reduced from 30% to 15% a country's minimum permitted holding of its SDR allocation over a five-year period. Against a background of greatly increased use of SDRs[1] two further important steps were taken in January 1979. First, the formula relating SDR interest rates to market interest rates was revised to make the SDR rate 80% rather than 60% of the composite market rate. Second, the first increase in SDR allocations since 1970 was implemented with SDR 4bn being allocated to raise total SDRs to 13.3bn. A similar allocation of SDR 4bn was made in January 1980, with a final such allocation planned for January 1981. It was also agreed that when the Seventh General Increase of Quotas becomes effective in 1980, members will contribute 25% of their increase in quotas in SDRs. More recent steps include the extension of the right to hold and exchange SDRs to non-member organizations, e.g. BIS, and legalization of the use of SDRs for the making of currency swaps and forward transactions.[2]

Despite these developments aimed at enhancing the status of SDRs, the fact remains that SDRs only accounted for 4.1% of total world reserves at end-1979 and only 2.0% when gold reserves are valued at their market price. While SDRs have been made more attractive in relation to currencies, the continued appreciation of gold during the late 1970s has shown that gold is a far more effective hedge against inflation than are SDRs. At best, all the IMF can press for is a continued enhancing of SDRs relative to currencies. In this respect the proposed Substitution Account at the IMF, in which members would deposit currency reserves in return for SDRs, could be an important means of increasing the weight of SDRs in world reserves. Whether the proposals will come to anything during 1980 is doubtful, unless there is a sustained collapse in the dollar relative to other currencies.[3]

The future of the SDR scheme is thus for the moment uncertain, not least because the tremendous growth in world reserves over the 1970s has created fears of an excess of world liquidity rather than a shortage. Even valuing gold at the old official price, world reserves increased by 94% between end-1970 and end-1974 and by a further 68% between end-1974 and end-1979. As a result the ratio of world reserves to world imports has remained steady at approximately 29% during the 1970s, though if gold is valued at its market price rather than the old official price the ratio increases from 32% in 1970 to 47% in 1974 and 54% in 1979. Indeed, on reflection, it is plausible to argue that the downfall of the Bretton Woods system proved to be its propensity to generate world liquidity, and from this stemmed the inflationary tendencies of the 1970s and the collapse of the par-value system in 1973.

1971-9: Crisis and Evolutionary Reform: Any illusions that the creation of the SDR scheme had inaugurated a new period of stability for the par-value system were quickly shattered. Following a period of considerable uncertainty in foreign

---

1 IMF, *Annual Reports*, 1978 and 1979, chapter 2, give relevant details.

2 IMF, *Survey*, 10 December 1979.

3 Cf., 'The Proposed Substitution Account in the IMF', *MBR*, Winter 1979.

exchange markets and massive short-term capital outflows from the US, the US government announced in August 1971 that the dollar was no longer convertible into gold and that to eliminate the disequilibria in the international economic system other countries must revalue their currencies relative to gold. To add pressure toward this end, a 10% surcharge was imposed on US imports of manufactures and the US proclaimed its intention to obtain trade concessions from Japan and the EEC. Detailed and intensive official discussions culminated in a meeting of the finance ministers of the Group of Ten countries at the Smithsonian Institute in Washington in December 1971. The main points agreed were: (i) a new set of values of exchange rates which involved a revaluation of the deutschmark and the Japanese yen; (ii) that 'pending agreement on longer-term monetary reforms' the permitted IMF margins of fluctuations around par values would be increased to ± 2.25%; (iii) that the US would devalue the dollar in terms of gold by 7.89%, so creating a new official price for gold of $38 per oz., and that this would form the new par value of the dollar; (iv) that the 10% import surcharge would be abolished; (v) that new discussions should be undertaken, under the auspices of the IMF, to consider the long-term reform of the international monetary system in all its major aspects.

The forum for discussion of international reform was set up in June 1972 and became known as the Committee of Twenty, holding meetings between September 1972 and June 1974 when the final report was presented. Three items dominated the deliberations of the C-20: firstly, methods of absorbing and recycling short-term capital flows; secondly the creation of an exchange-rate system with stable but adjustable par values, and with recognized and widely acceptable criteria for instigating changes in par values; and thirdly, the future reserve base of the international monetary system and in particular the role of the SDR in any reformed system. The deliberations of the C-20 could hardly be described as successful, the final report making it clear that substantial differences of view existed on fundamental issues.[1] The most concrete outcome of the C-20 activities has been its perpetuation in the form of an Interim Committee which continues to discuss proposals for reform. However, it would have indeed proved remarkable had any concrete reform proposals emerged, for the reform discussions were overtaken by two important events, the adoption of generalized floating by the major industrial countries in March 1973 and the massive increase in the price of oil in December 1973.

Managed Floating and the Oil Price Issue: Confidence in the Smithsonian exchange parities proved to be short-lived and in the period to March 1973 frequent speculative crises disturbed the international monetary system, the only effective counter to which was the adoption of floating exchange rates by the major industrial nations. By April 1973 the par-value system had collapsed, perhaps the predictable outcome of the drift of the Bretton Woods system into a reluctant dollar standard.

The experiences of 1972 and 1973 have underlined a major problem faced by an exchange-rate system in current circumstances, viz. coping with the massive volume

---

1 The final report of the C-20 'Outline of Reform' was published in IMF, *Survey*, June 1974. See also, *International Monetary Reform, Documents of the Committee of Twenty*, IMF, 1974. For a valuable account of the activities of C-20 and its failings see J. Williamson, *The Failure of World Monetary Reform, 1971-4*, Nelson, 1977.

of short-term funds which can be switched very rapidly between financial centres. Short-term capital flows forced the abandonment of Smithsonian parities and have played an important part in the fluctuations experienced by floating rates. Various attempts have been adopted to limit such flows, for example, a two-tier foreign exchange market by Italy, direct controls on overseas borrowing by Germany and an extension of inter-central bank currency swap arrangements, but these are of a somewhat *ad hoc* and inadequate nature.

The inception of a period of managed floating raises several difficulties for the international monetary system, in particular those of mutually inconsistent exchange-rate stabilization policies, the possibility of competitive, beggar-thy-neighbour exchange-rate management, and the problem of exchange instability in the face of speculative pressure. To help avoid these problems the IMF issued guidelines for exchange-rate management in June 1974 which were subsequently revised in April 1977 in anticipation of the revisions to Article 4 of the IMF agreement.[1] The revised guidelines emphasize the point that exchange-rate policy is a matter for international consultation and surveillance by the IMF and suggest three criteria to guide exchange-rate policy: (i) the avoidance of exchange-rate manipulation to gain an unfair competitive advantage or to prevent effective balance of payments adjustment; (ii) the prevention of disproportionate and disorderly short-term movements of exchange rates; and (iii) the recognition that exchange-rate management involves joint responsibilities. Members consult with the IMF on a regular basis concerning their exchange-rate policies and the IMF can initiate discussion if it feels that policies are being adopted, for example abnormal changes in reserves or the imposition of restrictions on trade and capital flows, which run counter to its guidelines. The experiences of the period of heavily managed intervention have been mixed. On the one hand, short-term movements in exchange rates have been more volatile than advocates of flexible rates would perhaps condone, while, on the other hand, exchange rates have been managed without any overt clashes of national interest and have changed to compensate for substantial national differences in inflation rates.[2]

More damaging to the reform movement was the increase in the price of oil which created an unprecedented imbalance in the international economic system, in the form of a massive payments surplus for the oil producers and a corresponding deficit for the oil-importing countries. The problem is simply that the ability of the oil producers to spend their oil revenues on imports of goods and services has not so far matched the increase in their revenues. Thus the major oil producers enjoyed aggregate current-account surpluses of $67.8bn in 1974 which progressively declined to give average annual surpluses of $28bn in the four years 1975 to 1978. The 40% increase in average oil prices during 1979 can only mean a prolonging of the oil-related deficits and structural imbalances in the world payments system. Indeed the oil producers' current-account surplus for 1979 has been estimated at a figure as high as $43bn. Since, as is generally agreed, the OPEC countries have no serious alternative but to invest their surplus revenues in the advanced industrialized nations, so returning on capital account the purchasing power extracted from the

---

1 Cf., IMF, *Survey*, 17 June 1974, and IMF, *Annual Report*, 1977, Appendix 2.

2 IMF, *Annual Report*, 1979. On the volatility of exchange rates see P.A. Tosini, 'Leaning Against the Wind: A Standard For Managed Floating', in *Essays in International Finance*, No. 126, Princeton, 1977, and J.R. Artus and A.D. Crockett, 'Floating Exchange Rates and the Need for Surveillance', ibid., No. 127, Princeton, May 1978.

current accounts of the oil-importing nations, the oil problem raises three serious issues for the stability of the international monetary system. First, there is the potential havoc which would be wrought to foreign exchange markets if surplus oil funds are invested in liquid assets and switched between currencies in search of interest return and the expected capital gain from exchange-rate alterations. The gyrations of sterling during 1976 and the depreciation of the dollar since 1977 are good examples of the effects of asset-switching. Clearly some means must be found of placing the funds in less liquid investments and/or creating sufficient central bank co-operation to undertake large scale recycling operations. Secondly, and more important, is the fact that the attractiveness of different oil-importing nations as havens for OPEC investment need bear no relation to the way in which their respective current-account balances have been affected by oil price increases. The possibility is therefore reinforced that individual countries will try to eliminate their deficits by deflation, trade restrictions or currency depreciation, the only outcome of which would be to depress world trade and output. Finally, there are the problems faced by the developing nations which have seen the real values of aid inflows virtually eliminated by the increase in oil prices.[1]

The initial response to these problems involved the introduction of a variety of measures to supplement the IMF's normal resources with special borrowing facilities. One of the first developments was the creation of the Extended Facility, introduced in 1974, through which a member can borrow for balance of payments purposes for periods longer than are normally allowed under the normal credit tranche policies. Borrowings under this Facility must not increase the Fund's holdings of the borrower's currency above 265% of the member's quota. As with all Fund finance, borrowing is conditional upon Fund approval of internal domestic policies to correct the payments deficit. In 1974 and 1975 the IMF created two temporary oil facilities to recycle oil-exporter funds to countries in severe payments difficulties following the increase in oil prices. The two arrangements channelled about SDR 7bn to countries in difficulty, including SDR 1bn borrowed by the UK in 1975. These temporary arrangements were replaced by the Supplementary Financing Facility, which came into effect in February 1979 with total resources of SDR 7.75bn. Despite these developments it is important to note that the recycling of oil-surplus money via the IMF has been small relative to the total amounts recycled via the international banking system and the intermediation of Eurocurrency and Eurobond markets. Between the years 1973 and 1975, for example, the euro-dollar deposits of the major oil exporters grew from SDR 4bn to SDR 21bn, the latter figure accounting for 45% of total Eurocurrency deposits at the time. During 1975 and 1976 total Eurobond issues amounted to SDR 21.3bn of which, however, only 6% was lent directly to the less developed countries.[2] Lending through the Euro markets has continued at a high rate since 1976 and it seems clear that the IMF has probably recycled less than 5% of the oil-surplus revenues. During 1979, however, the scope for further private lending came into question with the default on loans by Iran and the risks of increasing the scale of

---

1 For discussion of the adverse effects on developing countries and possible means of easing their problems, consult C. Michalopoulos, 'Financing Needs of Developing Countries: Proposals for International Action', *Essays in International Finance*, No. 110, Princeton, 1975.

2 Cf., R.I. McKinnon, 'The Euro Currency Market', *Essays in International Finance*, No. 125, December 1977, Princeton.

lending to debt-laden developing countries. It remains to be seen whether the euro markets can cope with the projected oil surpluses of the early 1980s as well as they have those of the 1970s. If not, the IMF, central banks and other international institutions will have to play a far greater role than in the past. Failure to recycle oil revenues would undoubtedly lead to a major world recession and default by many countries on their external debts.

The Jamaica Agreement and the Second Amendment: The final report of the C-20 advocated an evolutionary approach to the problems of world monetary reform and, despite the problems noted in the previous section, substantial progress has subsequently been made. During 1975 the Interim Committee held several meetings and agreement on four important issues was obtained in January 1976 at a meeting held in Jamaica. From this meeting emerged the most important development in the international monetary system since 1945, the Second Amendment to the Articles of Agreement, which came into effect in April 1978.

Without doubt the most fundamental outcome of the Jamaica meeting was the agreement to amend Article 4 of the IMF agreement. The main points of the new Article are as follows:[1] (i) a general return to stable but adjustable par values can take place with the support of an 85% majority in the IMF; (ii) par values may not be expressed in terms of gold or other currencies but can be expressed in terms of SDRs, the margins of fluctuation around par values remain at ± 2.25%; (iii) with the concurrence of the IMF, any country may abandon its par value and adopt a floating exchange rate; (iv) the exchange-rate management of a floating currency must be subject to IMF surveillance and must not be conducted so as to disadvantage other countries; (v) the agreed practices with respect to floating rates will operate until such time as a general return to par values is attained. In effect these changes legitimized floating exchange rates within the framework of the IMF system and without any diminution of the powers of the IMF.

The second aspect of the Second Amendment dealt with the relative positions of SDRs and gold. We have commented above on the attempts to enhance the reserve status of the SDR. The associated measures to demonetize gold were equally significant. In particular the official price of gold was abolished and members were no longer allowed to use gold to make their general quota contributions. Furthermore, members were again allowed to trade in gold at gold market prices. At Jamaica it was also agreed that the Fund would divest itself of one-third of its stock of gold. One-sixth would be transferred to members, in four annual instalments at the official gold price and in amounts proportional to their general quotas. The remaining one-sixth was to be sold to the world market at monthly intervals over the four-year period to May 1980 and the profits on these sales (the difference between the sale price and the old official price at which the IMF had received the gold) was to be used to establish a Trust Fund, to provide balance of payments assistance on concessionary terms to those poorer countries with a per capita GNP of less than SDR 300 in 1973. In the first three years of this scheme the total profits amounted to $2.52bn, of which SDR 1.7bn was allocated to the

---

1 The text of the proposed new Article 4 is contained in IMF, *Survey*, 19 January 1976, pp. 20-1. Full details of the revised articles of agreement may be found in *The Second Amendment to the Articles of Agreement of the International Monetary Fund*, Cmnd. 6705, HMSO, 1977.

Trust Fund and the remainder was distributed to 104 eligible developing-country members. Trust Fund loans are for a maximum of eleven years and carry interest at ½%.

The third and final outcome of the evolutionary reform process has been the decision to make two general increases in quotas. The 1976 review increased quotas by 32.5% to SDR 39bn and the Seventh Annual Review, expected to come into effect by November 1980, involves an increase to SDR 58.6bn. These changes make an important addition to Fund liquidity at a time of continued payments imbalance in the world economy.

The reforms embodied in the Second Amendment are undoubtedly important and reflect well on the IMF as an effective forum for international co-operation. However, the reforms fell short of the ideals outlined by the C-20 and their long-run effects may be in doubt.[1]

On exchange-rate management the revised guidelines for surveillance over exchange-rate policy are vague and the difficult question of whether surveillance should extend beyond exchange-rate policy has yet to be faced. Certainly 1979 proved to be a year of considerable unrest in gold and currency markets, with sharp declines in the dollar and the London market gold price rising by 60% from the end of October 1979 to reach $615 per oz. at the beginning of January 1980. On liquidity, it is plain that the SDR is currently the least significant reserve asset in the system, and that the aim of demonetizing gold is far from reached. Inflationary fears and political uncertainties in the Middle East have continued to make gold an attractive reserve asset. Indeed by allowing the revaluation of monetary gold in line with free-market prices the reserve-asset status of this metal has been greatly enhanced. Only the US continues to value its monetary gold at the old official price and the decision by the EMS members to value the gold component of the ECU (see section III.8 above) at market-related prices puts the IMF demonetization programme at risk. Important questions concerning the future of US dollar liabilities, which over the 1970s have accounted for between 70% and 80% of total foreign exchange reserves, their co-existence with other reserve currencies, for example the German mark, and the scope for a Substitution Account, also remain unresolved.[2] Until answers to these problems are found there seems little hope of re-creating a stable international monetary system based on a par-value mechanism. But perhaps the lesson to be learned from the 1970s is that the welfare of the major trading nations is best served by a system of managed, floating exchange rates.

Postscript: A partial solution to the contentious issue of the UK's contribution to the EEC budget was achieved in June 1980, with a refund to the UK for 1980 and 1981 of £1.57bn and the prospect of a further refund, following the same general principles, in 1982. This solution does nothing to come to terms with the structural difficulties which created the budgetary problem, nor to correct the excessive influence of the CAP on Community finances. (See also chapter 4, p. 190, footnote 2.)

---

1 For somewhat jaundiced views of the Jamaica agreement see Bernstein *et al.*, 'Reflections on Jamaica', *Essays in International Finance*, No. 115, Princeton, 1976, and A. Kafka, 'The IMF: Reform without Reconstruction?', *Essays in International Finance*, No. 118, Princeton, 1976.

2 For a recent appraisal see G. Richardson, 'The Prospects for an International Monetary System', *BEQB*, September 1979.

REFERENCE AND FURTHER READING

Sir Alec Cairncross (ed.), *Britain's Economic Prospects Reconsidered*, George Allen and Unwin, 1971.

Sir Alec Cairncross, *Control of Long-Term Capital Movements*, Brookings Institution, 1973.

R.E. Caves and Associates, *Britain's Economic Prospects*, Brookings Institution and George Allen and Unwin, 1968.

H.G. Grubel, *International Economics*, Irwin, 1977.

H.G. Johnson and J.E. Nash, *UK and Floating Exchanges*, Hobart Paper 46, Institute of Economic Affairs, 1969.

C.P. Kindleberger and P.H. Lindert, *International Economics*, Irwin, 1978.

F. Machlup, *Remaking the International Monetary System*, Committee for Economic Development and Johns Hopkins, 1968.

R.L. Major, *Britain's Trade and Exchange Rate Policy*, Heinemann, 1979.

C. McMahon, *Sterling in the Sixties*, Oxford University Press, 1964.

J.E. Meade, *UK, Commonwealth and Common Market: A Reappraisal*, Hobart Paper 17, Institute of Economic Affairs, 1970.

R.L. Miller and J.B. Wood, *Exchange Control for Ever*, Institute of Economic Affairs, London, 1979.

W.B. Reddaway, *Effects of UK Direct Investment Overseas: An Interim Report*, Cambridge University Press, 1967; *Final Report*, Cambridge University Press, 1968.

B. Tew, *The Evolution of the International Monetary System, 1945-77*, Hutchinson, 1977.

S.J. Wells, *British Export Performance*, Cambridge University Press, 1964.

J. Williamson, *The Failure of World Monetary Reform, 1971-74*, Nelson, 1977.

OFFICIAL PUBLICATIONS

Bank of England Quarterly Bulletin

British Business (weekly) (previously *Trade and Industry*), Department of Trade and Industry.

Economic Trends (regular analyses of balance of payments in March, June, September and December issues) (CSO).

IMF, *Annual Report* and IMF, *Survey* (twice monthly).

NEDC reports, especially *Export Trends* (1963) and *Imported Manufactures* (1965).

Report of Committee on the Working of the Monetary System, Radcliffe Report, Cmnd. 827, 1959.

UK Balance of Payments (*Pink Book*, annual), CSO.

4

Industry and commerce

J.R. Cable (assisted by I. Tonks)

I   INTRODUCTION: SOME THEORETICAL BACKGROUND

Whenever we attempt to analyse the behaviour of firms and industries we have, at some stage, to rely on theoretical models. Orthodox theory has it that firms behave as if their objective was to maximize profit. The theory offers us many insights and can lead to important policy implications for the government and others. But there are alternative models which will be drawn upon in this chapter for additional insights.

One strand of recent theoretical development has resulted in a group of 'managerial' models. These recognize that in modern, large firms there has been a divorce of ownership (by shareholders) from control (by salaried executives).[1] In this situation profit remains important to policy-makers within the firm both for survival and also because it may be directly linked to executive salaries through incentives such as stock-option schemes and bonuses linked to profits. But it is argued that where top management exercises the degree of control over policy that it appears to do in practice, firms are most likely to behave as if maximizing the value of variables yielding utility to managers, subject to some profit or other financial constraint. The variables in question vary from model to model. In Baumol's model the firm is assumed to maximize sales revenue, subject to a profit constraint.[2] Marris has developed an alternative, growth-maximizing model, with a security (stock market valuation) constraint.[3] Williamson put forward a more general model of managerial utility, in which the objective function incorporates salary, the number and quality of subordinates, control over discretionary investment and expenditure on managerial perquisites.[4]

Firms pursuing such objectives would usually arrive at equilibrium outcomes which differ from those of a profit-maximizer, e.g. in terms of price and output levels. In some cases they would also adjust decision variables in the opposite direction to a profit-maximizer, in response to changes in the business environment, e.g. changes in tax rates. Hence in analysing firms' behaviour and in assessing the

---

1   See A.A. Berle and G.C. Means, *The Modern Corporation and Private Property*, revised edition, Harcourt, Brace and World, N.Y. 1968; P. Sargent Florence, *Ownership Control and Success of Large Companies*, Sweet and Maxwell, 1961; R. Marris and A. Wood, *The Corporate Economy*, Macmillan, 1971; A. Wood, *A Theory of Profits*, CUP, 1975, and M. King, *Public Policy and the Corporation*, Chapman and Hall, 1977.

2   W.J. Baumol, 'On the Theory of Oligopoly', *Economica*, Vol. XXV, No. 99, August 1958, pp. 187-98, and *Business Behaviour Value and Growth*, Macmillan, 1959.

3   R. Marris, 'A Model of the Managerial Enterprise', *Quarterly Journal of Economics*, May 1963, and *The Economic Theory of Managerial Capitalism*, Macmillan, 1964.

4   O.E. Williamson, 'Managerial Discretion and Business Behaviour', *American Economic Review*, December 1963, and *The Economics of Discretionary Behaviour: Business Objectives in the Theory of the Firm*, Prentice Hall, 1964.

effects of government policy we may reach different conclusions depending on which theoretical model of behaviour we apply. Unfortunately there is at the moment no clear way of telling which model should be adopted. Empirical testing of the hypotheses so far has produced some evidence in support of each, but none of the theories − including profit-maximization − has yet been accepted as demonstrably superior. In this situation perhaps the most we can do when looking at the behaviour of firms and industries is to be very clear on the theoretical assumptions we make and, especially when appraising public policy issues, consider the various responses which might be expected under different theoretical assumptions.

Alongside the managerial theories is another, somewhat more radical, new theoretical departure. The 'behavioural' theory emphasizes the organizational aspects of firms and the limited amount of knowledge available in decision-making.[1] In the behavioural theory the firm is seen to pursue a number of goals in the form of independent, aspiration-level constraints, e.g. a particular sum of profits, or level of sales, or a target rate of return on capital, which firms attempt to 'satisfice'. Goals are imperfectly rationalized, may conflict, and receive sequential rather than simultaneous attention. Over time, aspiration levels for a particular goal will change according to past achievements in relation to past aspirations. The firm is seen as an adaptive organism, solving pressing problems rather than attempting to apply plans leading to optimal equilibrium values or growth paths of decision variables, as in more conventional approaches. In a situation of imperfect knowledge, search (the acquisition of information) is neither continuous nor determined optimally as an investment decision. Rather, search is 'problemistic', requiring to be motivated e.g. by adverse feedback on goal fulfilment or by some external event or evidence of failure. Search is 'limited' or 'narrow'; solutions are sought at first in the neighbourhood of problem symptoms and current alternatives and search widens only as satisfactory solutions fail to be found. In choosing among alternative strategies 'satisficing' procedures are adopted, the first acceptable strategy being selected. The firm's behaviour is constrained by standard procedural rules governing search, choice, etc., and these are abandoned only under duress. However, in the long term organizational learning occurs, and search and choice rules are adapted in the light of experience. Typically, firms exhibit organizational slack in the form of excess resources within the organization.

In order to derive quantitative predictions of firms' behaviour from the behavioural model it is necessary to develop specific computer simulation models. However, the theory does permit of some qualitative analysis without this. Like the managerial theories, the behavioural theory is important because it may lead us to conclusions about firms' behaviour which are different from those of other models. However, one distinguishing feature of the behavioural model is that it specifically sets out to embody the decision process. Thus, unlike all the other models so far mentioned, the behavioural model *does* attempt to tell us how various outcomes are arrived at as well as what the outcomes will be.

The theoretical approaches to firms' behaviour so far discussed have generally been conceived with the private sector of the economy in mind, and especially

---

1   H.A. Simon, 'A Behavioural Model of Rational Choice', *Quarterly Journal of Economics*, February 1955; R.M. Cyert and J.G. March, *A Behavioural Theory of the Firm*, Prentice Hall, 1963, and H.A. Simon, 'Theories of Decision Making in Economics and Behavioural Science', *American Economic Review*, June 1959.

'secondary' manufacturing industry rather than the 'primary' sector (agriculture and extractive industries) and the 'tertiary' sector (transport, distributive trades, professional and other services, government administration, etc.). Nevertheless there are some insights which they can give in all areas of industry and commerce, whether public or private, and the scope of this chapter is not limited to the private manufacturing sector. Some of the issues we shall consider do mainly concern the private sector (e.g. the question of monopoly control). But in another section we also consider the public-sector issue of pricing and investment criteria for nationalized industries. And a number of the issues considered are common to both the public and private sectors and all industry and commerce, e.g. the whole question of efficiency, productivity and technical progress.

II   THE SIZE STRUCTURE OF INDUSTRIES AND TRADES

An idea of the size structure of UK industrial groupings is given in the second column of table 4.1. Size is measured in terms of output. Alternative measures would be employment and capital stock. In some cases these would produce a rather different picture, because of inter-industry differences in capital/labour ratios. For instance, in 1972 the UK coal, petroleum and chemical industries together accounted for 21.4% of total capital employed in manufacturing but only 5.7% of manpower and 11.4% of output. Evidently there is need for some care in choosing the most appropriate size measure for any particular, given purpose.

Industry boundaries are based on the Standard Industrial Classification for the UK. The SIC groups the UK economy into Orders, which are subdivided into Minimum List Headings. The latter are generally the nearest one can get in official statistics to what we would normally mean by an 'industry', although even these subdivisions are too broad in some cases.[1] The industry groups in the table are mostly Orders, or even groups of Orders, and it must be remembered that they may be composed of a very large number of sub-trades, often quite disparate. Although there may be quite strong technological links among the industries concerned, it is by no means certain that their various products necessarily have high cross-elasticities of demand. In general industrial classifications tend to be production-oriented.

In comparison with other major European countries the UK has a relatively small agricultural sector, reflecting a greater reliance on food imports in the past (see below, p. 187), but some larger tertiary industries, notably finance, insurance, etc. The manufacturing sector as a whole is not large in relation to GDP by international standards, and certainly accounts for a much smaller share of all economic activity than in West Germany.

Table 4.2 enables more detailed comparisons to be made among the major West European countries for the manufacturing sector. This shows a comparatively small UK chemicals sector, and significantly larger metal products group, which includes the engineering and allied industries. The UK textiles and clothing industry is larger than in France and West Germany, but much smaller than in Italy.

---

1   For example, see p. 209 below.

TABLE 4.1

Size Structure and Growth of UK Industries, 1957-79

Industry	Annual rate of growth, 1957-79	GDP by industrial origin, 1978 (£m)[3]
Agriculture, forestry and fishing	2.26[1]	4,251
Mining and quarrying	2.62	4,516
Manufacturing:		
Food, drink and tobacco	2.08	4,611
Chemicals and oil products	4.95	3,906
Metal manufacture	−0.26	2,472
Engineering and allied industries	2.17	14,500
Mechanical	1.85	5,007
Electrical	4.41	3,978
Vehicles	0.80	4,098
Textiles, leather clothing	0.73	3,435
Printing, paper publishing	2.19	3,269
Total Manufacturing	2.06	42,948
Construction	1.35	8,731
Electricity, gas and water	4.35	4,918
Transport and communications	2.78[1]	11,699
Distributive trades	1.95[1]	15,596
Insurance, banking, finances and business services	4.18[1]	11,268
Miscellaneous services	2.09[1]	18,899
GDP[2] at factor cost	2.10	141,999

Sources: NIBB, 1979; NIER, 1980.
Notes: 1 1957-78.
        2 Includes public administration and defence, ownership of dwellings, public health services, local authority educational services, adjustment for financial services and residual error.
        3 Contribution of each industry to GDP before providing for depreciation, but after providing for stock appreciation. Figures for selected individual manufacturing industries are estimates.

Changes in the size distribution will obviously occur when industries grow at different rates. As the next section will show, there have been considerable differences in growth experience among individual UK industries since the early 1950s. These have produced some significant changes in the proportion of GDP originating in broad sectors of the economy.[1] In particular, the share of manufacturing fell from 36.7% in 1955 to 30.2% in 1978. Other industries whose share has declined include agriculture and construction, from 10.6% to 9.1%. Public utilities and commerce (distribution, transport, insurance, etc.) increased their share of GDP from 26.6% to 30.6%, and the share of miscellaneous services, public administration and defence also rose. The figures for mining and quarrying imply that its share remained fairly constant over the period, 3.5% in 1955 and

---

1 For a stimulating and controversial discussion of Britain's alleged structural malaise, with too few resources committed to marketed goods, see R. Bacon and W. Eltis, *Britain's Economic Problem: Too Few Producers*, Macmillan, 1976.

TABLE 4.2

Relative Importance of Manufacturing Industries, UK and Selected European Countries, 1975[1]

	Percentage of manufacturing output			
	UK	France	W. Germany	Italy
Food, Drink, Tobbacco	11.0	12.7	13.7	12.6
Chemicals	13.3	17.9	17.4	14.4
Basic Metals	7.2	12.4	5.9	7.7
Metal Products	42.2	37.6	38.8	29.9
Non-Metallic Mineral Products	4.2	4.6	4.8	5.9
Textiles, Clothing and Leather	9.0	8.3	6.6	16.2
Wood, Wood Products	3.5	0.3	5.1	5.6
Paper and Paper Products	8.3	6.2	4.6	5.0
Other Manufacturing	1.3	–	3.1	2.8
All Manufacturing	100.0	100.0	100.0	100.0
Manufacturing output in thousand millions of EUA[2]	45.8	74.5	125.0	41.8

Sources: Indicators of Industrial Activity, 1979, OECD; *National Accounts of OECD Countries*, 1978, 1975.

Notes: 1 These figures have been extracted from tables containing weights for mining, electricity and gas as well as manufacturing.

2 European Units of Account are an EEC monetary unit based on the gold content of the US dollar prior to December 1971. Conversion tables are given in National Accounts, ESA, Eurostat 1978.

3.1% in 1978, but this hides two significant trends. Throughout the 1960s the coal-mining industry was gradually run down, so that by 1973 its share was only 1.3% of GDP. The subsequent oil crisis, which restored the competitive position of the mining industry and halted its decline, plus the extraction of North Sea oil, has meant that energy output has dramatically increased in a very short time. Between 1957 and 1974 mining and quarrying declined at an annual rate of 3.33%. Over the last six years this trend has been reversed and the growth rate of the industry averaged nearly 38% per annum. This staggering growth rate is due to one particular sector. The output of petroleum and natural gas has risen from 0.4 million tons in 1973 to 77.6 million tons in 1979.

III INDUSTRIAL OUTPUT GROWTH, 1957-78
III.1 General Output Trends

The growth of UK industrial output over the past two decades, at a rate of approximately 2.4% per annum, has been extremely modest by international standards. Table 4.3 compares the annual growth rates for total industrial production (manufacturing, mining, electricity and gas) between the UK and the six original EEC members. Most of the other countries grew at around twice the UK rate or more, except for Belgium and Luxembourg, and of these two the Belgian rate was also well above the UK's. If differences in growth rates such as these persisted for only short periods there would be little change in relative output levels and, ultimately, living standards among the various countries. When they persist for a time period as long as that covered in table 4.3 the differential impact is large. Whereas UK industrial production grew by a little under 70%, that for the EEC as a whole rose to over two and a half times the original level, while the Italian and Dutch production more than trebled. At the beginning of the period (and indeed up to 1967) national income per head was higher in the UK than in the EEC as a whole, although the French and German GDP per head had exceeded the UK's since 1961. By 1972 the UK had become one of the poorer Western European nations.

Table 4.1 shows a fair measure of diversity among the growth rates for various industry sectors in the UK over the same period, with the chemical industry, electrical engineering, the public utilities and financial services expanding at around twice the average rate, and with one industry actually declining. Yet even the faster-growing sectors have scarcely matched the average performances in the EEC countries previously discussed. As one would expect, examples of more impressive expansion do emerge upon further disaggregation, e.g. plastics, electronics and man-made fibres. The physical quantity of synthetic-resin production increased more than eightfold between 1950 and 1973, and total production of man-made fibres more than trebled between 1958 and 1973. More recently, however, these rapid growth rates have slowed down and even fallen. In the chemical industry, this has been due to the movement out of its 'new industry' phase into a more mature one; and in the textile industry its products have become uncompetitive in import and export markets.

What the eventual effects of EEC membership on individual UK industries will be is hard to say. Various forecasts were made at the time of UK entry. One of the most comprehensive produced a ranking of some 230 manufactured products in order of those most likely to benefit from entry.[1] The products belonged to nine industrial sectors: chemicals; manufactures of leather, wood, rubber, paper, etc.; textiles and clothing; iron and steel; non-ferrous metals and metal manufactures;

TABLE 4.3

Output Growth and GDP per head in the UK and EEC, 1957-78

Country	Annual growth of industrial production[1] 1957-78 (%)	Total growth of industrial production 1957-78 (%)	GDP per head (in EUA)	
			1960	1978
UK	2.39	68.1	1286	3953
France	4.42	158.8	1245	6500
Germany	4.35	155.7	1231	7618
Italy	5.40	225.4	653	3108
Belgium	3.39	107.4	908	7066
Netherlands	5.20	207.9	1157	7071
Luxembourg	1.65	43.8	1559	7097
EEC (the six)	4.50	163.3	1041	5921
EEC (the nine)	3.74	101.5[2]	1095	5498

Sources: Industrial Production, OECD, 1955-71, 1960-75; *National Accounts*, Eurostat, 1978; *Indicators of Industrial Activity*, OECD, 1979; *Eurostatistics*, 1980.
Notes: 1   Includes manufacturing, mining, electricity and gas.
                2   1960-78.

1   S.S. Han and H.H. Liesner, *Britain and the Common Market*, University of Cambridge, Department of Applied Economics, Occasional Paper No. 27, 1971.

TABLE 4.4

Degree of Self-Sufficiency in Agricultural Products in the UK and EEC (Value of Domestic Consumption as % of Domestic Production)

	1976/7 (%)	
	UK	*Eur-9*
Wheat (soft)	58	105
Wheat (hard)	—	86
Rye	54	95
Barley	90	94
Oats	93	91
Potatoes	82	96
Sugar	27	104
Vegetables	69	92
Fresh fruit	31	78
	1977	
Skimmed milk	202	114
Cheese	68	104
Butter	32	107
Eggs	100	100
Meat	73	96

Source: Yearbook of Agricultural Statistics, 1978, Eurostat.

mechanical engineering; electrical engineering; transport equipment; and a miscellaneous category. The broad conclusion was that none of these industrial sectors was likely to fare much better or worse than any other across the board. Rather, each sector had its more promising and more vulnerable parts. This result accords well with previous findings that the creation of the EEC influenced the economies of the original partners mainly by a redistribution of resources within rather than between industries.[1] However, the findings for individual products did not in all cases agree with an official list of products thought likely to benefit from entry.[2] This included footwear, machine tools and food-processing equipment, all of which figured among those expected to do least well of all among the 230 products in the first study.

III.2 Agricultural Development and Policy

As in almost all other developed countries, UK agricultural production has been maintained and developed since the war at a higher level than would otherwise be the case, given the costs of domestic production and world price levels for agricultural products. The method by which support was given prior to the entry of

1 B. Balassa, 'Tariff Reductions and Trade in Manufactures among the Industrial Countries', *AER*, June 1966, pp. 466-73, and I. Walter, *The European Common Market: Growth and Patterns of Trade and Production*, New York, 1967.

2 *BTJ*, 8 July 1970, pp. 41-3.

the UK into the EEC differed in some respects from the Common Agricultural Policy (CAP) operated by the EEC.

Under the UK scheme up to 1973, farmers received assistance in two main ways, through deficiency payments and through direct grants for capital investment and farm-improvement schemes. The deficiency-payments scheme operated as follows. Agricultural products sold in the UK at world price levels, with more or less free access to the UK market for foreign producers, and some preferential treatment for Commonwealth producers. Where these prices were below the level of a guaranteed price, set by the government to encourage a certain level of home production, taking production costs and farm incomes into account, farmers received from the government a deficiency payment equal to the difference. Thus the UK maintained open markets to foreign producers, and consumers enjoyed the relatively low world food price levels, but home production was encouraged and farm incomes were stabilized and controlled. The cost fell on the Exchequer and varied inversely with the level of world prices. Early experience of the mounting cost of an open-ended support scheme, with no upper limit on quantities produced at home and hence on the liability of the Exchequer, led to a modification in the early 1960s. Around 1963 'standard quantities' were introduced for most products, and the guaranteed price fell as these were exceeded.

The farm capital grants scheme provided assistance for investment in farm buildings, fixed machinery, land drainage, hill-land improvements and remodelling works for farm amalgamations, etc. The rates of grant-aid tended to differ among projects, although steps were taken in 1970 towards a comprehensive scheme with a basic rate of 30%. In addition to capital grants, subsidies were offered for certain current expenditures, e.g. those associated with the use of fertilizers and lime. The guaranteed prices, grants and subsidies were reviewed annually and published in the *Annual Review and Determination of Guarantees*.[1]

One overall result of the old UK policy was certainly to make domestic production higher than it would have been without official support (and assuming other countries continued to support their own farmers). The policy also affected the composition of agricultural output and the efficiency of the industry. In the later years of the policy especially, guaranteed prices were manipulated to produce selective expansion. Similarly, selective use was made of grants and subsidies to bring about desired changes in the structure of the industry, and to mechanize and modernize it. The fact that between 1955 and 1972 output grew by 2.7% per annum and capital by 3.0%, while employment fell by roughly 3.1% is some indication of the extent to which this happened.

EEC arrangements for agricultural support under the CAP have objectives which are very similar to those of the previous UK policy. Article 39 of the Treaty of Rome mentions securing increases in agricultural efficiency, stabilizing agricultural markets, guaranteeing regular supplies, and ensuring reasonable prices to consumers and fair living standards for the agricultural populations. The two policies are also similar in that support to farmers comes partly in the form of price guarantees and partly in capital and current grants or subsidies. However, the methods of operation are different, especially on the price-support side.

---

1 Since 1977 the *Annual Review* has been published separately, now that the scope for determining prices, etc. at national level is limited.

The CAP was designed to bring about free intra-community trade in agricultural products, with uniform prices among the members and a common external tariff. Since the early 1960s 'target' prices have been negotiated for many products which, like the old UK guaranteed prices, make domestic production profitable. However, under the EEC arrangements consumers pay the full target price, or a price close to it. To ensure that this is so, there is a system of variable levies on imports from the outside world, broadly designed to equalize the supply of foreign produce (including transport costs) and the target price. In addition, there is provision for support-buying of unsold produce when prices fall below an intervention-price level. In some cases the intervention price is set close to the target price. For instance, the intervention price for grain is within 5-7% of the target price. For some products, however, such as fruit and vegetables, prices can fall significantly before support-buying occurs. The central authority responsible for the policy is the European Agricultural Guidance and Guarantee Fund. Price support is managed by the Guarantee wing of this authority. The fund receives its income ultimately from the Exchequers of member nations, contributions being determined partly in proportion to the size of the import levies arising from each nation's external trade in agricultural products.

Grant aid to farmers comes under the Guidance wing of the EAGGF but grants are actually made by each national government. Up to 1971 the assistance schemes of each country had not been harmonized, but over the 1960s an increasing proportion of the relevant expenditure was reimbursed by the Fund. The rate of grant aid for approved schemes varied up to a maximum of 25%, and as in the UK some grant aid was available for current expenditures (i.e. towards the cost of non-capital inputs).

The relative merits of the old and new systems are worth considering. From a world standpoint many observers have commented unfavourably on the protectionist attitude of the CAP towards non-Community produce, in contrast to the 'open door' aspect of the earlier UK policy. Secondly, the high domestic price characteristic of the CAP has been adversely compared with the former UK 'cheap food' policy, especially as food expenditure accounts for a higher proportion of total expenditure among poorer families. Thirdly, many observers would say that compared with the UK system the CAP is an inefficient scheme in a number of technical respects.

Thus one problem is that of surpluses of major products. The CAP's high prices and support-buying arrangements stimulate production and remove the normal market sanction on over-supply (i.e. downward price adjustment) while simultaneously discouraging demand. In the absence of other non-market controls on supply, such as the 'standard quantities' under the old UK system, this produces a chronic tendency towards the appearance of surpluses. At one time or another there have in fact been surpluses of butter (purchased to sustain a high target price for milk), grains, sugar, beef, fruit and wine. A second technical deficiency, which also arises from the open-ended nature of the support system, is that there is in principle no upper limit to the cost of support. Thirdly, the CAP as at present operated, places must less emphasis on raising farm efficiency than did the old UK system. Despite the *Mansholt Plan* of 1968, which was designed to shift the emphasis of CAP away from price support towards structural reform, price support retains the major share of expenditure. Yet almost three-quarters of the total EEC expenditure (estimated at £10,000 million in 1980) goes on farm price support, benefiting farmers who make up less than 8% of the EEC workforce.

Financing the milk surplus alone takes up about 35% of the budget. The guidance wing of the policy accounted for a little more than 1% of the total cost in 1978 compared with 60% or so going on grants and subsidies under the old UK system.

The CAP has always been a source of problems among the member countries, with their differing domestic agricultural situations and interests. Setting suitable common target prices against a background of widely differing productivity levels from country to country has been a major and recurring problem. Lengthy and often heated negotiations also occur over the size of the Farm Fund and of individual member contributions to it. In a situation where Britain in particular, and also West Germany and Italy, are net losers in terms of budgetary contributions and receipts, the remaining countries either benefit or receive roughly what they give. Britain's share of financing the budget in 1980 will be 20.5%, but its share of receipts from the CAP is expected to be only 10.3%. Small amounts do come to Britain through the regional and social funds, but these fail to compensate. The reasons for Britain's excessive net contribution to the Community budget are that her extensive import trade with non-EEC countries and her small agricultural sector results in a high gross contribution to the budget from customs duties and VAT, and only a small return from the CAP. This structural pattern is unique among the Nine. The estimated net loss for Britain in 1980 is £1,200m, in a situation where Britain is the third poorest member of the Community in terms of per capita GDP. Yet this net accounting loss measured by receipts less payments does not reflect the true cost, which should include the loss in consumer surplus from prices being higher than their world levels. There will be a deadweight welfare loss suffered by the community as a whole. The true cost of the CAP to the UK is estimated at being £2,200 million.[1] At the time of writing, negotiations are taking place to reduce Britain's net contribution to the budget. The British government is demanding a cut of £1,000m, a five-year freeze on the cost of the farm policy and an open guarantee to spend extra money in Britain for each of the next five years at whatever level would be needed to lift our net receipts to at least 80% of the Community average. Its European partners are unwilling to concede to any of these demands, and in fact are pushing for a 5% rise in EEC farm products' prices. So far they have offered Britain a £350m refund and are unwilling to give any more unless Britain also retreats on some of its more contentious issues such as fishing rights and oil policy.[2]

In the 1970s currency problems have also loomed large: since agricultural prices are fixed in EUA, changes in official parities within the Community create a need for adjustments to maintain agricultural price uniformity in real terms. In the case of Britain, the 'green pound' – the exchange rate between sterling and EUA for agricultural purposes, which does not float – was devalued by a total of 15% in 1974 and 1975, and a further 7.5% in early 1978. However, the total devaluation since 1973 is much less than the overall decline of sterling against major trading currencies over the same period.

---

1   J. Kay, *Fiscal Studies*, February 1980.

2   The terms of these negotiations have since been agreed. Britain's net contribution to the budget will be reduced to £380m in the current year and £456m in 1981. In return, Britain will withdraw its veto of the proposed 5% farm price increase.

III.3   Energy

The growth of total energy consumption, at less than 1% p.a. over the past fifteen
years (see table 4.5), has clearly been much less than the expansion of GDP over the
same period. The introduction of technical economies in fuel use, and relatively
slow growth in some fuel-intensive industries such as iron and steel and rail, are
among the factors which explain this differential growth. In addition energy
demand has been reduced due to the sudden large price increases, particularly in
petroleum prices, since 1973; between 1973 and 1975 total energy consumption
actually fell by 8.5%, though this was followed by a rise of 5.9% up to 1978.

The discovery of natural gas and then oil in the North Sea, together with the
quadrupling of world petroleum prices by OPEC countries in 1973-4 and subsequent
increases, have produced dramatic changes in the pattern of UK energy
procurement. Gas was the first industry to be affected, moving from stagnation
to resurgence in the mid-1960s, as cheap, imported gas became available to replace
town gas. Growth then accelerated under the impact of even cheaper and growing
North Sea supplies in the 1970s. From 1969 to 1976 sales rose at over 16% p.a.
and by 1979 99.8% of gas used was natural.

Direct use of coal was in very sharp decline over the period 1960 to 1974. (The
reduction in coal output was much less rapid however (cf. tables 4.5 and 4.1)
because coal has been retained, by a deliberate act of government policy, as a
primary energy source in electricity generation.) Up to the mid-1970s there was
rapid growth of electricity demand, and the electricity industry's share in total coal
sales rose from 21.8% in 1957 to 66.3% in 1978. The reason for coal's decline over
the period was primarily that after 1956 petroleum had become relatively much
cheaper. The 1973-4 oil price rises, however, restored coal's price competitiveness,
and the industry's prospects have also been improved by the discovery of large
reserves at Selby and in Warwickshire, and by technical developments in mining
technology. Thus far, however, the net result has been only that the long-term
decline of coal has been halted. In the period 1971-2 to 1978-9 production has
fluctuated around an average level of just over 111 million tons per annum,
compared with an average of around 180 million tons during the 1960s.

Large-scale production of North Sea oil began in 1976, production rising from
12 million tonnes in that year to 77 million tonnes in 1979. Present forecasts are
for further expansion to 110 million tonnes in 1981, and a maximum 146 million
tonnes in 1984, after which output is expected to level off or decline. Department
of Energy estimates are that the total recoverable reserves in the UK Continental
Shelf could lie in the range 2,400 to 4,400 million tonnes. However, these
estimates should be treated with caution. North Sea oil, though of high quality,
is expensive and economically viable only if world price levels are high.
(Production costs in the North Sea are approximately ten times those of the most
accessible Middle East sources.) As with coal, actual future production will depend
on the trend of extraction costs, the price of imported oil, and world political
developments which affect the strategic value of a secure, domestic source of
supply.

Because government policy is to keep the North Sea oil price in line with world
levels, its availability is not expected to lead to dramatic changes in the future
pattern of fuel use. In fact, oil consumption in 1980 is expected to be not much
different from the 1970 level. The main benefits from North Sea oil lie elsewhere,

Industry and commerce

TABLE 4.5

Total UK Inland Energy Consumption, 1960-78: Heat Supplied Basis (million therms)

Type of fuel	1960	(%)	1970	(%)	1974	(%)	1978	(%)	% change 1960-78
Coal									
(direct use)	23433	(46.4)	11839	(20.4)	7519	(12.9)	5738	(9.7)	−75.5%
Gas	3187	(6.3)	6182	(10.7)	12123	(20.7)	15382	(26.0)	+382.7%
Electricity	3372	(6.7)	6567	(11.3)	7282	(12.5)	7676	(13.0)	+127.7%
Petroleum	12385	(24.5)	27198	(46.9)	27193	(46.5)	27060	(45.7)	+118.5%
Other fuels[1]	8154	(16.1)	6167	(10.6)	4371	(7.5)	3335	(5.6)	−59.1%
Total	50531	(100.0)	57953	(100.0)	58488	(100.0)	59191	(100.0)	17.1% i.e. 0.9% p.a.

Source: AAS, 1980.
Note: 1 Includes coke, breeze, solid and liquid fuels derived from coal.

in particular in the form of a significant increase in the growth of GNP,[1] and favourable effects on the balance of payments and government revenue.

Energy consumption per head in the UK is higher than in Europe − by 5.8% in total than in the nine EEC member countries, and 1.8% higher in the household consumption sector.[2] However, UK dependence on imported fuel is much less, 25% as against 56%. This partly reflects the effect of North Sea oil, but is also the result of an even more rapid run-down of coal production and switch to petroleum on the continent than in the UK. In 1950 coal supplied nearly 75% of energy needs in the Six, and petroleum only 10%. In 1977 the proportions of coal and oil among the different primary fuels in gross inland consumption in the UK and in the Nine were:

	UK	EEC-9
Hard coal	34.2%	18.9%
Crude petroleum	43.2%	53.9%

Like agriculture, energy is the subject of a common policy in the EEC. However, the energy policy is rudimentary compared with the elaborate CAP. It is also very different, in that the Community opted for a cheap energy policy during the 1960s based on imported crude oil, with some subsidies to internal coal producers. These characteristics typify the old UK agricultural support system rather than CAP. One reason for the rather limited agreement over energy policy which has been achieved is that before 1967 responsibility for the various fuel industries was divided. Coal was the responsibility of the European Coal and Steel Community (ECSC); oil,

1 A recent estimate suggests that, taking into account the oil price increase of 1973-4, total growth of GDP from 1975-85 is raised by about 4%, about half this increase coming in 1977-9, when the annual measured growth rate is on average 0.7% higher due to oil. See *NIESR*, February 1978.

2 Source: Eurostat, *Energy Statistics Yearbook*, 1979. Figures are for 1977. The gap is closing however: comparable figures for 1971 are 15.6% and 19.7% respectively.

natural gas and electricity were covered by the EEC; and nuclear power was the province of the European Atomic Energy Community (Euratom). After the merger of the three communities in 1967 the full extension of the Treaty of Rome to the energy sector was agreed; i.e. a common market in energy was created. Since then the European Commission has undertaken short- and medium-term forecasts of energy demand and supply, analysed the problems likely to occur up to 1985, and identified various policy options. A number of directives, orders, regulations and decisions have also been made. Through these, members have agreed to maintain certain levels of oil stocks and to supply regular information on oil and natural gas imports and on certain investments in oil refineries, oil and gas transport and storage facilities, and in electricity production. Support of coal production by member governments had been authorized, e.g. by financing stocks, and a subsidy introduced for EEC production of coking coal and coke. Other proposed measures have included harmonization of fuel taxes (at a proposed level lower than the present UK fuel-oil tax) and a detailed package containing 46 measures, proposed in 1972, covering such things as environmental protection; developing relations between petroleum exporting and importing countries; and defining medium-term guidelines for the coal industry.

In the nuclear-energy sector Euratom was set up to promote and co-ordinate research; help disseminate technical information; facilitate capital investment; establish a common market in specialized material and equipment; free movement of capital and manpower in the nuclear field; and maintain links with other countries and international organizations. Some progress has been made in each of these areas, but generally less than was envisaged originally. In particular Euratom has not been successful in co-ordinating the national nuclear R and D programmes of members.

III.4 Transport

Provision of transport services has grown faster than the output series for the transport and communications sector suggests, at least on the passenger side (cf. tables 4.6, 4.7 and 4.1). This is mainly because the output series takes no account of private motoring, which is where the main increase in passenger mileage occurred (despite a temporary check in 1974 due to a sharp increase in fuel costs). The impact of rising incomes on car ownership has been a major factor. (The number of private cars currently licensed rose from 4.2m in 1957 to 14.0m in 1978.) Before 1974 relative price movements would also have been a reinforcing factor; both rail and bus fares rose very much faster over the period than did private motoring costs. In the inland freight sector the two growth rates are much more nearly in line, but there too there has been a major re-allocation of traffic towards road services (table 4.7).

Because so much of public transport is nationalized, developments in the transport sector are more than usually subject to government policy.[1] A consultative document published in April 1976 highlighted a number of problems.[2]

---

1 See also section IV.

2 'Consultative Document on Transport Policy', Department of the Environment, 13 April 1976. Also N. Lee, 'A Review of Current Transport Policy and Objectives in Britain', *TBR*, March 1977.

One was the lack of a proper framework for the co-ordination of transport policy, at both the national and local levels. A second was the problems facing certain vulnerable groups, in particular the 50% of households without a car, whose mobility has been reduced as the growth of private motoring adversely affected the revenue base of public transport and the level of services provided. This problem is especially severe in rural areas (where the proportion of households without cars is 30%). Thirdly, environmental problems were listed as requiring a greater degree of priority in the future. Finally, the document stressed the problem of transport subsidies (which rose from £174m in 1968 to £797m in 1978). The bulk of this money has gone to the railways; despite subsidies and the writing-off of more than £3,000m debt over 20 years, the rail subsidy had risen to £546m in 1978. The document stressed that these subsidies, especially to rail users, do not necessarily represent transfers to the poorer sections of the community; thus the richest 20% of households account for 50% of rail travel, whereas the poorest 40% are responsible for only 15%.

TABLE 4.6

GB Inland Passenger Mileage, 1960-78[1] (000m passenger-miles)

Year	Air	Rail	Road		Total
			Public service vehicles	*Private transport*	
1960	0.5 (0.3%)	24.8 (15.6%)	43.9 (27.7%)	89.4 (56.4%)	158.6 (100.0%)
1965	1.0 (0.5%)	21.8 (10.6%)	39.2 (19.0%)	144.7 (70.0%)	206.7 (100.0%)
1970	1.2 (0.5%)	22.2 (8.7%)	34.8 (13.7%)	196.2 (77.1%)	254.4 (100.0%)
1974	1.5 (0.5%)	22.4 (8.1%)	34.2 (12.4%)	217.5 (78.9%)	275.6 (100.0%)
1978	1.5 (0.5%)	21.9 (7.3%)	32.3 (10.8%)	244.8 (81.5%)	300.5 (100.0%)
% change 1960-78	+198.0%	−11.8%	−26.4%	+173.8%	+89.5% i.e. 3.4% p.a.

Source: AAS, 1980.
Note: 1   % figures in brackets show respective contributions to the total in any one year.

The document did not detail specific proposals, although some suggestions and probable directions of future policy were intimated. The idea of switching freight from road to rail was rejected, mainly on the ground that the impact would be slight. Thus, even if all journeys over 100 miles were transferred to rail, only a 2-4% reduction in road traffic would result. Also the document did not suggest that any drastic measures to curtail private motoring were being contemplated. Continued subsidies to rail transport were described as unjustifiable,[1] though there might be a case for increased subsidies for bus services which, unlike rail subsidies, do tend to find their way to poorer people and those without cars. Changes in the vehicle licencing system were discussed, to favour buses and local transport, but penalize heavy lorries. In new road investment, priority was recommended for

---

1   The document underlined the case for fare increases in order to raise revenue, citing 1975 evidence of the inelasticity of demand for rail services; prices rose by 50% and traffic fell by 5%, implying a (short-run) elasticity of −0.1%.

TABLE 4.7

GB Inland Freight Transport, 1960-78[1] (000m ton-miles)

Year	Road	Rail	Coastal[2] shipping	Inland waterways	Pipelines[3]	Total
1960	30.1 (49.3%)	18.7 (30.6%)	11.9 (19.5%)	0.2 (0.3%)	0.2 (0.3%)	61.1 (100.0%)
1965	42.1 (57.1%)	15.4 (20.9%)	15.3 (20.8%)	0.1 (0.1%)	0.8 (1.1%)	73.7 (100.0%)
1970	50.0 (60.6%)	16.4 (19.9%)	14.2 (17.2%)	0.1 (0.1%)	1.8 (2.2%)	82.5 (100.0%)
1974	53.0 (65.1%)	14.3 (17.6%)	11.9 (14.6%)	0.1 (0.1%)	2.1 (2.6%)	81.4 (100.0%)
1978	60.6 (64.3%)	12.2 (12.9%)	15.3 (16.2%)	0.1 (0.1%)	6.1 (6.5%)	94.3 (100.0%)
% change 1960-78	+101.3%	−34.8%	+28.6%	−50%	+29.50%	+54.5% i.e. 2.3% p.a.

Source: AAS, 1980.

Notes: 1 % figures in brackets show respective contributions to the total in any one year.
2 Coastal shipping figure for 1978 is estimated, since the survey on which previous coastal shipping figures were based has been discontinued.
3 Excludes the movement of gases by pipeline, and pipelines less than 10 miles long (prior to 1965).

by-passes around sensitive and congested areas, and a National Transport Council was proposed as a forum for policy formulation.

Specific policy proposals were outlined in a 1977 White Paper.[1] Total planned expenditure at £2.2bn in 1980 (in 1976 prices) represented a significant reduction from the £2.6bn in 1976-7 and compared with £2.0bn in 1971-2. The main policy emphasis was to remain on public transport. Expenditure on roads was reduced in absolute terms, to remain at about 51% of total expenditure, as in 1976-7, compared with 76% in 1971-2.[2] No subsidies were to be given to rail freight and inter-urban passenger services. But major cuts in the rail network were ruled out, and support for passenger services was to continue, though at a level of £295m in 1980, compared with £325m in 1976-7. Bus services were also to continue to receive support, especially in rural areas, via concessionary fares, grants and fuel duty rebates.

Recent statistics show that since 1976, when the consultative document appeared, spending on new roads has actually been cut by just over a quarter, overall rail subsidies have increased slightly (but with a 45% increase on local services), while subsidies for buses and other services have actually fallen around 20% in real terms.[3]

EEC transport policy originates from a European Commission memorandum of 1961 (the Schaus Memorandum) and an Action Programme of the following year. One of the general aims was to prevent transport from blocking the development of an effective common market for other goods and services. Transport is an important element in the cost of many commodities. If, for instance, transport

1 *Transport Policy*, Cmnd. 6836, June 1977.

2 See also annual reports on the road programme promised in Cmnd. 6836: *Policy for Roads: England 1978*, Cmnd. 7132, April 1978 *Policy for Roads: England 1980*, Cmnd. 7908, June 1980.

3 Source: *Social Trends*, HMSO, 1980, table 10.22.

undertakings in one country gave preferential treatment to certain industries or firms, this would frustrate attempts to secure competition among member states on equal terms. A second general aim was the more positive one of fostering transport developments which would stimulate trade and the opening up of markets, e.g. in the development of transport networks. Thirdly, the Community was to endeavour to create in the transport sector (as elsewhere) 'healthy competition of the widest scope'.

Subsequent detailed agreements have gone only part of the way towards achieving these objectives. Prohibitions have been introduced on discrimination in the transport sector on grounds of nationality, and on tariffs designed to give the kind of preferential treatment outlined above. An inquiry was held into the way costs of infrastructural investments were met in the member countries, in the first instance to see whether the costs fell broadly on those to whom the benefits accrued, or whether, on the other hand, infrastructural developments tended to result in tariff structures not truly reflecting the costs of providing the relevant services. There has also been harmonization of the regulations governing lorry-drivers' ages, qualifications, hours, rest periods, etc., and the use of tachographs is mandatory. Some agreement has been reached whereby bilateral arrangements between members for quotas for public service licenses would be replaced by Community-wide agreements. Some uniformity in tariffs has also been agreed, e.g. in the form of maximum and minimum road-haulage rates, between which any rate negotiated between contractor and customer should settle. It has been established that the EEC rules of competition apply to the transport sector. Finally agreement has been reached on the 'normalization' of railway accounts to take account of any social burdens placed on the systems, with common rules for granting subsidies in such cases and a common definition of obligations that could be imposed in return for such subsidies. More recent policy announcements restate that major transport planning and investment will remain the responsibility of national governments, but it is envisaged that the Community can play a useful role in co-ordinating national plans. From February 1978 member countries must inform the EEC Commission about their transport development projects and programmes. Future proposals are that financial support should be made available for projects that can be identified as being of Community interest.

IV   POLICY TOWARDS THE NATIONALIZED INDUSTRIES
IV.1   Background

On a wide definition, public enterprise exists where there is an undertaking which is publicly owned and directed by a branch of the government, or a body especially set up for the purpose by the government. This would include all public administration and defence, and the public health and education services, together with a number of government agencies such as the British Tourist Authority, the Forestry Commission, the Herring Industry Board, etc.[1] Our present concern is with the narrower area of the nationalized industries, which in general are distinguishable from the rest of the public sector by the fact that the goods and

---

1   See R. Maurice (ed.), *National Income Statistics: Sources and Methods*, Central Statistical Office, HMSO, 1968.

services they supply are marketed. Paradoxically, it might seem, these goods are non-public goods in the theoretical sense.[1]

The nationalized industries have for a long time dominated four strategic sectors of the economy: energy, public transport, communications, and iron and steel. In 1976 the involvement in the energy field was extended by the formation of the British National Oil Corporation, and in 1977 the aerospace and shipbuilding industries were added to the nationalized industry sector. Together the nationalized industries employ around 1.7 million people (7% of the total work force) and in 1976 they accounted for 14% of total fixed investment in the economy and for 10% of output.[2]

In EEC countries it is fairly general for there to be some form of state control of electricity, gas and water, postal services, railways and parts at least of broadcasting and the national airlines. Steel, however, is generally in private hands. The French have a particularly large public sector and own among other things the Renault car manufacturers. The Italians have two giant state companies, IRI – a wide-ranging holding company – and ENI, an oil and chemicals firm. There is also the uniquely continental phenomenon of a state monopoly in certain goods for taxation purposes; that is, the state retains a monopoly profit as part of its fiscal revenue. The match industry (in France, West Germany and Italy) and the tobacco industry (in France and Italy) are examples.[3]

IV.2   Price and Investment Policy: Theory

The economists' prescription for nationalized-industry pricing is that prices should be set equal to marginal cost.[4] The overall objective is to ensure an efficient allocation of resources as between these industries and the private sector. A simple rationale can be given for such a policy. On the one hand the demand curve for a nationalized-industry product tells us how much consumers will pay per unit for different quantities supplied, and so we interpret the demand curve as consumers' evaluation of the good or service as output is varied. On the other hand the marginal cost curve tells us the incremental cost of producing each unit, and if we can equate the money costs actually incurred by the undertaking with the true opportunity cost of diverting extra resources from alternative uses to the undertaking in question, we can construe the marginal cost curve as recording consumers' evaluation of the forgone alternative product. If consumers value the public enterprise good more than the alternative (demand price exceeds marginal cost), then welfare can be increased by diverting more resources to the public enterprise, so increasing output, and vice versa. Hence, for an optimum level of output, price should equal marginal cost.

---

1   A public good is one whose consumption by one person does not reduce the amount available for consumption by others (e.g. defence and broadcasting). Public goods will be undersupplied by the market and must generally be supplied and paid for out of taxation.

2   Source: *The Nationalised Industries*, Cmnd. 7131, HMSO, March 1978. These figures do not include the activities of companies within the responsibility of the National Enterprise Board, such as British Leyland and Rolls-Royce. See below, p. 000.

3   See D. Swann, *The Common Market* (3rd edition), Penguin Books, 1975, and Stuart Holland, *The Unequal Mix: European Public Enterprise*, Martin Robertson, 1978.

4   For a fuller discussion, see Ralph Turvey, *Economic Analysis and Public Enterprise*, Allen and Unwin, 1971 and *Public Enterprise*, Penguin Books, 1968.

Unfortunately, this apparently straightforward principle raises many difficulties in practice. Firstly, an optimum is reached only if a large number of other conditions are met, including the equality of all other prices with marginal cost. Otherwise the 'second best' solution will very likely require a price not equal to marginal cost.[1] A modification of the marginal cost pricing rule which takes some of this into account is to set price equi-proportional to marginal cost. Thus if price is on average, say, ten per cent above marginal cost in the economy, this same margin should be included in public enterprise prices. So long as we are concerned with the allocation of resources between alternative end uses, this does yield an optimal outcome. But it will not produce an overall optimum, since the relative prices of commodities (in general) and primary inputs such as labour will be affected. Thus, labour will be paid less than its marginal value product, leading to its being under-supplied. In sum, optimality conditions will be fulfilled in commodity markets but not in factor markets, and the level of total output will be too low.

Secondly, even if all necessary conditions are met, the ensuing resource allocation is optimal only within the existing distribution of income among consumers. If this distribution is not accepted as being ideal, it would be perfectly justifiable for the government to modify some or all nationalized-industry prices in the name of social justice. (It could be argued that this is precisely what the government does in not charging or making only token charges for some public-sector goods and services, e.g. health and education.)

Thirdly, price must be set equal to marginal social cost, rather than marginal private cost. Where, for instance, increased output in one industry confers external benefits by reducing production costs in other industries, marginal private costs in that industry will exceed marginal social costs, and vice versa for an industry imposing net external costs. Therefore, even if all other necessary conditions for a welfare maximum were met, a nationalized industry equating price with marginal private cost would be producing too much, from the community standpoint, if it gave rise to net external costs and too little if it conferred net external economies. Hence, for maximum welfare, external effects of this sort must be taken into account in both the nationalized sector and elsewhere.

Fourthly, economists are themselves divided as to whether price should be equated with short-run marginal cost (the rate of change of total costs in the short run, i.e. when some factor or factors are fixed), or with long-run marginal cost (the rate of change of total costs in the long run, when there are no fixed factors). Finally, except where there are constant returns to scale, neither short-run nor long-run marginal cost pricing will automatically ensure that total costs will be recovered from revenue. Marginal and average costs are equal only at that output at which average costs are at a minimum. Hence marginal cost pricing will exactly equate total costs and revenues only if, by chance, the output level which results happens to be this one. Otherwise, either a deficit (marginal cost is less than average cost) or a surplus (marginal cost exceeds average cost) will result. In practice, most of the nationalized industries are thought to be ones where average costs decline continuously over the relevant range of outputs, so that marginal cost is less than average cost and a deficit is likely to result. Since there is

---

1   See R.G. Lipsey and K. Lancaster, 'On the General Theory of Second Best', *RES*, Vol. SSIV, 1956-7, pp. 11-32.

no agreed method of financing deficits (or distributing surpluses) in a way which will not affect resource allocation, there is a basic conflict between financial rectitude and pricing policies designed to optimize resource allocation.

For optimal investment by public enterprises, the two main requirements are that the costs and benefits of any project over its life are correctly evaluated, and that estimates of future costs and benefits are correctly related to the present decision-making period.[1]

In evaluating costs and benefits, due account must be taken of external effects on other producers and consumers. Moreover, since market-determined prices in a 'second best' world will not necessarily reflect the true worth of inputs and outputs to the community, it will usually be necessary to attempt the difficult task of adjusting these on a socially desired basis.[2]

The method of relating together costs and benefits in different periods that is generally thought best is to express the returns to an investment project in terms of net discounted present value.[3] Generally speaking, the rate of time discount used in evaluating public-sector projects should be the same as is used elsewhere (and any allowance made for uncertainty should also be the same). Otherwise the relative merits of private- and public-sector projects will be distorted.[4]

Even if public-sector projects were treated scrupulously in the manner outlined, the maximum benefit would not be derived from the total of funds available for investment in the economy unless private projects were treated in exactly the same way. In practice, private-sector investments will almost invariably be evaluated with no regard for external effects; various ways of treating uncertainty are likely to be used; and a substantial amount of decision-making will be undertaken by rule-of-thumb methods.[5] In so far as the government is unable to regulate all private-sector-investment appraisal appropriately, the best that can be hoped for is a form of sub-optimization, the correct principles being applied in the public sector only.

IV.3   Price and Investment Policy: Practice

The postwar nationalization Acts merely require the industries to break even, taking one year with another. Later, in 1961, the financial responsibilities of the

---

1 For a description of the methods used to evaluate investment in nationalized industries, see R. Pryke, *Public Enterprises in Practice*, MacGibbon and Kee, 1971, chapter 15.

2 For an extended discussion of cost-benefit analysis, see A.R. Prest and R. Turvey, 'Cost Benefit Analysis: A Survey', *EJ*, December 1965, and R. Layard, *Cost Benefit Analysis*, Penguin, 1972.

3 Net discounted present value (R) for any product with a life of n years is given by

$$R = \sum_{t=1}^{n} \frac{B_t - C_t}{(1 + r)^t} - I,$$ where B_t, C_t are benefits and costs respectively in the year t, r is the

rate of discount and I is the initial cost. The main merits of this method over its chief rival (internal rate of return or marginal efficiency of capital) are that it always gives a unique solution and always ranks projects correctly.

4 A discussion of the implications of using different rates of time discount appears in R. Pryke, op. cit., chapter 16.

5 See NEDO, *Investment Appraisal*, HMSO, 1967.

industries were tightened in a number of ways, and financial targets were introduced, usually expressed as a rate of return on assets employed.[1] However, until 1967 explicit guidelines on pricing and investment policy were lacking. Then long-run marginal cost pricing was introduced as the official policy, together with the net-present-value approach to investment decisions.[2] A test discount rate (TDR) of 8% was laid down, later raised to 10%.[3] The 1967 policy focused very much on the pricing of individual goods and services, and on individual investment projects. Arbitrary cross-subsidization amongst different groups of consumers was to be avoided, and the need to distinguish social as distinct from purely commercial operations was stressed. The government undertook financial responsibility for non-commercial operations, e.g. by specific subsidies or grants. The existing system of financial targets was retained, as a measure of expected performance against which to compare actual achievements.

For a year or two after 1967 there was some progress towards revising pricing methods, especially in the Post Office and British Rail. However, in the early and mid-1970s macroeconomic and financial considerations had become of overriding importance once more, as they had tended to be before 1967. Up to 1974 severe price restraint was applied by the government, and investment programmes were cut. This led to mounting deficits, indiscriminate subsidies to the consumer from taxpayers, and in some cases sharp reductions in investment and employment. Then followed a period of very rapid price increase, with the prime objective of first holding and then eliminating Exchequer support. By 1978 significant improvements in financial performance had occurred in most cases, though with some exceptions, including the much-publicized steel industry.[4]

This 'interference' with the nationalized industries' price and investment policies did not contravene the 1967 White Paper's recommendations, which explicitly reserved the right of the government to intervene on national economic grounds. In the event, however, the price restraint of the early 1970s and its subsequent correction led to suspension of both the financial targets and attempts at economic pricing policies which the White Paper sought to introduce. The most recent White Paper on nationalized-industry policy,[5] whose publication follows an earlier report by the Select Committee on the Nationalized Industries,[6] and an independent review by NEDO,[7] seeks to reintroduce and reinforce the 1967 White Paper, and avoid repetition of the 'mistakes' of the early 1970s.[8]

---

1 *The Financial and Economic Obligations of the Nationalised Industries*, Cmnd. 1337, HMSO, April 1961.

2 *Nationalised Industries: A Review of Economic and Financial Objectives*, Cmnd. 3437, HMSO, November 1967.

3 The rate chosen was expressly intended to match the return looked for by private industry on marginal, low-risk investment. Because of differences in financing methods and tax liability, the equivalent private-sector rate will be higher than any given nationalized-industry rate; the original 8% was held to be equivalent to 15-16% in the private sector.

4 See *British Steel Corporation: The Road to Viability*, Cmnd. 7148, HMSO, March 1978.

5 *The Nationalised Industries*, Cmnd. 7131, HMSO, March 1978.

6 *Ministerial Control of the Nationalised Industries*, H of C 371-I, II and III, 1968.

7 *A Study of the UK Nationalised Industries: Their Role in the Economy and Control in the Future*, NEDO, November 1976.

8 See also R. Rees, 'The Pricing Policy of the Nationalized Industries', *TBR*, June 1979.

The 1978 White Paper shares with its 1967 predecessor the objective of optimal resource allocation, reiterates the need to avoid cross-subsidization amongst consumers and to distinguish social from commercial services, and retains the use of marginal cost pricing policies and of TDR in investment decisions. However, the limitations of the latter two in practice are recognized, and they no longer occupy the forefront of policy. The 1978 White Paper recognized that in many cases prices are 'market determined' and that even where this is not so, the difficulties of practical application in marginal cost pricing can be severe. It is admitted that TDR has not lived up to expectations, in part because much investment which is undertaken forms part of an existing system, or is 'necessary for safety or security'. The main focus of current policy is therefore shifted from these matters affecting individual services and projects to the opportunity cost of capital in the industry as a whole. A 'real rate of return on assets' (RRR) is defined which is to be achieved by the industries on new investment as a whole. The RRR is principally related to the real rate of return (and its expected trend) in the private sector, taking into account questions of the cost of finance and of social time preference. It is set initially at 5%, and is to be reviewed every three to five years. The RRR is not the same as the financial target rate of return for each industry, which varies, and takes into account the earning power of existing assets, sectoral and social objectives, and so forth.

Thus the main matters over which the government has sought to exercise control since 1978 are the RRR and the financial target together with the 'general level of prices'. Individual prices and investment priorities are left largely up to the industries themselves, subject to the vague admonition to 'pay attention to the structure of prices and its relation to the structure of costs' and to the need to consult sponsoring departments on certain major investment proposals.

In some ways current policy represents a retreat from the ambitious 1967 position. Although a commitment to marginal cost pricing is retained, even the White Paper exhibits at points a certain resignation over how much is to be expected in this direction. More important, though, is the fact that the latest White Paper contains no policy change or promise that macroeconomic considerations will not again overrule questions of nationalized-industry policy *per se*. Indeed, current policy if anything increases this possibility in that it is proposed to introduce powers for Ministers to give specific directives in addition to the general directive presently provided for. Given the large size of the nationalized industries it is easy to see how governments are tempted to use them directly to help manage the economy. While this possibility remains open, so also does that of current policy going the way of its predecessor.

IV.4   Organization, Control and Productive Efficiency in the Nationalized Industries

Many of the problems of internal organization and efficiency which arise in the nationalized industries are of the same kind as those encountered in private industry. There are, however, differences in degree. Because of the extremely large scale of the operations under one administrative control, the organizational problems exceed those of all but a few, giant private firms. Moreover, in seeking solutions to these problems the nationalized industries are inevitably subject to much more publicity and outside criticism than private enterprises.

Several important organizational developments have taken place in recent years. A number were embodied in the 1968 Transport Act which, inter alia, eliminated the regional divisions of British Rail; set up a National Freight Corporation and Freight Integration Council; created Passenger Transport Authorities for four major conurbations (now increased to five), and transferred the London Transport Board to the GLC, making, effectively, a sixth, and established a National Bus Company for England and Wales, and a Scottish Transport Group. In 1969 the status of the Post Office was changed from that of government department to public corporation, to be run on more commercial lines, and from 1979 it has been run as two separate corporations, one for postal services and one for telecommunications. The British Steel Corporation was reorganized into a system based on product divisions (four steel-making, one for constructional engineering, and one for chemical activities). Earlier there had been four large groups, under which system most products fell within more than one group. At the time of writing, further fundamental changes have been proposed in the steel industry. It is intended to reduce capacity from 21.5 million tonnes a year to 15 million, in line with demand predictions. If effected these proposals mean that employment in the industry will have been cut back by more than half since 1974, from 228,000 in that year to a proposed 110,000. Finally, there has been a major reorganization of the gas industry. The Gas Council and the area boards have been replaced by a single authority, the British Gas Corporation. A recurring theme in these organizational changes was clearly to provide for better co-ordination and planning throughout the whole of the particular industries concerned.

Where the problems of running the nationalized industries differ most from those of private industry is over the need to reconcile operating efficiency on the one hand with public accountability on the other. The one arguably requires maximum autonomy, delegation and decentralization in nationalized industries; the other inhibits this.[1] In the latest White Paper this conflict is recognized, but the government stresses that it must be concerned with strategy in such basic industries; with their efficiency in the absence of a bankruptcy sanction and (in some cases) significant market pressures; and with securing an acceptable return.

Many difficulties have arisen in this area in the past. In 1968 the Select Committee on the Nationalized Industries concluded that Ministers have tended to do the opposite of what Parliament originally intended.[2] Whereas they were supposed to lay down policies, but not intervene in management, they have in practice given very little policy guidance but been closely involved with many aspects of management. The NEDO report proposed a formal two-tiered structure as a solution of this problem, the industries to be run by Corporation Boards but under the strategic direction of Policy Councils. However this was rejected in the 1978 White Paper on grounds of likely confusion of responsibility between the Policy Councils, Ministers and sponsoring departments, and a consequent slowing-down of decision-making.

No major structural alternative was offered in the White Paper, though a number of procedural changes were proposed. As we have seen, the RRR and financial targets were to form a central focus of government/nationalized-industry relations,

---

1 In comparison with private industry, the nationalized industries also have much less discretion over certain strategic issues, such as diversification of their activities.

2 *Ministerial Control of the Nationalised Industries*, H. of C. 371-1, II and II, 1968.

within the corporate planning context. In addition, the industries were to be asked to select and publish an appropriate set of other performance indicators, to supplement the financial targets which could, of course, otherwise be met in various anti-social ways, e.g. monopoly pricing.[1] The introduction of powers for Ministers to make selective directions was regarded as superior to the present system of informal persuasion, not least because it makes for greater clarity of accountability. It was proposed that a civil servant be appointed to corporation boards, to improve the understanding by sponsoring departments of industry problems. In line with its general policy in the area, the government has asked chairmen for proposals concerning the implementation of industrial democracy. For a short time the industries also remained open to the quasi-independent sanction on their efficiency represented by the Price Commission, which from July 1977 to its demise in 1980 had discretion (subject to ministerial veto) to investigate most nationalized-industry price increases.

Throughout the White Paper there was a recurring emphasis on the need for more publication of nationalized-industry affairs; actual versus target performance in Annual Reports; historical series of other performance indicators; the extra costs due to ministerial intervention; and so on. The aim seemed to be to satisfy the public-accountability requirement directly, by making the performance of the industries and intervention by the government more obvious and publicly available. This intention is wholly admirable provided it does not make the task of running the industries unattractive to managers who can otherwise work in private industry, not subject to the same exposure. The ability of the nationalized industries to attract highly qualified management in any case tends to be reduced by the levels of remuneration offered. In 1969 the NBPI found that top salaries and retirement pensions were substantially lower in nationalized industries than in comparable private-sector jobs, and large increases for chairmen of the main undertakings were subsequently implemented.[2] However, throughout the seventies the real value of the salaries was allowed to fall behind again. In 1978 the government implemented the findings of another study, which recommended an average total increase of 31% in top salaries.[3]

IV.5   EEC Provisions

The EEC members have not so far devised a common policy on the control and financing of public enterprise. On the other hand the publicly-owned industries and firms are, of course, affected by Community policies towards industry, such as the competition and regional policies, and the common policies towards energy and transport. All of these are discussed elsewhere in this chapter. Two other issues are of relevance for the UK in this context.

The first concerns the use of subsidies by member governments. As we have seen these have been an important feature of the UK policy, but they are contrary to the

1   The National Coal Board, in its *Annual Reports*, now publishes information on selected performance indicators, such as output per manshift, daily output per face and average costs of production.

2   NBPI Report No. 107, *Top Salaries in the Private Sector and Nationalized Industries*, Cmnd. 3970, March 1969.

3   *Second Report on Top Salaries*, Cmnd. 7253, June 1978.

spirit and rules of the Community. This is because if one particular member government subsidizes a loss-making industry of its own, the free play of competition within the Community-wide industry would be inhibited. However, in practice it can be hard for the Community to apply meaningful sanctions on such behaviour. Moreover, it could be that UK subsidies for the strictly non-commercial activities taken by the nationalized industries would be sanctioned, e.g. under the 'harmonization of accounts' procedure agreed for railways.[1] On the other hand some limitations could be set on the precise nature of the social obligations placed upon the industries. More difficulty is likely to arise over any remaining annual revenue supports to cover operating deficits after allowance for social obligations is made, and cases where, from time to time, the accumulated deficits of UK industries like coal and rail in particular are written off, or interest payments suspended.

Secondly, two of the UK nationalized industries come within the sphere of influence of the ECSC, the history and role of which is of some importance. The ECSC is the oldest of the three communities (ECSC, EEC and Euratom) and was the first step towards European integration, i.e. the first common market. The 1951 Treaty of Paris abolished duties and quotas on trade in coal and steel among member states; discrimination in prices, delivery terms and transport rates; and restrictive practices leading to collusive sharing or exploitation of markets. Up to 1967 the ECSC had separate institutions but the relevant bodies are now those of the three merged communities; the European Commission and Parliament, the Council of Ministers and the European Court of Justice. One additional body which survived from the earlier period was a high-level consultative committee, composed of producers, consumers, workers and dealers.

The ECSC maintains a policy of free trade in coal and basic iron and steel products. Producers are required to publish all prices at selected basing points, and transport charges also have to be published or notified. Levies are made upon coal and steel producers, currently equivalent to around 0.3% of production value but with some variation according to product. The European steel industry is undergoing something of an upheaval. Faced with present capacities for crude steel production of 200 million tonnes per annum, estimated as being 10% greater than forseeable demand in the mid-1980s, capital investment in the industry is declining and large-scale redundancies are being made, at a time when there is a need to improve the competitiveness of the steelworks by modernization. The various kinds of central benefits paid by the ECSC reflect these trends. They include contributions to technical research projects, loans at attractive rates for investment projects capable of employing redundant ECSC workers in the declining coal and steel areas; housing for ECSC workers and investment projects to facilitate the capital investment programmes of the coal and steel industries; financial assistance to redundant or transferred coal and steel workers (provided this is at least matched by the member government). In 1979 £33m was provided in redundancy payments to 27,000 workers, mainly in France, Luxembourg and Britain. It is intended that the proportion of the ECSC budget spent on aid to redeployment will rise to 36% in 1980.

The ECSC regulations obviously provide an additional set of considerations for the industries, affecting pricing in particular. In steel, and to some extent coal and

---

1   See above, section III.4.

transport, modifications of existing practices have been required. In principle, however, there is no reason why the ECSC requirements should clash with the basic marginal cost pricing rules and investment procedures which remain recommended practice in the UK nationalized industries.

V COMPETITION POLICY AND CONSUMER PROTECTION[1]
V.1 The Case for Policy Measures

Monopolistic market structures and practices raise questions of public policy under any theory of the firm, though the precise criticisms vary with the choice of theoretical model. Under profit-maximizing assumptions, monopoly price exceeds marginal cost, with consequential resource misallocation and reduced consumers' welfare. In addition, supernormal profits will be earned if price also exceeds average cost, so that income is redistributed in favour of producers. Possession of market power also permits firms to undertake practices such as price discrimination among consumers and cross-subsidization among activities. These two will generally reduce welfare and may be used to protect a monopoly position. Fourthly, some argue that monopolists tend to be technically inefficient, costs being higher than they need be because the presence of excess profits blunts the desire to seek out and apply cost-minimizing techniques. However, this argument is not strictly consistent with profit-maximization, since it implies pursuit of some other objective, e.g. leisure, at a certain point.

The main significance of monopoly under the managerial theories is that the existence of market power is likely to increase the tendency for firms to pursue managerial objectives other than profit. The criticisms of monopoly derived from the profit-maximizing model may not apply, but managerial behaviour need not lead to genuine cost-minimization (e.g. in Williamson's model, organizational slack is typically present)[2] and, in general, a part of the stream of resources being generated by the firm is diverted for the satisfaction of managerial aims (sales, growth, discretionary investment, staff, slack, etc.) and away from consumers' welfare. The behavioural principle of 'satisficing' behaviour suggests that although monopoly potential may exist it will not necessarily be exploited. Whether the type of market structure will affect efficiency under the behavioural theory would depend on the effect on search and decision procedures, and little is known about this at present. In general, if the behavioural theory is adopted, the whole basis for discussing monopoly in terms of resource allocation and supernormal profits is lost.

There are many alternative, and often conflicting, theoretical models of why firms merge. But clearly one effect may be to create monopoly situations, even though this need not be the sole objective, with consequences as outlined above under the different theories. Official thinking on mergers emphasizes the potentially anti-competitive effects of both horizontal and vertical mergers, but believes that there may be substantial efficiency gains from scale economies,

---

1 See also J.D. Gribbin, 'Recent Anti-Trust Developments in the UK', *Antitrust Bulletin*, Vol. XX, No. 2, Summer 1975; Alex Hunter, *Competition and the Law*, Allen and Unwin, 1966, and *Monopoly and Competition*, Penguin, 1969.

2 See above p. 181.

rationalization of production, etc.[1] The general run of the empirical evidence, however, makes the expectation of efficiency gains very doubtful.[2] Conglomerate mergers are seen as a special category. Both the anti-competitive effects and the potential for increased efficiency are considered likely to be smaller than for horizontal and vertical mergers, but there is concern that many may take place for purely financial reasons, and yield very little benefit in terms of increased efficiency, but at some anti-competitive risk. Moreover, it is argued that conglomerate mergers could lead to substantial losses in operating efficiency.[3]

Under profit-maximization the argument against restrictive trade practices is, broadly, that by concerted action a group of firms may achieve the same result as a single-firm monopolist. Thus the formal model explaining joint-profit-maximization by two or more firms is identical with the one explaining multi-plant monopolist behaviour.[4] Less formally, it is also argued that if prices are set at a level which allows the least efficient to survive, many firms will earn abnormal profits without difficulty, the inefficient will not be eliminated, and the general competitive spur to efficiency will be lost; and that restrictive agreements may also provide a base for collusive action to forestall the entry of new competition, suppress new techniques and developments, etc. How the managerial theories might qualify these arguments has yet to be shown. In a behavioural analysis we should probably be much less suspicious of the motives underlying restrictive practices than if we assume profit-maximization. Assuming profit-maximization, restrictive practices would not exist unless profits were thereby raised; under behavioural analysis this need not be so. Moreover, restrictive practices fit fairly easily into the behavioural concept of the 'negotiated environment', the implication being that they are primarily uncertainty-reducing phenomena, perhaps with advantages in facilitating forward planning, etc.

Clearly the criticisms of monopoly and monopolistic practices do vary somewhat according to our choice of theoretical model. Moreover, one of the problems confronting policy-makers is that, whichever model we take, monopoly or

---

1 See the Green Paper, *A Review of Monopolies and Mergers Policy*, HMSO, Cmnd. 7198, May 1978. Horizontal mergers are between competitors in the same market, vertical mergers are between customer and supplier. The first will, other things being equal, increase market concentration (the share of supply in the hands of a few large suppliers). Vertical mergers threaten competition where, for instance, a manufacturer takes over the firm supplying raw material both to himself and to his competitors, and would be able to charge disadvantageous prices to them, or where a manufacturer secures control over the sales outlets for both his own and his competitors' products.

2 For recent studies of UK mergers see G. Meeks, *Disappointing Marriage: A Study of the Gains from Merger*, CUP, (DAE Occasional Paper 51) 1977 and K.G. Cowling *et al.*, *Mergers and Economic Performance*, CUP, 1980. Other studies are reviewed in the 1978 Green Paper.

3 Conglomerate mergers are those where there has previously been neither a vertical nor horizontal link between the parties. Efficiency gains would probably be mainly financial and managerial; efficiency losses might arise because of the complexity of operations under one control. Competition might be harmed if the conglomerate firm, by virtue of its size, became accepted as a price-leader in a particular market, or fought its way to a monopoly position in that market via a price war, accepting temporary losses in that market, compensated for by profits earned elsewhere.

4 See, e.g., K.J. Cohen and R.M. Cyert, *Theory of the Firm*, Prentice-Hall, 1956, p. 235. In practice the degree of co-ordination of activities required is greater than would normally occur under a restrictive agreement between firms.

monopolistic practices may confer advantages as well as disadvantages. For instance, against adverse effects of monopoly on resource allocation and income distribution under the profit-maximization hypothesis is the fact that, if scale economies are to be exploited, there may be room for only one firm of minimum optimal scale in some markets. Moreover, it has been vigorously argued (though not universally agreed) that the security and profitability of monopoly is an important enabling condition for technical progress.[1] It has also been pointed out[2] that an active merger market may make firms more efficient than they would otherwise be, for the companies most likely to be taken over are those which are operating at a high level of slack, have a correspondingly low level of profit, and so are poorly rated on the stock market. A 'take-over raider' who hopes to make the firm more efficient will thereby make a capital gain. However, such a threat, presumably accompanied by threatened displacement of management, may well serve to keep the present management 'on its toes'.

A further problem confronting policy-makers, though one arising only if profit-maximizing assumptions are retained, concerns the 'second-best'. Where competition does not prevail in every other market, removal of an individual monopoly or monopolistic practice cannot be relied upon to increase welfare (as a result of the ensuing change in resource allocation), and may indeed reduce it.[3]

The control of anti-competitive market structures and practices is itself a form of consumer protection, since the exercise of market power is typically at the expense of the consumers' interests. This aspect apart, economic theory does not place much emphasis on the need for consumer protection. In the theory consumers are assumed to have a complete ordering of their preferences for different goods and services based on full information about the characteristics of the commodities and the utility to be gained from consuming them. Consumers then attempt to maximize their utility, faced with their income and market-determined prices. Provided these prices (including the price of labour and hence income) are competitively determined, the theory implies that all is well with the consumer. In practice the consumer is not fully and costlessly informed, and may not be able to judge the utility he will derive from a certain good.[4] He may not, for example, realize that a drug may be unsafe under certain conditions, or that food may be too old for use and he may be faced by confusing packaging or subject to misleading claims by advertisers or retailers. Lastly, he may not be able to choose how much or how little service he obtains with a good.

There is nothing to guarantee that it is in the manufacturers' best interests for consumers to exercise a totally free and informed choice. It is this potential divergence of interests which creates the need for policy measures.

---

1 See section VII below, and J. Schumpeter, *Capitalism, Socialism and Democracy*, Allen and Unwin, 1943; K.J. Galbraith, *American Capitalism*, Hamish Hamilton, 1956 (revised edition), chapter 7; J. Jewkes, D. Sawers and R. Stillerman, *The Sources of Invention*, Macmillan, 1969.

2 See B. Hindley, 'Capitalism and Corporation', *Economica*, November 1969.

3 See above, p. 198 and R.G. Lipsey and K. Lancaster, op. cit.

4 For an opposing view see Milton and Rose Friedman, *Free to Choose: A Personal Statement*, Secker and Warburg, 1980.

V.2   Structural Conditions in UK Markets

According to orthodox micro-theory the main structural characteristics of markets which determine market conduct and performance are the degree of actual competition, measured by seller concentration; the degree of potential competition, reflected in the height of barriers to the entry of new competition; the extent of product differentiation in the market; and the rate of growth or decline of demand.[1] All of these have a bearing on the degree of market power enjoyed by firms in a market, and it is control over the exercise of such power that competition policy attempts. Unfortunately, systematic information on structural conditions in the UK is limited to the first characteristic only, seller concentration.

The most comprehensive source of concentration data is the Census of Production. The latest available figures are for 1976 and refer to Minimum List Headings (MLH), which are rather broad industrial categories from an analytical point of view. A frequency distribution of 120 MLH industries by concentration class (range of five-firm concentration ratio) is given in the right-hand column of table 4.8. From a number of published studies it emerges that concentration has been increasing over time. One pioneering study found that in 41 out of 200 industries for which accurate comparisons were possible concentration increased in 27 trades over the period 1935-51 and fell in only 14.[2] Between 1951 and 1958 there was apparently a somewhat similar tendency, concentration increasing in 36 of 63 industries and falling in 16, with two showing no change and nine undetermined.[3] An analysis of the period 1958-63 reveals that the unweighted average concentration ratio for 214 market or product areas rose from 55.7% to 58.6% (in terms of the average weighted by total sales in each market, the rise was from 65.8% to 69.0%).[4] Analysis of a sample of 30 markets out of the 214 suggested that merger activity had been responsible for around one-third of the net change in concentration overall and one-half of the total change in those cases where concentration had increased. Between 1963 and 1968 there was a further and more rapid increase in concentration levels, especially pronounced where concentration levels were already high.

The most recent and comprehensive study of concentration trends considered the period 1919-76.[5] Changes in concentration were divided into two component parts: due to merger between firms, and due to internal growth within firms. Two merger booms were identified, one in the 1920s and one in the 1960s. The former, reinforced by internal growth as firms benefitted from increasing returns to scale at the plant level, produced a 'spectacularly large' increase in concentration 'broadly equivalent in its effect on market structure to that of two thirds of all firms being eliminated from the manufacturing sector'. It was during this period that some of today's giant firms, such as I.C.I. and Unilever, were born. Mergers continued to

---

1   See J.S. Bain, *Industrial Organization*, 2nd edition, Wiley, 1968, and R. Caves, *American Industry: Structure, Conduct and Performance*, 2nd edition, Prentice-Hall, 1967.

2   R. Evely and I.M.D. Little, *Concentration in British Industry*, CUP, 1960.

3   See W.G. Shepherd, 'Changes in British Industrial Concentration 1951-58', *OEP*, 1966, and K.D. George, 'Changes in British Industrial Concentration 1957-58', *JIE*, July 1967.

4   P.E. Hart, M.A. Utton and G. Walshe, *Mergers and Concentration in British Industry*, CUP for the NIESR, 1973.

5   L. Hannah and J. Kay, *Concentration in Modern Industry*, London, 1977.

TABLE 4.8

Seller Concentration: Selected UK Markets

Concentration Class[1] (range of five-firm concentration ratio, %)	Product Group Basis 1968[2] Number of product groups in class		MLH Basis 1976	
	(No.)	(%)	(No.)	(%)
0-9	0	0.0	2	1.3
10-19	8	2.4	12	7.7
20-29	20	5.9	16	10.3
30-39	28	8.2	23	14.7
40-49	34	10.0	32	20.7
50-59	47	13.8	17	11.0
60-69	36	10.6	15	9.7
70-79	38	11.2	14	9.0
80-89	46	13.5	16	10.3
90-100	83	24.4	8	5.2
Total	340	100.0	155	100.0

Source: Census of Production, 1968, 1976.
Notes: 1 The meaning of this column is that, taking the 1968 data, there is no product group/MLH in which the largest five firms account for less than 10% of total sales, eight in which they account for 10-19%, and so on.
2 The markets included are sub-Minimum List Heading product groups in mining and quarrying and manufacturing, for which five-firm concentration ratios are available.

occur over the next three decades but were offset by the internal growth of small and medium-sized firms, so that concentration actually fell during this time. Large firms, on the whole, failed to maintain their high rates of internal growth, probably reflecting the fact that the minimum point on their long-run average cost curves had been reached. This continued offsetting influence also meant that the net impact of the merger boom in the late 1960s was not as great as the earlier boom.

While the analysis of MLH data gives an indication of the way concentration has increased over time, because MLH categories span more than a single market the level of concentration at a given time tends to be underestimated. This is brought out clearly in table 4.8 which also includes a frequency distribution by concentration class for 340 more narrowly defined markets, or product groups. The striking feature here is that in almost one-quarter of the 340 markets five firms held 90% or more of total sales, while in only 16.4% of markets was the top five firms' share under 40%. In comparison, the MLH statistics for the later year 1976 show only 5.2% of industries with concentration ratios over 90%, and 34% with ratios under 40%.

From an analytical viewpoint the main question is how far UK markets fall into the 'atomistic', oligopolistic or monopolized categories, for which theoretical models exist. Since concentration ratios tell us nothing about the size distribution among the largest firms, Census data can tell us only about the division between atomistic and non-atomistic markets, the latter including both oligopoly and monopoly. Without supplementary information even this division is not easily made. The first two concentration classes are almost certainly atomistic, but when the five-firm ratios exceed 30% the possibility of some recognized interdependence among the market leaders, or of one firm among the five exerting some form of leadership, must be recognized. When the ratio exceeds 50%, the probability of this must be reckoned very high. Thus, on the basis of the more disaggregated market-level data in table 4.8, no more than 8.3% of the 340 markets can safely be assumed non-atomistic. An alternative approach is to base the division on previous empirical results relating seller concentration in different markets to their performance and especially to differences in profit rates, which we should expect from neo-classical theory to be higher in non-atomistic markets. One pioneering study for the US found systematic differences according to whether or not the seven-firm concentration ratio exceeded 70%.[1] Making a notional adjustment for the fact that table 4.8 has five-firm ratios, we might guess that at least 40-45% of the 340 markets came above the critical line in 1968.

An indication of the incidence of single, dominant firms was contained in a Parliamentary answer in 1970. This suggested that in 1965 there were 156 product areas where one firm had 50% or more of the market.[2]

Alongside the trend towards a higher degree of seller concentration in individual markets there has been a similar, accelerating increase in overall concentration, as measured by the share in net output of the 100 largest firms in the economy. Before World War I this was less than 20%, rising to 33% in 1958. Over the next twelve years the rate of increase roughly trebled, and in 1970 the largest 100 firms accounted for nearly 50% of net output.[3] The precise connection between overall concentration and seller concentration in individual markets is not well documented. But of the largest 100 manufacturing companies between 1968

TABLE 4.9(a)

Seller Concentration in Selected Markets, UK and some EEC Countries, 1963[1]

Concentration class (range of four-firm concentration ratio, %)	UK		France		Italy		Netherlands		Belgium	
	(No.) (%)		*(No.) (%)*		*(No.) (%)*		*(No.) (%)*		*(No.) (%)*	
0-9	7	5.98	42	43.30	36	36.73	13	13.40	13	13.83
10-29	47	40.17	43	44.33	43	43.88	44	45.36	34	36.17
30-59	43	36.75	11	11.34	18	18.36	23	23.71	32	34.04
60-100	20	17.08	1	1.03	1	1.02	17	17.52	15	15.96
Total number of industries	117	(100.0)	97	(100.0)	98	(100.0)	97	(100.0)	94	(100.0)

Sources: M.C. Sawyer, 'Concentration in British Manufacturing Industry', *OEP*, November 1971, pp. 352-78 for the UK figures, and Louis Phlips, *Effects of Industrial Concentration, A Cross Section Analysis for the Common Market*, North Holland, 1971.

Note: 1   The markets are roughly equivalent to Minimum List Heading level for the UK and the other countries. The figures are derived in very similar ways.

1   J.S. Bain, op. cit.

2   *Hansard*, April 1970. Reprinted as Appendix A in G. Walshe, *Recent Trends in Monopoly in Great Britain*, CUP, 1974.

3   S.J. Prais, *The Evolution of Giant Firms in Great Britain: A Study of Concentration in Manufacturing Industry in Britain 1909-70*, CUP, 1976.

TABLE 4.9(b)

Seller Concentration in West Germany, 1975

Concentration class (range of concentration ratio, %)	Three-firm CR		Six-firm CR	
	(No. of industries)	*(%)*	*(No. of industries)*	*(%)*
0-9	15	9.4	4	2.7
10-29	61	38.1	39	26.4
30-59	59	36.9	58	39.2
60-100	25	15.6	47	31.8
Total	160	100.0	148	100.1

Source: Monopolkommission, Hauptgutachten II, 1976-7, *Fortschreitende Konzentration bei Grossunternehmen*, Nomos Verlagsgesellschaft, Baden-Baden, 1978.

and 1974 approximately half were known to have two or more 'monopolies' (25% shares in particular markets, and of these twenty companies had five or more monopolies).[1]

The inescapable conclusion is that UK economic activity is relatively highly concentrated in the hands of a fairly small number of firms, and that this concentration is increasing. 1963 data suggests the UK level of market concentration was much higher than in France and Italy (table 4.9(a)) and much the same as in Belgium and the Netherlands. Strictly comparable data for West Germany is not available, but the data which does exist suggests a pattern similar to that in the UK (c.f. the last two columns of table 4.9(b) and of 4.8).

V.3   Policy Measures

Legal powers to promote competition derive from a number of enactments beginning with the 1948 Monopolies and Restrictive Practices Act. The principal pieces of legislation on which current policy rests are, however, the Fair Trading Act of 1973, the Restrictive Trade Practices Act of 1976, and the Resale Prices Act of 1976.

The Fair Trading Act is now the basis of the law dealing with dominant-firm monopoly and merger. It also codified and extended previous legislation offering a variety of safeguards to consumers. Thirdly, it introduced important organizational changes in the application of the policy, providing for the appointment of a Director of Fair Trading to centralize the application of competition and consumer protection policies. Previously this responsibility had been rather widely shared.

On the monopoly front, the 1973 Act repealed the earlier Monopolies Acts of 1948 and 1965, which had created powers of control over dominant-firm monopolies. However, the 1973 Act contained provisions similar to but more wide-ranging than those enacted in the earlier legislation. Monopolies in the UK are not presumed illegal *per se*, as they are in the United States, but there is provision for review of monopoly situations by the Monopolies Commission (MC), which is an independent administrative tribunal, supported by a research staff. Monopoly

---

1   J.D. Gribbin, 'The Conglomerate Merger', *Applied Economics*, 1976, 8, 19-35.

references may be made either by Ministers or the Director General (subject to veto). The latter is expected to provide a broader-based view of the state of competition in the economy, to which end he has a responsibility to collect data on market structure and the behaviour of firms, on which the MC may draw. An economic information system has now been set up in the Office of Fair Trading for this purpose. Merger references are the sole prerogative of the Secretary of State.

Dominant-firm situations may be referred if the firm holds at least one-quarter of total sales in the relevant market. (Prior to 1973 the figure was one-third.) The market-share rule also applies to reference of proposed merger cases, which may alternatively be referred if the gross assets are £15m or more. One new feature introduced by the 1973 Act is that the market-share test may be applied to sales in a particular local area, rather than at the national level only. Responsibility for acting upon the recommendations of MC reports rests with the appropriate Minister, whose task it is to make the necessary statutory orders. In practice the Director General of Fair Trading has been asked by the Secretary of State to discuss the recommendations with the firms concerned, and when appropriate secure undertakings to implement them.

Anti-competitive practices of firms are now subject to constraints imposed under the 1973 Fair Trading Act, and the 1976 Restrictive Trade Practices and Resale Prices Acts. Under the Fair Trading Act, uncompetitive practices adopted by firms in their capacity as employers, uncompetitive practices adopted by nationalized industries and restrictive labour practices, are all liable to investigation by the MC. In the latter case, however, the intention is to stimulate informed discussion only, and there is no power to make orders based on the MC's conclusions.

Other types of anti-competitive practice are dealt with by the Restrictive Practices Court, originally set up under the Restrictive Practices Act of 1956. At this stage the scope of the legislation was limited to the supply of goods: specifically it embraced agreements under which two or more persons accept restrictions relating to the price of goods, conditions of supply, quantities or descriptions, processes, or areas and persons supplied. In 1968 'information agreements' were also included, that is agreements under which no restrictions are accepted, but information concerning prices, conditions etc., are exchanged. The 1973 Act permitted the extension of the legislation to cover the supply of services, and action implementing this provision was taken in early 1976. The 1976 Act merely consolidated the legislation contained in previous Acts.[1]

The general procedure with restrictive agreements is that they must be registered, and it is the Director General's responsibility (formerly that of the Registrar of Restrictive Practices) to bring them before the Court. This has been the status of a High Court, and consists of five judges and ten other members appointed for their knowledge and experience of industry, commerce or public affairs. Agreements are presumed contrary to the public interest, and the onus is on the parties to prove the reverse by seeking exemption under one or more of eight escape clauses or 'gateways'. Valid grounds for exemption may be found if it can be shown that the restriction gives protection from injury to the public; benefits consumers; is necessary to counteract measures taken by others to prevent competition, or to counterbalance a monopoly or monopsony; avoids local unemployment; promotes

---

1 A further Restrictive Practices Act in 1977 was introduced primarily to exempt agreements involving restrictions accepted in loan-finance agreements that were caught by the extension of the legislation to cover services.

exports; is required to maintain some other restriction which the Court finds to be not contrary to the public interest; or does not directly or indirectly restrict or discourage competition to any material degree. If a case is made out on one or other of these grounds, the Court has to be further satisfied that, on balance, benefits to the public outweigh detriments. Otherwise the agreement is declared void, and continuation would be in contempt of court.

There is a time limit for the registration of agreements, and penalties for non-registration, and interim orders may be made on registered agreements, while a final decision on them is being made. The relevant Minister may exempt certain agreements which he deems to be in the national interest or intended to hold down prices.

One particular restrictive practice is the subject of its own act. This is 'resale price maintenance' which is not dealt with by the Resale Prices Act of 1976. Prior to 1964, when individual RPM was first controlled,[1] it was the manufacturers' general practice to specify actual (as opposed to maximum) prices at which their product should be retailed, with sanctions for non-compliance. Procedure with resale price maintenance is very similar in form to that for restrictive practices in general, involving a general prohibition and 'escape clauses'. Although resale price maintenance remains in a few trades, for instance in the supply of books, it has in many cases been superseded by the device of 'recommended' retail prices, which are in effect maximum prices. This device has been investigated by the MC which concluded that it operated with different effects in different industries, not always contrary to the public interest.

Monopoly and restrictive-practice legislation is now both comprehensive and detailed, after more than a quarter of a century of modifications to remedy shortcomings and fill in perceived gaps in the earlier Acts. By contrast, the concept of overall government responsibility for consumer protection (as opposed to piecemeal responsibility) is quite new. Under the 1973 Act the Director General of Fair Trading is again assigned a key position.

He has a duty to collect and assess information about commercial activities, in order to seek out trading practices which may affect consumers' economic interests. If he finds areas in which there is cause for concern, he then has two options. The Director General may either make recommendations to the relevant Minister as to action which might be useful in altering the malpractice, whether it concerns consumers' economic interest or their health, safety and so on. Or, presumably where more severe action is demanded, he may set in motion a procedure which could lead to the banning of a particular trade practice. To do this he makes a 'reference' along with proposals for action to the Consumer Protection Advisory Committee (CPAC), which considers whether his proposals are justified, given that the practice is covered by the legislation. This body, after taking evidence from interested parties, reports to the relevant Minister, who then makes an Order, when appropriate, with the agreement of Parliament.

Another of the Director General's main functions in the area of consumer protection is to make sure that those who are persistently careless of their existing legal obligations to consumers mend their ways, either by his seeking written assurance or, failing this, in the courts. Lastly, the Director General has obligations to pursue an informal dialogue with industry; to publish information

---

1 Collective RPM (i.e. RPM maintained by the sanction of a group of firms withholding supplies) was prohibited by the Restrictive Practices Act of 1956.

and advice for consumers; and to encourage trade associations to use voluntary codes of practice to protect consumers.

V.4　　Policy Impact[1]

A total of over 60 monopoly situations had been investigated by the Monopolies Commission by the end of 1978. In addition, several hundred merger cases had been screened since 1965. However only a small proportion were actually referred to the Commission. For instance, between November 1973 (when the Fair Trading Act came into force) and the end of 1979 over one thousand merger cases were screened, of which only thirty were referred. The total number of restrictive practices registered by end-1979 was 3,810, of which 3,193 had been abandoned. Of course, not all these cases were heard by the Court. Many were terminated voluntarily after the results of key cases became known, and others were simply left to expire. By end-1979 363 cases relating to the supply of services had accumulated on the register of restrictive practices.

On the consumer protection side, a number of references have been made to the CPAC. By end-1979 a total of eighteen voluntary codes of practice had been introduced, including the servicing of electrical appliances, package holidays, the sale of new and used cars, the sale and repair of shoes, mail-order catalogue trading, laundering and dry-cleaning, and so on. The Office of Fair Trading has also investigated various other practices (e.g. advertising, bargain offer claims, party-plan and door-to-door selling and one-day sales) and reviewed the conduct of a large number of individual companies, of which 29 subsequently gave assurances about their future business practices. The working of the 1968 Trades Description Act has been reviewed, and the Office of Fair Trading issued nine consultative documents concerning the implementation of the 1974 Consumer Credit Act, and carried out the licensing provided for under the Act.

In very bare outline, these are the results of competition policy as developed in the UK over thirty years. Bearing in mind the comparatively small number of single-firm monopoly cases investigated, reservations about the quality of the analysis in some cases,[2] and an unaggressive approach in applying remedial measures, it seems unlikely that this particular strand of the policy has had a marked general effect on seller-concentration levels or on the behaviour of dominant firms. In the merger field, a small number of proposals has been stopped, or allowed to proceed only after certain assurances had been given. Again, in purely numerical terms the impact of policy can hardly be said to have been widespread.

The control of restrictive practices had undoubtedly done away with a great mass of overt price-fixing that had existed before 1956. But this is not necessarily conclusive evidence of success. Firstly, both the escape clauses in the 1956 Act and the quality of the Court's reasoning and decisions have been adversely criticized.[3]

1　See also the *Annual Reports,* HMSO, 1974-7.

2　See C.K. Rowley, *The British Monopolies Commission,* Allen and Unwin, 1966 and A. Sutherland, *The Monopolies Commission in Action,* CUP, 1970.

3　See, e.g., R.B. Stevens and B.S. Yamey, *The Restrictive Practices Court,* Weidenfeld and Nicolson, 1965, and D. Swann *et al., Restrictive Practice Legislation in Theory and Practice,* Allen and Unwin, 1974.

Indeed, doubts have been expressed over the suitability of judicial practices for resolving complex economic issues. Secondly, it is questionable how far the abandonment of restrictive practices has actually affected behaviour in the markets concerned. Especially where the practices abandoned are in fairly concentrated, oligopolistic markets, they may merely formalize the mutually accommodating behaviour which would in any case occur. Removal of an agreement in these circumstances would not touch the underlying, structural cause of this behaviour.

The variety and detail of the consumer protection activities undertaken since 1973 is in some ways impressive. As expected, the overwhelming emphasis has been on voluntary solutions: negotiated codes, assurances and the like. The advantages of this approach, its flexibility, cost-effectiveness and constructiveness, are heavily stressed by the Director General of Fair Trading in his first two Annual Reports.[1] Its main drawback is perhaps that voluntary co-operation is most likely to be forthcoming and effective where it is least needed.

Misgivings over the effectiveness of competition policy as a whole led to the setting up in 1977 of an inter-departmental review. Two Green Papers were subsequently published.[2] No fundamental changes in policy were recommended and, contrary to expectations, there was no proposal to shift the onus of proof in merger cases, to allow merger only if the companies could demonstrate positive benefits. Had this occurred, merger activity would have been drastically reduced. The Green Papers did recommend some procedural changes, and also that there should be provision for the investigation of 'uncompetitive practices' other than within the context of a full monopoly investigation. Provision for this was made in the 1980 Competition Act. The Act also provided for the investigation of efficiency, services and possible abuse of monopoly positions in certain public bodies, such as transport and water undertakings and agricultural marketing boards, and empowered the Secretary of State to order investigation of specific prices where there are 'major public concern'.

V.5   EEC Provisions[3]

Articles 85 and 86 of the Treaty of Rome set out EEC regulations dealing with monopolies, mergers and restrictive practices. The European Commission is the body responsible for applying the policies and investigating breaches in them.

The most fully developed parts of the regulations are those relating to restrictive practices. These prohibit all agreements, such as price-fixing and market-sharing, which prevent, restrict or distort competition in the EEC and extend over more than one member country. As in the UK, however, exemption may be gained via a 'gateway' if the agreement improves production or distribution or promotes progress. There is also provision for block exemptions. At present these apply in two narrowly-defined cases — one deals with certain types of exclusive dealing agreement between a supplier and a distributor, and the other with certain

---

1   H of C, 370, 21 May 1975, and H of C, 288, 7 April 1976.

2   *A Review of Monopolies and Mergers Policy*, Cmnd. 7198, May 1978 and *A Review of Restrictive Trade Practices Policy*, Cmnd. 7512, March 1979.

3   For a useful summary of the Community's competition policy see D.W. McKenzie, 'Fair Competition in the EEC', *TI*, 13 December 1973. See also D. Swann, op. cit., pp. 55-68 and 159-75, and K.D. George and C. Joll, 'EEC Competition Policy', *TBR*, March 1978.

arrangements for specialization of production. Finally, the Commission has indicated that certain general areas of agreement are not caught by the regulations, mainly because of their limited impact on inter-member trade, or because they deal with rather peripheral or partial co-operation between firms. Firms wishing to test whether their agreements conflict with the legislation are invited to apply for 'negative clearance' while their cases are being investigated.

EEC monopoly regulations are less clear-cut since, although any abuse of a dominant position within the EEC is prohibited if it affects trade between member countries, it is not clear as yet what sort of market-share criterion constitutes dominance, or what abuses will be covered by the regulations. Even less clear up to 1971 was the position of mergers. Until the case of Continental Can (an American firm) in that year, it was unsettled whether Articles 85 and 86 could be applied to merger cases. Although this particular merger was allowed on appeal to the European Court of Justice, the implicit extension of the legislation to mergers was accepted. Since then a proposed regulation concerning mergers has been approved by the European Parliament.[1] This empowers the European Commission to prohibit mergers involving combined assets of 200 million EUA or 25% of a national market where the merger in question creates or strengthens a position of the parties 'to hinder effective competition in the common market or in a substantial part thereof', and to exempt such anti-competitive mergers in particular cases where this is 'indispensable to the attainment of an objective which is given priority treatment in the common interest of the Community'. It further provides for a compulsory system of advance clarification in cases of large mergers involving combined assets of 1 billion EUA unless the acquired firm has assets of less than 30 million EUA.

It is perhaps appropriate that EEC competition policy should focus rather more on restrictive practices than monopolies, given the lower seller-concentration levels in at least some EEC countries, and given the long history of cartelization in countries such as Germany. Besides, economic integration of the member countries obviously involves breaking down many such restrictive agreements. Even in the area of restrictive practices, however, it is only comparatively recently that the Commission has been shown to have any teeth in dealing with severely anti-competitive cartel practices, by imposing fines on such groups as the 'Aniline Trust' who negotiated more-or-less simultaneous price increases in the Market, and on a group of firms fixing prices and market shares in the market for quinine. Some agreements between UK firms may well fall foul of the EEC regulations. For example, the agreement by which Imperial Tobacco and British American Tobacco shared common brand names, but only sold cigarettes in certain specified agreed markets, has undergone extensive modication.

EEC case-law on monopoly is virtually non-existent as yet. This is partly due to the concern in the Community that EEC industry should be competitive in world markets with US industries, and the arguments that this needs large firms in order to obtain full economies of scale. It could be argued, however, that some of these scale economies, such as economies of scale in Research and Development, might better be achieved by means of common research work, since this particular kind of restrictive agreement is not proscribed in the treaty.

---

1 For a discussion of the regulation, which is under consideration by a special working party of exports from member states, see Kurt Market, 'EEC Competition Policy in Relation to Mergers', *Antitrust Bulletin*, Vol. XX, No. 1, Spring 1975.

VI   REGIONAL POLICY AND THE LOCATION OF INDUSTRY
VI.1   The Regional Problem and the Rationale for Government Action

According to one writer a regional problem might be said to exist as long as there is somewhere a sense of regional grievance.[1] This could arise over regional discrepancies in unemployment and activity rates, average income per head, output growth, net emigration and so on. Statistical information on some of these disparities will be found in chapter 5, section I.3. A major influence on the character of the UK regional problem since the mid-1950s has been the decline of certain staple industries, especially coal, cotton textiles and shipbuilding, and falling agricultural employment. However, the UK regions are nearly all mixed urban-rural areas with a fair spread of activities and by international standards the imbalance between them is fairly slight.[2] For instance there is nothing to compare with the 'southern problem' in Italy, where income per head was estimated to be less than half the national average and less than one quarter of that in the richest part of the EEC in 1975. Other main aspects of the EEC regional problem are some low-income agricultural areas in France and the Irish Republic, and certain older industrial areas developed around iron-ore and coal – the Ruhr, Saar and Lorraine.[3] The industrial centres of the EEC outside the UK lie mainly along the Rhine-Rhone valleys, from the Netherlands to Northern Italy. These are estimated to have accounted for some 60% of the Gross Product of the EEC before its enlargement in 1973.

The original objective of UK regional policy was to reduce the very high unemployment rates in the regions in the 1930s. Although there are now other policy considerations, such as securing economic growth, the efficient utilization of national resources and demand management, concern over regional unemployment is still very much to the fore. Persistent regional unemployment indicates a continuing labour-market disequilibrium, with excess supply of labour at the ruling wage levels. One justification for government intervention is that such disequilibria have proved themselves non-self-curing through normal market mechanisms. Presumably this has been due to the immobility of capital and especially housing, and of labour for various reasons, including social ties, imperfect knowledge of job opportunities elsewhere and, perhaps, downward rigidities in wage rates.

A second justification for government regional policy is the likely divergence of social and private costs and benefits in firms' location decisions. Thus, left to their own devices firms might choose locations which permitted minimum cost production (or at least a satisfactorily low level of costs) when the costs actually entering their accounts are the only ones considered. But when the social costs are taken into account (e.g. arising from increased congestion and differential effects on unemployment as between high- and low-employment areas), we might find that the most desirable location was a quite different one.

---

1   A.J. Brown, 'Surveys of Applied Economics: Regional Economics, with Special Reference to the United Kingdom', *EJ*, Vol. LXXXIX, No. 316, December 1969. See also the same author's *The Framework of Regional Economics in the UK*, CUP, 1972; G. McCrone, *Regional Policy in Britain*, Allen and Unwin, 1969; H. Richardson, *Elements of Regional Economics*, Penguin, 1969; and *MBR*, November 1975, pp. 11-19. For an official treatment see *Regional Development in Britain*, COI Reference Pamphlet 80, HMSO, 1976.

2   The standard regions of the UK are: Northern, Yorkshire and Humberside, E. Midlands, E. Anglia, S. East, S. West, Wales, W. Midlands, N. West, Scotland and N. Ireland.

3   D. Swann, op. cit. See also *ET*, August 1979, pp. 90-98, for relative income data.

VI.2   Regional Policy Measures

These have been implemented by the Special Areas Act 1934, the Distribution of Industry Acts since 1945, the local Employment Acts since 1960 and various Finance Acts. The basis of current policy is the 1972 Finance Act and also the 1972 Industry Act (which gave effect to the White Paper Industrial and Regional Development (Cmnd. 4942) published in that year), though with significant alterations in the application of policy in 1975 and 1979.[1] The history of regional policy since 1945 is one of repeated experiment. The following description looks first at the types of area designated to receive assistance, and then at the forms this assistance has taken.

Up to 1966 the criterion used for designating areas for assistance was simply the level of unemployment. Since then the criterion has been widened to 'all circumstances, expected and actual' which allows account of, for example, population migration to be taken as well. The first areas to be selected were the pre-war 'special areas' (South Wales, North East England, West Cumberland, and the Clydeside-North Lanarkshire area). In 1945 these were extended to produce fairly large 'development areas'. These were replaced in 1960 by some 165 smaller development districts, based on local-employment-exchange areas, the idea being to channel assistance to the most severely affected centres of unemployment. But this change in the policy gave rise to considerable uncertainty about the continuing status of individual districts, and in 1966 there was a reversion to the policy of specifying broad development areas. This remains the basis of current policy, although two other types of areas have been designated in addition to the development areas. These are the 'special development areas' and the 'intermediate areas'. Special development areas, lying within the development areas, were first created after 1967 in areas affected by colliery closures because of the imminence there of high and persistent unemployment, but were later extended to other areas. Intermediate areas were designated after the Report of the Hunt Committee in 1969,[2] being areas outside development areas suffering problems similar in kind if not in acuteness, and likely to decline relative to areas which either had natural advantages or were already receiving assistance.[3]

The geographical extent of the assisted areas at the time of writing is as follows: development areas cover all of Scotland and the Northern Region of England; Wales (except for its eastern fringes, both north and south); Yorkshire and Humberside; and North Devon and Cornwall. Special development areas exist in West Central Scotland (centred on Glasgow); the Tyneside-Wearside area and West Cumberland in the north of England; Merseyside; part of North Wales including Anglesey and a large area of South Wales around Cardiff. Intermediate areas cover those parts of the North West and Wales not already mentioned, as well as the Chesterfield area and part of Devon. Altogether, the assisted areas account for 43% of total employment in Great Britain. Northern Ireland is treated as an additional special case.

In looking at the assistance measures which have been adopted at one time or

---

1   See below, p. 220.

2   *Report of the Committee on Intermediate Areas*, Cmnd. 3998, HMSO, 1969.

3   A fourth type of area, the North Midlands 'Derelict Land Clearance Area', received certain subsidies to encourage the modernization and construction of industrial buildings from 1972 to 1974.

another it is convenient to distinguish between measures designed to prevent expansion in areas considered to be sufficiently developed, and financial assistance designed to encourage expansion in the regions. The principal member of the first group is the Industrial Development Certificate (IDC), required for factory building or extension. Up to 1972 they were required in all areas for projects above a certain minimum size, and after 1966 their issue was strictly controlled in the Midlands and South East. From 1972 IDCs have not been required in development areas, and since 1974 a three-tier system has applied to the rest of the country, the maximum size limit for exemption being 15,000 sq.ft in the intermediate areas, 5,000 sq.ft in the South-East planning region and 10,000 sq.ft elsewhere. The 1974 change represented a tightening of the system in the non-assisted areas, although in the recession situation which followed IDC control has apparently not been applied strictly.

In some ways similar to IDCs are the permits required for office development. This control began in London in 1964, and was later extended to certain other areas, although it subsequently lapsed in some. In February 1969 the exemption limit in outer London was raised from 3,000 sq.ft to 10,000 sq.ft. This form of control was retained in 1972 in view of the planning pressures in the South East. However, control of office development has never been regarded as a major policy instrument for dispersing jobs to the regions, and has tended to operate more with regard to intra-regional considerations.

Up to 1963 the financial inducements offered to firms moving to, or located in, the assisted areas were mainly in the form of discretionary grants and loans which were conditional upon the creation of sufficient employment (at a capital cost not exceeding certain limits, albeit flexible ones). In addition, there was government provision of 'advance factory units' for sale or lease to firms at attractive rates. From 1963-6 these measures were supplemented by a system of tax allowances favouring firms in development areas. In January 1966 the tax allowances were replaced by a system of cash grants on plant and machinery, combined with initial allowances[1] on industrial buildings. From September 1967 to 1976 manufacturers in development areas also received a regional employment premium (REP), the value of which was doubled in 1974. For a time they also benefited relatively to firms elsewhere under Selective Employment Tax. In October 1970 cash grants gave way once more to differential tax allowances in the regions, but in 1972 these latter benefits were made nationwide. Extra assistance for the regions was then added in the form of grants. In 1973 a special scheme was introduced to assist removals to the assisted areas by firms in service industries, offering fixed grants per employee transferred and rent-free periods in the new premises.

In 1975 a major reshaping of regional policy took place. The incentives offered from then on included regional development grants for building, new plant and machinery; selective assistance loans or interest-relief grants; removal grants; advance factories; tax allowances on machinery and industrial buildings; finance from European Community funds (e.g. from the European Investment Bank or the European Coal and Steel Community); REP, until late 1976, manpower training assistance; help for transferred workers; and contract-preference schemes relating to

---

1 An initial allowance is an additional proportion of the cost of an asset which may be written off for tax purposes in the year in which the capital expenditure takes place. See chapter 2, section IV.6.

contracts placed by government departments and nationalized industries.[1]
Obviously not all of these applied in every case. Some were conditional on the
amount of employment created and the rates of benefit varied among the different
types of area, Northern Ireland generally offering the highest rates.

The main changes in policy since 1975 have been the phasing out of REP in
1976, and a drastic curtailment of the policy by the Conservative government
elected in 1979. The government's present proposals are to reduce the proportion
of total employment which benefits from regional incentives from 43% to 25% by
1983. This will be achieved by progressively downgrading or abolishing many of
the assisted areas listed earlier. It is intended that the regional support budget of
£609m in 1979 will be cut by £233m within three years. The Regional
Development Grant will be maintained at its present level of 22% in Special
Development Areas, reduced to 15% in Development Areas and abolished altogether
in Intermediate Areas. The minimum levels for these grants will be raised from
£100 to £500 for plant and machinery and from £1,000 to £5,000 for buildings.

The regional measures described so far have existed alongside another, to some
extent competitive, policy. Under the New Towns Act 1946 and Town
Development Act 1952, some twenty new towns have been established and rather
more enlarged. The principal objective here has been to relieve congestion and
assist urban renewal in large conurbations. But this policy impinges on regional
policy since the new and enlarged towns have by no means all been in development
areas, and their creation may have been a counter-attraction to firms which might
have moved to development areas.

VI.3   Some Issues in Regional Policy

One criticism that has been made of government intervention in the location of
industry is that it will give rise to an efficiency loss in the form of higher real costs
of production.[2] This real cost must be set against the social benefits of regional
policy, and might overwhelm them. The argument makes two assumptions. The
first is that firms will locate at cost-minimizing sites if left alone, and the second is
that location significantly affects costs.

There is some evidence, on the first of these, that firms do not approach
location as a cost-minimizing exercise, but, in practice, more as is predicted by the
behavioural theory of the firm.[3] Thus, apparently, firms do not seek an optimum
location but rather an adequate site which satisfies certain minimum requirements.
Choice is usually from among a very limited number of alternatives, perhaps no
more than two or three. The decision to move is usually stimulated by some
problem such as expiry of a lease or a cramped, physically constrained site, rather
than by the attractions of alternative locations alone. Search for a new site is
'narrow' in the literal sense of not spreading far from existing operations. By
itself this evidence does not enable us to dismiss the argument that interference

---

1 For full details see Department of Industry: *Incentives for Industry in the Areas for
   Expansion*, HMSO, 1978 and *Regional Development Incentives*, HMSO, Cmnd. 6058,
   May 1975. See also A. Whiting (ed.), *Economics of Industrial Subsidies*, HMSO, 1976.

2 See, e.g., A.C. Hobson, 'The Great Industrial Belt', *EJ*, September 1951.

3 See B.J. Loasby, 'Making Location Policy Work', *LBR*, January 1967; W.F. Luttrell,
   Factory Location and Industrial Movement, NIESR, London, 1952; and R.M. Cyert and
   J.G. March, op. cit., pp. 54-60.

necessarily results in an efficiency loss. For the sites selected might be lower-cost locations than ones to which government policy directs firms, although not optimal ones. On the other hand, they might be higher-cost locations. Thus, once cost-minimizing assumptions are abandoned, it becomes impossible to predict whether intervention will on balance lead to an efficiency gain or loss, assuming that location significantly affects cost.

On this second question there is some evidence to suggest that location may not significantly affect costs, at least for the majority of manufacturing. One study estimated that some 70% of manufacturing is 'footloose', i.e. not critically affected by costs at different locations.[1] Another writer suggests that some two-thirds of manufacturing is probably footloose with respect to transport costs, which are obviously an important consideration in this context and have always received much attention in location theory.[2] A third, very comprehensive, study found little evidence of continuing excess costs in plants which had moved in relation to the levels in parent or original plants, although it could take five years for initial excess costs to disappear.[3] Thus it appears that a serious efficiency loss would not be inevitable if at least a good deal of manufacturing industry were relocated, though there could obviously be specific exceptions.

A second criticism of UK regional policy has been over its capital bias. Prior to 1967 the various grants, loans and tax allowances offered as financial incentives related exclusively to capital expenditures. As a result the policy was especially attractive to firms with capital-intensive operations, and this was clearly not helpful to the policy objective of creating new employment. Moreover by lowering the relative price of capital inputs, the policy would tend to increase capital/labour ratios of firms receiving the assistance, perhaps causing this ratio to depart from what it should be for efficient utilization of resources. However, while in force REP (and also SET subventions) would have worked in the opposite direction.

A number of other issues have arisen concerning the nature of the policy instruments used at various times. Firstly, the widening of financial incentives after 1963 to include tax allowances or cash grants for investment and the REP, etc. has been criticized on the ground that a larger and larger proportion of the aid given has become unconnected with the creation of new jobs; it is available to firms already in development areas as well as to those moving in. As this has happened, it is argued, the cost-effectiveness of the policy in creating new jobs must have fallen. However a profit-maximizing firm, with reasonably full information and already situated in a development area, would presumably now find it profitable to expand output and employment and seek to do so, and even satisficing firms with only limited perception would tend to do so, in so far as aspiration levels adjust to what is attainable and if there is sufficient publicity surrounding the new measures. Secondly, it has been argued that where tax allowances give way to cash grants assistance is paid to the inefficient as well as the efficient, since their receipt does not depend on profits being earned, as do the benefits through tax allowances. Thus a policy including grants may result in propping up ailing firms. On the other hand, the arguments in favour of grants carry some force. Broadly, these

---

1 R.J. Nicholson, 'The Regional Location of Industry', *EJ*, 1956. But see A.J. Brown, op. cit., on the reliability of this result.

2 L. Needleman, 'What are We to do About the Regional Problem?', *LBR*, January 1965.

3 W.F. Luttrell, op. cit.

are that grants are more likely to be taken into account in decision-making, since there is evidence that returns in investment are often calculated pre-tax;[1] that grants are more conspicuous and the benefits offered easier to calculate; and that the longish time-lag in the 'payment' of tax allowances can be avoided, as can the uncertainty of benefits under the allowance system, since these depend on future, unknown, profitability. Especially if firms' location policy is on behavioural lines, it could well be that a system of grants is necessary for incentives to be effective, even if on other grounds tax allowances might be preferable. Thirdly, it could be argued that the use of a negative prohibition like the IDC's as a policy instrument may be less acceptable than positive financial incentives. For, if rigidly applied, IDCs could do harm by choking off investment and expansion altogether in some cases (e.g. in non-footloose trades). Financial incentives on their own would not entail this risk and, moreover, footloose industries would presumably select themselves, thus automatically minimizing the real costs of, e.g., achieving a given reduction in regional unemployment. This argument is quite strong so long as profit-maximization is assumed. On a behavioural analysis, however, the IDC comes off rather better in some respects. If firms 'satisfice', financial incentives on their own are unlikely to succeed, or will work only sluggishly. For although higher profits are made attainable in development areas, the response (especially from existing firms) may well be slight if adequate profits can still be earned elsewhere. On the other hand, failure to secure an IDC, like expiry of a lease, is exactly the kind of problem to which firms are stimulated to respond in the behavioural theory, and the obvious response is to move. Two pieces of empirical evidence may be cited in this context: the conclusion that the stimulus to move comes from the 'exporting' area not the 'importing' area[2] and the belief among the administrators of the policy that at least up to the mid-1960s it was the IDC rather than the financial incentives which had most effect. Thus, like cash grants, the IDCs may be necessary for an effective policy, even if there could be other drawbacks. Moreover on a behavioural analysis the IDC or similar controls may have other merits. Thus, we no longer assume cost-minimizing location decisions and, by promoting wider search than would otherwise occur, the IDC could increase the chances of lower-cost locations being found. Indeed, it could even be that the IDC is a necessary adjunct to financial incentives because it plays an attention-focusing role in bringing their existence to the notice of firms.

Finally, let us look at two rather contentious issues in regional policy. One is that offering incentives to individual firms is not an effective way of inducing them to move to areas which are otherwise unattractive to them. More effective would be to create positive, real attractions like new towns or other 'growth points', and by the government undertaking more infra-structural investment in roads, docks and other items of social capital stock. Resolution of this argument requires a good deal more knowledge than we have at present about firms' motivation.

Secondly, there has been some dispute over the respective merits of the present 'work to the workers' policy and of the alternative solution of encouraging migration ('workers to work'). The alternative policies may be thought of as eliminating unemployment (excess supply of labour) by shifting the demand curve

---

1 See NEDC, *Investment Appraisal*, HMSO, 1965.

2 B.J. Loasby, op. cit.

to the right (work to the workers), and shifting the supply curve to the left (workers to the work). The migration solution, even if successful in eliminating regional unemployment, would not necessarily remove all inter-regional differences. In particular it would increase net emigration from some areas. Arguments against the migration solution would be that the most mobile workers are probably also the fittest and most skilled, so that the areas they leave become even less attractive to firms; that social overhead capital might be wasted; that congestion in receiving areas would intensify; that the community life and culture in the emptying regions would deteriorate, and so on. However, some limited sorts of migration might avoid these effects (e.g. marginal population movements from large, old, industrial centres to expanding towns outside major conurbations in the prosperous regions). It is very unlikely that a thorough comparison of the costs and benefits of migration and of existing policy would indicate that present policy should be scrapped. But it may be that the two policies are not mutually exclusive and, especially in view of the very small scale of assistance towards migration at present,[1] it could be that some readjustment of the relative weight given to the two policies is desirable. The 1972 policy changes did include more financial help for workers moving house in search of work, but did not go very far in this direction.

VI.4 The Effectiveness of Regional Policy[2]

The statistical evidence shows that, despite the existence of regional policy, the regional problem is still with us. There has been no long-term trend for regional disparities in unemployment to disappear. None of the depressed regions acquired rates of output-growth significantly faster than the UK average, though regional policy has undoubtedly helped Scotland to equal, and occasionally overtake, the overall rate in the 1960s, after a period of very slow relative growth in the late 1950s. Except for Northern Ireland and the South West, the 'problem' regions all had higher personal incomes in relation to the UK average in 1954-5 than in the subsequent ten years. Finally, although the drift to the South East was checked in the later 1960s, net emigration from Scotland, the worst affected region in this respect, increased markedly in the 1960s.

Yet studies do suggest regional policy has had some impact. Two studies of investment grants in the period 1966-8 concluded that planning regions showing predominantly 'development area' status enjoyed a greater level of investment of plant and machinery per employee than the other planning regions,[3] with the marked exception of the South East in the case of one study. A third study analysed patterns of relocation of manufacturing over the period.[4] From 1945-51 about two-thirds of all moves in manufacturing were to development areas. But this was largely because in this period of post-war reconstruction the chief factor stimulating moves was the availability of factory space, which was under

1 See chapter 5, section I.3.

2 For an assessment of regional policy impact see *Cambridge Economic Policy Review*, Vol. 6, no. 2, June 1980.

3 See A. Beacham and T.W. Buck, 'Regional Investment in Manufacturing Industries', *Yorkshire Bulletin of Economic and Social Research*, May 1970; and C. Blake, 'The Effectiveness of Investment Grants as a Regional Subsidy', *Scottish Journal of Political Economy*, February 1972. The former relates to 1966, and the latter to the 1967-8 period.

4 R.S. Howard, 'The Movement of Manufacturing Industry in the UK 1945-65', *Board of Trade*, 1968.

government control and mainly in development areas. Between 1952-9 this control had disappeared, the shortage eased, financial inducements under regional policy were not yet strong and IDCs were not too difficult to get outside development areas. As a result the proportion of moves to development areas fell below 25%. But stricter control over IDCs and larger financial incentives subsequently raised this figure to 50% by the mid-1960s. More recently published studies tend to confirm that regional policy had had a significant effect, suggesting that the strengthening of the policy in the 1960s may have increased the number of moves to development areas by 70-80 per annum (in relation to a maximum of around 160 per annum) with a total employment effect of about 220,000 jobs by 1970. Apparently all three major policy instruments – IDCs, financial incentives and REP – exerted a separate significant influence.[1]

If the regional problem remains, but regional policy has had some mitigating effects, there is only one conclusion. But for the existence of the policy, the regional problem would now be worse than it is.

VI.5   EEC Provisions

Subsidies given to assist the development of backward regions are explicitly permitted by the Treaty of Rome. In the early development of the EEC and up to 1969 the member governments gave a variety of regional aids with very little supervision or guidance from the central EEC institutions. As a result there was very little harmonization of attitudes towards regional problems and of types and rates of assistance. There is even some evidence of competition among member governments to attract foreign investment to their own problem regions. However there was some activity at Community level. The European Investment Bank, provided for in the Rome Treaty, financed projects in less-developed regions and made loans to firms for rationalization required because of the creation of the Common Market; these loans were at commercial rates of interest and intended to top-up funds raised from other sources to the required level. Also, some of the activities of the ECSC and Agricultural Guidance and Guarantee Fund contributed to the Community regional policy effort, especially as the EEC regional problems have much to do with agriculture and the coal and steel industries. Finally, the Social Fund financed training schemes for unemployed workers, though mainly on an industry-by-industry rather than regional basis.

In 1969 a memorandum from the European Commission expressed the need for a more cohesive policy and made certain proposals. These included annual examination of each nation's regional problems; the establishment of a standing committee to review aid schemes; and a Regional Development Rebate Fund to give financial aid to member governments from Community sources (in the form of abatements of interest) for approved aid schemes.

Lengthy and inconclusive negotiations over EEC regional policy measures took place in late 1973 and early 1974, ultimately being suspended because of elections in Britain and France. The size of the Regional Fund was a major source of disagreement, the UK originally proposing a large sum of £1,500m over three years

---

1 B. Moore and J. Rhodes, 'Evaluating the Effects of British Regional Policy', *EJ*, Vol. 83, 1973, pp. 87-110; and 'Regional Economic Policy and the Movement of Manufacturing Firms to Development Areas', *EC*, 43, pp. 17-31, February 1976.

compared with the £250m proposed by West Germany when negotiations broke down. Agreement was finally reached at a Meeting of Heads of Government in December 1974. The Fund was established from 1 January 1975 at a level of £540m for the three years 1975-7. The UK share was set at 28%, second largest after Italy (40%) with a net gain to the UK of about £60m after deducting our contribution through the EEC budget. This figure compares with a total of around £500m spent on regional aid within the UK in 1975. Moreover, receipts from the Fund go to the government rather than to the promoters of individual projects, and so form part of the UK total spending rather than an addition to it.

At one time there were some doubts about the compatibility of UK regional measures with overall EEC policy, but this issue has now been resolved. In general the EEC philosophy appears to favour selective rather than automatic aids, and aids directed towards investment rather than operating costs. Thus automatic aids like the UK Regional Development Grants do not find favour, while the REP, which was both automatic and related to operating costs, was positively disliked. Nevertheless, the existing UK measures have been accepted in the EEC, albeit after a certain amount of rewording of the Community's principles during the renegotiation of the UK's terms of entry. EEC policy distinguished between 'central' and 'peripheral' areas, with 20% and 30% ceilings on the level of assistance respectively. In the UK non-assisted and intermediate areas have been classified as central, and development and special development areas as peripheral, with Northern Ireland being treated as a special case.

VII   INDUSTRIAL EFFICIENCY
VII.1   Introduction

In earlier sections of this chapter we have seen that industrial growth in the UK has proceeded at a very modest rate by international standards, to the point that in terms of GDP per head Britain has now to be regarded as one of the poorer countries in Western Europe. In the search for explanations various questions have been asked. Has Britain fallen behind because of a lack of technical progressiveness and R and D spending? Are UK firms too small to compete with those of other countries in world markets? Does UK management and workforce exhibit inefficiency to an unusually large degree? There are no complete answers to these questions, but in the following pages we shall consider some of the evidence relevant to them and especially the role of the government.

In all, five aspects of the problem and their accompanying strands of policy are isolated and discussed. These are R and D performance; industrial structure (in particular the size distribution of plants and firms); problems of financing investment; the role of planning and information exchange; and the micro-level significance of price control.

VII.2   R and D and Technical Progressiveness

The latest available statistics show that in 1975 total UK R and D expenditure was £2,151m.[1] This represented about 2.0% of GDP, rather lower than the level of 2.6%

---

1   Source: *AAS*.

in the 1960s. Private industry carried out most of the work but provided only 34% of the funds. 52% was financed by the government. The league table of industries undertaking most work is headed by electrical engineering (26.0%, with electronics and telecommunications alone contributing 16.8%), followed by aerospace (21.6%), chemical and allied industries (18.5%), motor vehicles (6.5%) and mechanical engineering (7.7%). Other industries had less than 4%. R and D activity is known to be very much the preserve of large firms. A survey in 1959 of nearly 5,000 firms showed that 350 large firms (employing over 2,000 workers) accounted for about 85% of the total R and D expenditure, with medium and small firms contributing only a minor share, and small firms virtually nothing.[1] Although the data is now twenty years old, it would undoubtedly still give a fair idea of the present situation.

UK spending on R and D is creditably high by international standards. Historically, Britain and especially America have been regarded as international 'creditor' countries in R and D, while Europe is in deficit.[2] However, more recent data, although restricted to public spending only, gives a somewhat different impression (table 4.10). In relation to GNP, UK spending falls slightly below that of W. Germany and only just above that of France. And while America still spends most relative to GDP, the lead has been cut significantly since 1970, especially relative to West Germany, where spending has increased markedly.

TABLE 4.10

Public Sector R and D in Relation to GDP, in UK, USA and Major European Countries, 1970 and 1975

	R and D as a Percentage of GDP				
	UK	West Germany	France	Italy	USA
1970	1.25	0.96	1.24	0.46	1.56
1975	1.18	1.22	1.16	0.40	1.33

Source: Eurostat, *Public Expenditure on Research and Development*, 1974-6.

A high level of R and D effort does not necessarily go hand in hand with rapid growth of GNP. Thus America and Britain, which research most, have grown less rapidly in recent years than has Europe, which invests less in R and D. Nevertheless, encouragement of research activity is a longstanding element in government policy. The large share of R and D which is government-financed has already been mentioned. The benefit to private industry from this work would not be as great as if, for instance, grants of equivalent value were made for firms' own projects. Nevertheless, a substantial overspill of new developments into the firms' other operations does occur, especially in such fields as aircraft, electronics, metallurgy, engines and machine tools. In some cases, notably computing, aircraft and machine

1 See C. Freeman, 'R and D: A Comparison between British and American Industry', *NIER*, May 1962.

2 See C. Kennedy and A.P. Thirlwall, 'Technical Progress: A Survey', *EJ*, March 1972.

tools, the government has provided funds for the development of firms' own projects. Additionally, the government sponsors work on behalf of industry in its own research establishments; funds research through various Research Councils; gives grants to co-operative research associations in various industries; and, via the National Research and Development Council (NRDC), finances development of inventions made in government laboratories and by private individuals, where this is in the public interest.

All of these measures impinge directly on R and D activity. Two other strands of government policy may have had an indirect bearing: policies to encourage larger firm size, and competition policy. These policies are discussed elsewhere.[1] Here we consider only the reasons for their connection with R and D.

As we have seen, R and D activity is heavily concentrated in large firms in Britain and America, and one school of thought is that large firm size is a necessary condition for technical progressiveness, primarily because of the large financial requirements.[2] However, not all stages of the innovation process are expensive. Invention itself can still involve only negligible expenditure. It is the subsequent stage of development up to the point of commercial application, and the actual introduction of the new product or process, which are typically expensive. In the past many important inventions have been the work of individuals or small firms.

This sort of evidence puts the contributions of large firms, as measured by R and D inputs, into a different perspective. There is some evidence that in Britain and elsewhere large firms are a comparatively minor source of fundamental breakthroughs,[3] and that the R and D resources they commit are devoted mainly to relatively minor product improvements and modification.

The question of large absolute size and technical progressiveness intertwines with the argument that market power (large size relative to market supply) is an important facilitating condition.[4] Empirical tests of this hypothesis and its rival — that competition is conducive to technical progress — have so far proved very inconclusive.[5] It is difficult to say why this is so. It might be because of practical difficulties in measuring technical progressiveness, of which there is no direct measure. Alternatively, the explanation could be that both competition and market power carry with them both advantages and disadvantages from the point of view of securing technical advances, and the balance between them is either roughly equal or varies from case to case. Thirdly, it may be that there are other important factors at work.

1 See sections VII.3 and V respectively.

2 See J.K. Galbraith, *American Capitalism*, Hamish Hamilton, 1956.

3 See, e.g., J. Jewkes, D. Sawers and R. Stillerman, op. cit., and F.M. Scherer, op. cit.

4 See also section V above.

5 The evidence is mainly for the US. Scherer, in *Industrial Market Structure and Economic Performance*, Rand McNally, 2nd edition 1980, after providing an excellent summary, notes 'What is needed for rapid technological progress is a subtle blend of competition and monopoly, with more emphasis in general on the former than the latter and with the role of monopolistic elements diminishing when rich technological opportunities exist' (p. 438).

VII.3 Scale, Unit Cost and Structural Reorganization

The ideas that there are widespread and large economies of scale in production, and that they fairly frequently fail to be exploited, are recurring themes in discussions of UK industrial growth. The extent of potential scale economies can be gauged either by observing the physical relationship between inputs and output in production (i.e. by estimating production functions) or by direct observation of long-run average costs as scale is varied. To assess how fully such scale economies as exist are exploited we would need to relate additional information on the actual size distribution of plants and firms to these estimates of potential scale economies. There is a fair amount of information on the first of these questions. The second has received very little attention in the literature, but certain limited conclusions can be drawn from Census of Production data.

In general, empirically estimated production functions in both the UK and most other countries have revealed remarkably few results that are inconsistent with a constant-returns hypothesis.[1] By contrast, empirical cost functions have suggested that average costs decline rapidly at first as scale increases, but that the rate of decline lessens as scale is increased further, the cost curve tending to flatten out until it is virtually horizontal. Thus an 'L'-shaped long-run average cost curve is observed, indicating substantial economies to increases in scale over smaller size ranges; further, but less substantial, economies at higher size levels; but with no evidence of eventual diseconomies of scale.[2] According to the evidence there is much inter-industry variation in the magnitude of scale economies. One study shows the percentage increase in total cost per unit faced by plants producing at only 50% of estimated minimum efficient scale (m.e.s.) for various industries;[3] in brick production, for instance, costs would be some 25% above the level of m.e.s. whereas for a sulphuric-acid plant the increase would be only 1%. In view of this inter-industry variation, only very rough generalizations can be made. But from the available evidence it seems that scale economies in most trades are likely to have been secured by plants five times as big as the smallest and even where economies continue to be enjoyed at larger size levels, they will almost certainly have been exhausted by plants ten times the size of the smallest.

This tentative conclusion enables us to draw from Census data some equally tentative inferences about the degree of exploitation of scale economies. Table 4.11 shows the size distribution of plants in 1976. It shows that small plants are numerically predominant. This can mean one of several things. Either these plants are all in industries, or subsections of industries, where there are few, if any, economies of scale; or the larger plants are run inefficiently, so that there is room for small efficient plants which nevertheless fail to exploit scale economies fully; or the owners of these small plants are content to accept a very low rate of return on their investment; or, finally, scale economies are of very little importance, so

---

1 See A.A. Walters, 'Production and Cost Functions: An Econometric Study', *Econometrica*, 1963.

2 Ibid.; see also J. Johnston, *Statistical Cost Analysis*, McGraw-Hill, 1960; C.F. Pratten, *Economies of Scale in Manufacturing Industry*, Cambridge University Press, 1971; and Z.A. Silberston, *EJ*, March 1972.

3 C.F. Pratten, op. cit. M.e.s. is the point on the L-shaped long-run average cost curve at which average costs cease to fall.

that the size distribution is the outcome of purely random effects.[1] Attempting to allow for the first suggestion, we might say that the smallest plants which generally exist in an industry employ 100 workers. Then, if we take plants employing 500 workers or more and apply the conclusion of the previous paragraph, we find from table 4.11 that nearly 60% of total output is produced in plants in which the bulk of scale economies can fairly safely be assumed to have been exploited. On the same basis, around 44% of total output is in fact accounted for by plants at least ten times the size of the smallest. The same general picture emerges for manufacturing enterprises (groups of establishments under common ownership) (table 4.12). Without close study at the individual-industry level, firm conclusions should not be drawn. But it could be that the efficiency loss believed to arise from the existence of sub-optimal scale has been exaggerated.

Over time, there has certainly been a marked trend towards larger plants and firms. Plants with over 1,500 workers accounted for 15.2% of total employment in private-sector manufacturing industry in 1935, and for over 30% in 1976; those with under 100 employees accounted for 25.6% in 1936 and for 20.4% in 1976. Perhaps, therefore, the importance of plant scale economies is increasing, but if so the evidence indicates it is being taken up to some extent. Also, it is interesting to observe that the number of establishments (plants) per enterprise is quite small, 1.33 in 1968,[2] so that if firms *are* efficient then economies of multi-plant operation must be very limited in most industries.

TABLE 4.11

Distribution of Manufacturing Establishments[1] by Employment Size, UK, 1976

Employment size category	No. of units	%	Total employment (000)	(%)	Total net output (£m)	(%)
1-10	56,979	53.1	267.2	3.7		
11-19	17,087	15.9	245.8	3.4	7,533.4	17.0
20-49	14,366	13.4	444.6	6.1		
50-99	7,542	7.0	526.5	7.2		
100-199	4,967	4.6	693.7	9.5	3,834.6	8.6
200-499	3,854	3.6	1,190.1	16.3	7,227.6	16.3
500-999	1,391	1.3	964.8	13.2	6,126.4	13.8
1,000-1,499	442	0.4	539.2	7.4	3,500.0	7.9
1,500 and over	606	0.6	2,433.1	33.3	16,212.3	36.5
Total	107,234	100.0	7,305.1	100.0	44,434.2	100.0

Source: Annual Census of Production, 1976.

Note: 1 An establishment is the smallest unit capable of supplying census information, usually a factory or plant at a single site or address.

1 It has been pointed out that the configurations we observe are similar to those one might expect if firms, initially of equal size, were subjected over a longish period to a succession of pieces of good or bad luck, each having a proportionate effect on firm size. For a discussion of this idea see, e.g., F.M. Scherer, op. cit., chapter 4.

2 *Census of Production 1968.* On this point see F.M. Scherer *et al., The Economics of Multi-Plant Operation*, Harvard University Press, 1975.

TABLE 4.12

Distribution of Manufacturing Enterprises[1] by Employment Size, UK, 1976

Employment size category	Enterprises (No.)	(%)	Establishments (No.)	(%)	Total employment (000)	(%)	Total net output (£m)	(%)
1-99	83,466	93.3	87,117	81.5	1,189.4	17.1	5,751.9	13.5
100-199	2,813	3.2	3,930	3.7	386.9	5.6	2,014.7	4.7
200-499	1,698	1.9	3,344	3.1	518.8	7.4	2,936.4	6.9
500-999	674	0.8	2,289	2.1	471.2	6.8	2,872.8	6.8
1,000-4,999	609	0.7	4,861	4.6	1,275.4	18.3	8,136.8	19.1
5,000-9,999	98	0.1	1,811	1.7	669.8	9.6	4,616.2	10.9
10,000-49,999	78	0.1	2,549	2.4	1,441.2	20.7	9,388.4	22.1
50,000-99,999	9	0.01	669	0.6	572.0	8.2	3,618.0	8.5
100,000 and over	4	0.05	336	0.3	446.3	6.4	3,223.8	7.6
Total	89,446	100.0	106,396	100.0	6,971.2	100.0	42,559	100.0

Source: Census of Production, 1976.

Note: 1 An enterprise means one or more establishments under common ownership or control.

As a means of securing greater efficiency and growth, structural reorganization has tended to receive emphasis under Labour governments, particularly from 1964-70. Thus an Industrial Reorganization Corporation (IRC) was set up, which initiated and aided a number of mergers, including some spectacular ones such as Leyland-BMC and GEC-AEI-English Electric. The 1968 Industrial Expansion Act was also designed to provide government support for schemes which would improve economic efficiency, expand productive capacity and promote technical improvements, and a specific programme of grant-aided help was provided to reorganize the shipbuilding industry under a 1967 Act.

Under the 1970-4 Conservative government emphasis tended to swing away from 'structural' solutions to industrial problems in favour of a greater reliance on the pressure of competition, and the IRC was dissolved in May 1971. The main emphasis of more recent government policy is described in section VII.5.

VII.4   Finance for Investment

Orthodox economics suggests two possible reasons for government intervention in private-sector capital formation. One would be that, for some reason, the social returns on investment projects undertaken by firms are greater than the private returns. If so it is legitimate to reduce the cost of capital services to the firm in order to raise the level of investment in capital goods from the privately-optimal to the socially-optimal level. The divergence between social and private benefits might arise from the impact of investment on unemployment, or on the balance of payments or even on national prestige. Secondly, intervention would be justified if there was evidence of 'market failure' in the supply of funds for investment: that is, if shortcomings in the organization of financial institutions, or in the information flows on which they base their decisions, left firms unable to borrow at 'appropriate' interest rates given the profitability and degree of risk of their investment plans.

Alternative explanations, implicitly drawing on rather different theoretical models of the firm, might be that firms facing an uncertain future simply tend to underestimate the private returns to investment, or that investment policies resulting from the gradual adjustment of firms' aspirations to their past achievements would result in growth rates that were unacceptably low to the government.

In practice, the rate of investment in UK manufacturing is widely regarded as being too low. Also, new investment tends to earn relatively poor returns, and capital-market imperfections are believed to exist, mainly affecting the supply of medium- and longer-term funds. A number of measures to improve investment performance were embedded in a broader government industrial strategy outlined in a White Paper published in November 1975.[1] The investment measures themselves stemmed from the Industry Acts of 1972 and 1975. The 1972 Act affirmed the (Conservative) government's determination to provide a substantial and lasting impetus to profitable industrial expansion, modernization and a higher growth rate by increasing the government's incentives to investment in all regions of the UK. The main investment incentive was the allowance of free depreciation (whereby firms set capital expenditure against tax at whatever rate suits them best)[2] on new plant and machinery, and an initial tax allowance of 50% on industrial buildings and structures throughout the UK, measures which had previously applied only to the assisted areas.[3] Further, there was a system of grants to industry for capital expenditure in the assisted areas and in some cases elsewhere.

One other provision of the 1972 Act was that grants might be given only in exchange for state shareholdings in the companies concerned. This provision was not used by the Conservative government, but has been used subsequently by the Labour government, for example in its rescue of British Leyland in 1975.

The 1975 Act greatly increased the emphasis on extending state ownership in the provision of assistance to industry. Part I of the Act set up the National Enterprise Board,[4] with initial finance of up to £1,000m to assist firms, or the reorganization of industries, exercising the powers of selective financial assistance under the 1972 Act. A controversial feature of the NEB is that it is empowered to extend public ownership not only to companies asking for help (as Upper Clyde Shipbuilders, Rolls-Royce and British Leyland had earlier done) but also into profitable companies. The NEB is required to promote industrial democracy in the undertakings controlled by it, and to hold and manage securities and other property in public ownership which is transferred to it (including Rolls-Royce, Alfred Herbert, Feranti and BL). The Act required the NEB to earn an 'adequate' return on its capital, and made acquisitions exceeding £10m in a company, or 30% of a company's share, subject to the consent of the Secretary of State.[5] However,

---

1 *Approach to Industrial Strategy*, HMSO, Cmnd. 6315, November 1975.

2 In most cases free depreciation amounts to a 100% initial allowance.

3 See also section VI and chapter 2, section IV.6.

4 Other parts of the Act dealt with planning agreements and information disclosure, which are discussed in section VII.5.

5 Guidelines published in 1976 restricted the NEB's freedom of action without reference to the Secretary of State to £0.5m in cases of share purchases contested by shareholders.

present government policy serves to modify the functions of the NEB. An Industry Bill currently before Parliament ends the NEB's function of extending public ownership, promoting industrial reorganization and industrial democracy.

At one time there was optimism in left-wing circles and apprehension elsewhere that the NEB would lead to a major extension of public ownership, to include at first 100 and then 25 of the biggest UK companies. It is now clear that the NEB as previously organized and financed would not, and was not intended to, attempt such a task.

The question of possible institutional shortcomings in the private-sector supply of investment funds to industry was one of the issues reviewed by the government-appointed Committee set up under the chairmanship of Sir Harold Wilson on The Functioning of Financial Institutions.[1] More generally, the financial problems of smaller companies have recently received considerable public discussion and attention, notably in 1978 and subsequent budgets.

VII.5   Information Exchange and Planning

In most textbook descriptions resource allocation takes place in market economies without the need for economic agents to meet, exchange information and co-ordinate their behaviour in any direct way. Planning is effected via the price mechanism. In the UK, especially under Labour governments, steps have been taken to supplement the impersonal price signals in the market with other types of information, and to create a measure of non-market planning in the resource allocation process.

The first major effort in this direction was the National Plan of 1965. As a planning exercise this was short-lived. However some of the institutional structure associated with the Plan survived, in particular the Economic Development Committees for different industries. Twenty-one EDCs were set up, under the aegis of the central National Economic Development Council, and they undertook a wide range of activities. These have included regular demand and supply forecasts and publication of information on export performance, sales opportunities in particular markets, and import trends. Other topics which have been covered include manpower problems; standardization; stockholding procedures; factors affecting investment; R and D; and the effect of decimalization, taxation and devaluation. The information has been disseminated within industries via newsletters and reports, and there has also been some exchange of information between industries.

A 1974 White Paper introduced a different type of policy instrument, the planning agreement.[2] These were intended as a means of exchanging information between the government and individual companies on long-term objectives and medium-term expectations and plans.[3] Agreements would be concluded annually,

---

1   Cmnd. 7937, HMSO 1980. A minority group on this Committee proposed the setting up of a public investment bank. However, the majority of the Committee believed that existing financial mechanisms are sufficient.

2   *The Regeneration of British Industry*, Cmnd. 5710, HMSO, 1974.

3   For a description of the possible contents of such agreements, see *TI*, 8 August 1975, pp. 338-42.

though subject to revisions, and they would also be voluntary. However, companies could find themselves under considerable pressure to volunteer, in order to secure maximum benefits from government assistance measures. Thus, for instance, the 1975 Industry Act provided safeguards to firms with Planning Agreements over the rates of grant and qualifying conditions for regional development grants and selective financial assistance. Moreover part IV of the same Act provided a procedure — albeit a cumbersome and lengthy one — whereby companies could be compelled to disclose information of a planning nature. (In return it obliged the government to publish 'in due course' a model of the economy so that the public could make forecasts using their own assumption about GDP, unemployment, the balance of payments, retail prices, average earnings and other matters.) However, the Planning Agreements system never really got off the ground, and does not feature in the current (Conservative) government's approach. Thus the 1980 Industry Bill would repeal the provisions of the 1975 Act with respect to planning agreements and to the disclosure of information by companies.

Another strand of the last (Labour) government's thinking on planning was described in a 1975 White Paper, *An Approach to Industrial Strategy*.[1] It proposed that a systematic statistical and analytical framework be set up, covering the past performance of individual manufacturing sectors, and the implications for each of alternative medium-term growth assumptions. Subsequently some 40 Sector Working Parties have been set up, covering about 40% of total manufacturing output. The Sectors chosen were industries 'intrinsically likely to be successful', or with the potential of being so (together with industries 'whose performance (as in the case of component suppliers) is most important to the rest of the industry)'.

The SWPs bring together representatives of government, management and unions to analyse their own industry and agree on medium-term programmes of action to improve their sector's competitive performance. This means increasing productivity, increasing the level and quality of investment, improving the 'non-price' competitiveness of the products, concentrating the products on the right markets, and ensuring that enough people have the skills that industry needs. Management and union representatives ensure that the programmes are practically viable at the industry, company and firm level, and the government representatives see that these programmes are harmonized nationally.

The current (Conservative) government's approach to industrial policy is one of deep scepticism towards planning and government interference, and of reliance on market forces. Not only between different governments, but also amongst non-involved observers (including economists) there is often marked disagreement about the relative merits of market solutions versus planning, and there is a dearth of objective theoretical knowledge and empirical evidence to help resolve the issues. Moreover, it is particularly hard to evaluate mixtures of planning and the market mechanism, as distinct from 'ideal' stereotypes.

On the one hand, it is possible that the government, if it succeeds through some form of 'planning' in discovering more about the micro-implications of its macro policies, could avoid some of the past errors which the 1975 White Paper listed: unduly sharp and frequent changes of economic regulators; pre-emption of resources for the public sector and personal consumption; and intervention in the nationalized industries. It is also possible that companies, if better informed about

---

1 Cmnd. 6315.

government intentions and less prone to suffer from the errors listed above, could improve their own planning and resource utilization. However, unless the present government radically alters its outlook (for example, if there were further spectacular industrial failures), it seems that policy for the immediate future will place most emphasis on restoring incentives to private-sector decision-makers, by reducing taxes, freeing resources for private industry (by public-sector spending cuts), relaxing government restrictions, especially those affecting small businesses, and relying on the market.

VII.6   Some Microeconomic Implications of Price Controls

Statutory price controls were first introduced by the Labour government in 1966, after a period of voluntary control. Applications for increases were reviewed by the now-disbanded National Board for Prices and Incomes (NBPI). Subsequently, statutory controls gave way to voluntary arrangements until November 1972. In the first stage there was a virtual standstill on most prices other than food for five months. Stage II of the policy saw the creation in 1973 of a Price Commission (PC). About 200 of the largest firms (later increased to around 1,400) were required to give prior notice of price increases to this body. Smaller firms had to report prices intermittently, and the smallest to keep records for inspection. Increases were accepted only on the basis of 'allowable' cost increases, that is, a rise in the price of materials, fuel, rents, transport, etc. and a proportion of labour costs, and as long as profit margins did not exceed a 'reference level', on the average level in the best two of the previous five years. The PC as originally constituted remained in being until 1977, during which time the basic nature of price control policy was unaltered, though many detailed changes were made, mainly towards relaxation of the 'Price Code', especially in December 1974 and August 1976. Over the period some 8,000 notifications were received each year, together with a total of 350,000 inquiries or complaints about pricing matters. From July 1977 until 1979 a reconstituted PC was in operation, operating what was in practice a somewhat looser and more flexible policy.[1]

The primary objectives of price control policies are macroeconomic ones. The final periodic report of the original PC[2] suggests that at the last peak of economic activity (in 1973-4) it may have kept prices 3-4% lower than they would otherwise have been. In the subsequent recession, however, its effect was minimal, and the binding constraint on price levels was almost certainly depressed trading conditions rather than price control.

Our present interest is less in the macroeconomic significance of price controls than on their incidental microeconomic effects, especially their impact on industrial efficiency. On orthodox theoretical arguments, we should expect these to be small or non-existent. If firms are already maximizing profits and pursuing cost-minimizing policies, the extra sanction of price control will be on output, employment levels and investment. Thus, if costs increase but prices do not adjust to the same extent,

---

1   See *Quarterly Reports of the Price Commission*, and, for a firsthand account of the original PC's role, Sir Arthur Cockfield, 'The Price Commission and the Price Control', *TBR*, March 1978.

2   HC 459, 1977.

the profit-maximizing output and employment levels will generally fall. If current and expected future profit levels fall, the incentive to invest is weakened, while at the same time the surplus available for re-investment is less.

Other models lead to somewhat different conclusions. As was noted earlier, in section I, the managerial and behavioural theories suggest that there is generally some discretionary expenditure and/or slack in the firm's operations. In the behavioural theory in particular, firms do not generally operate at or close to maximum efficiency, in the sense of choosing cost-minimizing factor ratios and obtaining the maximum output it is possible to get from any given bundle of resources. One set of empirical estimates of the degree of technical inefficiency – or X-inefficiency, in the writer's own terms – suggests that it may amount to 25% of output in many cases and up to 80% in some.[1] If these estimates are anywhere near the mark, the scope for raising efficiency is clearly considerable, and the sanction of price controls is one possible way of achieving it. Thus, in the Williamson model, the introduction of price controls could result in a more adverse business environment, causing discretionary expenditures to contract. In behavioural terms, price control could be exactly the kind of 'problem' to which firms will respond by cutting slack and widening search for new and better production methods. However, the gains will not always be unambiguous ones. For instance, where firms are forced to abandon managerial objectives there will be some loss of managerial utility to offset the social gain arising from cost savings, and organizational slack may serve a useful social function to some extent as a form of contingency reserve. Moreover, cutting slack will tend to have employment implications, with the attendant social costs especially at times when unemployment is already high.

What the actual effects of price control have been in this area is hard to assess. The NBPI reports contained a good deal of specific recommendations for improved efficiency and long-term productivity benefits. Similarly, the PC uncovered important areas of 'administered pricing' policy where significant improvements could be made to the benefit of the community, especially where competitive pressure is lacking. In its first periodic report the new PC tended to see its role to lie in investigating pricing in monopoly or imperfect-competition situations,[2] and at one point a merger of the Price Commission and the Monopolies Commission seemed likely. In the event, however, the Price Commission was finally abolished by the Conservative government in 1980, though one vestigial remnant of price control will remain. Under the 1980 Competition Act, the Secretary of State may refer specific prices 'of major public concern' to the Director General of Fair Trading for investigation.

REFERENCES AND FURTHER READING

F.M. Scherer, *Industrial Market Structure and Economic Performance*, Rand McNally, 2nd edition, 1980.

D.A. Hay and D.J. Morris, *Industrial Economics: Theory and Evidence*, OUP, 1979.

B.S. Yamey (ed.), *Economics of Industrial Structure*, Penguin, 1973.

---

1 H. Leibenstein, 'Allocative Efficiency vs. X-Efficiency', *AER*, 1966.

2 HC 117, 1977.

R. Turvey, *Economic Analysis and Public Enterprise*, Allen and Unwin, 1971; and *Public Enterprise*, Penguin, 1968.

R. Pryke, *Public Enterprise in Practice*, McGibbon and Kee, 1971.

R. Rees, *Public Enterprise Economics*, Weidenfeld and Nicolson, 1976.

The Nationalised Industries, Cmnd. 7131, HMSO, March 1978.

S.J. Prais, *The Evolution of Giant Firms in Britain*, CUP, 1976.

L. Hannah and J.A. Kay, *Concentration in Modern Industry*, Macmillan, 1977.

A. Hunter, *Monopoly and Competition*, Penguin, 1969.

A.J. Brown, *The Framework of Regional Economics in the UK*, CUP, 1972.

H.W. Richardson, *Regional and Urban Economics*, Penguin, 1978.

C.F. Pratten, *Economies of Scale in Manufacturing Industry*, CUP, 1971.

C. Freeman, *The Economics of Industrial Innovation*, Penguin, 1974.

D. Swann, *The Common Market*, 4th edition, Penguin, 1978.

For information on current developments in industry and commerce:

British Business (formerly *Trade and Industry*).

National Institute Economic Review (especially February issue).

5

Labour

David Metcalf and Ray Richardson

I EMPLOYMENT
I.1 The Working Population

In September 1979 the working population (or labour force) in the UK was estimated to be 26,528,000. This aggregate was composed of employees in employment (22,928,000), employers and self-employed (1,886,000), HM Forces (319,000) and the registered unemployed (1,395,000).[1]

Since 1971, when a new method of estimating the number of employees in employment was introduced, there has been a continual rise in the mid-year estimates of the working population. On the face of it, this implies a re-establishment of the pattern which prevailed from 1950-66, during which period the working population fell only in 1958, and a break with the sustained fall in working population estimated for the period 1966-71.[2]

To some extent, these changing labour-force patterns over time may reflect measurement and estimation difficulties. For example, it is difficult to estimate accurately the number of self-employed workers, and it has been suggested that certain tax and National Insurance changes have given substantial incentives for people to switch into or out of self-employed status. If this has happened it is quite possible that the estimated changes in working population are misleading because they would capture changes in the number of employees but not those in the number of the self-employed. In addition, the much discussed 'black economy' phenomenon, about which little is known with any certainty, may involve many people being at work but nowhere being counted as such in the official statistics. Here, however, we will assume that the official estimates are broadly correct and discuss what determines the size of and changes in the labour force.

One influence is the size and demographic composition of the population. For example, younger and older males are less likely to be in the labour force than males aged between twenty-five and fifty-five. In order to abstract from demographic changes it is convenient to discuss these issues in terms of activity rates (sometimes called labour-force participation rates). These express, for any age and sex group, the proportion of working to total population.

It is worth considering changes in the activity rates for the two sexes separately, if only because male activity rates have tended to fall, while female activity rates have tended to rise.

Economic growth tends to reduce male activity rates. In particular, younger males stay in the educational system longer and older males retire earlier, especially when growth is accompanied by improved retirement pensions. Thus, between 1961 and 1977 the proportion of boys who stayed on in school rose from 23% to

---

1 *DEG*, January 1980, p. 62.

2 *BLS*, p. 220; *DEG*, March 1977, pp. 250-2; and *DEG*, January 1980, p. 62.

51% for 16-year-olds and from 13% to 21% for 17-year-olds.[1] In addition, the number of males attending universities approximately doubled over the same period. For older men, the reported activity rates have fallen in each successive Census of Population; for example, the activity rate of 65-69-year-olds fell from 48% to 31% over the period 1951 to 1971.[2] All of these changes reflect the fruits of economic growth, both directly through increased incomes and indirectly through greater government support to education and retirement pensions.

Superimposed on the inverse relation between long-run growth and male activity rates is a complex, and not necessarily stable, reaction to fluctuations in growth. The dominant postwar reaction of the male labour force to fluctuations in growth has generally been positive; the male labour force has tended to contract (or grow less rapidly) during economic recessions and to grow (or contract less rapidly) during periods of economic expansion. There are exceptions to this general pattern, however, most notably in the recession which began in 1974. Between 1974 and 1977 the number of male employees (either in employment or unemployed) *rose* by more than 300,000; in contrast, during the recessionary period of 1969-72 the number of male employees *fell* by 340,000. The different experience in the two recessions is worth exploring more fully. In both periods, male unemployment rose; in the earlier period it increased from 440,000 to about 680,000; in the later period it increased from 460,000 to 1,050,000. Male employment fell in both periods; by 580,000 in the earlier recession and by 280,000 in the later one. It will be seen that by one measure, the loss of jobs, the second recession was much less severe; but by the other measure, the increase in registered unemployment, it was much more severe. No fully convincing reasons for these changes in labour-market behaviour have so far appeared.

It was suggested above that a typical response to long-run growth is that the male labour force contracts, while a typical response to short-run growth is that the male labour force expands. These two responses, the negative and the positive, are not contradictory, as they might seem at first sight. The first concerns people's responses to a permanent increase in wealth levels; the second concerns people's responses to what is presumed to be a temporary fall in employment prospects. This is an application of the fundamental notions in economics of income and substitution effects. If a worker is not planning to supply the maximum amount of labour at all times, he can choose the most advantageous periods when the supply is to be offered. On many calculations the most advantageous periods occur when wages are high and jobs are easy to find; that is, in expansionary conditions. Consequently, a recession is a period during which there is less point in offering one's services. This view therefore predicts that over the business cycle the size of the labour force will be positively related to the state of the economy. It is usually termed the 'discouraged worker effect', meaning that as the economy contracts, the number of people in employment falls by more than the increase in the number counted as unemployed.

There is an alternative and opposite view to the one just described, labelled the 'added worker effect'. It suggests that as 'primary' (i.e. permanent) members of the labour force are made unemployed in recessions, 'secondary' (i.e. temporary) workers are drawn into the work force so as to provide an additional source of income for

1   *AAS*, 1971, p. 106 and *AAS*, 1980, p. 122.

2   *ST*, 1975, p. 84.

the family; the result is that the number of unemployed rises more than the number disemployed. This view obviously has some validity but it is basically a qualification to the 'discouraged worker' hypothesis. It stresses that many households plan imprecisely, that unpredicted events are important and force changes even in carefully laid plans, and that savings, credit and social welfare payments may be inadequate to maintain family living standards for more than a relatively short period. These and other factors are all of obvious practical importance, but they should not be taken to imply that the 'discouraged worker' hypothesis, with its emphasis on rational calculation, is thereby unrealistic and likely to be misleading.

Whereas male activity rates have declined over the long run, female activity rates have increased very sharply. Ignoring the self-employed and HM Forces, females accounted for 41% of the labour force in 1979, as compared with just over 30% in 1950. In discussing long-run changes, however, a distinction should be made between married and non-married females. The activity rates for young non-married females have fallen, while those for older non-married females have risen; for example, between 1951 and 1971 they fell for 20-24-year-olds from 91% to 81%, and rose for 45-59-year-olds from 61% to 73%.[1] The reasons for the distinctive pattern for young non-marrieds are not clear but they are probably connected with (a) the rise in the extent of girls and young women staying on at school and attending universities, and (b) the rise in the number of one-parent families, financially supported either by the state or by alimony or other family resources.

For married women the picture is unambiguously one of increased activity rates, albeit at different rates for the different age groups. Table 5.1 shows the striking changes that are officially estimated to have taken place.

TABLE 5.1
Wives' Activity Rates by Age, Great Britain, 1951 and 1976

Age Group	1951	1976
16-19	38	52
20-24	37	55
25-44	25	56
45-59	22	61
60+	5	14
All ages	22	49

Source: ST, 1979, p. 84.

The importance of these changes can hardly be overstated, and their implications extend far beyond the labour market. What is of immediate importance here is to consider the reasons for the rise. One possibility is that there has been a widespread reduction in the extent of sex discrimination in the labour market. For this to have happened, however, there would have been either a consistent rise in the wages of females relative to those of males or a significant shift in the employment structure, with large numbers of females joining the better-paid and more attractive occupations. Neither of these developments seems to have taken place, certainly

---

1 *ST*, 1979, p. 84.

not on a major scale, in the first 25 years after the Second World War. Whether or not sex discrimination, usefully defined, has been extensive, there have been no conclusive studies demonstrating changes in its extent.[1]

Turning to influences primarily affecting married women, we can point first to the fact that the average number of children per family has fallen over time. Whether this is a cause or effect of higher participation is not known. What is known, for the US, is that activity rates have also risen for married women with young children. This suggests that declining family size is, at most, a partial explanation of rising activity rates.

A second possibility is that, due to the introduction of new products, there has been a rise in the productivity of the housewife, effectively allowing her to produce the same amount of services as before but in less time. By itself this improved productivity does not necessarily make for greater participation by the wife in the labour force because, at the same time, everyone's income has risen. With the rise in income one might expect both the family's demand for housewifely services and the housewife's demand for personal leisure to increase, thereby decreasing the incentive to join the labour market. Only if the domestic-productivity effect is strong will the net effect be to release housewives for market work. With this possibility there is again the question of whether the product improvements were cause or effect. That is, did they appear autonomously or were they induced and hurried along by the independent effect of a rise in the number of working wives caused by some other factor? To our knowledge, no study has given a satisfactory answer to this question.

A third possible explanation of the rise in activity rates for married women is that social attitudes have become increasingly tolerant of wives, and even of mothers, working. This explanation is probably the most popular of all and there is certainly no doubt that attitudes have changed. Again, however, there is the difficulty of deciding the extent to which changes in attitudes were an independent cause or were themselves a response to changes in practice. It does seem plausible that the two world wars were very influential in this matter. They were, as far as the labour market was concerned, exogenous events inducing many women to join the market for the first time. This process surely changed social attitudes, encouraging working wives. It is also notable that over the last twenty years the largest increases in activity rates for married women are associated with older women, who experienced to the full the turmoil of wartime. However, one note of caution is worth sounding as to the impact of wartime exigencies. The available data are very sketchy, but they suggest that the increase in the proportion of wives who work in the market is very much an international phenomenon, extending even to countries for which the direct impact of the war was quite modest.

The above explanations all run in terms of supply influences, implying that progressively more married women are willing to work in the market. Demand influences may also have been important. One possibility is that the attempts by successive governments to induce greater regional evenness of employment have been successful in bringing some work to women who previously had very limited job opportunities. Related aspects of this view are discussed in section I.3 below, but there are two qualifications to be noted. First, if this argument has much

---

1 For an analysis that suggests that there have only been small changes in the extent of occupational segregation by sex see C. Hakim, 'Sexual divisions within the labour force', *DEG*, November 1978, pp. 1,264-8.

weight we would expect that, region by region, more or less equal increases in activity rates for married and unmarried women would have occurred. It is not clear that this has happened. Second, if the point were merely that there has been a geographical redistribution of jobs we would expect a decline in female activity rates in the prosperous, job-losing regions. This has certainly not happened in absolute terms, but it is true that female activity rates have tended to rise more rapidly in areas where they have traditionally been low.[1] In fact there has not been merely a redistribution of jobs. Since the end of the 1930s the UK economy has been run at unprecedented and persistent tightness. It seems most plausible to us, in the absence of hard statistical confirmation, that it is this influence rather than deliberate geographical dispersion that explains a major part of the rise of women in the labour force.

A second, structural, argument relating to demand influences could be made. It might be suggested that female activity rates have risen because expansion has been particularly marked in industries employing a high proportion of female to male workers. It is shown below, in section I.4, that these female-intensive industries have indeed enjoyed a relative expansion, certainly since the Second World War. However, most of these sectors are not inherently female-intensive and we would again put principal stress on the general expansion of the economy when considering demand influences which account for the rise of female participation in the labour market. Essentially, what has been happening here has been the tapping of a labour reserve.

Recently there has been some interesting research in this area, specifically in explaining the variation in married females' activity rates between towns and cities in Great Britain.[2] It was shown that wives' activity rates were greater, the higher were female wage rates and the lower were male wage rates; wives' activity rates were also higher for the foreign-born, for those who lived in the larger cities and for those who lived in towns with low male unemployment rates.[3] In general where labour markets are tight, as judged by unemployment or wages, married women are more likely to be in the labour force.

I.2   Aggregate Employment Patterns

Total male employment in the UK is continuing to fall. Concentrating on the estimates of employees in employment, the number of male workers in the UK rose fairly consistently from about 13,560,000 in June 1950 to about 14,860,000 in June 1965; by June 1979 the number had fallen, again fairly consistently, to only 13,340,000.[4] The net result, over a nearly 30-year period, was a fall in male employment of 220,000 people.

Although the official estimates are subject to revision, it is interesting to note that the reduction in male employment has recently slowed down. Between 1973 and 1979 the average annual fall was no more than 70,000. This is about one-third

1 J. Bowers, *The Anatomy of Regional Activity Rates*, Regional Paper 1, NIESR, 1970, chapter 3.

2 C. Greenhalgh, 'Labour Supply Functions for Married Women in GB', *EC*, August 1977.

3 Somewhat similar, but not identical, results can be found in R. McNabb, 'The Labour Force Participation of Married Women', *MS*, September 1977.

4 *BLS*, p. 221; *DEG*, October 1975, p. 1,030; and *DEG*, January 1980, p. 62.

of the corresponding fall for the period 1966 to 1972, which is a very striking change given the sluggish growth of total output in the later period. In fact the relatively modest fall in male employment came as a great surprise to economic forecasters who were tracking the economy after 1974. It implies that there has been a very sharp reduction in the rate of increase of average labour productivity in recent years.

Female employment, again measured by employees in employment, has continued to be buoyant. Since 1959 there has been a 25% increase in the number of females at work and only three years during which female employment has fallen.[1] Further, there is no sign that the rate of increase is slowing down. It is worth noting that a substantial number of the female labour force consists of part-time workers, defined as those who normally work less than 30 hours per week. In 1977, the last year for which reliable estimates are available, fully 40% of employed females worked part-time; the corresponding figure for 1971 was 34%.[2] The very great majority of these part-time workers are wives.

The above discussion should serve to correct an impression easily gained from some of the recent public discussion of labour-market problems. There has been much talk, in newspapers, on television and in Parliament, of a combination of developments that are said to threaten our prosperity. There has been concern at the high level of unemployment, the decline in manufacturing activity and the possible employment implications of new technology, exemplified by micro-processors. In this context, it is striking that in spite of being afflicted by the deepest recession in the postwar period, the decline in the number of people in work has so far been fairly modest.

I.3   Spatial Employment Patterns

The spatial pattern of jobs and workers in Great Britain is changing rapidly both within and between regions.

For example, the resident labour force in the seven British conurbations fell by more than 650,000 between 1961 and 1971.[3] During the same period, Greater London lost more than 25% of its jobs in manufacturing, many of them to other parts of the country, particularly to the rest of the South East region. This reduction in workplace and labour-force densities, together with shifts between the standard regions, has sometimes been a response to natural market forces and sometimes a result of deliberate planning policy. Thus, in the period since the Second World War there has been a great planned expansion of new towns that ring many of our major cities. Often, firms have wished to expand their operations around their existing inner-city sites but have been denied planning permission. They have therefore been obliged to move either to a nearby new town or to a more distant depressed region. Of course, many firms have moved for reasons other than planning difficulties, for example because suitable nearby land was not physically available, because labour was increasingly scarce locally, because local transportation facilities were deteriorating, or because government subsidies made such moves profitable.

---

1   *DEG*, October 1975, p. 1,030 and *DEG*, January 1980, p. 62.

2   *DEG*, February 1980, p. 147.

3   J. Corkindale, 'The Decline of Employment in Metropolitan Areas', *DEG*, November 1977.

The loss of workplaces in many of the major cities may or may not imply higher urban unemployment. For example, in London there has been no obvious change in unemployment, relative to other areas, during the period of major job loss. This implies either that the population is leaving London at the same rate as jobs or that commuting patterns are changing. Clearly some cities are suffering from the loss of jobs (Glasgow is often said to be in this category), while others benefit from the reduction of congestion that decline implies.

Until recently, when specific urban problems became more acutely perceived, the most noticed national aspect of employment was the inter-regional one. In the latter context the pattern of unemployment across regions was of most concern but attention was also paid to variations in activity rates by region.

Up-to-date estimates of activity rates by region are not readily available but it is clear that spatial differences are tending to be reduced over time. Thus, the proportion of the civilian labour force accounted for by females range, in 1977, from a high of 40% in Scotland and the North West to a low of 37% in Wales, Northern Ireland and East Anglia.[1] A decade before, the range was from 36% in the South East to 31% in Wales.

I.4 Employment by Industry and Occupation

In September 1979 the manufacturing sector of the British economy employed only 31% of all employees at work.[2] Adding the number of employees in agriculture, mining, construction and gas, electricity and water we still get only 42% of all employees, implying that the service sector now accounts for well over half of the employment in the country. The recent tendency for the service-sector labour force to grow relative to the whole labour force began in the mid-1950s, when the manufacturing and service sectors each employed about 42.5% of the total number of employees. The marked absolute decline in manufacturing employment began in 1966. In that year, manufacturing employment stood at 8.4 million; subsequently it has fallen in nearly every year (1969, 1973, 1974 and 1977 are the exceptions) and in nearly every individual manufacturing grouping, so that in December 1979 there were only 7.0 million workers employed in manufacturing.

Within the service sector the main growth areas have been professional and scientific services, particularly in education and medical and dental services. In the ten years to June 1979, the numbers employed in professional and scientific services rose by more than three-quarters of a million. Some service sectors have become smaller over this period, for example, transport and communications (due mainly to the rapid decline in railway employment) but the general tendency is for growth.

Another way of examining the composition of the labour force is to examine the division between the private and the public sectors. Over the period 1961 to 1978 there was an increase in the proportion of the employed labour force working in the public sector, from 24% to nearly 30%. The rate of increase was most rapid in the years 1966-7, 1969-70 and 1974-5 when the level of private employment fell sharply and public employment was fairly stable.

---

1 *Regional Statistics*, 1979, pp. 92-4.

2 *DEG*, February 1980, p. 186.

Within the public sector, total employment in the public corporations (i.e. roughly the nationalized industries) has been fairly constant in spite of the growth in the number of nationalized industries. Local authority employment has risen sharply, by 61% between 1961 and 1978, mainly because of a growth in the education sector. Over the same period, central government employment grew by 30%, mainly because of the growth in the National Health Service.[1]

These structural changes are also reflected in the relative growth of female employment, referred to above, because much of the service sector has made intensive use of female labour. Thus, approximately 68% of the employees in professional and scientific services are female, as against 24% in agriculture, only 4% in mining and 7% in shipbuilding. It is true that the textile and clothing industries are also female-intensive, but their decline has not been great in comparison to the expansion of the service sector. It is also worth emphasizing again that a significant number of females, particularly in the rapidly expanding service sectors, work only part-time. Thus, in June 1977 55% of the 1.25m females working in education and 41% of the nearly 1m in medical and dental services were part-time workers.[2] This compares with only 23% for manufacturing and it may suggest that some of the sectoral shifts that have occurred are not a purposeful move away from manufacturing but the use of a previously unused labour reserve that would not be available for full-time work, or perhaps even for part-time work in other sectors.

I.5   Hours Worked

To clarify discussions of work one should distinguish between normal basic hours, normal hours and actual hours of work. The first term relates to the number of hours a person is expected to work at basic rates of pay; the second includes any guaranteed overtime paid at premium rates; the third, and for most purposes much the most interesting notion, includes all overtime, guaranteed or not. Actual hours are typically in excess of normal hours, but by including absenteeism and sick days in the picture the situation may be reversed.

As with activity rates, two lines of enquiry can be distinguished for hours worked by the labour force as a whole. First, one wants to explain the trend; second, one wants to explain temporary variations around it. Further, it is revealing to examine the structure of hours worked, e.g. by occupation or wage level.

Over a long period average actual hours of work have fallen, from around sixty hours per week in the early part of the century to just over forty hours by 1979. Initially, the fall was in hours per day; subsequent reductions have been first in days worked per week and second in weeks per year. There is therefore a clear tendency for extra leisure to be bunched, there being 'economies of scale' in leisure activities.

For many years, normal hours fell more rapidly than actual hours, implying an increase in the number of overtime hours. Thus, between 1948 and 1968 normal weekly hours of male manual workers fell from 44.5 to 40.1.[1] Actual hours in the

1   The most detailed discussion of public-sector employment trends is to be found in M. Semple, 'Employment in the public and private sectors 1961-78', *ET*, November 1979, pp. 99-108.

2   *DEG*, February 1980, pp. 147-54.

1   *BLS*, p. 160.

same period tended to rise until the mid-1950s and fall thereafter. Since the late 1960s, however, normal hours have been relatively constant but actual hours have tended to fall.

Hours of work fluctuate a good deal from year to year. The changing tempo of the economy is the principal explanation of these variations, with the length of work-weeks falling in recessions and rising in expansions.

In the recession that began in 1974 the reduction in the work-week, as measured by the percentage of operatives in British manufacturing who worked overtime, was somewhat smaller than might have been expected.[1] A possible explanation for this relative buoyancy in overtime working is the increasing burden over the years of hiring and firing costs on employers, which makes them economize on the number of workers they employ.

There are wide variations between industries in actual hours worked. In 1975 the average annual hours worked per employee in Great Britain was 2,165 in construction as against 1,616 in mining.[2] Within manufacturing the range was from 1,995 in the bricks and pottery sector, to 1,582 in clothing and footwear.

Some of the variation observed in such a cross-section is due to different industries being at different stages in their own business cycle. Additionally, some industries have relatively old labour forces whose work-weeks are naturally shorter. Nevertheless, there are persistent real variations across industries and occupations in hours worked and these certainly affect the attractiveness of the different jobs. Some research work is beginning to explain such variations. In a recent study[3] it was shown for a sample of ninety-six industries in Britain that the number of hours offered by the average manual male worker was positively affected by the hourly wage rate and low skill levels, and negatively affected by the number of fellow workers employed in the factory, residence in the South East and Midlands, and residence in conurbations. Further, the number of work hours demanded from the male worker was greater when the worker was more skilled, aged between 25 and 54, and working in industries that were fast-growing or highly concentrated; fewer hours were demanded from young males and from those who tended to work alongside females.

Manual workers have longer work-weeks than do non-manuals. For men in 1979 the reported difference averaged 7.4 hours per week; for women, the corresponding figure was only 2.9 hours. Also, males, particularly in the manual occupations, tend to work longer hours than do females.[4]

I.6   The Quality of the Labour Force

As time goes on, the average skill level of members of the labour force rises. This is one component of the increased quality of the working population, implying that, from a given number of workers and a given quantity of supporting factors of production, potential output grows over time. Other important sources of higher quality are better health levels, an improved spatial distribution of employment

---

1 *DEG*, March 1978, p. 390.

2 *DEG*, September 1977, p. 937.

3 D. Metcalf, S. Nickell and R. Richardson, 'The Structure of Hours and Earnings in British Manufacturing Industry', *OEP*, July 1976.

4 *DEG*, February 1980, p. 208.

and, up to a point, shorter working weeks. In quantitative terms the increase in skill levels has had much the largest impact on productivity of any of these sources.

There is no precise, independent measure of the increase in average skill level in the UK over any period and no comprehensive indication of the allocative efficiency of labour between various skill levels. In recent years, however, a number of studies have been made, mainly of the educational system. The formal education sector is not the only source of skill augmentation but the model testing its efficiency has general applicability. The problem at issue may be described as follows. If the sector is organized efficiently the net social value of a pound of expenditure will be the same at the margin for all types and levels of education. What we must do, therefore, is to equalize the social profit on all educational activities.

The terminology employed here may be disagreeable to some people. However, as long as account is taken of all sources of cost and benefit, whether they be material or psychic, there can be no real objection. It is true that some sources may not be measurable in practice and that others may be measured only imperfectly. These defects do not suggest that no measurement should take place, merely that decisions and judgments should not be based solely on what is measurable.

In fact the measurement of the profitability of education and training programmes is decidedly imperfect. The usual measure of benefits is some estimate of the expected increase in monetary earnings enjoyed by the trainee, i.e. his expected full earnings minus the earnings he would otherwise expect were he not to undertake the training under consideration. To take a concrete example, in estimating the profitability of a university degree a comparison is made between the observed earnings of people already graduated and those of people who stopped just short of going to university. This provides an earnings differential for each age group which stands for the earnings increase expected by the current trainee at each stage of his working life.

This estimate is extremely crude and a number of adjustments can be made to improve on it. For example, not all of the crude differential can be attributed to education because ability and motivation levels differ between the two groups from which data are drawn. Consequently, an effort should be made to estimate the independent effect of ability differences.

Once the estimate of benefits has been obtained it is necessary to estimate the costs of the training. The principal cost is the output that could have been produced by the trainee had he been in full-time work. Its value is usually measured by the monetary earnings he forgoes while being trained or educated. Added to the forgone earnings are the direct costs of instruction, represented by salaries of teachers, cost of buildings, etc.

Two early research efforts for the UK were by Blaug[1] and Morris and Ziderman[2] and both contain a clear account of the procedures and difficulties involved. The latter was more comprehensive and among its conclusions were (1) that postgraduate qualifications were not very profitable for society, and (2) that higher national certificates were very profitable indeed. If these calculations are correct

---

1   M. Blaug, 'The Rate of Return on Investment in Education in Great Britain', *MS*, September 1965.

2   V. Morris and A. Ziderman, 'The Economic Return on Investment in Higher Education in England and Wales', *ET*, May 1971.

they imply that society would be better off if there were more resources involved in HNC work and less in postgraduate work; they suggest that the UK educational system is inefficiently structured and is turning out the wrong mix of graduates.[1]

For many years British governments have been active in seeking to improve the skill composition of the labour force. The Industrial Training Act, passed by the Conservative government in 1964, was an important piece of legislation in this respect. Under the Act, Industrial Training Boards were set up in 30 or more industries. The Boards imposed a levy on the firms in the industry and financed approved training schemes with the proceeds. In 1972 the Training Opportunities Scheme (TOPS) was started; this greatly expanded the number of training places provided directly by the government.[2]

II UNEMPLOYMENT
II.1 Composition of the Unemployed[3]

Stocks, flows and durations: In 1979 the number of people unemployed in the United Kingdom averaged 1.4 million, equivalent to 5.8% of the labour force.[4] Males account for a little over two-thirds of this total. The flows through the unemployment register are very large relative to the stock. In 1979 there were some 4.5m unemployment registrations and 4.5m cases of people leaving the register occurred. These registrations and deregistrations do not refer to 4.5m separate people: some individuals have more than one spell of unemployment. The average duration of each completed spell of unemployment was approximately one-third of a year (1.4m/4.5m) or 16 weeks.

This average-spell duration is an important statistic because the main reason the stock of unemployed people rises is that the average duration of unemployment rises and not that more people become unemployed. For example in 1955 when unemployment was at an all-time (peacetime) low of 1.1%, the average duration of each spell of unemployment was only 3½ weeks.[5] Since 1966 flows into unemployment have been remarkably stable at around 4m per year even though the rate of unemployment has more than trebled. The higher unemployment rates primarily reflect longer spell durations.

---

1 For a useful, though complex, survey of the relevant work on Britain, see G. Psacharopoulos and R. Layard, 'Human capital and earnings', *RES*, July 1979.

2 For an excellent discussion of the issues involved in training see A. Ziderman, *Manpower Training: Theory and Policy*, Macmillan, 1978; see also B. Showler, *The Public Employment Service*, Longman, 1976, especially chapter 5.

3 For a fuller discussion see D. Metcalf and S. Nickell, 'The Plain Man's Guide to the Out of Work' in Royal Commission on the Distribution of Income and Wealth (Diamond Commission), *Selected Evidence* to Report No. 6, Lower Incomes, HMSO, 1978; S. Nickell, 'A Picture of Male Unemployment in Britain', *EJ*, forthcoming 1980. Both these papers are freely drawn on here. They both give extensive further references. See also K. Hawkins, *Unemployment*, Penguin 1979.

4 Official figures refer to people registered as unemployed. Some people register but are not available for work, e.g. occupational pensioners. However, on balance, official figures understate true unemployment because many people do not register as unemployed. The main such group are married women who traditionally have not always been eligible for benefits (though recent social security changes will moderate this non-registration).

5 F. Cripps and R. Tarling, 'An Analysis of the Duration of Male Unemployment in GB 1932-73', *EJ*, June 1974.

The incidence of unemployment among people is very unequal. With 4m registrations a year and a labour force of 24m, in 6 years the number of registrations equals the size of the labour force. Therefore if a person is in the labour force for 48 years he would, if unemployment were distributed equally, expect to have 8 spells of unemployment during his lifetime. Yet we know many people never suffer a single spell of unemployment. Indeed, in any year some 3% of the labour force account for 70% of the total weeks of unemployment.[1] Clearly a fraction of our labour force must be constantly at risk of long-term unemployment and/or recurrent spells of unemployment. Unfortunately the group who bear the burden of unemployment are concurrently towards the bottom of the pay distribution, work in the most risky occupations, and are those who also suffer a higher incidence of ill health — labour-market disadvantage is cumulative.[2]

Demographic characteristics: In April 1979 there was the following pattern of unemployment rates by age in Britain.[3]

	under 25	25-54	55+
Males	9.2%	5.3%	7.9%
Females	8.8%	2.7%	3.0%

Young workers have high rates of unemployment because on average they have a very high propensity to become unemployed and many have recurrent spells of unemployment, while some older workers have both a higher likelihood of entering unemployment than the 25-54 group, and once unemployed, remain so for a relatively long time.[4]

The under-20s have a 25% chance of entering unemployment in any given year. This reflects their frequent job-changing, relatively low current costs of unemployment and the ease of finding another job — reflected in their low unemployment durations.

There is no doubt that youth unemployment has worsened since the post-1974 recession. In 1973 males under 20 had an identical unemployment rate to all males (3.5%). But now their unemployment rate is nearly double the all-male rate. Why is this?[5] At least three explanations have been suggested. First, young workers are harder hit in a recession than adult workers and, conversely, their employment prospects pick up faster when the economy improves. Firms economize on labour in a recession and they reduce recruitment. This hits young workers because of their high turnover rates and lack of labour-market experience. This is the dominant factor in the rise in youth unemployment. Second, the relative pay of youths has risen substantially. Finally, if industries which employ youngsters suffer

1 R. Disney, 'Recurrent spells and the concentration of unemployment in Great Britain', *EJ*, March 1979. Richard Disney made helpful comments on the whole of section II. S. Owen, 'Do the faces in the Dole Queue change: the Distribution of unemployment amongst individuals 1970-4', Government Economic Service *Working Paper*, forthcoming 1980.

2 See R. Layard, D. Paichaud and M. Stewart, *The Causes of Poverty*, Royal Commission on the Distribution of Income and Wealth, Background Paper No. 5, HMSO, 1978.

3 *DEG*, June 1979, p. 569.

4 *DEG*, August 1979, pp. 789-90.

5 *DEG*, August 1978, pp. 908-16.

most in recessions then this would compound employment problems of young people. This last argument has not operated recently. It is manufacturing which has experienced the largest employment fall during the current recession. But youngsters are disproportionately employed in the non-manufacturing sectors like distribution, construction and insurance, banking and finance.

The concern over youth unemployment probably stems from the fear that it casts a life-long shadow. This fear does not seem to be justified. Youngsters who are unemployed for 3 months or more on leaving full-time education get just as good first jobs and subsequent jobs as their similarly qualified friends who slot straight into a job after leaving education.

The higher unemployment experienced by older workers partly reflects the fact that the structure of jobs and wages within the firm makes it difficult to allow for the waning productivity of older workers, who are therefore specially prone to redundancy.[1] And once older workers become unemployed they suffer long spells because firms tend to prefer younger workers. A quarter of all vacancies and a third of labouring vacancies have an explicit upper age limit of 50.[2] The higher unemployment of older workers also reflects their higher incidence of illness and disability.

Unmarried men experience unemployment rates half as large again as married men of the same age and socio-economic group. It is not clear whether this reflects the institution of marriage — single men have less pressure to take up another job — or whether married men are simply of higher quality than single men and so are desired both by women and by employers. The fact that unmarried men are more likely to suffer from mental instability and alcoholism than their married counterparts hints that the labour-quality point is important.

Once men are married their incidence of unemployment increases dramatically with the number of their dependent children. In 1972 the following male unemployment rates were extracted from the General Household Survey (GHS) for married men:

Number of dependent children	0	1	2	3	4	5+
Unemployment rate (%)	3.2	2.8	3.9	4.5	10.3	12.3

There are many reasons for this. First, the level of family support for those in work is substantially below that for those out of work. In 1980 a working 3-child family receives £12 a week child benefit but (if we assume the children to be aged 9, 11 and 13) gets almost twice that amount (£23.30) if on Supplementary Benefit. Second, families with a large number of dependent children are less mobile. Third, lower-skilled groups — those most at risk of unemployment — have slightly larger families, but the positive relation between family size and unemployment also holds for particular skill groups. Fourth, the sociological literature suggests that groups who are alienated from society and who suffer a feeling of powerlessness are prone to both higher fertility and higher unemployment.

---

1 See for example D. Mackay, 'After the shake-out', *OEP*, March 1972.

2 *DEG*, February 1978, pp. 166-72.

Socio-economic (SEG) Group and Industry: There are marked disparities in the incidence of unemployment by occupation. The 1972 General Household Survey indicates the following male unemployment rates:

SEG	Unemployment rate (%)
Senior and intermediate non-manual (e.g. managerial, professional)	1.2
Junior non-manual (e.g. clerical)	3.3
Foreman and skilled manual	4.0
Semi-skilled manual	6.7
Personal service (e.g. waiters, barmen)	19.3
Unskilled manual	14.2

Further, people classified by the Employment Service as general labourers account for around half the unemployed. Their lack of training causes unskilled workers to bear the brunt of macroeconomic fluctuations and firms' expansions and contractions. The persistently low level of vacancy to unemployment ratios also reflects the lack of demand for these workers which prolongs their unemployment spells. For example in March 1979 the registered vacancy to unemployment ratio for general labourers was 0.02, whereas for toolmakers it was 1.52. Our economic system puts the least skilled at the most risk of unemployment. Yet simultaneously some industries are experiencing difficulties in recruiting skilled craftsmen. This has been specially severe in engineering where inadequate apprenticeship recruitment in the late 1960s and early 1970s, coupled with narrowing of skill differentials and lack of job security have resulted in shortages of pattern makers, machine tool-setter operators, toolmakers, precision-instrument makers and instrument mechanics.[1]

Geographical structure: During the forty years 1930-70 the main geographical focus was 'the regional problem'. Although this had a number of dimensions, it was encapsulated in the variation in unemployment rates by region. For much of the postwar period Scotland, Wales and Northern England had unemployment rates some three times as large as those in the Midlands and the South East. As the amount of structural and frictional unemployment appeared to be rather similar in every region, commentators were led to suggest that differences in demand pressure across the regions were the key to the regional problem.[2] But the policy implications of such a finding are unclear. It is very difficult to boost demand in one region without the main impact of the extra spending leaking out into other regions.

In the 1970s regional differences in unemployment relativities have become much less severe. The coefficient of variation (i.e. standard deviation/mean) of unemployment rates across the 10 British regions fell from .42 in 1966 to .22 in March 1979.

Perhaps because the regional structure of unemployment is now so much less unequal the focus of attention has recently shifted to local labour markets and the decaying cores of our inner cities. Local labour markets which have a

---

1 *BEQB*, June 1978, pp. 158-9, September 1979, pp. 253-4.

2 R.J. Dixon and A. Thirlwall, *Regional Growth and Unemployment in the United Kingdom*, Macmillan, 1975; P. Cheshire, *Regional Unemployment Differences in GB*, NIESR Regional Papers II, CUP, 1973.

disproportionate number of people at risk of unemployment – the young, the old, the single and large families – have relatively high unemployment rates. These demographic factors account for the bulk of the variation in the 1971 male unemployment rate across 32 London boroughs.[1]

Unemployment in the central areas of our great conurbations is now seen to be the major spatial labour-market problem. The resident labour force in our conurbations declined by 7% between 1961 and 1971 while it rose by 11% in the rest of Great Britain.[2]

And while employment rose by 1.8% between 1971 and 1976 in Great Britain it declined in the inner areas of our major cities, by 15% in Liverpool, 10% in Birmingham and 9% in London and Manchester.[3] If we look at manufacturing the picture is even worse. For example inner London (defined as the Boroughs of Newham, Tower Hamlets, Hackney, Islington, Camden, Kensington and Chelsea, Hammersmith, Wandsworth, Lambeth, Southwark, Lewisham, Greenwich and the Cities of London and Westminster) lost 1 in 3 of its manufacturing jobs in the five-year period.

The Department of the Environment recently sponsored a number of Inner Area Studies. A typical conclusion from these studies was that the unskilled are 'trapped' in the inner city, and they suggested subsidised migration as a way of reducing the unemployment problem in the central cores. But, as the likelihood of unemployment for a person with given characteristics – a single, older, general labourer for example – is only modestly higher if he lives in the inner city than if he lives in the suburbs, it is not really clear how such subsidized migration would help.[4]

II.2   Why has Unemployment Risen?

Recorded unemployment is now three to four times as large as it was in the two decades following World War II:

	Unemployment (%), UK
1948-66 (av.)	1.7
1967-74 (av.)	2.8
1975-9 (av.)	5.7

Three sets of factors have been advanced to account for the higher unemployment. First, the 'full employment' rate of unemployment has risen. Second, profits have been squeezed and this has led to insufficient investment. Third, fear of inflation and adverse balance of payments have inhibited successive governments from using fiscal and monetary policy to reduce deficient-demand unemployment.

1 D. Metcalf and R. Richardson, 'Unemployment in London', in D. Worswick (ed.), *The Concept and Measurement of Involuntary Unemployment*, Allen and Unwin, 1976.

2 J. Corkindale, 'The Decline of Employment in Metropolitan Areas', *DEG*, November 1977, pp. 1,199-202. The conurbations are Greater London, Central Clydeside, Merseyside, South East Lancashire, Tyneside, West Midlands and West Yorkshire.

3 J. West and P. Martin, 'Employment and Unemployment in the English Inner Cities', *DEG*, August 1979, pp. 746-9.

4 A useful discussion of this problem is P. Cheshire, 'Inner Areas as Spatial Labour Markets: a Critique of the Inner Area Studies', *Urban Studies*, 1979, pp. 29-43.

The 'Full Employment' Rate of Unemployment: If we take the period 1948-66 as one of full employment there are grounds for thinking that at the same pressure of demand – measured for example by vacancies or capacity utilization – unemployment would now be above 1.7%.

Let us initially dismiss two reasons sometimes advanced to account for the upward creep in the full-employment unemployment rate. First, it is not due to the changed composition of the working population. Quite the reverse. Young and old workers, who have relatively high unemployment rates, now account for a smaller fraction of the labour force than they did 10 years ago.[1] And women, who have lower-than-average unemployment rates, comprise a growing fraction of the labour force. Second, the geographical, occupational and industrial mismatch between unemployment and vacancies has not worsened.[2] For example the coefficient of variation (standard deviation/mean) of unemployment across 172 local labour markets fell from .67 in 1966 to .53 in 1973.

The most controversial of the factors advanced to explain the rise in unemployment concerns benefits. It is widely believed that the replacement ratio, defined as unemployment benefit and/or supplementary benefit relative to earnings, has risen and that this causes working people to become unemployed or to prolong unemployment. The most careful statistical analysis indicates that the elasticity of unemployment duration with respect to the replacement ratio is +0.6.[3] To see how much of the extra unemployment this can account for, we can take boom years to standardize for any business-cycle influence:

	Replacement ratio (= benefit paid per recipient/post tax male manual earnings, full-time workers aged over 21)	Unemployment
1964-5	.33	330,000
1973	.37	580,000

The replacement ratio rose by 12.1%. So the extra unemployment generated is

$$12.1\% \times 0.6 \times 330,000 = 24,000$$

This is around one-tenth of the increase in unemployment of 250,000 between 1964-5 and 1973. Assuming such estimates are reliable, it is clear that the disincentive effects associated with more generous unemployment benefits account for only a modest fraction of the rise in unemployment. Anyway, these may be overestimates because, at a time of high overall unemployment the job opportunities not taken by those deterred by benefits may well be taken by other unemployed men.

---

1 In the early 1980s the proportion of older workers will continue to fall and the proportion of women will continue to rise, but the proportion of youngsters will rise rather than fall. See *DEG*, June 1979, pp. 546-51.

2 See R. Turvey, 'Structural Change and Structural Unemployment', *International Labour Review*, September/October 1977; N. Bosanquet, 'Structuralism and Structural Unemployment', *BJIR*, November 1979.

3 S. Nickell, 'The Effect of Unemployment and Related Benefits on the Duration of Unemployment', *EJ*, March 1979.

The main reason for the rise in the replacement ratio was the introduction of the Earnings Related Supplement (ERS) in addition to the standard flat-rate unemployment benefit in 1966. The econometric tests of the impact of ERS on unemployment were confirmed by a Department of Employment study[1] which concluded that it could have added, at most, 50,000 people to the unemployment register. Nevertheless many people believe that work disincentive effects associated with ERS are severe and the government has proposed to withdraw it in 1982. This, coupled with the decision to de-index unemployment benefit in 1980-1, so that it is no longer automatically adjusted in line with inflation, will result in a harsher treatment of unemployed people than has been customary in recent years. Unemployment is expected to rise to unprecedented postwar levels in the early 1980s yet it seems that the government is not prepared to protect the incomes of those hurt by its macroeconomic policies.

Three factors which concern the demand for labour may have resulted in a rise in the full-employment rate of unemployment. First, the number of unskilled jobs is decreasing. Between the 1961 and 1971 censuses, unskilled workers as a percentage of the labour force declined by 12.5%. Second, the effect of this change in the structure of labour demand or the duration of unskilled workers' unemployment has probably been compounded by the recent rise in the relative wages of unskilled workers compared with skilled workers. This narrowing of differentials has been specially noticeable in engineering. Third, employment protection legislation may, paradoxically, have increased unemployment. While it makes the jobs of existing employees more secure, firms will now screen job applicants much more carefully and so the likelihood of being hired falls.[2]

From the above estimates, the higher replacement ratio, the reduction in the demand for unskilled labour and employment protection have probably been associated with a rise in the full-employment rate of unemployment of around 200,000 since 1966. In this case if we would have been content with an unemployment rate of 1.7% before 1966 the equivalent rate now would be around 2.5%. But this is under half the current rate. So we must turn to other explanations for the rise in unemployment.

Too High Real Wages: There has been a striking rise in real wages in manufacturing relative to increases in labour productivity. The manufacturing real product wage (real cost of labour/output per employee) — essentially the share of labour in value added — rose (1970 = 100) from 95 in the 1960s to 105 in the 1970s, and simultaneously employment in manufacturing (1970 = 100) fell from 101 in the 1960s to 92 in the 1970s.

There are a number of reasons for this rise in real wages relative to the value of the output produced by labour. First, it is normal for the share of wages in value added to rise in a recession even though employment is falling. And the 1970s had more recession years than the 1960s. Second, employment became more sticky relative to output in the 1970s (resulting in a big fall in labour productivity in the 1974-7 recession). Third, a higher fraction of the labour force is now unionized and

1 *DEG*, October 1976, pp. 1,093-9.

2 S. Nickell, 'Unemployment and the Structure of Labour Costs', *Journal of Monetary Economics*, Supplement No. 11, 1979. See also articles about the operation of the Employment Protection legislation in *DEG*, June 1978, pp. 658-61 and July 1979, pp. 652-5.

the premium in pay that people covered by union collective agreements got over non-union individuals doubled between 1968 and 1972.[1] Finally, the rise in oil and other input prices in 1974 and 1979 worsened the terms of trade faced by the British economy but real wages did not fully adjust downwards in either instance.[2] In consequence profits have been squeezed. The share of real profits in net domestic income fell from 13% in the 1960s to 8% in the 1970s.[3] The profit squeeze was probably compounded by the lack of inflation accounting in manufacturing, price controls and international competition.

Scott has argued that the profits squeeze has, in turn, been associated with a reduction in investment and, in particular, in labour-using investment and this has been associated with a substantial fall in employment in manufacturing and a rise in aggregate unemployment.[4]

Deficient Demand: The following estimate of deficient-demand unemployment may not be too unreasonable:

		% unemployment
1980 rate		6
less		
1948-66 full-employment/unemployment rate	2	
increase in full-employment rate due to employment protection, etc.	1	
extra unemployment associated with profit squeeze[5]	1	
therefore		
deficient-demand unemployment		2

Successive governments have been reluctant to use fiscal and monetary policy to get rid of this deficient-demand unemployment — equivalent to 500,000 people. Yet there is strong evidence that unemployment can be reduced by expansionary fiscal and monetary policy. In wartime, for example, unemployment falls to near zero. In the 1950s in the US unemployment approached 10%. It was widely believed that this was due to technological factors. Yet the expansionary macroeconomic policy — tax cuts and the extra spending associated with the Vietnam war — soon halved the level of unemployment.

So if stimulating demand could do the trick, what stops us? There are four main constraints. First, government revenue as usually measured tends to fall short of public spending, and there is a public sector borrowing requirement. Second, the expansionary fiscal and monetary policy will probably result in higher wage settlements. Third, in an open economy like Britain the balance of payments

1   R. Layard, D. Metcalf and S. Nickell, 'The Effect of Collective Bargaining on Absolute and Relative Wages', *BJIR*, November 1978.

2   G. Maynard, 'Keynes and Unemployment To-day', *Three Banks Review*, December 1978.

3   *BEQB*, June 1979, p. 183. Real profits control for the distortions arising from inflation.

4   M. Scott, *Can We Get Back To Full Employment?*, Macmillan, 1978, chapter 5.

5   This is the most uncertain estimate. Some Keynesians would argue that the effect is 0%, while Keynes himself could be interpreted as saying that what is called here deficient demand is actually due to real wages being too high, giving a total impact of 3%.

worsens when macroeconomic policy is expansionary. Fourth, there is disagreement as to whether such reductions in unemployment could be sustained in the long run.

II.3   Moderating Unemployment

What can be done about unemployment, independent of macroeconomic policy? First, the incidence of unemployment could be made more equal and the income of unemployed people improved. Second, the range of Special Employment Measures already in use could be extended. These covered some 200,000 to 300,000 people in 1979-80. But we must not infer that this means employment is a quarter of a million higher than it otherwise would have been. Some of the people covered by the Special Measures would have been hired anyway. And it is possible that money spent on such Special Measures could have been spent differently, or used for tax cuts, which would also have raised employment.

Distributional Issues: The national insurance system has completely broken down in the face of higher unemployment. In November 1978 only 38% of unemployed people were receiving unemployment benefit. This poor coverage occurs because unemployment benefit is exhausted after 12 months, and for other reasons. Imagine the public outcry and legal shambles if 62% of those involved in car crashes were not covered by insurance. Yet that is exactly the coverage that our so-called 'national insurance' provides for the unemployed. The remainder are forced onto means-tested relief and, as successive reports of the Supplementary Benefit Commission (SBC) have shown, they are among the poorest of the British poor.[1]

Lengthening unemployment spells have caused many more people to be unemployed for over 52 weeks. In January 1976 unemployment was 1.3 million and 182,000 people had been unemployed over one year. Yet some 3 years later in April 1979, when unemployment was also 1.3 million, nearly twice as many people – 347,000 – had been unemployed over one year. Employment quotas and subsidies have been suggested as methods of reducing this long-term unemployment.[2] If such measures are thought to have too large efficiency costs, benefits could be raised.

The Manpower Service Commission is in a dilemma over the long-term unemployed. It has a whole series of managerial objectives like increasing its share of hirings (what it calls 'placing penetration'). Thus in 1978-9 2.7m vacancies were

---

1   See for example SBC, Annual Report 1978, Cmnd. 7725, HMSO, October 1979, paras. 3.20, 13.18. Supplementary benefit has short-term rates and (higher) long-term rates for those who have been on SB for more than one year. But the unemployed *never* qualify for the long-term rate. In 1980 this denial imposed a financial penalty of £7.95 on an unemployed married man. See D. Metcalf, 'Unemployment: History, Incidence and Prospects', *Policy and Politics*, January 1980, for a fuller discussion of the failure of national insurance in the face of high unemployment. The proposal in the March 1980 budget to price-protect supplementary benefits but to raise insurance benefits by 5% less than the inflation rate is a further nail in the national insurance coffin and will, of course, substantially increase the numbers on supplementary benefit.

2   See S. Nickell, 'A Picture of Male Unemployment in Britain', *EJ*, forthcoming 1980, for a fuller discussion of quotas and subsidies, and *DEG*, January 1980, pp. 9-12 for a discussion of long-term unemployment.

notified to the Employment Service, of which they filled 1.8m and those placements accounted for 20% of all engagements by firms.[1] If the MSC starts to submit 'difficult to place' individuals, employers may cease notifying their vacancies to the MSC. Consequently many individuals seldom get submitted for a job by the MSC. The number of submissions is inversely related to unemployment duration. While the MSC's managerial objectives are understandable, it does not seem right that the people who need the most help from the Employment Service in fact seem to get the least. One way round this problem, recognized by the MSC, would be for the Job Centre to try to match a man or woman to a job only after (say) one month of unemployment instead of, as now, on the day the person joins the unemployment register. Many people would have left the unemployment register during the 4-week period, so more MSC resources would then be concentrated on those facing poorer employment prospects.

A shorter work-week has been suggested as a method of sharing unemployment. If for example the work-week fell from 40 hours to 38, and no extra overtime hours were worked, average hours worked would have fallen by 2/40 or 5%. Would extra men and women be hired to fill the gap? If the hourly wage remains constant then the firm's labour costs will also have fallen by 5% and so it has an incentive to hire the extra labour. But there may be difficulties — reorganization of shift lengths, extra hiring costs and the fact that the unemployed are mainly unskilled when the firm may require skilled workers. If, as trade unions demand, the hours are reduced while weekly pay remains constant then the unit labour costs will be increased by 5% and, especially where the firm faces international competition, the incentive to hire extra labour is attenuated. It is often claimed that unit labour costs will not rise because labour productivity will rise. But presumably if it is possible to raise productivity this would already have been done. Anyway, if productivity goes up this vitiates the need for any extra employment, so defeating the original reason for the shorter work-week. The Department of Employment have calculated that if the potential output lost by a reduction in the work-week from 40 to 38 hours was made up as follows:

	%
increased employment	35
higher output per man	20
more overtime	35
lower output	10

then unemployment would fall by 210,000, net government spending would be lowered by £500m (lower unemployment benefit, and more tax and national insurance revenue) but labour costs would rise by 4.4%. The inflationary effect of the increase in labour costs would in turn weaken our competitive position and damage our longer-term employment prospects. In late 1979 and early 1980 over one million manual workers in engineering, plumbing, printing, retail food and the exhibition industry negotiated a cut in their standard work-week to below 40 hours. It will be interesting to see whether employment now rises in these trades.

---

1 See MSC, *The Employment Service in the 1980s*, London, 1979, and *DEG*, June 1979, pp. 558-63.

Special Employment Measures: The period 1975-80 saw an enormous growth of special measures to boost employment and reduce unemployment. There were 4 kinds of measure:

Subsidies, e.g. Temporary Employment Subsidy (TES), Small Firms
  Employment Subsidy (SFES), Youth Employment Subsidy
Job creation, e.g. Youth Opportunities Programme, Special Temporary
  Employment Programme
Measures to reduce labour supply, e.g. Job Release Scheme, Short-time
  Compensation Scheme
Training and work experience, e.g. Work Experience Programme

The maximum annual gross public spending on these programmes was around £400m. The net public spending on these programmes is, of course, substantially less than the gross spending. This is because the government receives extra tax and social security revenue and does not have to pay out so much unemployment benefit and supplementary benefit. Indeed, internal Department of Employment calculations suggested that the Temporary Employment Subsidy actually added to net Exchequer revenue. At their peak these Special Measures covered around 200,000 people.[1] The Conservative government has kept a similar range of measures but decided to limit their geographical coverage.

We tend to think of these measures as microeconomic. But how does spending £400m on them differ from using £400m to reduce income tax by around 1p in the £? A careful investigation of this issue concludes that, as compared with tax cuts, employment subsidies have a specially favourable balance of payments effect — the TES was so successful in exporting unemployment in textiles, clothing and footwear from Britain to the EEC that the EEC caused us to withdraw it. Job-creation measures have the advantage that they can be targetted to particular groups like the long-term unemployed. This is, however, double-edged if the wrong target is picked. For example the 1977-9 measures probably helped youths and women too much relative to older men. Further, it is peculiar to cut public spending on orthodox things which society clearly values like roads and schools and then, as a sop, have job-creation projects concentrating on employment we did not previously value, like cleaning beaches. The special measures also have a lower Exchequer cost than tax cuts. But there are also economic efficiency costs associated with these measures particularly if they are used to bolster jobs in declining firms rather than subsidizing new jobs, and for this reason successive governments have insisted that the schemes be temporary contra-cyclical measures.[2]

---

1 For a discussion of these measures see *DEG*, March 1978 (early retirement schemes, Youth Employment Subsidy, Work Experience Programme); April 1978 (Job Release Scheme); May 1978 (TES, SFES). A useful summary of these measures is given in *DEG*, November 1979, pp. 1,122-5.

2 R. Layard, 'The Costs and Benefits of Selective Employment Policies: The British Case', *BJIR*, July 1979; R. Layard and S. Nickell, 'The Case for Subsidising Extra Jobs', *EJ*, March 1980.

III   WEALTH, INCOME AND PAY

The distribution of wealth, income and earnings are topics which excite great controversy. In this section we describe the (unequal) distribution of wealth, income and pay, and discuss some of the theories advanced to account for these distributions. Our analysis of labour earnings looks at the pay-structure by industry, occupation and sex, and wages in local labour markets. We then turn to problems of poverty and low pay.

III.1   Distribution of Wealth[1]

The measurement of personal wealth, and its distribution, is notoriously difficult. There are three main methods by which the distribution of personal wealth can be estimated. First, a sample survey could be undertaken of individuals' assets and liabilities to determine net wealth (sometimes referred to as net worth). Such a survey is desirable in principle but would be difficult to execute because of such problems as a low response rate and the difficulty of determining the composition and valuation of items to be included in wealth. Second, the investment income method works backwards from statistics on investment income to determine the distribution of capital from which this investment income is derived. Third, under the present British tax system the only time an individual's wealth becomes known is at death when a return is filed for capital transfer tax (CTT). These estate returns to the Inland Revenue form the basis of most of our knowledge on the distribution of wealth. The calculations assume that the wealth of the individuals who die comprises a sample of the assets of the living. They are then adjusted for elements of wealth not accounted for in CTT data such as the wealth of those excluded from CTT statistics because they have relatively small wealth holdings.

The data in table 5.2 show that in 1976 the wealthiest 1% of the adult population held a quarter of all the marketable wealth (e.g. dwellings, land, shares, Building Society deposits) in the UK. This is more than the amount held by the whole of the bottom 80%. In 1976 more than half the adult population had net wealth of less than £1,000, while 4 in 1,000 had wealth in excess of £100,000. These very wealthy 146,000 individuals each had an average wealth over £300,000. Even if they received no real return on it this amount is greater than the typical person would earn in a lifetime of work.

The total value of personal wealth was £274 billion in 1976. Physical assets — dwellings, land, vehicles and consumer durables — and financial assets each account for around half of this total. Less wealthy individuals hold the bulk of their wealth in the form of houses and life-insurance policies while shares and land are proportionately much more important for richer people.

Wealth can be accumulated by savings out of inheritance, earnings, entrepreneurial fortunes, capital gains and financial windfalls. Overall some 60% of wealth represents savings out of earnings — thus older individuals have more wealth

---

1   The information in this section and that following is taken from Royal Commission on the Distribution of Income and Wealth (Diamond Commission), Report No. 7, Cmnd. 7595, HMSO, July 1979. This Royal Commission was set up in 1974 and, alas, closed down in 1979. It did sterling work on improving available information on wealth and income distributions. Its findings have been brought together in an excellent brief non-technical publication, *An A to Z of Income and Wealth*, HMSO, January 1980.

than new labour-force entrants — but those in the top 5% of the wealth distribution are much more likely to have accumulated their wealth via inheritance or entrepreneurial fortunes. It is clear that rich people inherit a disproportionate amount of their wealth.

So far we have only considered marketable wealth. If we allow for the imputed value of the stream of future pension benefits which are locked away and not marketable, the share of wealth held by the bottom 80% of the distribution doubles to 45%. This is because virtually all members of the adult population have accrued rights to state pensions and the number of people in occupational pension schemes is growing.

TABLE 5.2

Percentage distribution of Personal Wealth held by Adult Population, UK, 1923 and 1976

Quantile group	1923 Marketable wealth	1976 Marketable wealth	1976 Marketable wealth plus rights to state and occupational pension schemes
Top 1%	61	25	14
Next 2-5%	21	21	15
6-10%	7	14	11
11-20%	5	17	15
21-100%	6	23	45
Total amount (£bn)	Not available	274	505

Source: Diamond Commission, Report No. 7, tables 4.3, 4.5, 4.15.

The distribution of wealth has certainly become much less unequal over this century. The share of the top 1% fell from 61% to 25% between 1923 and 1976. This mainly reflects the higher rates of estate duty (now capital transfer tax) and the spread of owner-occupation from 10% of dwellings in 1900 to over 50% in 1980. Price changes are also important. Less wealthy people hold more of their wealth in the form of housing while the rich hold more shares. So if house prices are rising rapidly and share prices falling the distribution of wealth becomes more equal.

III.2   Distribution of Income

The distribution of total income from all sources (i.e. from employment, pensions, dividends, etc.) is less concentrated than the distribution of wealth. This is because earnings from employment are the main source of total personal income and these earnings are more equally distributed than the investment income provided by personal wealth.

The composition of total personal income in the UK may be seen from table 5.3. Over two-thirds of personal income comes from employment. Two important changes have taken place in the last 30 years. Social security benefits and other cash grants have doubled in importance. This reflects higher real benefits and the growing number of pensioners and unemployed people. Second, the changes in the housing market — the growth of owner-occupation and the decline of the private rented sector — are mirrored in the data.

The distribution of personal income in 1976-7 is shown in table 5.4. The data are derived from the Inland Revenue, supplemented by information from the Family Expenditure Survey on incomes which are not taxable (for example, unemployment benefits) or are below the tax threshold. The data refer to tax units, i.e. generally treat a married couple as one unit. The distribution of income is less concentrated than the distribution of wealth. The top 1% (10%) of each distribution only account for 5.5% (26.2%) of income but they hold 25% (60%) of the wealth.

The median pre-tax income was £2,662. 80% of the units had incomes below £4,750. Less than 10% of the units had incomes above £6,000. The fact that there are relatively few people with high incomes makes the redistribution of income, and greater provision of desirable health and education services, difficult. While it may be possible to squeeze many thousands of pounds of tax out of a rich individual, there are not many of them, so that the extra revenue raised by squeezing them harder is quite small. Nevertheless, the share of the top 20% of the income distribution, with 42.4% of income, is seven times the share of the bottom 20% who account for only 6.2% of the total. Likewise, the top half of the income distribution has three times the share of the bottom half. It should be borne in mind that these figures refer to the distribution at one specific point in time; many of those in the bottom half of the distribution in 1976-7 (e.g. some pensioners and students) will be in the top half at other points in their life. The inequality in lifetime incomes is less than the inequality of the income distribution observed at any particular point in time.

TABLE 5.3

Composition of Personal Income, UK, 1951 and 1978 (%)

Source	1951	1978
Income from employment	71.5	68.5
Income from self-employment	12.1	9.2
Social security benefits and other cash grants from public authorities	6.0	12.5
Imputed rent of owner-occupiers	1.7	3.7
Other rent dividends and interest paid to households	7.3	1.4
Other	1.4	4.7
Total	100	100

Source: ST, 1980 edition, No. 10, table 6.1.

Some of the inequality is redressed via taxes on income and benefits in the form of cash and services like education and health. Income tax makes the distribution a little more equal (see table 5.4). After tax the share of the top 10% falls from 26.2% to 23.1%, while the share of the bottom 40% rises from 16.6% to 19.2%. Likewise social security benefits and spending on education and health boost the incomes of the poor proportionately more than those of the rich. The present Conservative government is aiming to reduce public spending and income tax. If

TABLE 5.4

Distribution of Personal Income before and after Income Tax, UK, 1976-7

Quantile groups	Income before tax (£m)	Income before tax (percentages)	Average income before tax (£)	Income after tax (£m)	Income after tax (percentages)	Average income after tax (£)
Top 1%	5,153	5.5	18,051	2,866	3.8	10,038
2- 5%	10,011	10.8	8,766	7,276	9.7	6,372
6-10%	9,262	9.9	6,489	7,179	9.6	5,029
Top 10%	24,426	26.2	8,556	17,321	23.1	6,067
11-20%	15,068	16.2	5,278	11,962	16.0	4,190
21-30%	12,416	13.3	4,349	9,991	13.4	3,499
31-40%	10,329	11.2	3,618	8,427	11.3	2,952
41-50%	8,505	9.1	2,979	6,977	9.3	2,444
51-60%	6,877	7.4	2,409	5,762	7.7	2,018
61-70%	5,447	5.8	1,908	4,914	6.6	1,721
71-80%	4,285	4.6	1,501	3,818	5.1	1,337
81-90%	3,451	3.7	1,209	3,346	4.5	1,172
Bottom 10%	2,272	2.5	796	2,258	3.0	791

Source: ST, 1980 edition, No. 10, table 6.19.

Note: Based on tax units. The total number of tax units is 28.5 million.

their plans are fulfilled the post tax/benefit income distribution is likely to become more unequal in the early 1980s.

The income figures presented and discussed in table 5.4 should be treated cautiously for the following reasons: (i) the data ignore income in the form of imputed rent from owner-occupied houses, fringe benefits, home production and capital gains; (ii) the data are uncorrected for tax evasion and misreporting; (iii) the data refer to money but not real incomes. This is important because inflation affects people differently according to the basket of goods they consume. For example over the last twenty years the prices of food and fuel have risen faster than the overall index of retail prices. As pensioners and low-income families spend relatively large amounts of money on these items the changes in the distribution of real incomes will be different from those in the distribution of money incomes; (iv) income alone does not capture other aspects of welfare such as leisure, security and job satisfaction; (v) family composition has changed over time such that there are now more old and young people living alone; this will tend to increase the dispersion in income observed over time; (vi) the data refer to current and not lifetime income distributions.

III.3   Distribution of Earnings

The distribution of earnings, like the distribution of income, is positively skewed (median earnings are less than mean earnings). However, the earnings distribution is more equal than the distribution of income because the latter includes a return on wealth which, as we have seen (section III.1), is very concentrated.

The dispersion of earnings in April 1979 (full-time workers, men aged twenty-one and over, women aged eighteen and over, whose pay for the survey week was not affected by absence) was as follows.[1]

	Median earnings per week (£)	As a % of median			
		Lowest decile	Lower quartile	Upper quartile	Highest decile
Men	93.9	66.0	80.3	125.1	156.9
Women	58.4	69.4	82.1	124.7	158.6

Both men and women at the lowest 10% point earned around two-thirds of median pay, while the best-paid 10% earned over half more than the corresponding median.

There are two particularly important and interesting facts concerning the distribution of gross weekly earnings of male manual workers. First, the dispersion of the distribution has been quite stable for almost a century:[2]

Distribution of weekly earnings, manual men (% of median)

	1886	1979
Lowest decile	68.6	68.3
Lower quartile	82.8	81.7
Median	100.0	100.0
Upper quartile	121.7	122.2
Highest decile	143.1	148.5

This stability suggests that we might seek to explain the distribution of earnings by factors such as differences in ability, motivation and luck, which might be expected to remain fairly stable from one generation to the next, rather than by appeal to institutional factors such as the growth of unions, or social forces such as the extension of public intervention, which have changed dramatically in the last century.

Second, the position an individual occupies in the distribution changes from year to year. Evidence on the gross weekly earnings of all full-time adults who were in

1 *DEG*, October 1979, p. 972. The data in this section refer to individuals, not families or Inland Revenue income units. Many people only work part-time or part of the year and therefore the distribution of annual earnings of those who worked at any time during the year is different from the distribution above, because the annual earnings distribution has a concentration of people in the lower tail.

2 *Social Trends*, No. 6, 1975, table 5.15 and *DEG*, October 1979, p. 972. A very full discussion of the evidence on the distribution of earnings and evaluation of theories seeking to explain this distribution is contained in A.R. Thatcher, 'The New Earnings Survey and the Distribution of Earnings', in A. Atkinson (ed.), *The Personal Distribution of Incomes*, Allen and Unwin, 1975. E.H. Phelps Brown, *The Inequality of Pay*, OUP, 1977, contains much evidence on this topic.

the New Earnings Surveys in 1970 to 1974 (*DEG*, January 1977) indicates that the lowest-paid workers received by far the largest percentage increase in earnings between one survey and the next, while the higher-paid workers tended to experience much smaller percentage increases. Such movements are known as 'regression towards the mean'. Between 1970 and 1974 21% of male manual workers were in the lowest-paid tenth in at least one of the five surveys, but only 3% were in this tenth of all of the surveys. These movements refer to weekly earnings of full-time workers and therefore reflect the variable nature of many components of manual workers' earnings (e.g. overtime, short-time bonuses, piecework), the effects of job changes and the incidence of wage settlements. Movements in individuals' hourly earnings, which may more nearly reflect skill and motivation, or in annual earnings, which may reflect the incidence of unemployment, could be more or less dramatic than the fluctuations in weekly earnings.

One important explanation of the skewed distribution of earnings relates to the coupling of natural ability and training. In a smoothly functioning, competitive labour market, earnings will reflect productivity at the margin. Among all the determinants of marginal productivity we may concentrate here on a worker's 'natural ability' and training. If, for a given level of formal training, a man comes to the labour market with relatively great motivation, ability and drive he will tend to earn more than the average worker. Further, it is established that on average the more naturally gifted man tends to undertake more than average amounts of training. An unskewed distribution of ability combined with a skewed distribution of training produces a skewed distribution of productivity. The last, in an approximately competitive market, produces a skewed earnings distribution.

This simple picture is only a partial explanation of the actual earnings distribution. First, not everyone has equal access to the educational and training sectors, even where natural ability is the same for all. One implication is that relatively bright working-class children have difficulty in getting sufficient secondary and advanced education. This means that ability is not properly harnessed with education, thereby reducing the degree of earnings inequality.

Second, in some activities, including many of the professions, free entry of labour is restricted and earnings are pushed above the competitive level by union activity. The impact of such behaviour on the distribution of pay depends on (i) the numbers affected, and (ii) the size of the union mark-up. Union activity among male manual workers probably reduces inequality because although a similar proportion of skilled and unskilled workers are covered by union agreements, the pay premium associated with union coverage is higher for unskilled workers than for the skilled.

Third, luck plays a significant part in determining earnings, particularly in any one year. The last qualification is important because a more valid measure of material well-being than current earnings is the discounted sum of lifetime earnings. If a man is lucky one year but unlucky the next we would have a misleading view of his well-being by looking at either year in isolation. Similarly, if a man is receiving a low wage currently because he is training, but expected to do well when he is trained, it would be mistaken to view him as a poverty case. The same may apply to people approaching retirement.

The General Household Survey (GHS) provides each year information on individual earnings and related individual characteristics such as age, schooling, work experience, race and family background. The 1975 GHS has been extensively analysed.[1] Let us consider the factors which generated the distribution of pay among the 5,000 or so full-time male employees in the sample.

Consider first the distribution of hourly earnings. Years of full-time education have a substantial effect on hourly earnings. Holding constant father's occupation, work experience, ethnic background, health and marital status, each additional year of education raises pay by between 5% and 10%. Does this mean education is a good weapon against poverty? The trouble with ordinary education is that while a person is being educated you do not know whether or not he is going to end up poor. In any case there is such a spread of earnings for people with a given level of education that even if all education disparities were eliminated the remaining inequality would be still over 93% of what it is now.

Of course one could go further than eliminating educational disparity. Positive discrimination could be practised whereby those who had low earnings potential would be given *more* education than others. But this implies the ability to spot low earners while they are still being educated and it is doubtful whether this is practicable. It could, however, be done for adult training — by then people have shown what they can and cannot earn — and there is strong evidence that short periods of vocational training are able to improve a person's position in the occupational hierarchy.[2]

Family background, measured by father's occupation, influences hourly earnings directly and indirectly via education levels. An individual with a non-manual father had *ceteris paribus* hourly earnings 12% higher than those with unskilled fathers.

Marriage is also associated with higher pay. After controlling for other factors, married men had hourly pay 14% greater than single men. This may be because marriage puts pressure on individuals to work harder or may simply reflect the fact that better quality men are more likely to get married.

Pay is influenced by work experience. On average an individual with between 30-40 years of work experience earns, *ceteris paribus*, twice as much as a person with 5-10 years experience. But the individual who gets stuck in a particular manual job has little prospect of a real wage increase (other than from general economic growth) after the first 10 years.

One particularly important finding concerns the influence of colour and country of birth on pay. Other things being equal (i.e. holding constant age, experience, weeks worked, years of schooling, marital status, etc.), West Indian-born workers receive hourly earnings 14% lower than whites. Other non-whites receive, on average, some 22% less than whites. These differentials occur because black and brown workers tend (like women) to be crowded into low-paying occupations and industries. Thus while 58% of Pakistani males and 32% of West Indian males working in Britain are unskilled or semi-skilled, the corresponding figure for whites is 18%. Further, virtually no whites with degree-level qualifications do manual work but around one-fifth of such men from minorities do manual work, and

1 R. Layard, D. Piachaud, M. Stewart, *The Causes of Poverty*, Royal Commission on Distribution of Income and Wealth (Diamond Commission), *Background Paper* No. 5 (to *Report* No. 6, *Lower Incomes*), HMSO, 1978, especially chapter 4. This is by far the best discussion on the factors generating the distribution of pay in Britain. The remainder of this section draws freely on this source.

2 D. Metcalf and S. Nickell, 'Occupational Mobility in Great Britain', *Research in Labor Economics*, forthcoming, 1981.

minority men with high qualifications are much less likely than whites to be in professional and management occupations.[1]

This occupational structure discourages them from undertaking extra schooling or training because the pay-off to such investment is lower than it is for whites. Further, their occupational status may lead potential employers to conclude that non-whites are feckless when in fact their higher average turnover rate or higher average absenteeism rate are characteristics of their occupations and industries and not inherent racial characteristics. For example, a study of labour turnover at London Transport[2] showed that, other things being equal, blacks had a longer duration of employment than whites. It seems clear that the occupational composition of black and brown workers, as compared to white workers, will shortly (quite rightly) become a pressing policy issue. The problem is in many ways analogous to that facing women (see section III.6).

The factors above account for around a third of the variance of *annual* earnings. Another third is explained by differences in the number of weeks worked in the year by each individual. This is itself influenced by human capital factors. Individuals with relatively high hourly earnings work more weeks – it is the unskilled who bear the burden of unemployment and, to a lesser extent, sickness.

We now turn to examine some more narrowly defined aspects of the distribution of earnings. The next four sections analyse the pay structure by occupation, industry, sex and local labour markets. The lower tail of the income distribution is studied in the final sections on poverty and low pay.

III.4   Wage Structure by Occupation[3]

The foundations of wage theory are contained in two famous principles. First, Adam Smith's principle of net advantage states that when competition exists in the labour market the 'whole of the advantages and disadvantages' of different occupations will continually tend towards equality. Note that this principle does not imply that wages will tend towards equality, but that (suitably discounted) lifetime returns to one occupation will tend to equal those in another occupation. The returns that make an occupation attractive or unattractive are both pecuniary and non-pecuniary. Second, we have the principle of non-competing groups, which evolved from the work of John Stuart Mill and Cairnes; this states (broadly) that certain non-competitive factors may inhibit the tendency towards equality in net advantages.

Linked to these two principles are two sets of reasons for the existence of occupational wage differentials: compensatory wage differentials and non-compensatory wage differentials.

---

1 D. Smith, *Racial Disadvantage in Britain*, Pelican, 1977. See also DE (Unit for Manpower Studies), *The Role of Immigrants in the Labour Market*, 1976, for a comprehensive discussion.

2 J. Smith, *Labour Supply and Employment Duration in London Transport*, Greater London Paper No. 15, 1976.

3 The forces generating the occupational pay structure excite considerable controversy. Two good articles on the controversy are M. Fisher, 'The Human Capital Approach to Occupational Wage Differentials', *International Journal of Social Economics*, Vol. 1, no. 1, 1974, and G. Routh, 'Interpretations of Pay Structure', *International Journal of Social Economics*, Vol. 1, no. 1, 1974. See also E.H. Phelps Brown, *The Inequality of Pay*, OUP, chapter 2.

Compensatory wage differentials are those differentials which are consistent with competition in the labour market. If individuals were not compensated for the factors listed below (in the form of higher wages when at work) then the supply of labour to those occupations would tend to be deficient. All other things being equal, individuals will tend, for example, to be compensated in the form of higher wages for entering occupations that (1) require long periods of education and/or training, (2) are dangerous or dirty, (3) are subject to lay-offs or have a relatively short working life. (4) Also if they are risk-averters, they will desire to be compensated in terms of the mean earnings of the occupation if the dispersion of the earnings around the mean is very large. (5) Differentials will also accrue to wholly exceptional workers, such as professional sportsmen and entertainers, this being an example of economic rent applied to the labour market.

Non-compensating occupational wage differentials are different. They occur where economic or institutional reasons inhibit competition in the labour market. For example, closed shop agreements inhibit union members from non-union competition. Legal restrictions boost solicitors' pay for conveyancing work. And minimum-wage legislation might raise the pay of those at the bottom of the earnings distribution above the competitive level.

Earnings by broad occupational groups are presented in table 5.5. It will be seen that earnings of non-manual workers are greater than those of manual workers. This reflects in some large part the relative education/training intensities of the two groups. There is also evidence of other compensating differentials. Within group 14, furnacemen earn 232p per hour while plumbers earn 202p per hour. The furnacemen are being compensated for the unpleasant conditions in which they work. Bricklayers (group 16) earn 206p per hour, while general labourers (group 18) earn 169p: the bricklayers are being compensated for their relatively low earnings while apprenticed. Within group 7, firemen earn 220p per hour while security guards earn 182p. The firemen are being compensated because their job is more dangerous.

There is also evidence of individuals being compensated for being more able, or having more alternative job opportunities, or undertaking a more skilled task, even though the length of education and training is similar to that of their less-skilled colleagues. In group 3, for example, teachers in further education earn £130 per week which is £23 more than secondary-school teachers earn. Within group 17, the earnings of a lorry driver are positively related to the size of vehicle: drivers of heavy-goods vehicles (over 3 tons) earn 27p per hour more than other goods drivers.

Trade unions are able to influence the occupational earnings structure if the demand for labour is inelastic and/or if they can control the labour supply. For example, miners (group 16) earn 312p per hour, which is 78% more than postmen (group 7) earn. This reflects, in part, the strength of the National Union of Miners, conferred by the inelastic demand for domestic coal which results from the currently used methods of electricity generation, together with limitations on coal imports. In contrast the lengthy postmen's strike of 1971 certainly did not bring the country to a halt, partly because telephonists and other postal workers continued working and tolerable substitutes were therefore available for the postal workers' services.

TABLE 5.5

Earnings by Occupation: Full-Time Adult Men, April 1979

	Average gross weekly earnings (£)	Average gross hourly earnings (p)
Non-manual		
1 General management	171	–
2 Professional and related management and administration	129	–
3 Professional and related in education, welfare and health	113	–
4 Literary, artistic, sports	115	–
5 Professional and related in science, engineering and technology	119	–
6 Managerial	114	–
7 Clerical and related	84	204
8 Selling	95	231
9 Security and protective service	105	234
Manual		
10 Catering, cleaning, hairdressing	74	157
11 Farming, fishing and related	68	150
12 Materials processing (excluding metal)	94	201
13 Making and repairing (excluding metal and electrical)	94	207
14 Processing, making, repairing (metal and electrical)	101	214
15 Painting, repetitive assembling, product inspection	92	201
16 Construction, mining	95	205
17 Transport operating	93	188
18 Miscellaneous	85	180
Total: Manual	93	198
Total: Non-manual	113	290
Total: All occupations	101	232

Source: DE, *New Earnings Survey*, 1979; *DEG*, October 1979, table 8.

Note: Both sets of figures exclude those whose pay was affected by absence. The gross hourly earnings figure excludes the effect of overtime.

III.5 Wage Structure by Industry[1]

There are a number of reasons for studying the industrial wage structure. First, it is important to know whether labour can be allocated among industries independently of wages or whether expanding (contracting) industries must pay higher (lower) wages to get the labour they require. Such information is useful in designing a pay policy. Second, how are the gains in labour productivity distributed? They can go to labour in the form of higher wages or firms in the form of higher profits or consumers in the form of lower prices. Analysis of the industrial wage structure provides evidence on the topic. Third, it is important to know whether, independent of the characteristics of the individuals working in the industry, highly concentrated industries or industries with large plants pay higher wages; such data would be useful in, for example, designing our monopoly legislation.

1 The most substantial recent work on this issue is R. Wragg and J. Robertson, *Post-War Trends in Employment, Output, Labour Costs and Prices by Industry in the UK*, Research Paper No. 3, DE, June 1978.

Wage Changes and Employment Changes: Price theory implies that in the long run, given competitive conditions, each industry will, *ceteris paribus*, pay for a given grade of labour a wage identical to that paid by other industries. The *ceteris paribus* assumption implies that there are no differences in the non-pecuniary attractions of different industries or location or in the cost of living by location. In the long run therefore the growth in industry wage levels should not be correlated with the growth in the amount of labour employed. In the short run an industry which expands its demands for labour will tend to have to raise the wages it pays because of short-run inelasticities in labour supply. Therefore the theory predicts a positive association in the short run between changes in employment by industry and changes in wages by industry.

It is clear that in the long run there is no relationship between changes in pay and changes in employment. Wragg and Robertson studied 82 manufacturing industries over the period 1954-73. The pay changes in each industry were very similar but employment experience was very different. Indeed, the weaving industry suffered a loss of employment of 6.2% p.a. yet had a higher than average increase in earnings. They went on to study 22 sectors of retail distribution over 1950-71, with similar results. Annual employment growth varied enormously (the coefficient of variation (standard deviation/mean) was 7.64) while pay increases among the 22 sectors were very similar (coefficient of variation of 0.13). In the long run, therefore, expanding industries do not have to increase their pay at a rate above the average to meet their labour requirements, and industries where employment is contracting still give around average pay rises. This reflects the continual churning which goes on in the labour market — 10 million job changes a year, and around 0.75 million new entrants to the labour force and individuals retiring from it — which allows the labour force to adjust steadily to the changing requirements imposed by the economy.

But what of the short run? It appears that there is a positive association between earnings changes and employment changes.[1] This upward-sloping short-run market-labour supply curve implies that to avoid labour shortages developing a pay policy might need to permit such shortage sectors to pay above the norm.

Wage Changes and Productivity Changes: An industry may react to an increase in physical productivity by lowering its relative product price or raising the relative wages it pays. If wage changes among industries are significantly (positively) related to movements in value productivity (i.e. variations in physical productivity and product prices taken together), this implies that non-competitive forces, such as ability to pay, determine the wage structure. In contrast, if the differential wage changes are unrelated to change in value productivity by industry, this implies that competitive forces dominate in the explanation of wages. We anticipate such forces will be important because there is no reason, on equity or efficiency grounds, to expect that sectors with high labour productivity or growth in labour productivity will, *ceteris paribus*, pay high wages; working with bigger machines, if the intensity of work is unchanged, is no reason for higher pay.

The statistical associations found for 1954-73 for 82 manufacturing industries by Wragg and Robertson among the growth rates of output per head (i.e. labour

---

1   OECD, *Wages and Labour Mobility*, 1965, pp. 85-118; W.B. Reddaway, 'Wage Flexibility and the Distribution of Labour', *LBR*, October 1959; E.H. Phelps Brown and M. Browne, 'Earnings in Industries of the UK 1948-1959', *EJ*, Vol. 72, September 1962.

productivity), earnings, unit labour costs and prices, are clear and unambiguous. Earnings changes are very similar across the 82 industries while labour productivity changes differ markedly. In turn, there is a negative association between labour productivity changes and movements in unit labour costs and, finally, a negative relation between labour productivity changes and price rises. Likewise another study[1] found no association between industrial capital: labour ratios and earnings. Individuals who work with a lot of capital do not receive higher pay, *ceteris paribus*, than individuals working with little capital. These suggest that workers who cannot increase their productivity easily (such as musicians or nurses) do not find their relative position in the pay structure worsening persistently. Further, they also indicate that, after allowing for general inflation, the gains from increased labour productivity flow mainly to consumers.

Industry Characteristics and Wage Levels: There has been considerable interest recently in the idea that the labour market is segmented into two (or more) sectors, one of which is high-paying, with well-developed internal labour markets allowing for promotion within the firm, employing high-quality labour with low quit propensities, and the other with opposite characteristics. Some recent studies on the structure of earnings in British manufacturing industry throw some light on this idea.[2]

Industries which are highly concentrated or where large plants predominate pay more than atomistic small-plant sectors. Concentrated industries have relatively high average pay largely because they employ superior-quality labour, and because they are highly unionized. But even after controlling for labour characteristics and unionization, concentrated industries pay a little more than unconcentrated industries. This may reflect a sharing of monopoly profits with their employees in an attempt to buy good industrial relations or it might be an attempt by existing firms to forestall entry by new firms (though both reasons seem *a priori* unlikely).

Industries with small plants — Agriculture, Distribution and Miscellaneous Services (e.g. catering) — have lower pay than industries with large plants even when labour quality is held constant.[3] This reflects the disutility of working in large plants and the low incidence of shift work and payments-by-results in such small-plant sectors.

This evidence provides modest support for the notion of a segmented labour market. Big firms in monopolistic industries (the so-called primary sector) pay high wages relative to small firms in unconcentrated industries (the secondary sector). This wage differential is attributable, apparently, to higher labour quality, the

---

1 W. Hood and R.D. Rees, 'Inter Industry Wage Levels in the UK Manufacturing Industry', *MS*, 1974.

2 D. Metcalf, S. Nickell and R. Richardson, 'The Structure of Hours and Earnings in British Manufacturing Industry', *OEP*, July 1976; M. Sawyer, 'The Earnings of Manual Workers: A Cross Section Analysis', *SJPE*, Vol. XX, No. 2, June 1973; A. Tylecote, 'Determinants of Changes in the Wage Hierarchy in UK Manufacturing Industry: 1954-70', *BJIR*, Vol. XIII, No. 1, March 1975; K. George, R. McNabb and J. Shorey, 'The Size of the Work Unit and Labour Market Behaviour', *BJIR*, July 1977.

3 See R. Layard *et al.*, *The Causes of Poverty*, Background Paper No. 6, Royal Commission on Distribution of Income and Wealth, HMSO, 1978, Appendix table 18. It should be noted that once the industry-concentration ratio and unionization have been controlled for, plant size has no *independent* impact on pay, see R. Layard, D. Metcalf and S. Nickell, 'The Effect of Collective Bargaining on Relative and Absolute Wages', *BJIR*, November 1978.

disutility of working in large plants, the higher profits of concentrated industries and the higher density of union membership in the primary sector. However, the policy implications of such findings are far from clear. Should we, for example, encourage unionization in the secondary sector or discourage it in the primary sector? Should we encourage small plants to merge? Further, to the extent that labour quality is important, the evidence does not tell us which firms will choose a low-wage, low-labour-quality, low-productivity strategy as against a high-wage, high-quality, high-productivity strategy.

III.6   Wage Structure by Sex[1]

Evidence: Females account for 41% of employment in Britain, yet among full-time workers in 1979 men were 6 times more likely than women to be earning over £100 a week and 25 times more likely to be earning over £200 a week. Females earn less than males in each broad occupational and industrial group: the data in table 5.6 show that the hourly earnings of full-time female adult workers were, on average, 72% of male hourly earnings and that the percentage differential between male and female pay is higher for non-manual workers than for manual workers.

There are two broad reasons why average male pay exceeds average female pay. First, and more important, women are crowded into the low-paying occupations and industries. Second, within occupational groups women tend to be paid less than men. In education, for example, women are disproportionately represented in the relatively low-paying primary segment, and within primary-school teaching women earn 13% less than men. It must be noted, however, that even within primary teaching the main reason for the differential is not that women are paid less than men for doing the same job but rather that women are under-represented in the higher-paying headship and deputy headship jobs. This example could be repeated for other occupations and industries.

Reasons why women earn less than men: A major reason why women earn less than men is that their attachment to the labour force is weaker than that of men. This relatively weak attachment is in large part because it is widely believed that it is the role of women rather than men to drop out of the labour force to care for young children: the lower lifetime commitment of women to the labour force is a response to centuries of social conditioning rather than an inherent trait. Attitudes on the roles of the two sexes can certainly be influenced by economic factors; for example the two world wars, which caused the demand for female labour to rise substantially, were particularly important in raising the labour-force status of women. This suggests that the respective roles of men and women are thus amenable to change via economic and other influences. The observed weaker labour-force attachment causes females to be crowded into the lower-paying

---

1 A useful summary of the existing literature is B. Chiplin and P. Sloan, *Sex Discrimination in the Labour Market*, Macmillan, 1976. A readable, thorough, statistical analysis is S. Nickell, 'Trade Unions and the Position of Women in the Industrial Wage Structure', *BJIR*, July 1977. For details of the equal pay and equal opportunity legislation, see DE, *A guide to the Equal Pay Act 1970*, HMSO, 1975; Home Office, *A Guide to the Sex Discrimination Act*, 1975. For an excellent progress report on the legislation see *DEG*, September 1979, pp. 863-6. Restrictions on hours women may work are discussed in *DEG*, April 1979, pp. 331-2.

TABLE 5.6

Male-Female Hourly Earnings, Full-Time Workers, April 1979

	Female (p)	Male (p)	Female/male (%)
Total manual	139	198	70
Total non-manual	177	290	61
Total	167	232	72
All Wage Boards and Wage Councils			
Manual	122	156	78
Non-manual	128	212	60
Occupations: manual			
Catering, cleaning, hairdressing	130	157	83
Materials processing (excluding metals)	139	201	69
Making and repairing (excluding metal and electrical)	139	207	67
Processing, making, repairing (metal and electrical)	156	214	73
Repetitive assembling, etc.	145	201	72
Transport, etc.	142	188	76
Occupations: non-manual			
Professional: management	95	129	74
Professional: health, education, welfare	80	113	71
Professional: science, engineering, technology	75	119	63
Managerial	71	114	62
Clerical	60	84	72
Selling	47	95	49

Source: DE, *New Earnings Survey*, 1979; *DEG*, October 1979, tables 2, 3, 8, 9.

Note: Data refer to adult workers whose pay in the survey week was not affected by absence and excludes the effect of overtime.

segments of the labour force and, in some cases, to be paid less than men in a given task. Some manifestations of the relative labour-force attachments of men and women, which partially determine their occupational composition, include the following.

Labour turnover is higher for women than for men. Such turnover imposes costs on the employer; at a minimum these costs will be the hiring costs incurred when replacing employees. For example, the New Earnings Survey shows that in April 1974 the number of female employees who had been with their employer under twelve months was 29% while the corresponding male figure was 19%.[1] It is often argued that these figures reflect a composition effect, i.e. that females are disproportionately represented in industries and occupations which themselves have high turnover. This appears not to be true: in every industry and every occupation except one, female turnover is greater than male turnover. An alternative possibility, however, concerns the age composition of the labour force. Young workers have dramatically higher turnover rates than prime-age and older workers. Therefore some of the observed higher female labour turnover may occur because younger workers account for a higher fraction of the female labour force than the male labour force.

1 *DEG*, January 1975, pp. 25-6.

Females are also more prone to absenteeism. In April 1970, for example, 23.8% of full-time adult women were paid for less than their normal working hours because they were absent from work owing to sickness (certified or uncertified), late arrival or early finish, holidays or other approved absence, or unspecified reasons. The corresponding figure for men was only 15.9%. Absenteeism also causes costs to employers, for example, by disrupting production schedules.

Because women have higher turnover rates than men, employers have less incentive to pay for female training. A profit-maximizing employer will be willing to pay for his employees' training if he can get a return on his investment by paying the trainee less than the value of his services when the training is completed. Given that women are more likely to quit or to be absent from a firm than men, employers will prefer to train men. This is compounded by hours legislation prohibiting women from working over a certain number of hours per week or at certain times.

Similarly, girls have less incentive to finance their own education and training. Staying on at school or university or taking a computer programming course entails costs, for example tuition costs or foregone earnings (i.e. earnings that could have been received if working). If a woman has children this will involve a period out of the labour force; further, women retire at a younger age than men. Thus the time over which she will receive benefits (in the form of higher earnings) from the training is less than for a man. Thus, of those young persons entering employment in 1974, 44.3% of the boys entered apprenticeships to skilled occupations or employment leading to recognized professional qualifications, while only 8.3% of girls followed this route. In contrast 40.0% of the girls are immediately segmented into clerical employment. The contrast is even clearer if we consider highly qualified people (i.e. those holding an academic or professional qualification of degree standard). The DE estimates[1] that in 1971 the stock of such highly qualified males was 1,060,000, compared with 352,000 females.

If females go out of the labour force for a period in their twenties or thirties they will accumulate less experience and seniority (on the job training, learning by doing) than males. On all these grounds, females will tend to be less productive than males. They will therefore earn less within a given occupation and will be less likely to progress up the occupational hierarchy.

Females will also tend to be paid less than men if the firm draws them from a limited geographical area: they will incur lower transport costs on average than men. Also, women may tend to work in more pleasant conditions.

The structure of the industries in which females work is a further element in the explanation of the sex differential. Females are disproportionately represented in small plants and atomistic industries, which tend to pay less and offer poorer career prospects than larger plants and concentrated industries; also a relatively low proportion of the female labour force is unionized, which reflects in part the higher costs of organizing in industries consisting of small plants.

Discrimination: It is frequently alleged that the main cause of pay differentials is that discrimination exists against women. Studies suggest that in 1975 the hourly pay of men was between 8% to 29% higher than that of women with similar

---

1   DE, *Employment Prospects for the Highly Qualified*, Manpower Paper No. 8, HMSO, 1974.

education, experience and father's occupation.[1] More narrowly, employer discrimination means that if the net value of the woman's service is identical to that of the man the latter receives a higher wage. The only way that the woman can offset the employer's discrimination is to accept a lower wage. If *all other things are equal* yet firms pay, because of discrimination against women, higher wages to men than to women, then higher profits will accrue to the firm that replaces men with women. Male sales assistants are paid 173p per hour whilst females are paid 114p per hour. It is unlikely that if both males and females were equally productive, firms would not substitute female labour for male labour.

It should be noted that none of the above discussion implies that women are not discriminated against in society at large – they obviously are. The crucial question is how that discrimination can be ended, and the problem here concerns the causal relationship. We believe that if females could be given greater incentives than they have at present to remain in the labour force, accumulate experience, undertake training, travel longer distances, etc., then this will cause the distinction between the traditional roles of men and women to be eroded fairly speedily.

The equal pay and equal opportunity legislation which effectively came fully into force in 1976 should provide some incentive to stronger female labour force attachment. However, should this legislation prove too frail other policies exist to improve the lot of women in the labour market and these will be considered below.

The purpose of the Equal Pay Act is to eliminate discrimination against women in connection with wages and fringe benefits. A women is to receive equal treatment when she is employed (a) on work of the same or broadly similar nature to that of men; (b) in a job which, though different from those of men, has been given an equal value to men's jobs under a job-evaluation exercise. Thus the Act is designed to ensure that if the net value of a woman's services is identical to that of a man both will receive identical wages and conditions.

If discrimination does exist it is based on hostility to women employees or lack of information (e.g. employers think that women will be more likely to be absent or to quit and therefore pay them less than men or refuse to promote them). The Equal Pay Act by itself is likely to lead to a reduction in information about the relative performance of men and women both because of segregation and because female unemployment may rise on account of the higher costs of employing women.

Further, the intentions of the Act can be overcome in a number of ways. Men and women can be segregated by job. This has already happened. The standard occupational classification lists 396 occupations but the 1979 New Earnings Survey reports only 35 occupations with sufficient men and women to provide comparisons of their earnings. It seems possible that this Act will therefore compound rather than reduce occupational segregation. If women believe that they are nevertheless doing work of equal value, the jobs can be subjected to a job-evaluation scheme.

---

1 See R. Layard *et al.*, *The Causes of Poverty*, Background Paper No. 5, Royal Commission on the Distribution of Income and Wealth, HMSO, 1978, pp. 52-6 and Christine Greenhalgh, 'Male-Female Wage Differentials in Great Britain', *Economic Journal*, forthcoming, 1980. Broadly, these estimates are derived by computing separate earnings-functions for men and women. Then an estimated female wage is calculated by assuming that a female of particular characteristics is paid according to the male wage structure. The difference between the estimated female wage and the actual female wage is termed 'discrimination'. Such calculations are, as the authors recognize, very difficult to undertake accurately.

But the employer can give a relatively high weight in such a scheme to attributes such as physical strength where men have a relative advanfage, and a low weight to manual dexterity where women have the advantage (although there is a right of appeal on the 'fairness' of the job-evaluation scheme). Legislation precludes women from night work and limits the number of overtime hours women may work; an employer may therefore pay large shift-work or overtime supplements.

Despite these qualifications and reservations it is clear that implementation of the Equal Pay Act was associated with a narrowing of the sex differential. Average hourly female earnings rose from 65% of male earnings in 1974 to 74% in 1977. This is a very large compression in such a short space of time. It is probably mainly due to the requirement in the Equal Pay Act that in collective agreements female hourly earnings must not be set below the lowest male hourly earnings. But the changing occupational composition of the female labour force, such that females are increasingly represented in the higher-paying occupations, and flat-rate elements (e.g. a cash increase of £6 a week rather than percentage increases) in the 1975-7 pay policy, probably also played a part in narrowing the sex differential.

Although the narrowing of the pay differential is to be welcomed it is not without offsetting disadvantages. It is noticeable that between 1976 and 1978, the first three years of the full operation of the Act, female unemployment rose around 50% while male unemployment fell. The disproportionate rise in female labour costs surely contributed to this relative rise in female unemployment. Nevertheless female *employment* continued to rise during this period.

The Sex Discrimination Act is potentially important in overcoming the current under-representation of women in high-paying sectors. It covers education and the supply of goods and services as well as employment. The Act says that women must be given equal treatment in the arrangements for selecting a candidate for a job, in the terms on which a job is offered, on access to promotion, transfer and training or any other aspects of the job and on dismissal. The Act established the Equal Opportunities Commission with fairly wide powers: it can help individuals to bring cases if it considers them of wider interest; it can conduct formal investigations compelling people to give evidence; it can serve non-discrimination notices and seek injunctions against persistent discriminators. Unfortunately the EOC has so far done little to raise the status of women. Indeed, since this hapless organization was established male-female pay differentials have widened!

The Employment Protection Act (1976) should also favourably influence women's labour-force commitment. It provides for six weeks' paid maternity leave and twenty-nine weeks' unpaid leave with no loss of seniority or status. This legislation is of particular significance for women in highly skilled sectors.

The government could consider a number of alternative strategies to improve the labour-force status of women. First, it might encourage them to join unions: the male-female wage differential is, *ceteris paribus*, smaller in those industries which are highly unionized. Second, more girls could be encouraged to take apprenticeship or college training by providing them with differentially large training grants. Third, female quotas, especially in the higher occupational grades, could be enforced. Finally, women's pay could be forced up relative to men's pay by subsidizing women's employment.

III.7   Local Labour Markets

A local labour market may be defined as 'the geographic area containing those actual or potential members of the labour force that a firm might induce to enter its employ under certain conditions, and other employers with which the firm is in competition for labour'.[1] Evidence suggests that, for a given occupation, substantial dispersion of earnings exists within the local labour market. For example Robinson, examining earnings in ten occupations in engineering plants within an (unspecified) local labour market, found that the range in pay between the highest- and lowest-paying plants was never less than 55% and was over 100% on two occasions. A fascinating study of local labour markets in Australia, Great Britain and the US showed very similar dispersion of pay among plants for a given occupation in each of the three countries.[2] For example for typists:

	Coefficient of variation (%) of earnings
Adelaide (201 individuals)	11.8
Chicago (557 individuals)	14.4
Coventry (400 individuals)	11.3

It is possible that this wage dispersion indicates the existence of healthy competition in the labour market, in contrast to an institutional domination of wage determination which would establish a common rate across all plants. It may also reflect the fact that information about wages and conditions in other plants is costly to obtain, thus allowing inter-plant wage differentials to persist for a long time.

Earnings in local labour markets in engineering are positively related to plant size.[1] The rank correlation coefficients found between earnings and plant size by industry in 1966 were:

Electrical machinery	+0.85	Radio and telecommunications	0.00
Motor vehicles	+0.78	Mechanical engineering	+0.19
Insulated wires	+0.65	Metal working	+0.37
Scientific instruments	+0.73		
Miscellaneous electrical	+0.73		

The rank correlation coefficients for the industries on the left-hand side are statistically significant. Before such evidence is used to refute the hypothesis that wages are determined by competitive factors, it is necessary to show that the quality of labour is the same in all plants; it could be that the large plants pay high

---

1   D. Robinson, 'External and Internal Labour Markets', in D. Robinson (ed.), *Local Labour Markets and Wage Structures*, Gower Press, 1970, chapter 2. This book contains a wealth of evidence on earnings within local labour markets and within individual plants. See also D. Mackay, D. Boddy, J. Brack, J. Diack and N. Jones, *Labour Markets under Different Employment Conditions*, Allen and Unwin, 1971. This book contains precise summaries of previous literature on local and internal labour markets and synthesis of theory and facts. It also contains a full discussion of factory (i.e. intra-plant) wage structures and labour turnover, which pressure on space forces us to omit here.

2   W. Brown *et al.*, 'Occupational Pay structures Under Different Wage Fixing Arrangements', *BJIR*, 1980 (forthcoming).

3   S. Lerner, J. Cable and S. Gupta, *Workshop Wage Determination*, Pergammon, 1969, p. 32.

wages to get superior-quality labour. Indeed, in their conclusions the authors stress the importance of competitive conditions in determining engineering wages: 'There was recurring evidence in all studies of the need for earnings to conform in some degree to prevailing local levels. In engineering it was found that if the average earnings in a works were below the modal level for a district this was usually sufficient grounds for securing a wage increase from the local employers' association'. Firms which paid less than the going rate in an area tended to find that they experienced problems recruiting and retaining adequately qualified labour.

One particularly interesting strand of local labour-market analysis concerns how long workers stay with their firms. For individual employers quits are usually costly, for a number of reasons. First, they either disrupt production and delivery dates or require the employer permanently to take on excess labour in order to minimize the impact of such disruption. Secondly, they directly raise costs by increasing the number of employees dealt with in any year, thereby raising total training costs, personnel department costs and orientation costs. Thirdly, they affect the stability of the work group and lower its morale. Apart from raising costs, the instability associated with frequent quits may have an additional social cost in inhibiting a number of valuable manpower practices. Thus, an employer facing a high quit rate often feels less concern for the welfare of his workforce and may, for example, be less inclined to provide the best training facilities.

Quit rates have been examined in detail recently for London Transport, British Road Services, the Metropolitan Police and the Department of the Environment.[1] For London Transport (LT) three cohorts — drivers, male conductors and female conductors — were studied. Their respective mean employment duration at LT was thirty, twenty-one and twenty-one months.

A number of influences had a clear impact on lengths of stay. Workers younger than thirty spent considerably less time with London Transport than did older workers; five months less in the case of drivers, nine and eight months less in the case of conductors. Colour also had a marked association with length of stay. Non-whites consistently stayed longer: ten months more for drivers and up to twelve months more for conductors. Those who were willing and able to work overtime, and hence had relatively high earnings, also tended to stay longer, so that a 1% increase in earnings raised length of stay by between 1.1% and 2.6%. A fourth variable that was associated with length of stay was the number of quits in the three years prior to joining London Transport. For each of the three cohorts, the larger the frequency of previous quits the shorter the stay with London Transport.

The results of analyses like this have important pointers for firms' manpower planning and for overcoming labour shortages in particular occupations. When selecting new recruits it should be possible, while considering all applicants on their merits as individuals, also to take account of what is known about the average effect of various factors on quit rates.

Firms react to labour shortages in a variety of ways. In a thorough study of busmen, teachers and draughtsmen it has been shown that explicit pay increases are only used in a modest way to overcome shortages.[2] Two other avenues bear the brunt of the adjustment. First, great attempts are made to shift the labour supply curve. Bus companies take on labour that they previously considered unsuitable for

---

1 R. Richardson, C. Robinson and J. Smith, 'Quit Rates and Manpower Policy', *DEG*, January 1977.

2 B. Thomas and D. Deaton, *Labour Shortages and Economic Analysis*, Basil Blackwell, 1977.

driving – like women. Part-time staff are hired to meet peak demands at rush hours or in the summer months. In teaching it is specially noteworthy that part-time work, so prevalent when there was a shortage, is now virtually non-existent. Local shortages of draughtsmen are overcome by subcontracting. Second, the nature of the product is changed. Bus companies axe their route mileage and local education authorities let the pupil-teacher ratio rise. By focusing on the supply of labour and the nature of the product firms are able to circumvent the more costly pay increase which would otherwise be necessary to overcome local labour shortages.

III.8   Poverty[1]

One aspect of income distribution which causes widespread concern is the problem of poverty. Low earnings from work are only one part of the poverty problem, which also encompasses hardship faced by, for example, old people, sick or disabled people, families with large numbers of children, fatherless families, and the unemployed.

In this section we discuss measurement problems, the characteristics of low-income families, and the role of the social security system. Low pay is discussed more fully in the next section.

Measurement

Poverty can be defined as an absolute or relative standard. Absolute standards are based on consumption of necessities. The quantity of necessities consumed is valued at current prices to obtain a monetary poverty standard. Relative standards are normally related to some measure of income in the general population. So, broadly, absolute standards attempt to estimate subsistence needs which do not vary with social progress, while relative standards relate poverty to rising living standards.

If poverty is defined on the basis of the *absolute* living standard in 1971, numbers in poverty declined from about a fifth of the population in 1953 to about a fortieth in 1973. In twenty years, on this absolute standard, the numbers in poverty declined dramatically – by a factor of eight. But in *relative* terms there was little change. The net income of the poorest 5th percentile was about the same proportion of median income in both years.[2]

Recent practice in Britain has been to base poverty standards on the current values of the supplementary benefit scale rates. This defines poverty in the *relative* sense because the scale rates are set in such a way that they increase broadly in step with general standards of living.

---

1   For a full discussion see Royal Commission on the Distribution of Income and Wealth, *Lower Incomes*, Report No. 6, Cmnd. 7175, HMSO, 1975; R. Layard, D. Piachaud and M. Stewart, *The Causes of Poverty*, Background Paper to Cmnd. 7175; and P. Townsend, *Poverty in the United Kingdom*, Pelican, 1979.

2   G. Fieghan, P. Lansley and A. Smith, *Poverty and Progress in Britain 1953-73*, CUP, 1977.

At the end of 1977 the number of families and people with incomes normally below their supplementary benefit (SB) level were:[1]

	Families	People
before supplementary benefit added to income	4.0m	6.2m
after supplementary benefit added to income	1.3m	2.0m

Nearly two-thirds of the 4.0m figure are pensioners. The remainder consist of sick and disabled people, the unemployed and the low paid. Naturally, once social security benefits are taken into account the number of families with incomes below SB levels falls, but it is still very worrying that over a million families have incomes below SB. This occurs mainly because some people who are eligible for SB do not claim it.[2]

A number of problems exist in measuring living standards. Should the income unit, for example, be the individual, the family or the household? How are we to control for household size and composition? Presumably larger households need more income than smaller households to get a similar standard of living. Likewise older children cost more to maintain than younger children. Therefore to measure comparative living standards sensibly, normal net household income must be adjusted for these size and composition effects. The adjustment factors are known as *equivalence scales*. The effects of adjusting the distribution of normal net household income for household size and composition are substantial. The equivalent income distribution is considerably more equal: fewer households have low or high incomes and more have intermediate levels of income.[3]

Role of Social Security

The Current Position: Poor people are aided by the state in three main ways: (i) National Insurance benefits, e.g. retirement pensions, sickness and unemployment benefit, are paid to those satisfying the statutory conditions; (ii) benefits for children (child benefit) and disabled people (e.g. mobility allowance) are paid without a means test but also without National Insurance conditions; (iii) supplementary benefit is paid to non-working persons aged 16 and over who involuntarily fall below a prescribed level of income laid down by Parliament, below which it is felt to be wrong that any family's income should be allowed to fall. Family Income Supplement, an income-related addition to pay, is used to

---

1 *ST*, No. 10, 1980 edition, p. 141.

2 There are other ways of measuring poverty than merely counting heads. One way is to calculate a 'poverty gap' in money terms. The poverty gap is simply the amount by which income falls short of the official poverty line. In 1975 before social security benefits (i.e. national insurance benefits plus supplementary benefits) were paid the poverty gap was £5.86 billion or 5.8% of GDP. But after social security benefits were paid the gap was only £0.25 billion or 0.25% of GDP. When put like this the performance of the British social security system is not unimpressive, though this is not to deny that families who are still falling below the poverty line face real hardship. Also the official poverty line itself is held by many people to be inadequate. For an excellent exposition and application of this method of analysing poverty see W. Beckerman, 'The Impact of Income Maintenance Payments on Poverty in Britain 1975', *EJ*, June 1979.

3 R. Van Slooten and A. Coverdale, 'The characteristics of low income households', *ST*, No. 8, 1977.

boost the net incomes of low-paid working family men. In addition there is an array of means-tested benefits both in kind (e.g. school meals and dental treatment) and in money (e.g. rent and rate rebates). In 1979-80 (1979 prices) social security spending totalled £19bn, a quarter of all public spending.

It was originally hoped that the National Insurance system as proposed by Beveridge in 1942 would provide a level of benefits equal at least to the official poverty line, and that supplementary benefit would wither away except as a last resort for the few people who fell through the National Insurance net. This hope has not been realized. Over 10% of the population live in families which rely on SB to bring them up to poverty-level incomes.

Criticisms: The current system has been criticized on a number of grounds, although some of the criticisms are contradictory. First, the growth in the numbers receiving SB shows that some groups are not adequately catered for by the other anti-poverty measures. Important groups here include retirement pensioners, unemployed people and fatherless families. Aggregate unemployment rises not because more people become unemployed but because on average each person is unemployed longer. So rising unemployment is associated with more people losing the earnings-related supplement (ERS) to unemployment benefit which is paid for the initial six months of unemployment (from 1982 the ERS is to disappear, pushing yet more people onto SB). And more people become unemployed for over 1 year (350,000 in January 1980) and so exhaust entirely their National Insurance unemployment benefit. Lone parents are another group who have grown rapidly in recent years (750,000 in 1980) and many have no income source other than SB.

The second criticism of the current arrangements is that, despite a battery of measures to alleviate poverty, a substantial number of people still exist below the poverty line defined by the supplementary benefit level. Some 1m families or 2m people lived below the official poverty line in November 1977. There are two main reasons for this. First, many people, especially pensioners, while eligible for supplementary benefit do not claim it. Second, many individuals are poor despite working: their weekly earnings are below the official poverty line. The Family Income Supplement was introduced in 1971 to mitigate poverty associated with low earnings.

The third criticism concerns the income-related nature of many benefits. The core of the problem is whether benefits should be related to income or whether the National Insurance system should be designed to ensure that everyone has a tolerable minimum income, with the tax system taking back some benefits from those who do not need them. The criticism has a number of strands. (i) Benefits which are related to means are traditionally unpopular and discourage a full take-up. Many of those eligible for supplementary benefit do not claim; the take-up rate of rent and rate rebates appears only to be around 50% of those eligible. (ii) It may result in absurd marginal tax rates for those with low incomes. This is known as the poverty trap: as the earned income of the family rises it loses not only monetary supplementation such as FIS but also benefits in kind such as free school meals or prescriptions. DHSS estimates that at the end of 1977 50,000 families with children might have been liable to receive no increase in net income from a £1 rise in earnings and a further 60,000 might have received less than 25p.[1] Given the government's belief that high marginal tax rates discourage proper work effort,

---

1 *ST*, No. 10, 1980 edition, p. 145.

this is clearly anomalous. (iii) The discretionary nature of the SB system makes it difficult for clients and officials to understand fully. There may also be indirect administrative costs such as social workers.

Fourth, it is widely held that many people have little incentive to work because payments when out of work are greater than or approximately equal to payments in work. This problem is real but exaggerated. It occurs primarily in the case of individuals with large families who receive ERS and tax rebates (both of which last for only a limited period) on becoming unemployed. One reason for the income in and out of work problem is that some individuals both receive benefits and pay income tax. This is mainly because in recent years income-tax allowances have not kept pace with inflation but social security payments have.

The final criticism concerns the benefits in kind. These distort the price system, the consumer paying less than the cost of providing the service (e.g. 'free' school meals or milk). Critics argue that individuals should be assured of some minimum money income and then left to spend it as they wish, with the purchases priced according to cost. This raises much wider issues than poverty relief and will not be pursued here.

Reform of Social Security: A number of important reforms are taking place in the social security system. These affect the National Insurance system, family support, supplementary benefit and new benefits for the disabled.

National Insurance contributions are earnings related. Employees in the full state pension scheme pay 6¾% of their pay as National Insurance contributions (up to a ceiling, equal to £165 in April 1980) and employers pay 10.2%. These contributions include components to help finance the National Health Service, Redundancy Fund, and Unemployment and Sickness Insurance as well as Old Age Pensions.

The benefit side is changing too. The New Pension Scheme introduced in April 1978 consists of two components. The *basic* flat-rate pension is uprated annually in line with the prices index. The *additional* pension is earnings-related. The employee will get one-eightieth of his earnings (between a specified floor and ceiling) for each contribution year after 1978, subject to a maximum of twenty eightieths. The average married couple will, when the scheme is fully mature in 1999, receive a total pension equal to at least two-thirds of the man's real take-home pay. So this scheme will help to eliminate poverty in old age. If an employer runs an occupational scheme which is at least as good as the state scheme he can opt out of the additional segment of the state scheme and he and his employees pay correspondingly lower contributions.

Sickness benefit and unemployment benefit are to be taxable from 1982. This is correct in principle but poses practical difficulties. Therefore as an interim measure the real value of these benefits is to be cut by 5% points in 1980. In addition the ERS to sick and unemployed people and others is to be withdrawn in 1982. And from 1982 the burden of paying and administering sickness benefit for the first 8 weeks of sickness is to be moved from the state to the employer.[1] These proposals – part of the overall public-spending cuts announced in the 1980 budget – raise a number of thorny issues of principle. First, they reverse efforts of successive governments to reduce the numbers on SB – cuts in insurance benefits will, as the government recognize, cause more families to rely on SB. Second, individuals who are sick or unemployed and find they no longer receive

---

1 See *Income During Initial Sickness: A New Strategy*, Cmnd. 7864, HMSO, April 1980.

earnings-related benefits might wonder why they have to pay earnings-related contributions in the same way as before. Third, the proposal that the employers administer sick pay represents a retreat from the principles of the Beveridge Report.

The system of family support has been reconstituted. Child benefit, a universal tax-free weekly amount per child, has replaced the old system of child tax allowances (CTAs) and family allowances. The new system has three important advantages. First, individuals who had low incomes and paid no tax gained no advantage from CTAs, but they do get child benefit. Second, child benefit is paid for all children whereas family allowances were paid only for second and subsequent children. Third, child benefit is paid to the mother whereas the benefit of CTAs went to the father.

It should be noticed that child benefits — £4.75 per week per child from November 1980 — are primarily designed to achieve horizontal equity rather than vertical equity. They help ensure that, at given income levels, families with children do not have wildly different living standards from families without children. While they may incidentally help low-income families, this is a secondary consideration. If relief of poverty were the main reason for child benefits, there would be little point in paying a tax-free universal benefit which costs over £600m per year extra public expenditure for each £1.00 per week per child increase. It is an open question whether or not family support should be more concerned with relief of poverty and less with horizontal equity. The government will also have to decide in time whether to index child benefit to earnings or prices so that it is automatically uprated annually; and whether to stick with a flat amount per child or to vary the amount by age of child, family size or some other factor.

The system of supplementary benefits is also being changed with a view to simplification. The discretionary nature of the system makes it inevitable that it becomes complicated and, possibly, anomalous over the years. Special needs payments, heating addition, rent allowances, children's rates varying by age, etc., all make the system difficult to understand. The aim is to reduce discretion and produce a simpler system.

A number of new benefits have been introduced for disabled people in the 1970s. These include attendance allowance for people who need looking after constantly or nearly constantly; mobility allowance to help disabled people offset the costs of getting around (previously only those with invalid trikes received such help); non-contributory invalidity pension (NCIP) to provide a weekly income as a right to disabled people of working age, including a special NCIP for housewives. The Pearson Report[1] has also recommended a new benefit for disabled children. It seems probable that this patchwork of benefits will shortly be ripe for review to see whether they could be integrated into a unified benefit for the disabled which would vary according to degree of disability.

Alternative Reforms

Despite the changes taking place many other proposals for reforming social security are put forward. This is not surprising. The criticisms of the system are

---

1 Pearson Report, *Report of Royal Commission on Civil Liability and Compensation for Personal Injury*, Cmnd. 7054, HMSO, March 1978.

still relevant and it is right that a programme which accounts for one quarter of
public spending should be under constant scrutiny.

There have been three main sets of suggestions concerning the direction of
reform.[1] They have a superficial similarity, in that under each scheme individuals
will be guaranteed a minimum income at around supplementary benefit level and
the need for supplementary benefits will be substantially reduced. In fact, however,
the schemes are very different.

The first suggestion is for a 'new Beveridge Plan'. Under the original Beveridge
proposals it was proposed that social *insurance* should guarantee everyone a
minimum standard of living. This subsistence income was to be provided as a right,
without a means test; the part played by SB was to be virtually phased out. In the
postwar period, however, National Insurance benefits have usually been below the
prescribed minima laid down by supplementary benefits. The suggestion is therefore
to implement fully the original Beveridge proposals. One of the aims of the new
pension scheme (discussed above) is to ensure pension benefits of sufficient size
virtually to eliminate the need for pensioners to turn to supplementary benefits to
augment their income. Higher child benefits are also held to be important.
Advocates of this universalistic approach to curing poverty, generally qualify it by
suggesting that the benefits from raising social security payments could be taxed
and thereby directed towards those with lower incomes.

This policy would obviously be successful in raising the incomes of non-employed
disadvantaged individuals. It does not involve high marginal tax rates and is
therefore less likely to have disincentive effects on working harder. Further it
would not involve any major administrative problems. It does have two
disadvantages. First, it would be costly. The Meade Report calculates it would
cost an additional 4-7p on the basic rate of income tax. However, this is merely
another way of stating the seriousness of the poverty problem. Second, the
problem of the employed with low incomes remains. This problem would be
moderated if income-tax thresholds were raised. But minimum-wage legislation –
the policy most frequently advocated to raise earnings by the back-to-Beveridge
protagonists – may result in unemployment among the very groups it is designed
to help.

The second scheme for reform, the Social Dividend, is the boldest. Under this
scheme a non-taxable flat-rate sum would be paid weekly to every individual
irrespective of income. This would be accompanied by a proportional personal
income tax. All other elements of the social security system (insurance
contributions and benefits, supplementary benefits and family allowances) would
be abolished. This system has the advantage that the benefit paid is insensitive to
income. Work incentives may nevertheless be impaired because it is generally
agreed that the proportional tax rate would have to be over 50%. The scheme also
has the administrative drawback of extending income tax to everyone, however
small his income.

The third alternative, which has many variants, is the Negative Income Tax. This
scheme involves a minimum-income guarantee and a break-even income. If an
individual is employed and earns between the minimum and the break-even income

1 See Meade Report, *The Structure and Reform of Direct Taxation*, IFS, 1978, chapter 13
   for a clear exposition of the Social Dividend and New Beveridge Schemes. For a concise
   description of the difficulties involved in reforming social security see A. Prest, 'The
   Structure and Reform of Direct Taxation', *EJ*, June 1979.

his earnings are supplemented (by the negative income tax); beyond the break-even income he pays positive income tax. The FIS is thus a prototype NIT. This scheme could be all-embracing, covering the whole range of government welfare programmes, or could be oriented towards particular problems such as poverty caused by large families. The essential problem with this scheme is that a choice must be made between high marginal rates of negative income tax and low minimum levels of payments. For example, from 1980 the point at which a single individual starts paying income tax is £1,375 p.a. If the NIT is operated with a rate of 50% this means that 50p is payable to an individual for every £1 by which his income is less than £1,375. Thus the basic minimum payment is only £688. If this basic minimum is too low the tax rate could be raised to 75% giving a minimum of £1,031. Such a high marginal tax rate is likely to have disincentive effects on labour supply. Further problems with the NIT, which could be overcome with time and ingenuity, are (i) that the unit to which it applies, the individual, the family or the household, must be determined; (ii) that the NIT must be on a weekly basis, but (positive) income tax has always been assessed yearly; (iii) that people not in employment have to claim the NIT; (iv) that assets may be difficult to incorporate into the NIT scheme.

III.9 Low Pay[1]

Low pay is one part of the poverty problem. Industries which are at the bottom of the earnings structure tend to be characterized by high proportions of small plants, of women workers, of unskilled workers and of falling demand for labour. It is also clear that low-paid workers are heavily represented in the service sector. In the five main service sectors (distributive trades; insurance, banking and finance; professional and scientific services; miscellaneous services; public administration) 8% of full-time male manual workers earned under £50 a week in April 1979, while the corresponding figure for manufacturing industry was 1%.

Low pay is also related to age and skill. Teenagers, workers in their early twenties and workers over fifty are disproportionately represented. Older and unskilled workers not only tend to have relatively low earnings, but also to suffer higher rates of unemployment. Unemployment rates referring specifically to unskilled workers are at least three times the national average unemployment rate. The annual earnings differential between them and other workers is therefore greater than apparent from a comparison of the earnings of those in work.

Two important features of the structure of the low-pay problem are worth noting. First, if the low paid are described as those in the lowest tenth of the distribution of manual earnings, we observe considerable movement across the boundary of this lowest tenth. 21.4% of manual men were in the lowest-paid tenth at least once in the five years 1970 to 1974, but only 2.9% were in this tenth in each of the years.[2] Second, low pay must be seen as part of a general problem of labour-market disadvantages in that it is associated with a high incidence of job instability, ill-health and lack of fringe benefits. The low-paid worker is more vulnerable to the interruption of earnings power, cannot save for old age or

---

1 For a comprehensive survey of the low-pay problem see Chris Pond, 'Low Pay', in
   N. Bosanquet and P. Townsend (eds.), *Labour and Equality*, Heinemann, 1980.

2 *DEG*, January 1977.

emergencies, and can only borrow at very high interest rates such as through HP. Thus low pay is an important element in the cycle of poverty.

In Britain we approach the problem of low pay in two main ways. First, the FIS is a form of negative income tax. Second, the wages councils provide a form of minimum-wage legislation.

FIS was introduced in August 1971 to help mitigate poverty caused by low pay. When family income falls short of a prescribed level (from November 1980 £67 per week for a one-child family plus £7.00 for each additional child), the family is paid a benefit equal to one half of the difference between its total gross income and the prescribed level (with a maximum supplement of £17 for a one-child family and £1.50 for each additional child). This is a potentially powerful policy to raise the welfare of the low-paid. Even though it is necessary to claim this income-related supplement, the take-up rate is over 90% in cash terms. Further, families who receive FIS are also automatically entitled to certain other benefits including free school meals, free milk and vitamins for expectant mothers and children under school age, and exemption from NHS charges for prescriptions, glasses and dental treatment. FIS has the considerable merit of attacking *family* poverty. This is important because the bulk of low-paid people are young workers and married women and most such workers do not live in the poorest families. So raising low pay via a national minimum wage would leave much family poverty untouched.

Elements of a minimum-wage policy exist via the wages councils which set minimum rates in certain industries. Direct state intervention in fixing minimum wages first occurred in 1909 with the Trade Boards Act. In 1945 trade boards were renamed wages councils. There are forty wages councils. They are generally believed to be ineffective in helping low-paid workers and are thought to inhibit the development of voluntary collective bargaining arrangements.

A national minimum wage (assuming it is set above the existing wage for low-paid workers) will raise the money earnings of those who remain employed, but will cause some unemployment. Recall that the old and unskilled, the people the minimum wage is designed to help most, already have the highest unemployment rates. It may also give only a temporary boost to the low paid. Overseas evidence suggests that the original wage differentials are quickly restored. Proponents of minimum-wage legislation also argue that it raises the productivity of labour. So it will if capital is substituted for labour, but this is an inefficient substitution and unemployment will also result. It is sometimes said, however, that the minimum-wage legislation will have a 'shock effect' and thereby raise productivity without any loss in employment. This is unlikely to be widespread in that it implies that firms currently have a careless attitude towards profits. Further, many of the low-paying industries are competitive and are therefore unlikely to need a national minimum wage as a spur to efficiency.

This suggests that provision of more training facilities, better information about wages and opportunities both locally and nationally, inducements to labour mobility, wage subsidies, and running the economy with lower, more evenly distributed unemployment levels, are likely to be more effective solutions to the problem of low pay than is a national minimum wage.

IV TRADE UNIONS AND INDUSTRIAL RELATIONS
IV.1 Trade Unions

At the end of 1978 there were estimated to be 13,112,000 trade-union members in the UK. This implies that 54% of the nation's employees (in employment plus unemployed) were trade-union members, a significant expansion from the corresponding figure of 42% for 1964. Historically, the 1970s will be seen as a decade of relatively rapid trade-union expansion, with 17% growth already having been recorded. It is also worth noting that union membership has been growing particularly rapidly among females, up by 35% between 1970 and 1978 – their membership rate, however, is still below that for males.[1]

The number of unions is still tending to fall, down from 630 in 1965 to 462 in 1978, in spite of small increases in 1973 (probably the result of the 1971 Industrial Relations Act) and 1977. Nevertheless, in 1978 there were still 72 trade unions with less than 100 members each.

In addition to those in formal trade unions, many workers belong to other associations that engage in collective negotiations and bargaining; for example, many individual business concerns have what are sometimes called 'company unions'. Other workers are in industries that have wages councils, public bodies that are designed to reproduce many of the features of collective bargaining where trade-union growth is inherently difficult.

In 1973 the *New Earnings Survey* for the first time gave disaggregated estimates of the number of workers covered by various types of collective agreement. It was suggested there that 17% of full-time male workers and 28% of full-time female workers were not party to a collective agreement. For both sexes the service sectors, particularly the distributive trades and personal services, were heavily characterized by individual negotiation; in the manufacturing sector, clothing and footwear had relatively little collective bargaining.

Formal unionization is particularly extensive among male workers, manual workers, semi-skilled workers and workers in the manufacturing and public sectors. There are no absolutely reliable figures, but one recent study[2] suggests that in 1974 unionization was almost 100% in coal mining, railways and sea and road transport, but only around 5% in hotels and catering and other professional services.

Unionization is more limited in newer industries and in the expanding white-collar trades.[3] Where unions have been involved in the latter sectors they have traditionally differed from those in the blue-collar sectors in their aims, attitudes and militancy. Recently, however, the extent of white-collar organization has been growing, and with it has come more aggressive union behaviour.

It is interesting to know which factors are associated with year-to-year changes in total union membership. It appears that price inflation, changes in money wages, unemployment and the size of the potentially unionizable labour force are all related to movements in aggregate unionization.[4] What is now required is a convincing theoretical rationale for such associations.

---

1 *DEG*, December 1979, pp. 1,241-8.

2 R. Price and G. Bain, 'Union Growth Revisited', *BJIR*, November 1976, pp. 339-55.

3 G. Bain, *The Growth of White Collar Unionism*, Oxford, 1970.

4 G. Bain and F. El-Sheikh, *Union Growth and the Business Cycle*, Basil Blackwell, 1976. See also the review by R. Richardson in *BJIR,* July 1977.

IV.2   Economic Analysis of Unions

The existence and activities of trade unions raise very large questions in the fields of politics, sociology and law. On a somewhat narrower and more practical front, trade unions have had a considerable influence on the operation of work rules, consultation procedures and worker representation. Economists, however, have tended to concentrate on the impact of trade unions on wages and resource allocation. We shall do the same here.

The theoretical analysis of union behaviour by economists is not very satisfactory. At its simplest, the union is implicitly assumed to have organized all the relevant workers and to be facing a set of unorganized employers. In many respects, the analysis is analogous to the standard treatment of monopolies in product markets. In this context, the decision that the union has to make is to trade off jobs for higher wages.

The union is seen to face a given demand curve for its members' services. Higher wages mean fewer jobs (a) because they tend to raise product prices and reduce consumer demand, and (b) because they raise the price of the labour relative to other factors of production and encourage factor substitution. In this model, therefore, it is the prospect of reduced employment possibilities that disciplines the union wage claims. In order to predict what a union will decide to press for, it is necessary to know both the elasticity of the demand curve facing it and the relative value placed by the union on job opportunities and wages. In order to know the second of these it is necessary, in the spirit of this model, to know something about how decisions are arrived at within the union.

Economists frequently ignore some of these qualifications and simply predict that unions will secure a greater wage where they face a relatively inelastic demand curve. As a corollary of this prediction, it is also suggested that in situations where demand elasticities are high a union may have nothing to offer its potential members and may therefore not exist. If we add to this some consideration of the costs of successful organization, we have at least an embryo theory of union density patterns. It is usually said that such costs are low when the workforce in question is (a) stable and so not subject to high rates of quits or lay-offs, (b) concentrated among relatively few employers, (c) concentrated goegraphically, and (d) possessed of certain attitudes, sometimes labelled 'class consciousness'.

The simple theory of union behaviour sketched above is greatly weakened by the assumption that employers are not organized but act atomistically. When they too are organized, as they usually are in the UK, we enter the world of bargaining and bilateral monopoly. The theories relating to such a world are often elegant and are sometimes entertaining but they are rarely fruitful. Certainly they have not yet produced operational models that have been widely accepted by those who wish to understand the real world. This failure is not confined to the analysis of union behaviour but appears throughout economics whenever strategic, or 'game', situations are central. We therefore have in this area a very fragile theoretical platform from which to survey and analyse the real world.

So much for a sketch of the principles of effective unionization. A number of recent studies have attempted to measure the impact of collective bargaining on the structure of relative wages.[1] It appears that average hourly pay in an industry

---

1 See J. Pencavel, 'Relative Wages and Trade Unions in the UK', *EC*, May 1974; C. Mulvey, 'Collective Agreements and Relative Earnings in UK Manufacturing in 1973', *EC*, November 1976; articles by J. Pencavel, D. Metcalf, A. Thompson *et al*. and S. Nickell in *BJIR*, July 1977.

whose labour force is completely covered by a collective agreement is around 20% greater than the average wage in a completely uncovered industry.

In the 1960s many industrial-relations specialists became concerned at the apparently haphazard nature of local bargaining which was often superimposed on official bargaining and which, it was claimed, contributed to strike activity and inflation. For example, the Donovan Report[1] suggested that many sectors of British industry had two systems of collective bargaining, with informal workplace-bargaining between shop stewards and plant management existing simultaneously with formal company or industry-wide bargaining; the Report expressed its distaste for the informal element. It is interesting, therefore, to examine how the wage premium associated with union coverage varies by type of agreement. It appears that in manufacturing industry the wage premium associated with a national agreement is, at best, small, while those covered by district, local and company agreements have a wage advantage in excess of the overall average union mark-up of around 20%. Remember, however, that many such supplementary agreements have a national flavour. The industrial-relations literature is rich in descriptions of institutional mechanisms whereby local bargains struck in one plant are transmitted to plants of the same firm in other areas or to plants of different firms. Thus even supplementary district, local or company agreements may have national dimensions.

It is not clear at whose expense unions extract this wage premium. For much of this century the share of wages in national income was broadly constant.[2] This would imply union members gain at the expense of non-union members. Such unorganized workers tend either to be relatively low paid or relatively high paid, but it is not known which of these two sets of workers loses from unionization.

Further, in the last decade or so labour's share in national income appears to have risen.[3] Indeed, between 1968 and 1970 union membership and the share of wages in manufacturing national income both rose by 10%. In this case, unions may have secured their wage gains at the expense of profits rather than at the expense of their fellow, non-union, workers. This may, in turn, result in lower investment and a slower growth in real wages in the future.

IV.3   Strikes and Industrial Relations

Strikes: It is officially estimated that more than 29 million working days were lost through industrial disputes in the UK in 1979.[4] This is by far the largest annual figure for the whole postwar period; even so, it represents only about 10 hours per employee per year. During the last 10 years the typical figure of days lost has been about one-third or one-quarter of the 1979 figure. By international standards, to the extent that comparisons can be made, this makes the UK a rather average country; some countries, like Australia, Canada, Spain, Italy and the US lose more

1 *Report on the Royal Commission on Trade Unions and Employers' Associations 1965-1968*, (Chairman Lord Donovan), Cmnd. 3623, HMSO, 1968.

2 E.H. Phelps Brown, *Pay and Profits*, Manchester UP, 1968.

3 A. Glyn and R. Sutcliffe, *British Capitalism, Workers and the Profits Squeeze*, Penguin, 1972; M. King, 'The UK Profits Crisis: Myth or Reality', *EJ*, March 1975.

4 *DEG*, January 1980, pp. 28-30.

days per worker, while other countries, notably West Germany, Holland and Sweden, lose less.[1]

Of the total of 29 million lost days in 1979, no fewer than 16 million were due to the series of one- and two-day stoppages by the roughly 1½ million engineering workers. The other major dispute, involving local government manual workers, accounted for a further 3 million lost days. It is therefore clear that the incidence of strikes is very unevenly distributed across workers, firms, industries and occupations.

Thus, over the period 1966-73 mining lost an average of 4,300 days per year per 1,000 employees; the next most strike-prone sector was vehicles with 2,100 days, followed by shipbuilding with 1,820 days; in contrast, the distributive trades lost seven days per year per 1,000 workers.[2] Another feature of strike behaviour is the strong inverse relation between plant size and days lost through strikes. For manufacturing plants employing more than 1,000 workers, days lost averaged 2,050 per 1,000 workers over 1971-3, compared with 15 days per 1,000 workers in plants employing between 11 and 24 workers.

It is important to note that the vast majority of plants are not affected by stoppages. For example, between 1971 and 1973 95% of plants in manufacturing industry were free of stoppages. Thus, only 5% of manufacturing plants had at least one stoppage in these three years. Of these, two-thirds had only one stoppage but a small minority had a large number. Britain apparently suffers from a concentration of stoppages in the docks, in coal mining and in a small proportion (between 2 and 5%) of plants in manufacturing industry, especially motor vehicles and shipbuilding.[3]

More generally, strikes seem more likely when inflation is rising and when unemployment is low, and less likely when recent wage changes are high. Comparing different industries, strikes are more likely in those industries with relatively few female workers, extensive payments-by-results systems, rapid technical change and slowly growing wages.

There has been comment in recent years on payment of supplementary benefit to strikers' families.[4] It is certainly true that state support to strikers' families increased in the 1970s compared with the earlier postwar period. This increase was associated, in part, with a change in the pattern of strikes. There has been an increase in the number of longer, official strikes, particularly in the public sector (e.g. postmen 1971, miners 1974, firemen 1977, and steelworkers 1980). But, in recent years, the proportion of those eligible who actually received supplementary benefit was, at most, around one-third. Further, SB plays only a minor role in the budgets of those on strike. Only 15% of the postmen's income while on strike came from the state. Strikers and their families rely far more on running down their savings, deferring HP, rent and mortgage payments, living off wives' pay and back-pay and tax rebates. Gennard provides persuasive evidence that state income support does not cause or prolong strikes; he also suggests that modifications in the availability of SB to strikers' families would, in some cases, cause much hardship and would probably sour industrial relations. In spite of this, the present

---

1 *DEG*, February 1980, pp. 161-2.

2 *DEG*, February 1976, pp. 115-23.

3 *DEG*, November 1976, pp. 1,219-24.

4 For a full discussion, see J. Gennard, *Financing Strikers*, Macmillan, 1977.

government has decided to seek changes in the rules governing transfer payments to the families of strikers. At the time of writing (April 1980), the proposals would reduce the weekly supplementary benefit paid to strikers' families by £12, would eliminate the rule by which the family's first £4 of tax refunds be disregarded when deciding benefit entitlement and would, as from 1982, make supplementary benefit payments subject to income taxes.

Industrial Relations: Strike activity is the most heavily publicized aspect of industrial relations but is by no means the most important one. It arouses considerable public comment and often provides dramatic situations with great political significance but, in so doing, it tends to obscure other aspects of the relationships between employer and employee which make up industrial relations. The British 'system' of industrial relations has been the subject of much analysis and debate, particularly since the mid-1960s. There are a number of reasons for this.

Most generally, there has been a growing unease over the power that trade unions are thought to be acquiring. Whether they have grown in power in any meaningful way, and in what respects this might have happened, and in what ways any such changes might affect behaviour or events, are all questions whose answers are by no means easy to establish. But if opinion polls are to be believed, there is a considerable body of opinion in the country which holds that in a variety of ways unions are too powerful.

There is certainly a strong feeling that unions cause or exacerbate inflation. There is also a debate as to the tactics that are proper in the pursuit of wage claims. There is finally a debate on the question of the closed shop, the circumstances in which it should be allowed and the rights and position of individual workers who do not wish to be union members.

Among professionals in the field of industrial relations, there has been a narrower, more technical debate. For at least the last 10 to 15 years there has been much concern over the British 'system' of industrial relations, sparked off by two principal worries.

In many sectors the traditional industry-wide collective bargaining has become less important. Sustained full employment in the postwar period has appeared to make the role of shop stewards and local negotiations much more important; in many manufacturing industries, local agreements are mounted on the back of industrial agreements, causing substantial 'wage drift'. Also, the majority of strikes are unofficial.

These concerns, coupled with certain legal judgments particularly affecting the position of individuals, led to the establishment of a Royal Commission[1] to investigate the industrial-relations system.

The Commission thought that the principal problem in industrial relations was that two systems – the formal and the informal – existed. It further believed that certain industries where the conflict between the two systems was very apparent, e.g. engineering, were industries whose bargains set a pattern for others. It saw the remedy in integrating the informal systems and stressed the desirability of both plant bargaining and full employer recognition of unions. However, it strongly believed that the reform should be voluntary rather than imposed by law. It

---

1 *Report of the Royal Commission on Trade Unions and Employers' Associations 1965-1968* (Donovan Report), Cmnd. 3623, HMSO, 1968.

recommended the establishment of a Commission on Industrial Relations, a form of investigatory tribunal, to facilitate this voluntary reform. It believed implicitly that if reform could be achieved in a few key sectors this would percolate through the rest of the system. The report was not well received by independent observers, who felt that it merely pushed people in the direction they were already going anyway, and that it did little to change the ground-rules of the industrial-relations system or to get at the problem of excessive wage inflation.

Legislation: The report resulted in action from both Labour and Conservative governments. Labour established a Commission on Industrial Relations whose functions the Conservatives subsequently altered; on returning to power in 1974, the Labour government abolished the CIR. In 1969-70 the Labour government proposed additional reforms but withdrew them in the face of strong union and backbench opposition. It was left to the Conservatives to legislate substantial reform but their Industrial Relations Act (1971) had a stormy history, arousing bitter hostility in the trade-union leadership, before it was repealed in an early action by the Labour government of 1974. That action, the Trade Union and Labour Relations Act, together with the associated Trade Union and Labour Relations (Amendment) Act (1976), in many ways restored the pre-1971 situation, but in some respects the position of trade unions was further strengthened. For example, under the controversial closed shop provisions, it was no longer unfair for an employer to dismiss employees for refusing to join a union in those situations where employers and unions had agreed to a 100% union-membership provision.

Additional industrial-relations legislation was also introduced. The Employment Protection Act (1975) encouraged constructive union activity. Employers were required to disclose certain information judged to be relevant to collective bargaining, consult with unions on the handling of redundancies, and face more pressure to recognize independent trade unions when their employees wished to be represented. The legislation also gave powers to the Advisory, Conciliation and Arbitration Service and extended the legal rights of individual employees, e.g. in maternity pay and leave provision. The position of unions was also strengthened by the passing of the Health and Safety at Work Act (1975) and the Industry Act (1975). The latter gave worker participation in an embryonic form by encouraging Planning Agreements, i.e. agreements between individual employers, union and the government relating to the operations of firms.

Worker participation in its fullest form was considered by the Bullock Committee.[1] The majority of the Committee recommended that when employees numbered 2,000 or more in a firm they should have the same number of board seats as shareholder representatives. Together, these two groups would co-opt a (smaller) third group of independent directors. Worker directors could continue to act as shop stewards and would not be excluded from any boardroom discussion when, for example, the subject was wages. These proposals would have affected about 1,800 private companies grouped into 738 enterprises, employing around 7 million people. Reaction to these proposals was mixed, and the Labour government was unable to present agreed legislation to Parliament. Under the Conservative government it does not seem that worker participation will be encouraged by legislation.

---

1 *Report of the Committee of Inquiry on Industrial Democracy*, Cmnd. 6706, HMSO, 1977.

After its return to power in 1979, the Conservative government announced a new series of measures designed to affect industrial relations. At the time of writing (April 1980), the legislation is being considered by Parliament and may well be subject to further amendments, but the major proposals are as follows.

The government proposes that closed shop agreements should become more difficult to enter into, and that individuals who suffer damage from the operations of a closed shop agreement should have some additional legal redress. Second, the government proposes the provision of public money to encourage the taking of secret ballots on certain questions such as union elections and strike calls. Third, the government has proposed to redefine the limits of lawful picketing so as to influence who may picket and where picketing may take place. The government is also seeking to amend certain parts of the Employment Protection Act relating, for example, to trade-union recognition, unfair-dismissal provisions and maternity provisions. Finally, the government is seeking to change the immunity which the law provides for so-called 'secondary' industrial action, such as blacking and strikes.[1]

It is not clear what effects these changes will have, not least of all because the proposals have already been modified in detail on their way through the legislative process. What does seem clear is that the debate on the proper structure of the law in the field of industrial relations will not fade away quickly or quietly.

V   WAGE INFLATION AND PUBLIC POLICY

Of all the areas of controversy and disagreement in economics, the one that is most confused and least resolved is probably that of inflation, particularly its causes and cures. It is widely agreed that the most important immediate determinant of price inflation is changes in money wages. This is because wages are the major component of production costs and, as a matter of fact, the prices of finished goods usually change only after costs have changed. There are, of course, other components of costs, and changes in these may also affect prices. Thus, the course of price inflation is additionally affected by changes in (a) non-wage labour cost, e.g. training costs or National Insurance costs, (b) productivity, (c) taxes or subsidies on goods and services, (d) the foreign currency price of imported goods, (e) the exchange rate and (f) profit margins. In the recent past, each of these has had an influence on the price level for a time but changes in wages have been even more important.[2]

The determinants of at least some of these non-wage cost components are not a matter of very great controversy, though they are usually very difficult to forecast at any given time. However, there is very little agreement as to what determines the course of wage costs, and correspondingly little agreement on how that course might be changed by policy. As a consequence, we are now unable to forecast at all accurately future changes in average wages in the UK. As wage changes are so central to many economic events, this inability is one reason why all macroeconomic forecasting is extremely hazardous and conjectural. In recent years it has been necessary for forecasters to take a range of possible wage changes and to make

---

1 The government working papers and proposals on this set of topics can be followed in a series of reports in the *DEG*, starting July 1979 and continuing to December 1979.

2 See chapter 1, section V, for further discussion.

separate calculations for each. For example, economists making forecasts in mid-1980 for the following two years would probably have a wage-inflation range for 1980-1 stretching from 20% p.a. down to well under 15% p.a. The range for 1981-2 would have to be even more notional because it would be heavily influenced by the actual out-turn for 1980-1. With such large unknowns, traditional economic policy formation becomes very difficult.

V.1   Explanations of Wage Inflation

A traditional view is that average wage changes are largely the result of changes in the aggregate demand for labour relative to its supply. This may be true in two senses. One is that as demand increases relative to supply, people in work tend to work more overtime and hence have increased total earnings. The other, and this is what is being considered here, is that as demand increases relative to supply, earnings increase for a given number of hours and amount of effort − this may be called wage inflation. Many different types of economists believe that wage inflation is caused by tight labour markets, i.e. where the demand for labour is high relative to its supply.

At least until the mid-1960s many economists, following the work of Phillips,[1] believed that there was a stable relationship between wage inflation and the state of aggregate demand as measured either by unemployment, or vacancies or an index of unused industrial capacity. It was not, however, thought that aggregate demand was the sole determinant of wage inflation. Phillips noted that wages also seemed to respond to a very rapid rise in import prices, and other economists felt that recent price changes, whatever their source, might influence current wage inflation.

They also added further variables to the Phillips framework, for example, the level of industrial profits or the degree of industrial concentration. In addition to these influences it was felt that the position and shape of the Phillips Curve was the result of the institutional arrangements in the economy, for example, the collective-bargaining structure. Thus, a change in these institutions might affect unemployment and inflation simultaneously.

All these additional arguments having been made, it was nevertheless widely felt that changes in the rate of wage inflation from year to year were mainly the result of changes in the level of aggregate demand relative to supply. It was also felt that the principal way the government could influence the level of aggregate demand was by varying its fiscal policy, which meant a change in taxes or government expenditure that produced a change in the public-sector financial deficit or surplus.

Since the mid-1960s faith in the Phillips' framework has been progressively reduced in the UK. In other countries, for example the United States, many economists have continued to see value in it, although there too it is being increasingly questioned. The main reason for the change in view is that wage inflation and unemployment have tended to move in the same direction rather than inversely (see table 5.7). At the same time there has been a revival of interest in monetary analysis, which tends to restore to a position of importance the rate of increase in the supply of money as an explanation of the rate of inflation. Thus, an

---

1   A.W. Phillips, 'The Relation between Unemployment and the Rate of Change of Money Wage Rates in the United Kingdom, 1861-1957', *EC*, November 1958, pp. 283-99.

increase in the money supply is thought to raise the demand for goods and services and hence for labour; this will subsequently raise wages and prices. The transmission from changes in money supply to prices is thought to be complex, and is associated with time-lags that are believed to be both long (averaging perhaps eighteen months) and varied. In addition to re-affirming a link in the short run between aggregate demand and wage inflation, the revival of monetarism has also emphasized the importance for wage inflation of expectations of future price increases. Monetarists do not believe that there is more than a 'temporary' trade-off of any significance between wage inflation and aggregate demand (as measured, for example, by unemployment). Instead, they believe that there is a single equilibrium employment rate, the 'natural' rate, and that any departure from that rate can only be temporary (although 'temporary' could mean many years). Starting from a position of equilibrium, a sustained increase in the rate of monetary expansion is seen to lead to a sequence of events first lowering and then raising unemployment, to produce, in the new equilibrium, the initial level of unemployment but a higher level of inflation, for both wages and prices. Thus wage inflation is seen to be heavily influenced by price expectations that are themselves a direct or indirect result of monetary expansion.

TABLE 5.7
Unemployment and Wage Inflation 1955-79

	% Change hourly wage earnings, manual workers	% Unemployment males, GB
1955-60 (average p.a.)	6.2	1.6
1961-9 (average p.a.)	6.7	2.3
1970	15.3	3.4
1971	12.9	4.5
1972	15.0	4.9
1973	14.1	3.5
1974	21.4	3.5
1975	26.9	5.2
1976	12.1	7.2
1977	8.4	7.4
1978	13.8	7.0
1979	16.6	6.5

Source: DEG, various issues.

In some respects these two groups, the followers of Phillips and the monetarists, agree. Both believe that a policy of reducing the level of aggregate demand relative to supply will reduce wage inflation. One group would say that this would result in permanently higher unemployment, the other would deny this and claim that the rise in unemployment was temporary; they might therefore disagree as to whether the policy is desirable. Monetarists would say that the change in aggregate demand can be engineered only by a change in the rate of monetary expansion, whereas others would stress fiscal policy. In practice, however, there has not been much disagreement because in the UK a change in the public-sector deficit has usually been followed by a change in the rate of monetary expansions.

It has been rare, except perhaps in the last two or three years, for a change in the public-sector deficit to be offset wholly, or even largely, by a changed level of public debt sales, to leave the money supply substantially unaffected. With the recent arrival of official monetary targets the situation may have been fundamentally changed in this respect.

Finally, both groups believe that other policy changes could influence wage inflation. Many of those who worked within the Phillips framework saw in incomes policy a chance to shift the whole Phillips Curve, producing less unemployment and lower inflation. Monetarists have tended to be sceptical of incomes policies, partly because the latter have often been accompanied by monetary expansion. However, a monetarist certainly could argue that an incomes policy might reduce inflationary expectations and thus make a tight money policy work more quickly and smoothly. It would, however, be difficult for a monetarist to argue that monetary control and incomes policies were alternatives. In addition, both groups could agree that a whole range of microeconomic institutional changes might affect either the position of the Phillips Curve or the natural rate of unemployment.

In contrast to those who stress changes in fiscal or monetary policy, there are many observers who believe that wage inflation is the result of the configuration of unions or of collective-bargaining structures. The latter group also tends to believe that the course of wage inflation is largely uninfluenced by variations in such indicators as the unemployment rate. Thus Sir Kenneth Berrill, then Chief Economic Adviser to the Treasury, remarked to a Committee of the House of Commons in June 1974 that 'we do not believe the Phillips Curve over quite a large band, but starting at the top end, when you reduce unemployment you can begin to see shortages of skilled labour, bottlenecks and so on developing which affect the balance of payments and also earnings and prices. Then there is a large flat band. What happens at the heavy levels of unemployment we do not know because we have not had that since the 1930s.'[1]

A relatively early expression of this diverse group is to be found in the work of Hines, who attributed wage inflation to trade-union pushfulness.[2] Hines set out an index of trade-union pushfulness ΔT (= $T_t - T_{t-1}$, where T_t denotes the proportion of the labour force unionized, or union density, in year t). His thesis was that ΔT is a measure of union activity which manifests itself simultaneously both in increased union membership and density and in pressure on money wage rates. He tested this hypothesis with aggregate data from 1893-1961 and found, broadly, that through time excess demand for labour had become less important as a cause of inflation and that in the postwar period wage pushfulness was a key factor in the explanation of inflation. The importance of unions in industry-level wage adjustment was confirmed in a subsequent article.[3]

Given the controversial nature of this topic and the originality of Hines' contribution it is not surprising that the latter has been subjected to careful scrutiny. The most wide-ranging critique is that of Purdy and Zis,[4] who examine Hines' theory, data, estimation technique and interpretation.

---

1 Ninth Report from the Expenditure Committee, *Public Expenditure, Inflation and the Balance of Payments*, Session 1974, HMSO, p. 136.

2 A. Hines, 'Trade Unions and Wage Inflation in the UK 1893-1961', *RES*, 1964.

3 A. Hines, 'Wage Inflation in the UK 1948-62: A Disaggregated Study', *EJ*, 1969, pp. 66-89.

4 D. Purdy and A. Zis, 'Trade Unions and Wage Inflation in the UK', in D. Laidler and D. Purdy (eds.), *Inflation and Labour Markets*, Manchester UP, 1974.

Their main criticism is that Hines presents no theoretical underpinning for the proposition that militancy (ΔT) shows simultaneously in increased membership and in upward pressure on wage rates: 'There is a presumption in his theory that unions aim to drive up their members' real wage by exerting pressure on money wages; that unions aim to extend the organized proportion of the labour force lying within their jurisdiction and that the rate at which they succeed in carrying out this latter objective is a major determinant of their success in pursuing the former.' However, none of this comes out of a formal model of union behaviour or a discussion of what unions do when conflicting objectives, e.g. higher wages associated with lower employment, occur. Even more important, theoretically, is that the pushfulness view pays little attention to the employer. Hines argues that, through time, employer resistance is of less consequence because of the wage round and because of administered prices. While this may be true it still seems likely that the secular reduction in employer resistance will have some cyclical variability superimposed on it — that in the motor industry, for example, employer resistance is related to the demand for cars; indeed there is evidence that employers initiate strikes when demand is slack — and this should be discussed in the wage-adjustment model.

A second criticism of the union-pushfulness model is that it is not clear what ΔT measures: it is defined as a measure of militancy, but the contribution of unions to the process of inflation may depend more on their strength than on their militancy. This distinction is slippery but not trivial. If unions are strong they may get large money wage increases with a small show of militancy (indeed if they operate a closed shop, ΔT, the militancy measure used by Hines, is by definition zero). Further many labour historians (Phelps Brown,[1] Rossi[2])believe unions were more powerful (militant?) in forestalling and minimizing money wage cuts in the interwar period than they are in obtaining wage increases — in the words of Phelps Brown, unions are stronger when they act as the anvil rather than as the hammer.

Two semi-statistical problems concern (i) simultaneity between union density and wage changes, and (ii) the fact that union density may not be independent of excess demand. The proportion of the labour force unionized is a function of the costs of organization, as measured by factors such as the number of workers per plant, the benefits of membership and simply whether the union member can afford his dues. It is well known[3] that over long periods union membership is positively related to economic activity; for example, union membership fell steadily between 1926 and 1933 and rose steadily during the mid and late 1930s. It seems likely therefore that the level of union membership depends both on money wage changes and on the level of excess demand.

Purdy and Zis point to data problems within the union-pushfulness model. One such problem is that until recently there has been little variability in ΔT in the postwar period. More important, where a closed shop exists the basis of using ΔT as a measure of militancy is unclear because union membership will only rise or fall as employment in the closed-shop sectors rises or falls. Purdy and Zis quote

1 E.H. Phelps Brown, *Pay and Profits*, Manchester UP, 1968.

2 A. Ross, 'Changing Pattern of Industrial Conflict', in *Proceedings of Twelfth Annual Meeting of Industrial Relations Research Association*, edited by G. Somers, 1959.

3 E. Hobsbawm, *Labouring Men: Studies in the History of Labour*, Weidenfeld and Nicolson, 1964.

evidence from McCarthy,[1] who estimated that in 1964 3.75 million workers were
employed in closed-shop establishments and a further 1.35 million were in open
shops within trades where the closed-shop practice predominated, and which were
therefore quasi-closed shops enforced by informal sanctions. In all, 22% of manual
workers were covered by closed-shop arrangements and these constituted 49% of
manual unionists. A recent estimate of the extent of closed shops suggests that
their importance has increased. According to this work, closed-shop practices now
cover at least 5.2 million employees and are found over a wider spectrum of
industries than in the early 1960s.[2] It is clear therefore that in a large number of
plants increased union activity is unlikely to be reflected in ΔT because the
employees are already completely organized.

Finally, Purdy and Zis found that when they re-estimated the union-pushfulness
model to take account of their various criticisms, the impact of ΔT on wage changes,
although still positive, was much reduced. This is confirmed by Wilkinson and
Burkitt,[3] who used carefully constructed data on unionization by industry and
found that ΔT is significantly associated with wage changes in only one industry,
textiles, out of the eleven they studied.

The statistical studies discussed above have neither confirmed nor rejected the
central place of unions in the inflationary process and, in consequence, the debate
concerning the underlying causes of inflation continues unabated. It is generally
agreed that a correlation exists between the growth in the money supply and the
rate of inflation and that this correlation is stronger in the long run than in the
short run. What is in dispute is whether inflation is caused by excessive growth in
the money supply or whether union power or some other social force causes money
wages to rise which in turn induces the authorities to expand the money supply in
order that unemployment does not result.

V.2   Incomes Policy

History: Since the mid-1960s different governments in the UK have used incomes
and prices policies for a number of purposes.[4] The principal aim of these policies
has been to reduce the rate of inflation, but important subsidiary aims have, from
time to time, been to reduce the extent of restrictive labour-market practices, to
increase labour productivity generally, to encourage a shift in the structure of
earnings and to improve the competitive environment in industry. Here we shall
concentrate on the anti-inflationary aim.

There has been a wide variety of forms in the policies. For example, they have
differed as to whether they were voluntary or compulsory, as to whether they had
a flat-rate norm (i.e. so many pounds per week) or a percentage norm, and as to
whether they permitted exceptions or not.

1   W. McCarthy, *The Closed Shop in Britain*, Blackwell, 1964.

2   J. Gennard, S. Dunn and M. Wright, 'The Extent of Closed Shop Arrangements in British
    Industry', *DEG*, January 1980.

3   R. Wilkinson and B. Burkitt, 'Wage Determination and Trade Unions', *SJPE*, June 1973.

4   For a discussion of earlier policies see A. Fels, *The British Prices and Incomes Board*,
    Cambridge UP, 1972, particularly chapter 1.

From April 1965 to June 1966 the incomes policy was voluntary, i.e. there were no sanctions on those who chose to disregard its guidelines. From mid-1966 to mid-1967 the policy became both compulsory and more severely anti-inflationary in intent. After July 1967 there was a more ambiguous period where compliance with a somewhat more relaxed policy was 'essentially voluntary'.[2] Shortly after coming into power in June 1970, the Conservative government discontinued the incomes policy, but by mid-1971 they felt obliged to resume some direct action, with particular emphasis on achieving a gradual decline in the level of settlements in the public sector. By the autumn of 1972 they were trying to get TUC and CBI agreement on a more comprehensive but still voluntary policy; when this was not forthcoming, they announced a compulsory and initially severe incomes and prices policy in November of that year. This had three phases and lasted until a Labour government was elected in March 1974. After that time the statutory disciplines were ignored and a number of 'special cases' were recognized.

While in opposition between 1970 and 1974, the Labour Party had become officially hostile to incomes policies, particularly to those having statutory provisions. This was partly because there was scepticism of the economic advantages of such policies but much more because of political imperatives. In 1969 relations between the trade-union movement and the Labour government had become extremely strained following the publication of a White Paper on industrial relations (*In Place of Strife*). During the subsequent period of opposition there were moves to restore friendly relations, and a particular expression of the rapprochement was the so-called Social Contract. Under this, a future Labour government would enjoy generalized and specific support from the trade-union movement in return for legislation and policies designed to strengthen the position of the trade unions and their members. Among the matters on which the trade-union leaders felt strongly was the undesirability of statutory incomes policies. They felt that such policies, by undermining the role of free collective bargaining, struck at the very core of the justification for trade unions, at least as they are organized in the UK.

As a result, and in spite of quite exceptionally high wage inflation, the Labour government did virtually nothing directly to affect wage inflation between spring 1974 and summer 1975. However, a continuation of such a posture was widely thought to be impossible. It was not widely believed that in the absence of direct action wage inflation would quickly fall below 25-30% p.a. and it was recognized that such inflation as had already been experienced was going to be difficult to digest. On the other hand, there was great scepticism that a purely voluntary incomes policy, even if negotiated, would work.

In the event a very simple voluntary policy, albeit one with explicit sanctions held in reserve, was agreed between the government and the TUC and was adhered to very widely. This was followed, in the summer of 1976 and the summer of 1977, by two more stages, both fairly simple and neither backed with explicit sanctions, although during the third stage the government did take various disciplinary actions against firms that paid more than the suggested guidelines. In the summer and autumn of 1978 the Labour government tried to secure trade-union adherence to a fourth successive year of the largely voluntary policy, but the trade-union movement was unwilling to comply.

---

2 The description is that of Fels, op. cit., chapter 1.

   The Conservative government, which came to power in May 1979, has been uninterested, indeed hostile, to incomes policies, voluntary or statutory. With wage inflation back up to 20% in early 1980 some observers are becoming sceptical whether this hostility will continue for very long. Most seem to be of the view that if incomes policies are to be disinterred yet again they will be of a statutory rather than voluntary nature.

   As with the choice between voluntary and statutory there have been changes in the type of norm used. Most of the early policies had percentage norms, but the Conservative government's Phase II, from April 1973 to September 1973, had a flat-rate component (the exact formula was a permitted £1 + 4%). In July 1975 the Labour government announced a norm of £6 per week for everyone except those earning more than £8,500 per year, who were not allowed any increase at all. This was followed in the next year by a more complex formula of a minimum of £2.50 per week and a maximum of £4.00 per week, or, within those limits, 5%.

   The effect of these flat-rate guidelines, of course, is to reduce the relative earnings differentials within pay groups. This erosion of differentials certainly created political and industrial-relations problems and probably began to affect adversely the allocation of labour. As a result, in Stage 3 of the Labour government's policy there was a reversion to a percentage norm (10% of earnings) plus some allowance for genuine productivity deals.

   Three other aspects of the norms are worth mentioning. First, in November 1973 the Conservative government permitted a form of indexation, whereby workers could make agreements under which they would receive wage increases if the price level rose above a certain threshold. The intention here was that prices would not so rise and that the indexation clause would not in fact be triggered. This was an interesting idea and reflected the belief that wage settlements incorporate an allowance for expected future inflation. If most settlements include such a hedge against the future they will, in aggregate, raise costs and produce the very price rise they are seeking to protect against. If, therefore, the inflation hedge can everywhere be eliminated, the rise in costs, and hence in prices, might be avoided. The indexation scheme was an attempt to eliminate the inflation hedge by making the compensation for price increases conditional on their arrival rather than their prospect. Unfortunately the policy was a failure. The price index chosen was one that reflected the prices of imported goods, and many of these rose dramatically in 1973 as the major economies of the world boomed together. Once the threshold clauses were triggered a wage/price/wage spiral was set off because the wage compensation for price inflation was virtually 100%. Had a different index been used, or had commodity prices not exploded, or had the compensation not been roughly one-for-one, the policy might, in retrospect, have been judged more favourably.

   The second point about norms is that there is no longer an attempt to relate them seriously to productivity increases. In the 1960s the ostensible purpose of the policy was to limit average wage increases to average productivity increases, thus securing constant unit labour costs for any given level of output. More recently, with inflation generally so much higher, the goal of constant unit labour costs is seen to be far too ambitious and has been substituted for by the more modest aim of reducing the increase in unit labour costs over what it would otherwise have been.

   The third point about norms is that some incomes policies have been combined with tax policies, in that the Chancellor of the Exchequer has announced income tax reductions that are conditional on incomes-policy success. For example, in March 1977 Mr Healey announced a 2p cut in the standard rate of income tax contingent upon the successful negotiation with the trade-union movement of Stage 3 of the incomes policy. The theory behind this is that disposable incomes can rise (via the tax cuts) even if wage rates, and hence unit labour costs, do not. It also means that the wage rate or earnings norm is somewhat misleading because to it must be added the tax cuts, and these differ in value to different taxpayers.

The 1965-70 incomes policies permitted wage increases greater than the norm on four grounds: where there was a serious labour shortage in a particular industry, occupation or region; where the wages of a particular group of workers were 'seriously out of line' with their traditional place in the wage structure; for low-paid workers; and for productivity deals. More recent policies have also allowed exceptions for 'unsocial hours', and to allow the phased equalization of wage rates between the sexes to take place. The problem with most of the permitted exceptions is that they can often be used by powerful groups to circumvent the spirit of the policy. This is felt to be particularly true for productivity deals, which are often seen to be phoney.

Effectiveness of Incomes Policy: An incomes policy is likely to lead to some loss of allocative efficiency in the economy, by inhibiting changes in relative wages. Does it provide some compensating benefits by slowing down the rates of wage and price inflation below what they would otherwise have been?

The accumulated evidence on the effect on wage inflation of incomes policies as they have been applied in the UK suggests very strongly that they have generally been ineffective. Earnings increases are usually reduced below what they would otherwise have been in the early stages of the policy; but increasingly, and most notably when a government is compelled to dismantle the policy, earnings rise again to reach a level very close to that which they would have reached had no such policy ever existed.

For example a Department of Employment Working Party[1] estimated that over the years 1965, 1966 and 1967 earnings rose about 4% less than they otherwise would have done without a policy, whilst in 1968 and 1969 earnings rose 4% more than they would have done had there never been a policy. The total impact of the policy was nil. This raises the question, why are incomes policies taken off? Presumably the answer is that, at least as they have been applied in the UK, they become politically or economically unsustainable after a while.

This is also the conclusion reached by two extremely thorough studies of the effect of incomes policies over the whole postwar period. In one study the authors summarize all the recent literature and conclude 'incomes policy apparently has little effect either on the wage determination process or on the average rate of wage inflation'.[2]

In the other study, a careful and subtle statistical analysis, the conclusion was that wage increases in the period immediately following the ending of the various policy experiments matched any reductions gained during their operation.[3]

---

1 DE, *Prices and Earnings in 1951-69*, HMSO, 1971, para. 57.

2 M. Parkin *et al*., 'The Impact of Incomes Policy on the Rate of Wage Change', in M. Parkin and M. Sumner (eds.), *Incomes Policy and Inflation*, Manchester UP, 1972.

3 S. Henry and P. Ormerod, 'Incomes Policy and Wage Inflation', *NIER*, August 1978, pp. 31-9.

One reason for these findings is that incomes policies have often been introduced while the economy was being expanded. This was notably the case with the policies of the Conservative government in 1972 and 1973. It is precisely in such circumstances that one might expect least success because tight labour markets lead both workers and employers to try to circumvent the policy, the former because they want higher wages and the latter because they want more labour. Arguably one of the few incomes policy successes was with Stage 1 of the Labour government's policy in 1975. At the time, unemployment was rising rapidly and output was stagnant or falling, so that macroeconomic policy and the incomes policy were working in harmony against inflation. It could be argued that in these circumstances the incomes policy contributed nothing, that the success in reducing inflation should be ascribed to macroeconomic or monetary policy alone. However, most observers agree that the incomes policy at least caused the reduction in wage inflation to come earlier than it would otherwise have done.

Another strand of thinking on incomes policies is that in some circumstances they might raise the rate of wage inflation. This view is based on the proposition that the policy norm might become a floor rather than a ceiling – the norm might be seen as a minimum entitlement. This view probably influenced the Labour government in 1978 when it pitched the norm quite low, at 5%, and hoped that any excess, or drift, would still keep wage inflation in bounds. In the event, the tactic was transparent and the experiment backfired. 5% was judged to be far too low in comparison with most workers' expectations and any small chance that the continuation of the policy might secure official union support disappeared.

REFERENCES AND FURTHER READING

A.B. Atkinson, *Economics of Inequality*, Clarendon Press, 1975.

British Journal of Industrial Relations, July 1977. Symposium of Labour Economics and Industrial Relations.

Department of Employment, *British Labour Statistics: Historical Abstract 1886-1968*, HMSO, 1971.

Department of Employment, *New Earnings Survey, 1979*, HMSO, 1979.

E. Hobsbawn, *Labouring Men*, Weidenfeld and Nicolson, 1968.

W.J. McCarthy (ed.), *Trade Unions*, Penguin, 1972.

E.H. Phelps Brown, *The Inequality of Pay*, Oxford UP, 1977.

Royal Commission on the Distribution of Income and Wealth, *An A to Z of Income and Wealth*, HMSO, 1980.

Statistical Appendix

TABLE A-1

UK Gross Domestic Product, Expenditure (at 1975 prices), 1969-79 (£m)

Year	Consumers' Expenditure		General Government Final Consumption	Gross Domestic Capital Formation		Value of Physical Increase in Stocks and Work in Progress	Exports of Goods and Services	Total Final Expenditure at Market Prices	Imports of Goods and Services	Adjustment to Factor Cost[1]	Gross Domestic Product at Factor Cost[2]
	Durable Goods	Non-Durable Goods and Services		Excluding Dwellings	Dwellings						
1969	3,675	52,494	18,808	14,634	4,290	927	20,364	114,994	−22,955	−8,823	83,091
1970	3,987	53,689	19,076	15,485	3,940	798	21,471	118,279	−24,168	−9,163	84,822
1971	4,750	54,807	19,642	15,549	4,186	188	23,025	122,014	−25,331	−9,510	87,051
1972	5,770	57,229	20,451	15,404	4,363	152	23,291	126,611	−27,788	−10,239	88,385
1973	6,064	59,847	21,426	16,959	4,152	3,043	26,109	137,600	−31,052	−10,914	95,634
1974	5,056	59,362	21,732	16,810	3,826	1,655	27,671	136,112	−31,242	−10,633	94,237
1975	5,008	58,897	23,050	16,399	4,146	−1,477	27,010	133,033	−28,994	−10,447	93,592
1976	5,391	58,639	23,477	16,351	4,260	457	29,476	138,051	−30,223	−10,857	96,971
1977	5,005	58,193	23,250	16,216	3,961	1,193	31,420	139,238	−30,532	−10,842	97,864
1978	5,895	60,785	23,704	16,609	3,950	1,740	32,026	143,709	−31,653	−11,867	100,189
1979	6,260	63,138	23,971	16,490	3,516	1,867	32,657	147,899	−35,142	−12,281	100,476

Sources: *NIBB*, 1979; *ET(AS)*, 1980; *ET*, April 1980.

Notes: 1 Adjustment to Factor Cost represents taxes on expenditure less subsidies valued at constant rates.

2 For the years before 1973 the value of GDP as shown in the last column differs from the sum of its components. This is because the various items have been separately linked to the later series based on 1975 prices. See *NIBB*, 1979, p. 111.

TABLE A-2

UK Prices, Wages, Earnings, Productivity, 1969-79: Index Numbers (1975 = 100)

Year	Retail Prices (All Items)	Weekly Wage Rates	Hourly Wage Rates	Average Weekly Earnings	Average Earnings Non-manual Employees (GB)	Output per Person Employed (GDP)	Output per Man-hour Worked (manufacturing)
	1	2	3	4	5	6	7
1969	51.0	40.1	39.7	42.3	46.0	92.3	83.0
1970	54.2	44.1	43.7	47.1	49.3	94.2	84.5
1971	59.3	49.8	49.5	52.4	55.1	97.3	88.5
1972	63.6	56.9	56.4	58.9	61.4	99.6	94.3
1973	69.4	64.5	64.3	67.1	68.0	103.3	99.6
1974	80.5	77.2	77.1	79.1	77.4	101.3	100.6
1975	100	100	100	100	100	100	100
1976	116.5	119.3	119.3	115.6	120.5	102.7	104.6
1977	135.0	127.2	127.2	127.3	131.7	105.1	104.6
1978	146.2	145.4	145.4	145.7	147.9	107.9	106.2
1979	165.8	167.2	167.3	168.5	165.7	109.3	108.3

Sources: Col. 1. *ET(AS)*, 1980 and *ET*, April 1980.

Cols. 2, 3, 4. *NIER*, November 1979 and May 1980. Series cover workers in all industries.

Col. 5. *DEG*, October 1979 and March 1980. The series relates to GB and covers employees in all industries. The series is compiled on the basis of surveys for April of each year with a base year April 1970 = 100. For this table the figures have been recalculated to give 1975 = 100. The figure for 1969 is derived from the old series relating to 'Salaries' of non-manual workers.

Col. 6. *ET(AS)*, 1980 and *ET*, April 1980 .

Col. 7. *NIER*, November 1979 and May 1980. This is an estimate by the NIESR, based on output per person and the average weekly hours worked.

TABLE A-3

UK Personal Income, Expenditure and Saving 1969-79 (£m)

PERSONAL INCOME BEFORE TAX

Year	Wages and Salaries	Forces Pay	Employers Contributions	Current Grants from Public Authorities[1]	Other Personal Income	Total[2]	Transfers Abroad (Net)	UK Taxes on Income (Payments)
	1	2	3	4	5	6	7	8
1969	24,187	539	2,428	3,937	8,073	39,164	44	5,178
1970	26,975	658	2,771	4,331	8,537	43,272	17	5,744
1971	29,676	758	3,049	4,781	9,565	47,829	6	6,490
1972	33,136	862	3,616	5,845	10,759	54,218	53	6,623
1973	38,018	925	4,398	6,420	13,223	62,984	99	7,848
1974	46,000	1,071	5,687	7,875	15,447	76,080	121	10,349
1975	58,972	1,283	7,944	10,283	17,880	93,362	143	15,077
1976	66,586	1,473	9,955	12,762	20,648	111,424	13	17,526
1977	73,622	1,500	10,859	15,097	23,657	124,735	44	18,329
1978	83,587	1,643	12,136	17,849	26,980	142,195	218	19,672
1979	97,234	2,015	14,244	20,942	32,362	166,797	374	21,620

Sources: NIBB, 1979; *ET(AS)*, 1980; *ET*, April 1980.

Notes: 1 The figures exclude the net cost to public authorities of school meals and welfare foods provided free or at subsidized prices, also expenditure on legal aid. These are now included in public authorities' current expenditure on goods and services.
2 Before providing for depreciation and stock appreciation.
3 Before providing for additions to tax reserves.
   Column   6 = 1 + 2 + 3 + 4 + 5
   Column 10 = 6 − 7 − 8 − 9
   Column 13 = 14 − 11
   Column 15 = 10 − 14

National Insurance and Health Contributions	Total Personal Disposable Income[3]	CONSUMERS' EXPENDITURE				PERSONAL SAVINGS		
		Durable Goods		Other				
		Amount (£m)	As % of P.D.I.	Amount (£m)	Total	Amount (£m)	As % of P.D.I.	Year
9	10	11	12	13	14	15	16	
2,242	31,700	2,063	6.5	27,124	29,187	2,513	7.9	1969
2,655	34,856	2,394	6.9	29,339	31,733	3,123	9.0	1970
2,826	38,507	3,074	8.0	32,435	35,509	2,998	7.8	1971
3,337	44,205	3,862	8.7	36,152	40,014	4,191	9.5	1972
3,937	51,100	4,228	8.3	41,244	45,472	5,628	11.0	1973
5,000	60,610	4,081	6.7	48,007	52,088	8,522	14.1	1974
6,848	74,294	5,008	6.7	58,897	63,905	10,389	14.0	1975
8,426	85,459	6,053	7.1	67,913	73,966	11,493	13.5	1976
9,508	96,854	6,622	6.8	77,388	84,010	12,844	13.3	1977
10,058	112,247	8,750	7.8	87,558	96,308	15,939	14.2	1978
11,518	132,285	10,361	7.8	101,884	112,245	21,040	15.9	1979

TABLE A-4

UK Population, Working Population, Unemployment and Vacancies, 1969-79 (thousands)

Year	Total Population (mid-year estimate)	Working[1, 2] Population	Unemployed[1] (including school-leavers)	Registered Unemployment (including school-leavers) Monthly Average	Unemployment[3] Rate (%)	Unfilled[4] Vacancies 'A' Monthly Average	Unfilled[4] Vacancies 'B' Monthly Average
	1	2	3	4	5	6	7
1969	55,263	25,375	518	576	2.4	289	—
1970	55,421	25,308	555	612	2.6	263	—
1971	55,610	25,123	724	792	3.5	179	—
1972	55,781	25,195	804	876	3.8	191	—
1973	55,913	25,547	575	619	2.7	403	—
1974	55,922	25,601	542	615	2.6	283	85
1975	55,900	25,798	866	978	4.2	150	33
1976	55,886	26,097	1,332	1,359	5.7	121	24
1977	55,852	26,282	1,450	1,484	6.2	158	22
1978	55,836	26,328	1,446	1,475	6.1	210	27
1979	55,881[5]	26,398	1,344	1,391	5.7	241	30

Sources: Col. 1, *MDS*, April 1980; Cols. 2 and 3, *MDS*, April 1980; Cols. 4-7, *AAS*, 1979, 1980; *DEG*, April 1980 and previous issues; *MDS*, April 1980. January 1980.

Notes:

1 Estimates are for June of each year (seasonally unadjusted).

2 The Working Population includes employees in employment, self-employed persons, HM Forces and the registered unemployed. Numbers in the sub-aggregates may be found in the listed sources.

3 The unemployment rate is obtained by dividing the relevant monthly average unemployment figure by the relevant total employees (including unemployed) for the June of that year. Self-employed and HM Forces are excluded from the figure for total employees.

4 For 1969 to 1973 column 'A' relates to total vacancies. After 1973, column 'A' relates to vacancies notified to employment offices and column 'B' to vacancies notified to careers offices. These columns should not be added because of duplication in the series. Since the change in the method of recording the statistics occurred a year later in Northern Ireland, the total for column 'A' 1974 includes some vacancies that should properly have been recorded in column 'B'. Because of 'industrial action', figures for 1974, 1975, 1976 and 1977 are averages of 11, 11, 10 and 11 months respectively.

5 Provisional – includes estimates for N. Ireland.

TABLE A-5
UK Money Stock, Domestic Credit Expansion and Public Sector Borrowing Requirement, 1969-79 (£m) and Interest Rates

Year	Money Stock[1,4] (M$_1$)	Money Stock[2,4] (Sterling M$_3$)	Money Stock[3,4] (M$_3$)	Change in Money Stock[5] (Sterling M$_3$)	Domestic Credit Expansion[6]	Public Sector Borrowing Requirement[7]	Yield on UK Treasury bills (%)	Yield on 2½% Consols (%)
	1	2	3	4	5	6	7	8
1969	9,647	16,339	16,919	374	-243	-466	7.80	8.88
1970	10,554	17,893	18,529	1,541	735	-18	6.93	9.16
1971	11,707	20,372	20,944	2,459	1,190	1,371	4.46	9.05
1972	13,295	25,355	26,245	4,927	6,691	2,049	8.48	9.11
1973	13,967	32,029	33,466	6,702	8,066	4,200	12.82	10.85
1974	15,457	35,282	37,685	3,255	6,926	6,370	11.30	14.95
1975	17,483	37,595	40,573	2,331	4,529	10,520	10.93	14.66
1976	19,467	41,160	45,129	3,565	7,474	9,130	13.98	14.25
1977	23,659	45,290	49,565	4,130	1,132	5,995	6.39	12.32
1978	27,535	52,062	56,968	6,772	8,085	8,353	11.91	11.92
1979	30,046	58,645	63,957	6,583	10,337	12,616	16.49	11.38

Sources: Cols. 1-6 Figures kindly supplied by the Bank of England. More recent figures may be found in *ET*, *FS* and *BEQB*. All cols. based on seasonally unadjusted data.
Cols. 7-8. *ET(AS)*, 1980 and *ET*, April 1980.

Notes: 1 M$_1$ consists of notes and coin in circulation plus sterling sight (or demand) deposits held by the private sector. Totals refer to amounts outstanding at the year end.

2 Sterling M$_3$ is a wide definition of the sterling money stock. It includes notes and coin together with all sterling deposits (including certificates of deposit) held by residents in the private and public sectors. Totals refer to amounts outstanding at the year end.

3 This is col. 2 plus all deposits held by UK residents in other currencies. Totals refer to amounts outstanding at the year end.

4 Cols. 1-3 are not necessarily the amounts outstanding as given in published series. The money stock series contain a number of breaks caused by the introduction of new banking statistics in mid-May 1975 and the reclassification of institutions as banks. The figures given here are smoothed series produced by the Bank of England which should give a more accurate indication of the trend growth of the money stocks. Actual year-end data may be found in the publications listed above.

5 Figures relate to the sum of quarterly changes in £M$_3$ (unadjusted). For reasons partly explained in Note 4, the annual change given in col. 4 is not equivalent to the first difference in col. 2.

6 DCE is the increase in the domestic money stock (£M$_3$) after adjustment for any change in money balances caused directly by an external surplus or deficit. See chapter 2 and *BEQB*, March 1977.

7 The public sector includes the central government, the local authorities and public corporations. The borrowing requirement is discussed in chapter 2.

TABLE A-6

UK General Government: Current Account, 1968-78 (£m)

	1968	1969	1970	1971	1972	1973	1974	1975	1976	1977	1978
RECEIPTS											
Taxes on income	5,846	6,489	7,388	8,003	8,100	9,275	12,514	16,632	18,872	20,378	22,321
Taxes on expenditure	6,809	7,782	8,416	8,787	9,267	10,122	11,469	14,163	16,546	20,230	23,238
National Insurance, etc. contributions	2,161	2,242	2,655	2,826	3,337	3,937	5,000	6,845	8,430	9,495	10,023
Gross Trading Surplus	132	153	151	178	146	139	148	155	137	172	184
Rent	546	623	702	737	771	922	1,243	1,522	1,848	2,025	2,208
Interest and dividends, etc.[1]	711	809	899	1,030	1,171	1,375	1,776	2,058	2,439	2,780	2,951
Imputed charge for consumption of non-trading capital	224	244	272	309	354	445	537	700	839	947	1,039
TOTAL	16,429	18,342	20,483	21,870	23,146	26,215	32,687	42,075	49,111	56,027	61,964
EXPENDITURE											
Current expenditure on goods and services	7,416	7,729	8,689	9,902	11,272	12,882	16,021	22,350	25,844	28,220	31,654
Non-trading capital consumption	224	244	272	309	354	445	537	700	839	947	1,039
Subsidies	895	842	884	939	1,153	1,443	3,004	3,716	3,466	3,313	3,598
Current grants to personal sector	3,678	3,937	4,331	4,781	5,845	6,420	7,875	10,283	12,762	15,097	17,853
Current grants abroad	179	177	177	205	210	359	320	367	784	1,111	1,700
Total expenditure excluding debt interest	12,392	12,929	14,353	16,136	18,834	21,549	27,757	37,416	43,695	48,688	55,844
Debt interest[1]	1,794	1,929	2,025	2,087	2,286	2,737	3,608	4,212	5,395	6,371	7,302
Total current expenditure	14,186	14,858	16,378	18,223	21,120	24,286	31,365	41,628	49,090	55,059	63,146
Balance: Current surplus before providing for depreciation	2,243	3,484	4,105	3,647	2,026	1,929	1,322	447	21	968	−1,182
TOTAL	16,429	18,342	20,483	21,870	23,146	26,215	32,687	42,075	49,111	56,027	61,964

Source: NIBB, 1979.

Notes: 1 Excluding interest on loans from central government to local authorities.

Statistical Appendix

TABLE A-7

UK Balance of Payments, 1969-79 (£m)

				CURRENT ACCOUNT[1]			
	Visible Trade			Invisibles			
Year	Exports (f.o.b.)	Imports[2] (f.o.b.)	Visible Balance	Government Services and Transfers (net)	Private Services and Transfers (net)	Interest Profits and Dividends (net)	Invisible Balance
	1	2	3	4	5	6	7
1969	7,269	−7,478	−209	−467	648	500	681
1970	8,151	−8,183	−32	−486	741	559	814
1971	9,043	−8,853	190	−520	893	510	883
1972	9,423	−10,184	−1,761	−561	946	538	923
1973	11,937	−14,523	−2,586	−768	1,006	1,260	1,498
1974	16,395	−21,745	−5,350	−839	1,339	1,423	1,923
1975	19,330	−22,663	−3,333	−937	1,776	762	1,601
1976	25,193	−29,104	−3,911	−1,451	2,861	1,299	2,709
1977	31,734	−33,973	−2,239	−1,833	3,647	201	2,015
1978	35,071	−36,564	−1,493	−2,392	3,756	1,061	2,425
1979	40,689	−44,001	−3,312	−2,861	3,529	207	875

Sources: UK Balance of Payments 1979 Edition, ET, March 1980.

Notes: 1 All items listed represent a positive flow if unsigned. Negative flows are indicated by a − sign preceding the figure. For capital account items, a positive flow represents an increase in liabilities or a reduction in assets, whilst a negative flow indicates an increase in assets or a reduction in liabilities.

2 Including payments for US Military aircraft and missiles.

3 Includes Capital Transfers for 1973 (−£59m) and 1974 (−£75m).

4 The sum of columns 8, 13 and 14 is defined in official sources as 'Balance for Official Financing'. The balance is normally the negative of the item shown in column 15. For certain years this relationship is disturbed by special items which should be added to the sum of columns 8, 13 and 14 in order to get the appropriate figure for column 15. The special items are 1970, allocation of SDRs, +171, gold subscription to the IMF −38; 1971, allocation of SDRs, +125; 1972, allocation of SDRs, +124; 1979, allocation of SDRs, +195.

INVESTMENT AND OTHER CAPITAL TRANSACTIONS[1]

Current Balance	Official Long-term Capital	Overseas Long-term Investment in UK Private and Public Sectors	UK Private Long-term Investment Overseas	Other Capital Flows Mainly Short-term	Total Investment and Other Capital Transactions[3]	Balancing Item	Total Official Financing[4]
8	9	10	11	12	13	14	15
472	−98	620	−693	−4	−175	390	−687
782	−205	844	−829	736	546	−41	−1,420
1,073	−274	1,160	−860	1,765	1,791	282	−3,271
162	−253	918	−1,402	54	−683	−744	1,141
−1,088	−255	1,836	−1,760	324	86	231	771
−3,427	−287	2,556	−1,148	485	1,531	250	1,646
−1,732	−291	1,742	−1,290	−35	126	141	1,465
−1,202	−165	2,273	−2,232	−2,892	−3,016	589	3,629
−224	−319	5,249	−2,222	1,698	4,406	3,179	−7,361
932	−336	2,598	−4,268	−1,193	−3,199	1,141	1,126
−2,437	−401	4,248	−5,038	4,716	3,525	623	−1,906

Index